Financial Management
Fifth Edition

FINANCIAL MANAGEMENT

Fifth Edition

T.M. KENNEDY, B.COMM., F.C.M.A., M.S.SC.

M.J. MACCORMAC, M.A., M.COMM., D.ECON.SC., F.A.C.C.A.

J.J. TEELING, B.COMM., M.ECON.SC., M.B.A., D.B.A.

GILL & MACMILLAN

Gill & Macmillan Ltd
Goldenbridge
Dublin 8
with associated companies throughout the world
© T.M. Kennedy, M.J. MacCormac and J.J. Teeling, 1995
0 7171 2189 5

Index compiled by
Helen Litton

Design and print origination by
O'K Graphic Design, Dublin

Printed by
ColourBooks Ltd, Dublin

A catalogue record is available for this book from the
British Library.

Contents

Introduction

A young entrepreneur decides to take the plunge and return to Ireland to establish a business. He has worked in the fast food business in the US for three years and has, he believes, identified a niche in the Irish market for a speciality theme restaurant.

First and second among equals in the critical decisions facing the entrepreneur are:

Where will I get the money?

How will I invest the money I can get?

These two questions are the essence of financial management, the financing decision and the investment decision.

If the venture is successful, the measure of success is usually profit. Greater success may result in the business joining the stock market, an event generally accompanied by publicity and celebration. If a business fails, and many do, it is because there is no money to pay debts. The underlying reasons for failure may be many but lack of money is the final straw.

The prospect of success or failure brings into consideration another vital fact in financial management — risk. Risk is the kernel of business. If there was no risk, there could be no profit. This statement needs some explaining. If there was no risk of loss, then the money would be forthcoming for all ventures. The only cost would be an interest charge for the time the money was being used. Profit is a payment for risk taking.

Risk in business is of two types. There is the risk that the business itself might fail because the product is wrong, the prices are wrong, the location is faulty, the economy is poor and so on. This risk is known as business risk. Financial risk is the risk that the type of money used in the business is not suited to the investments made. An extreme example is where a bank overdraft is used to invest in research and development (R & D). R & D has a high risk of failure and usually takes a long time. A bank can ask for an overdraft to be repaid within twenty-four hours. Consider the impact on both the bank and the investor if the bank does call in the debt while the investor is conducting the research project. In many such instances, everyone loses: the investor goes bankrupt, the bank loses money as the value of an incomplete research project is negligible, and society in general may lose because worthwhile research is not brought to fruition. It is an essential part of financial management to match the sources of finance to the uses of finance.

1

For many years, financial management played a secondary role to business finance. Business finance concentrated on financial institutions, such as banks, and on the financial instruments provided by these institutions, such as term loans and overdrafts. Financial management was regarded as a function of the manager of a business. In reality the general manager often assigned the task of managing finance to the accountant. It was only during the 1970s that a central role was assigned to the management aspect of finance. It was realised that a poor investment decision could bankrupt a business. Projects with extended lives often depended for their profitability on cash inflows arising some years in the future. Experience — often bitter, sometimes fatal — taught managers to view distant cash flows with a jaundiced eye. To put the problem in perspective, think of the major social, political and economic upheavals that have occurred in the past decade. Many of those upheavals ultimately produced huge distortions in the incomes arising from many projects and made nonsense of the original investment decision.

Due to pressure from external forces such as inflation, currency volatility, technological innovation and the growing substitution of capital for labour, financial management has developed new and more sophisticated techniques for analysing and handling change and the uncertainties which surround change.

Not only has there been an explosion in the use and range of financial techniques but financial theory has grown apace.

To take one example, consider the impact of inflation. Inflation can make a nonsense of cash flows. This is of particular importance to long-term investment decisions but also causes significant problems in the day-to-day management of business. In settled times, with easy access to money and low annual rates of both inflation and interest, business could often afford the luxury of relatively lax management of working capital — that is, managing the investment in accounts receivable, inventory and cash. Higher rates of inflation meant that many profitable businesses did not earn enough each year to finance the consequent increase in the amounts invested in inventory and accounts receivable. One result was that many businesses borrowed heavily to finance growth. The term 'overtrading' was coined to describe the situation of a business that had too little ownership funds invested. Using other people's money is fine in good times but can be disastrous in bad times. The columns of *Stubbs Gazette* pay weekly tribute to the profitable businesses that have gone bankrupt due to the mismanagement of working capital. Techniques have evolved which can assist the financial manager in deciding how best to manage investments in accounts receivable, inventory and cash.

Managing finance from the viewpoint of the business is one very important aspect of business finance function. Of equal importance is the role played by the various financial institutions in providing finance and the many types of finance offered by these institutions.

Financial institutions means the banks, Stock Exchange, leasing houses and other providers of money. Ireland has a very well-developed financial infrastructure which is dominated by the four major banking groups: Allied Irish Banks, Bank of Ireland, National Irish Bank and Ulster Bank. In addition there is a variety of overseas banks, smaller Irish banks, leasing companies and now building societies supplying money for business.

The kind of money — so-called financial instruments — provided has also changed. The small domestic Irish economy has meant that many types of financial instruments are not available to Irish business but an ever-increasing range of products is being offered.

The state is probably the most important provider of money to Irish business. Through a number of agencies such as Forbairt, the Industrial Development Authority and Bord Fáilte, the state offers a selection of capital grants and incentives to assist in the creation and development of enterprise. On the regulatory side the Central Bank exerts control over all of the financial institutions in the country.

THE NATURE OF FINANCIAL MANAGEMENT

Financial management can be defined as:

Assisting in the achievement of the overall objectives of the firm through

(a) The provision of finance when and where required in a manner and at a cost which represents an acceptable level of risk to the business.
(b) The investigation and evaluation of investment opportunities open to the business.

Financial management generally assumes that the overall objective of the business is the maximisation of the owners' wealth. Note that wealth rather than profit is being maximised. Maximisation of profit is not very applicable to an ongoing business in that the concept is short-term: that is, it is possible to maximise current profits at the expense of long-term success. Maximisation of wealth is a useful objective in that it requires a set of corporate policies which maximise the present worth of the owners' investment.

For many years now a debate has proceeded over the relative merits of profit maximisation, wealth maximisation or wealth satisficing — that is, the objective of a satisfactory level of profit. Many individuals with little or no understanding of business, capital or economics have denounced wealth maximisation as immoral, unethical, antisocial or worse. To do so ignores the basic fact that wealth maximisation as an objective ensures that management will attempt to use all available resources in a manner which promotes the long-run efficient use of such resources. Should other policies be followed, then either the business will cease to exist or it will be taken over by others who can use better the resources involved. This text assumes that the objective of business is the long-run maximisation of the value of the owners' investment.

Decisions within companies are taken by managers, who are not always involved in ownership. Frequently, managers' objectives differ from those of shareholders as well as a number of other interested groups, such as the workers, customers and finally society as a whole. Management may seek to maximise sales, profit growth or market share given that its level of remuneration may be linked to one or more of these indicators. The greater the dispersion of shares among the owners of a company, the easier it is for management to ignore the shareholders' wishes and pursue motives and goals of its own. Significant changes have taken place in the past fifteen years in the pattern of share ownership due to the growth and interest of financial institutions in equity holdings. This makes it much more difficult for managers to ignore the wishes of these large shareholders, whose interest is more likely to be exerted privately than overtly. These sophisticated financial investors are themselves under intense pressure to produce returns which perform better than the market average.

Returning to the definition of financial management, it concerns two central and related questions: how firms should choose the investments they make — that is, the investment decision; and how they should raise the necessary finance — that is, the financing decision. The investment decision-making role of financial management is usually refined into

— strategic investment decisions that decide on the long-term asset investments of the firm. Capital expenditure is the name given to the long-term investments and capital budgeting is the decision-making process used to select the investment.
— short-term or tactical investment decisions in working capital: that is, investment in inventory, accounts receivable and cash. This area is often known as working capital management in that the manager attempts to match outflows of cash into accounts receivable and inventory with cash available from short-term sources such as creditors and bank overdraft.

The financing decision is also refined into

— capital structure: that is, the proportion of each type of finance — short-term, long-term debt and owners' investment — that goes to make up the funds available for investment;
— the dividend policy to be followed to compensate the shareholders of the firm.

The investment decision concerns both the long-term appraisal of many types of capital projects or investments and the efficient management of existing assets. Decisions on large-scale projects are usually designed to maintain the long-run profitability of the business while the short-term day-to-day decisions control the current profitability.

The financing decision is concerned with determining the best financing mix or capital structure. In a perfect capital market the capital structure of the firm would be irrelevant to its value, but in reality the market imperfections of taxation, bankruptcy costs and information costs have a profound impact. The other important decision that must be made from time to time is the firm's dividend policy. This involves striking a balance between the dividend payout ratio — that is, the percentage of earnings paid out in dividends — and the need to retain earnings for future growth financing. Considerable judgment is required in evaluating the firm's financing needs and the investor's preference for dividend income or capital gains.

THE JOB OF THE FINANCIAL MANAGER

Because finance is a critical function of business, the financial manager is almost always a senior member of management. The primary functions of the financial manager are:

(1) To advise on the investments which the business should make.
(2) To procure the finance necessary to fund the investments.
(3) To record and report on the activities of the business.

Major investment decisions will rarely be made solely by the financial manager. Certainly, day-to-day decisions on cash or credit are routine and may be subject only to periodic review, but larger decisions to acquire assets are normally made by the directors and/or owners of a business. Providing finance is often called the 'treasury function'.

The treasurer is generally responsible for relationships with financial institutions and for handling cash.

Recording and reporting on the activities of the business is the accounting or controllership function of finance. The simplest method of controlling the activities of a business is to reduce every activity to a set of financial statistics. As a rule the objective of a business is stated in financial terms; therefore the performance of the business must ultimately be translated into financial statistics. Many developments have taken place in this area of technology, with new quantitative techniques offering opportunities for greatly improved reporting and control. The systems established to produce management control data are known as Management Information Systems (MIS). Reporting to management has the generic name of Management Accounting. External reporting to shareholders and to the state is known as Financial Accounting or Auditing.

AN OUTLINE OF THE TEXT

The text is structured to analyse the various aspects of the job of managing corporate finance.

The early chapters set the scene. Chapter 1 deals with the various ways in which ventures can be established, ranging from the sole trader through limited liability companies on to co-operatives.

Knowing where a business stands and where it is heading is the theme running through Chapters 2, 3 and 4. An explanation of financial accounts in Chapter 2 is followed in Chapter 3 by the definition and explanation of a series of techniques which assist in understanding accounts. Chapter 4 extends the analysis to short-term future predictions. Chapters 5 and 6 look at short-term and long-term investment decisions.

Chapters 7 to 14 deal with the raising of finance. Chapters 7 and 8 examine Irish financial institutions. Chapters 9, 10 and 11 discuss respectively the short-, medium- and long-term sources of finance available to Irish business, and Chapter 12 looks at ownership sources of finance. A separate chapter, Chapter 13, analyses the extensive financial assistance provided to Irish business by the state. Chapter 14 examines the cost of the various sources of finance and demonstrates their effects on the capital structure of a business. Chapter 15 outlines the financial implications of mergers and acquisitions. The growing internationalisation of business and the increasing role of foreign activities in Irish business is reflected in Chapter 16, which provides an introduction to international financial management.

Throughout the text, techniques are applied to Ardmore Ltd, a small Irish engineering company.

FURTHER READING

E.J. McLaney, *Business Finance for Decision Makers* (London, Pitman Publishing, 1994).

S.A. Ross, R.W. Westerfield & J.F. Jaffe, *Corporate Finance*, 3rd ed. (New York, Irwin, 1993).

J.F. Weston & E.F. Brigham, *Essentials of Financial Management*, 10th ed. (Orlando, Harcourt Brace, 1993).

Legal Forms of Business Organisation

Business may take on a number of different forms of legal entity. Throughout this book the company is used as the standard organisation but in fact other forms are more numerous. The type of legal organisation assumed by a business is often a function of the amount of finance available. Once established, the legal form affects the taxation, financial and auditing requirements as well as the sources of finance which are available to the business. The following legal forms of business organisation are considered below: sole trader or sole proprietorship; partnerships; limited liability companies; co-operatives; state-owned enterprises.

SOLE TRADER

The sole trader is the dominant form of business organisation in Ireland. Exact numbers are not obtainable but practically every farmer, small shopkeeper and tradesman operates this form of legal organisation.

A sole trader or sole proprietorship is formed each time an individual trades in his own name. That is the major advantage of this form of organisation: simplicity. The sole trader is totally independent. Independence means that the owner usually makes all the important decisions.

Until recently, sole traders were relatively free to maintain or discard detailed financial records. This is no longer true. Now Value Added Tax, income tax and social welfare regulations require the sole trader to keep detailed financial records which must be available for state inspection.

The general features of a sole proprietorship are that:

(1) The owner has unlimited liability. A recent change in Irish law makes it difficult to foreclose on the family home.

(2) Profits are taxed at the rate of personal income tax appropriate to the owner. Any losses incurred by the business can be offset against other income sources. The public has no access to the accounts of the business. There are no requirements to be fulfilled under the Companies Act. The owner must pay income tax and pay related social insurance (PRSI) obligations by 1 November each year and submit a personal tax return by 31 January each year. Tax relief on pension funding is limited to 15 per cent of net relevant earnings.

(3) There are essentially no legal restrictions to the establishment of a sole

proprietorship. However, if a person intends carrying on business under any name other than his own, he must register certain particulars as required by the Registration of Business Names Act 1963. Some businesses require special qualifications, i.e. lawyers, pharmacists, etc., which must be complied with, while a licence is needed for such activities as money-lending, storing petrol, slaughtering animals and pawnbroking.

(4) The owner, with total control, can operate, invest and divest as he sees fit.

(5) Sole traders are not required to register details of loans secured by mortgages.

(6) A disadvantage is that one person may have difficulty in managing all of the functions of the business. This, of course, does not mean that functional specialists cannot be hired.

(7) In cases of the absence or illness of the owner, mismanagement can and does occur.

(8) As there is no continuity of existence, death effectively dissolves this legal form of organisation and often causes succession problems.

(9) Sole traders find it hard to raise finance other than their own funds and personal borrowing powers.

Despite the many problems, the sole trader form of organisation is useful for small businesses.

PARTNERSHIP

A partnership is legally defined as an association of persons carrying on a business in common with a view to profit. It may be formed by a verbal agreement among partners but it is usual to draft a Deed of Partnership. Without a Deed of Partnership, no new partner can be introduced without the unanimous approval of all existing partners. The number of partners may not exceed twenty, or ten in the case of a banking partnership. There is no limit for accounting and legal practices. As in the case of the sole trader, the liability of the partners for the debts and obligations of the partnership is unlimited. The Deed of Partnership would normally contain details of the following:

(a) The name of the partnership.

(b) The date of commencement of the venture.

(c) The duration of the venture.

(d) The retirement or admittance of partners.

(e) Capital subscription and division of profits.

(f) Signing powers for cheques.

Partnerships are legally controlled by the Partnership Act 1890 and the Limited Partnership Act 1907. There are two types of partnership:

(1) A general partnership where each partner contributes an agreed amount, is an agent of the partnership, and has full liability for all debts. Under the Partnership Act of 1890 it can be dissolved by

(a) agreement after a fixed term or on completion of a specified venture or at will by a partner giving notice to that effect,

(b) the bankruptcy or death of a partner,

(c) the courts, on the grounds of insanity, incapacity or misconduct of a partner,

(d) the courts, on the grounds of the hopeless state of the business or when they are of the opinion that it is just and equitable to do so.

General partnerships are common in Ireland, particularly among the professions — for example, lawyers and accountants.

(2) A limited partnership. Under the terms of the 1907 Act a limited partnership must consist of:

(a) One or more persons, called general partners, who shall be liable for all debts and obligations of the firm, and one or more limited partners, who shall at the time of entering into such partnership contribute thereto a sum or sums of capital or property valued at a stated amount, and who shall not be liable for the debts or obligations of the firm beyond the amount so contributed.

(b) Unlike a general partnership, a limited partnership allows continuity of existence in that it cannot be dissolved by the death, bankruptcy, lunacy or notice of a limited partner. It can be dissolved by the courts on the grounds of the hopeless state of the business or when the courts are of the opinion that it is the just and equitable thing to do. It allows a partner to be introduced without the consent of the existing limited partners and must be registered.

(c) A limited partnership is a medium whereby an investor can share profits without assuming the risk of unlimited liability. Limited partners may not take an active part in the business.

Note that a sleeping partner is not a limited partner. A sleeping partner is one who takes no active part in the management of the partnership but who retains unlimited liability for the debts of the venture. The number of limited partnerships registered in Ireland is small, averaging fewer than twenty per year.

Partnerships have greater access to capital than sole traders but the limitations set by the availability of additional partners (for example, limited capital and borrowing powers) still exist. The sharing of responsibility for the firm among a number of partners allows a larger type of firm to emerge under this form of organisation than under that of the sole trader.

Partners often have a blend of dissimilar skills and it is quite usual to find three partners, one of whom is a marketing person, one a production or technical expert and one a financial specialist. There is a high possibility, however, of disagreement developing between partners and the potential break-up of the firm. The Deed of Partnership may offer some insurance against this danger but it cannot cover all contingencies.

In law each partner carries full powers to commit the partnership — for example, in the purchase of goods — and even though partners may agree that these powers might be limited, there is no way in which this could be notified validly to third parties. Since all partners are liable for the debts of the firm, each partner must have complete trust in the way the other partners conduct business. In summary the general features of the partnership form of legal organisation are:

(1) Unlimited liability of all partners. In rare instances partners with limited liability may be admitted but they cannot take an active part in the business: if they do they become liable as general partners.
(2) Profits are taxed at the appropriate income tax rate of the partners.
(3) A partnership is an association of individuals and not a separate legal person.
(4) A partnership can obtain a wider range of skills and access to greater capital resources than is available to the average sole trader.

(5) Partnerships need not register details of loans secured by mortgages.
(6) Partnerships by their very nature are unstable and often dissolve over simple disputes.
(7) The instability of this legal form of organisation restricts the ability of the partnership to raise capital.

LIMITED LIABILITY COMPANY

In the seventeenth and early eighteenth centuries a new form of business organisation developed in England — the so-called joint stock company. Individuals were offered, at a price, shares in a particular venture. In this period English merchants were extending their trading routes all over the world and many new ventures needed finance. The joint stock company was an excellent way of providing this finance.

The advantage of the joint stock company was that each investor was entitled to share the proceeds of the trade in proportion to his investment. A period of wild speculation in the stock of the South Sea Company took place in early 1720. This led to the Bubble Act of 1720, which effectively made illegal the formation of all joint stock companies. The only way to establish a company was through royal charter or Act of Parliament. The Bank of Ireland was established by charter and the Dublin Gas Company by Act of Parliament. In 1768 the Warmsley Company petitioned parliament for a charter to establish a company. What was unique about this application was that the petitioners sought to have the liability of shareholders limited to the money which they had subscribed. The petition was granted. During the following seventy-five years, many companies were incorporated by parliament. Most of them sought, and obtained, limited liability. The Joint Stock Companies Act of 1856 was a major step forward in the organisation of business. Now a business could be legally organised by means of a joint stock limited liability company. Investors were liable only for the amount of capital which they agreed to invest. This Act was passed during the English Industrial Revolution so there was a rapid and sustained increase in the number of companies formed. The new technologies which spurred industrial growth were often both high risk and capital-intensive. Many investors were needed to raise the required capital but unless their risk could be quantified they would have been unlikely to invest. The limited liability joint stock company was the perfect answer. Over time, numerous refinements were introduced, so that by now joint stock companies have become the dominant form of legally organising large businesses.

It is important to understand what a company is. A company is a corporate body which has a legal existence quite distinct from the persons who are the shareholders. A company can have a perpetual life since ownership is represented by transferable shares. Many Irish companies have been in existence for over 100 years.

Formation of Limited Companies

The formation of a limited company is normally handled by a lawyer, who drafts the necessary documents for registration with the Registrar of Companies. The main documents required are:
   (a) Memorandum of Association.
   (b) Articles of Association.
   (c) Statutory declaration of compliance with all of the requirements of the relevant Companies Act.
   (d) Statement of nominal share capital.

(e) List of persons who have consented to be directors.

(f) Form of consent to act as director from those who have agreed to be directors.

The first two documents are of particular importance as they affect the company not only on incorporation but throughout its existence. Only these two are examined in detail.

Memorandum of Association. This document sets out, for the information of the public, the basic facts relating to the company. It governs the relationship of the company with others. The contents must include:

(a) The company name, with 'Limited' as the last word in the title in the case of a private company and 'public limited company' (PLC) in the case of a public company.

(b) The location of the registered office.

(c) The objects of the company — for example, the areas of activity in which the group operates or intends to operate; it is usual to make the objects cover as wide a range of activities as possible.

(d) A statement that the liability of the members is limited.

(e) The authorised or nominal capital of the company.

(f) The signatures of subscribers, generally directors, with their addresses and the number of shares they are initially taking in the company. The signatures must be witnessed. A public company must have a minimum of seven subscribers, while a private company must have at least two.

Articles of Association. The 'Articles' govern the internal workings or management of the company. In effect they are a set of rules and regulations which the company may draw up on its own or may adopt from a model set given in Table A of the Companies Act 1963. The Articles of Association form a contract between the company and the shareholders, defining their respective and relative rights and duties.

The model set of articles as set out in Table A of the Companies Act includes the following:

(a) A statement of the authorised share capital of the company and its division into shares.

(b) The rights attaching to these shares and their voting rights.

(c) Provisions relating to share issues, calls, transfers, forfeiture, alteration of share capital, etc.

(d) Appointment, retirement and powers of directors.

(e) Meetings of the shareholders and procedures at such meetings. The articles are subject to the memorandum and cannot confer or include any powers beyond those contained in the memorandum. They are signed by those who signed the memorandum. They must also be witnessed. The articles can be altered at any time by special resolution of the shareholders: that is, with the approval of 75 per cent of those voting.

The six documents outlined above are lodged with the Registrar of Companies. Within a short period, if everything is in order, the Registrar will issue a Certificate of Incorporation. The company is now registered and if private can commence business. A public limited company must wait until £30,000 of share capital has been subscribed. The fact that liability is limited means that investors are liable only for the amount of capital which they have agreed to subscribe. Once the capital subscription is fully paid, no further liability arises, irrespective of how much money a company loses.

Types of Joint Stock Company

There are four types: private limited companies; public limited companies; companies limited by guarantee; and unlimited companies.

Private Limited Companies. Private companies have the following characteristics:
(1) Between two and fifty shareholders. A minimum of two shareholders is necessary for incorporation.
(2) The right of transfer of shares is restricted.
(3) Business can commence immediately on incorporation.
(4) Up to the passing of the Companies (Amendment) Act 1986, private companies did not have to make copies of their accounts available for public inspection. Since the passing of that Act, which incorporated the European Community's Fourth Council Directive of 1978, all limited companies — with certain exceptions — must file their financial statements with the Registrar of Companies.
(5) The company is prohibited from inviting the public to subscribe for its shares or debentures. Consequently, a Stock Exchange quotation is not possible.

In mid-1994 there were over 135,000 private companies registered in Ireland, with a nominal paid-up capital of £1,570,000,000, an average of £11,630 per company. Annual formations average 14,000.

Public Limited Companies (PLCs). The main features of a public company are that:
(1) A minimum of seven persons is required for incorporation. The maximum number is governed by the number of shares the company proposes to issue.
(2) Shares are, generally speaking, freely transferable.
(3) Though incorporated, a public company cannot commence business until the Registrar of Companies issues a certificate to commence business. This is known as the Trading Certificate.
(4) Accounts must be audited each year and then filed with the Registrar of Companies. These accounts are available for inspection by the public.
(5) The shares and debentures of public companies may be quoted on the Stock Exchange subject to permission being granted by the Stock Exchange authorities (Chapter 8).

In 1994 there were over two thousand public companies registered in the twenty-six counties, less than one hundred of which were quoted on the Dublin Stock Exchange. Public companies are normally much larger than private companies. On average about forty public companies are formed each year.

Companies Limited by Guarantee. A very unusual type of registered company is one where members or shareholders agree to subscribe an agreed sum towards the assets of the company in the event of liquidation. Usually, the sum is a nominal amount.

This method of incorporation is used by non-profit organisations such as clubs, associations, societies, etc. There are over 380 companies limited by guarantee.

Unlimited Companies. An unlimited company is formed if shareholders decide that any or all of the following advantages offset the disadvantages of unlimited liability:

(a) The right to reduce issued capital without court permission.
(b) The right to purchase shares.
(c) Exemption from filing accounts.
In 1994 there were over 200 such companies.

Features of Limited Companies

The main features of limited joint stock companies are that:
(1) Investors' liability is limited.
(2) There is greater access to capital.
(3) The business survives the death or incapacity of the investors.
(4) Skilled managers prefer to work for companies which are regarded as more stable than either partnerships or sole proprietorships.
(5) Income is taxed at a specific corporation tax rate. This is usually lower than the top rate of personal tax but if profits are paid out as dividends then income tax must be paid in addition to the corporation tax.
(6) Large organisations tend to become bureaucratic. Organisational entropy is the technical description of increasing organisational inefficiency.
(7) The owners of the business may lose control to directors and/or managers who may not adequately safeguard shareholders' interests.
(8) Limited companies are more regulated than either partnerships or sole proprietorships.

Legal Requirements of Limited Companies

Company law in Ireland was initially consolidated in the 1963 Companies Act. This repealed a number of earlier Acts and its purpose was two-fold. Firstly, to bring all legislation on company law together, and secondly, to bring the law up to date by introducing greater protection to shareholders and creditors.

The Companies (Amendment) Act 1983 implemented the Second EEC Directive on company law. The directive was adopted by the Council of Ministers in 1976 and applies only to public limited companies. The 1983 Companies (Amendment) Act extended some of the rules to private companies.

The main provisions of the Act relate to the following matters:

(1) Name of a public limited company
Public companies will have to be clearly distinguished in their name from other types of company. This will mean that 'limited' will no longer be sufficient for both private and public companies, with public companies to be known as public limited companies (PLC) or the Irish equivalent, Cuideachta Phoiblí Theoranta (CPT).

(2) Registration and reregistration for companies
In the case of an old public company the directors of the company may apply to the Registrar of Companies to be reregistered as a public limited company. If, however, its allotted share capital is less than the authorised minimum for a public company (£30,000), then the company must either increase its share capital, reregister as another form of company or wind up voluntarily. There are also optional provisions for all companies to reregister in another form: for example, private company as a public limited company and vice versa; unlimited company as a limited company and vice versa.

A new public limited company may not commence business until it has registered and obtained a certificate from the Registrar of Companies certifying that it has complied with the relevant rules.

(3) Minimum share capital and the issue of shares

A public limited company must have a minimum of £30,000 share capital issued, though it need only be partly paid. The Act restricts the rights of the directors of a public or private company to issue shares in that company. The directors are prohibited from issuing shares in the company unless they have been specifically authorised to do so by the members of the company in a general meeting or by the Articles of Association. Members may remove, alter or renew such authority by ordinary resolution.

The offer of shares to the public by a private company is a criminal offence, although any issue of shares arising from such an offer is valid.

If a public company wishes to increase its share capital, it may not issue shares unless the capital offered for subscription is fully subscribed, or the terms of the offer allow an issue, notwithstanding a shortfall in subscription.

(4) Pre-emption rights

This part of the Act protects the right of existing shareholders to retain their percentage share in the company. Shares to be issued must be offered first to the shareholders pro rata to their existing holdings. These rights to first refusal are known as pre-emption rights and they apply to both public and private companies.

Pre-emption rights do not apply where shares are issued other than for cash (for example, takeover of another company). Nor do they apply to shares taken out by subscribers to the memorandum and shares in employee share schemes.

(5) Payment for share capital

The Act introduces extensive provisions to prevent shares being issued without adequate consideration, and in this respect must be regarded as an improvement on previous legislation.

Public limited companies are prevented from accepting as payment for shares a promise to work or perform services in the future. If they do so, the holder of the shares will be liable to pay cash for the shares. The provision does not extend to private companies, nor does it restrict the issue of shares for past services.

The issue of shares at a discount is prohibited, thereby repealing section 63 of the 1963 Act, which permitted issues at a discount subject to certain conditions.

In the case of public limited companies no share may be issued unless 25 per cent of the nominal value of the share and the whole of the premium, if any, has been paid.

Shares may be issued for a consideration that consists of non-cash assets. If so, in the case of public limited companies, the assets must be transferred to the company within five years of the date of issue. Otherwise, the shareholders are liable to pay in cash. It is also a requirement in such circumstances that a report be prepared by an independent person on the value of the consideration. The Act gives the independent person power to seek information and explanations from officers of the company.

(6) Maintenance of capital

The Act introduces safeguards for the maintenance of its capital by requiring that directors call an extraordinary general meeting of the company if they become aware that the value of the net assets has fallen to half or less than half of the called-up share capital. The meeting is to consider whether any, and if so what, measures should be taken to deal with the situation. The Act goes beyond the requirements of the Second Directive in that it imposes on auditors the duty of disclosing in their audit report the existence of a financial situation, i.e. net assets have fallen to half or less than half of the called-up share capital. Auditors should base their opinion solely on the amount of assets and liabilities included in the Balance Sheet on which they are reporting.

(7) Distributions of profits and assets
It is a fundamental rule of capital maintenance that dividends are paid only out of profits. Apart from the Companies Act 1963, which provides that dividends may not be paid out of unrealised surpluses arising from the revaluation of fixed assets, there were no statutory rules as to what profits may be distributed. As a consequence, the major rules governing distribution of profits were to be found in a number of judicial decisions, some dating from the late nineteenth century. The 1983 Act goes some way towards rectifying this situation by reaffirming the 1963 Act and laying down rules that supersede many of these judicial decisions. The rules, which apply to public and private companies, state that a company may make a distribution only out of profits available for dividend which are defined as 'its accumulated realised profits, so far as not previously utilised by distribution or capitalisation, less its accumulated realised losses, so far as not previously written off in a reduction or reorganisation of capital'. It will, therefore, no longer be possible for a company to pay dividends out of current profits unless past losses have been made good. Also, accumulated unrealised profits will not be available for distribution.

The Act contains further restrictions in that a public company may make a distribution only if the amount of its net assets exceeds the aggregate of its called-up share capital and undistributable reserves, and any distribution must not be greater than the excess. Distributable profits for a public limited company will, therefore, be net realised profits less net unrealised losses, if any. In effect if a company's unrealised profits are less than its unrealised losses, the deficit must be covered by realised profits before a distribution can be made.

Further changes were brought about by the Companies (Amendment) Act 1986 in implementing the Fourth EC Directive on Company Law. It laid down fixed formats for filing accounts and classified companies into large, medium-sized and small. In essence it meant that large companies have to publish a detailed Profit and Loss Account and Balance Sheet, medium-sized companies the same but in a little less detail, and small companies a summarised Balance Sheet only. To be classified as medium-sized or small, companies had to satisfy two of the following criteria:

Criteria	Medium-Sized (not exceeding)	Small (not exceeding)
• Balance Sheet Total	IR£5 m	IR£1.25m
• Turnover for the Year	IR£10m	IR£2.5 m
• Average No. of Employees in the Year	250	50

Any company exceeding the above criteria would be classified as a large company.

Further amendments in company law took place with the passing of the Companies Act 1990 and the Companies (Amendment) Act 1990. These Acts both amended existing legislation and brought new areas into company law. Against a background of the risk of insolvency of a large commercial operation, a new concept to Ireland, that of court protection for companies in difficulties, was introduced. This was done to facilitate the survival of viable businesses with short-term financial difficulties by enabling the court to appoint an examiner for a three-month period. During that period, the company is protected from its creditors and the onus is on the examiner to bring forward a 'scheme of arrangement'; otherwise, the company will lose the protection of the court and may be wound up. An application to the court for the appointment of an examiner can be made by the company itself, its directors, a creditor, or members holding not less than 10 per cent of the paid-up capital carrying voting rights.

In the case of an insurance company only the Minister for Industry and Commerce can apply to the court, and in the case of a licensed bank, only the Central Bank may apply. This Act covered other topics, such as insider dealing, disclosure of interests in shares, purchase of their own shares by companies, and variable capital investment companies.

The provisions in regard to directors' and other significant shareholdings were designed to make this information more freely available and allow more transparency as regards company ownership.

The provisions in regard to the purchase of their own or holding company shares were introduced to allow companies to redeem or purchase their own shares and to hold 'treasury shares'. Treasury shares are shares which are redeemed or purchased and not cancelled. They are available for reissue. The ability to redeem or purchase was subject to a number of restrictions, including the following:

— the repurchase must be financed out of distributable profits or the proceeds of a fresh issue of shares.
— the nominal value of non-redeemable shares in issue must not fall below 10 per cent of the nominal value of the total issued shares.

These provisions bring Ireland into line with what was generally accepted company practice in the USA and Europe for many years and in the UK since 1981. The flexibility it offers companies in managing their capital structure and the increased liquidity/marketability of private company shares were seen to outweigh the concern of creditors. They saw their interests and claims for payment being possibly undermined by excessive cash commitments to this process. The legislation serves to protect all parties and hence the need for a number of restrictions.

The establishment of variable capital investment companies was done to assist the development of the Irish financial services industry. Their sole objective was the collective investment of funds with the intention of spreading risk. They could have a variable share capital with no nominal value. The actual value of the share capital at any time is the net worth of the company, and any shareholder can require that his shareholding be purchased by the company at this value. These companies must be authorised by and operate under the supervision of the Central Bank.

CO-OPERATIVES

A co-operative society is formed by people who come together to undertake a venture which they could not undertake as individuals. Co-operatives are established for the benefit of all members. The co-operative movement in Ireland dates from 1889, when the first co-operative creamery was established in Drumcollogher, Co. Limerick. The Irish co-operative movement remained predominantly an agriculturally based movement relying almost totally on producers until the early 1990s. In recent years a growing number of tourism co-ops have been formed. This is in marked contrast to worker co-operation in the running of retail shops in other countries. Retail grocery co-operatives in Ireland are practically non-existent.

The initial efforts of the co-operative movement were mainly directed towards supplying farm raw materials. Early growth arose through the establishment of small creameries to ensure outlets for milk and markets for butter. Over 1,000 societies were later established for store trading, butter making and egg trading. In the 1920s and 1930s there was considerable growth in Agricultural Credit Societies. In the 1960s the number of societies dropped dramatically as many of the smaller societies went out of business, all the Credit Societies were wound up and most of the Creamery Societies amalgamated. There were ninety-three co-operatives in Ireland in 1993 (Table 1.1).

Irish co-operatives are registered under the Industrial and Provident Societies Acts of 1893 and 1934. They are required to make annual returns of their accounts to the Registrar of Friendly Societies. The maximum shareholding in a co-operative is £1,000 but there is no limit to the holding of one co-operative in another.

The features which distinguish co-operatives from other types of business units are that:

(1) Membership of a co-operative society is voluntary and open to anyone, subject to his being willing to accept the responsibilities of membership. Shares purchased are not transferable, but they are withdrawable.
(2) Voting depends on the number of members, not the number of shares held: that is, one man, one vote.
(3) Share capital receives a strictly limited rate of interest.
(4) At the year's end, after all payments and provisions for the future development of the business have been made, surpluses may be distributed among members in proportion to the business carried on by the individual members with the co-operative society.
(5) Provision is generally made for the education of the community in the principles and techniques of co-operation.

There should be co-operation among co-operatives at local, national and international levels. The co-ordinating body of the co-operative movement in Ireland, the Irish Co-Operative Organisation Society Limited (ICOS), the successor to the Irish Agricultural Organisation Society (IAOS), has done great work for the Irish co-operative movement in this respect. Founded in 1894 by Horace Plunkett, it exists to help Irish farmers and fishers and their families to enjoy higher living standards through better use of co-operatives.

The rapid growth in agri-business here led to the development of co-operatives, with sales higher than practically any other form of business in Ireland. However to compete internationally in the dairy industry, even greater size is needed so substantial merger activity is expected in the last half of the 1990s.

Table 1.1 gives an indication of the size of the movement, with total turnover of more than £6,078 million and 22,198 employees. The movement has grown dramatically in recent years and seen rapid improvements in managerial skills. Net profit as a percentage of sales at just over 2 per cent could be improved upon. This is probably due to a combination of growth strategies by the large and efficient and bad management by those staying static or in decline.

Table 1.1 Co-operative Statistics 1993

	Total	Dairies	Marts	Wholesale	Stores	Others
No. of Societies	93	34	32	3	3	21
Members	173,189	91,665	45,995	92	4,506	30,931
Employees	22,198	19,462	901	989	143	703
Trading Performance (£'000)						
Total Sales	6,078,300	4,953,642	633,565	420,525	15,321	55,247
Net Income	131,362	121,085	1,590	7,383	156	1,148
Net Income as % of Sales	2.16%	2.44%	0.25%	1.76%	1.02%	2.08%
Balance Sheet (£'000)						
Fixed Assets	1,206,599	1,112,510	20,981	59,222	1,530	12,356
Total Assets	2,449,457	2,229,201	40,049	148,838	5,503	25,866
Members' Funds	1,067,761	989,569	24,397	33,134	2,750	17,911
Bank Borrowings	513,940	472,256	5,244	34,125	376	1,939
Other Liabilities	867,756	767,376	10,408	81,579	2,377	6,016
% Debt/Equity	48.13%	47.72%	21.49%	102.99%	13.67%	10.83%

Source: Irish Co-Operative Organisation Society Annual Report 1993.

STATE-SPONSORED ENTERPRISE

In practically every developed country the state plays a vital role in business. In Ireland slightly less than 50 per cent of national expenditure is accounted for by the state. The largest business enterprises in the country are state-owned. Córas Iompair Éireann is one of the biggest employers in the country while the Electricity Supply Board has more invested capital than almost any other Irish business venture.

State enterprise in Ireland rarely competes with private business. As a rule, the state invests in areas where private enterprise is either unwilling or unable to provide the service. There are two methods used to establish a state enterprise:

(1) For a commercial operation, a state-financed company is registered under the Companies Acts: for example, Aer Lingus, Irish Steel.

(2) Where a non-competitive social service is involved, a statutory corporation is established by the passing of a specific Dáil statute: for example, Bord na Móna, Bord Iascaigh Mhara.

State bodies receive funds in any or all of the following ways:

(a) Invested share capital.

(b) Loans from the state.

(c) Loans from commercial sources.

(d) State subsidies.

(e) Indirect subsidies such as low interest loans or access to cheap raw materials.

Surprisingly, the owners of state bodies — that is, the public — cannot under existing laws question the activities of their organisations. Control rests with the government minister within whose area of responsibility the functions lie.

The world-wide movement towards the privatisation of state enterprise reached Ireland in the early 1990s. The Irish Sugar Company was the first to be sold to the public in 1991 by means of a Stock Exchange flotation. Now named Greencore PLC, the company is valued at more than £350 million. In 1991 Irish Life was also floated on the Exchange. Other state companies which are candidates for privatisation are An Bord Telecom and Aer Lingus.

There are a number of serious structural problems associated with state-owned business organisations. They frequently lack objectives, are bureaucratic and often inefficient. There are over 100 state enterprises in Ireland.

CONCLUSION

It is possible to relate the legal form of organisation to the size of business involved. Small one-man businesses are usually organised as sole proprietorships. As business expands, capital needs to increase and the private companies grow and develop into publicly owned corporations. Partnerships, co-operatives and state-sponsored businesses are relatively rare. Where they exist, they usually reflect the specific requirements of a particular situation.

In addition the increasing influence of the European Community has to be considered. This applies especially to its aim of encouraging fair trading and eliminating restrictive agreements and the abuse of dominant positions by firms operating within the Community.

FURTHER READING

Report of the Registrar of Companies, Stationery Office, Dublin, annual.
Report of the Registrar of Friendly Societies, Stationery Office, Dublin, annual.
Report of the Irish Co-Operative Organisation Society, Dublin, annual.
G. Clegg & C. Barrow, *How to Start and Run Your Own Business* (London, Macmillan, 1984).
Companies Act 1963.
Companies (Amendment) Act 1983.
Companies (Amendment) Act 1986.
Companies Act 1990.
Companies (Amendment) Act 1990.
R.C. Moyer, J.R. McGuigan & W.J. Kretlow, *Contemporary Financial Management*, 5th ed. (New York, West Publishing, 1992).
J.F. Weston and E.F. Brigham, *Essentials of Financial Management*, 10th ed. (Orlando Harcourt Brace, 1993)

QUESTIONS

Question 1.1
Define or explain each of the following:
> (a) Sole trader.
> (b) Partnership.
> (c) Company.
> (d) Co-operatives.
> (e) State-sponsored bodies.

Question 1.2
What are the differences between a general and a limited partnership?

Question 1.3
What are some of the advantages and disadvantages of being a sole trader?

Question 1.4
Explain how the sole trader, partnership and company forms of organisation differ in respect to management control and regulations?

Question 1.5
What are the different types of joint stock companies and their main features?

Question 1.6
In what way are co-operatives different from other types of business units?

2

Financial Statements

Control over the activities of a business venture is critical to success. In a small, easily managed operation, the owner/manager will usually be able to maintain adequate control by simply keeping an eye on things. Informal controls continue to play an important part in many organisations but they are inadequate for the needs of most modern businesses. Over centuries, a system of controls has grown and developed. These controls are known as financial statements. They are some of the basic tools used by managers to measure the health of a business.

The main indicators of financial performance are:
(a) The Balance Sheet.
(b) The Profit and Loss Account (Income Statement).
(c) The Cash Flow Statement.

These three statements, properly prepared and audited by qualified accountants, are the minimum legal requirements which must be met by most companies and co-operatives. The Cash Flow Statement is not necessary for 'small' companies and other companies operating in the financial services sector. Partnerships and sole proprietorships are not legally bound to prepare such accounts. It is proposed to exempt small limited-liability companies from the requirements to prepare audited accounts. The Revenue Commissioners, in order to assess taxation, require data which make the preparation of basic accounts essential.

The evolution of accounting standards has been a slow and tortuous process. The Institute of Chartered Accountants in England and Wales laid down a five-point plan through its 'Statement of Intent in Accounting Standards' in the 1970s. It was joined by the other main accountancy bodies to form the Accounting Standards Committee (ASC). The ASC issued over twenty standards called Statements of Standard Accounting Practice (SSAPs). These covered a wide range of issues and were finalised after publication of exposure drafts (EDs) and subsequent consultation.

In order to improve the standards process and make it more decisive and independent, a new body, the Accounting Standards Board (ASB), took over the functions of the ASC in 1990. The ASB can issue its recommendations, known as Financial Reporting Standards (FRSs), without approval from any other body and follows a similar process of consultation through the issuing of exposure drafts (FREDs). On its formation, the ASB accepted the SSAPs in force and to date has issued seven FRSs. All statements issued by the ASB are referred to the Institute of Chartered

Accountants in Ireland (ICAI) before publication.

While there is no general law compelling companies to observe the standards, compliance is ensured through the professional accountancy bodies using their own disciplinary procedures on their members. In the United Kingdom a review panel has also been set up by the ASB with powers to prosecute under civil law companies which are in breach of the standards.

The accounting standards are set with the objective 'to provide information about the financial position, performance and financial adaptability of an enterprise, that is useful to a wide range of users in making economic decisions'. Accounting policies or concepts are value judgments developed out of accounting theory and are the basis of the accounting standards (SSAPs and FRSs) currently in place. While all are important, most attention has been given to the concepts of 'going concern', 'accruals', 'consistency' and 'prudence'. These, allied to the attributes of relevance, materiality, reliability, timeliness and good presentation, form the basis of professional accounting practice.

The primary purpose of providing financial statements is to show the owners of the business how their capital has been utilised. But other objectives also exist. Lenders to a business generally wish to examine financial statements. Suppliers frequently set credit limits based on an analysis of the financial statements of a customer. Traditionally, Irish business people have shied away from producing accounts.

Business people are reluctant to publish financial information. The often quoted reason for secrecy is 'the danger of injuring the business by disclosure of information to competitors'. In most cases the danger does not exist. With the passing of the Companies (Amendment) Act 1986, the purpose of which was to implement the European Community's Fourth Council Directive of 1978, all Irish-registered public and private limited companies, with certain minor exceptions, are obliged to file statements with their annual returns to the Registrar of Companies. The most significant exemption is that which allows small private companies to file a Balance Sheet with relevant notes only — neither the Profit and Loss Account nor director's report has to be filed. However, the financial statements must meet the overriding requirement to give a true and fair view of the state of affairs.

THE BALANCE SHEET

Possibly the most important financial statement produced by a firm is the Balance Sheet. It is a list of the assets and liabilities of a business grouped into relevant categories. It is a statement of the condition of a firm at a particular date and usually shows the comparative position for a previous date. A Balance Sheet may be compared to a still photograph showing the financial condition of the firm at a given moment: it reflects the past rather than the future. A comparison of two Balance Sheets, at different dates, should provide some picture of the changes which have taken place. This information can then be used as a basis for decision-making.

Although a firm's Balance Sheet is prepared within guidelines of generally accepted accounting practice, the analyst must be aware of certain limitations in the statement. The following are some of the more important ones:
(1) The Balance Sheet does not reflect current values, as historical cost has been adopted as the basis for valuing and reporting assets and liabilities.
(2) Value judgments must be made in order to determine the true worth of several accounts. Examples include accounts receivable estimated in terms of collectability,

inventories based on realisable value, and fixed assets based on useful life.

(3) Appreciation or enhancement in most values is generally ignored, with depreciation of long-term assets being the accepted norm. This is particularly crucial in the case of property development companies and mining properties.

(4) Some items are omitted from the Balance Sheet because they involve extreme problems of objective evaluation. The three most obvious examples are the human resources of the firm, the business know-how or expertise built up over the years, and — most importantly — brands, e.g. Coca Cola. Items which appear in a Balance Sheet can be grouped as follows: assets; liabilities; net worth or owner's equity.

Assets

The assets are the resources of the business. They can be classified into five categories: current assets; long-term investments; fixed assets; intangible assets; and deferred charges.

(i) Current assets are those assets which are convertible into cash or capable of being used up within one year. Examples are cash, marketable securities, accounts receivable, inventory and prepaid expenses.

(ii) Long-term investments are investments in other companies' securities (ordinary or preferred shares or bonds) with the intention of holding them for more than one year. They are typically shown on the Balance Sheet at original purchase cost plus fees. If the intention is to hold these securities for less than one year, they would be classified as marketable securities under the heading of current assets. Few Irish companies have this item on their Balance Sheet.

(iii) Fixed assets are the permanent facilities of the business which are used to produce the product or services of the firm and have a life in excess of one year. They are tangible assets and are not being held for sale in the normal course of business. Examples include land, buildings, machinery, equipment, trucks and motor vehicles.

Fixed assets usually wear out over a period of time and so each year a part of the income of a business is set aside to account for this wear and tear. The amount set aside is known as depreciation. The objective of depreciation is to spread the cost of an asset over the useful life of the asset. In inflationary times depreciation does not provide adequate sums for replacement.

(iv) Intangible assets lack physical substance but give a long-term benefit to the firm. Examples include goodwill, trade names, trademarks, patents, copyright and franchise fees. Increasingly, brand names are being assigned a value.

(v) Deferred charges are certain expenditures already incurred but anticipated to generate future revenues. They represent an allocation of past costs to future years because of the clearly defined nature of the expenditure and the reasonable certainty of commercial viability. Examples include start-up costs, plant rearrangement costs and specific research and development costs.

Liabilities

Liabilities are sums owed to entities other than the owners of the business. They are generally grouped into the following categories:

(i) Current liabilities, such as accounts payable, short-term loans, overdrafts and other sums due for payment within twelve months.

(ii) Long-term or deferred liabilities, which cover all liabilities payable in more than twelve months.

(iii) Contingent liabilities — these do not yet exist but may come into being as a result of circumstances obtaining at the date of the Balance Sheet. Examples of contingent liabilities include guarantees given and consequences arising from legal actions.

Net Worth or Owner's Equity

Net worth is the owner's interest in the firm. It can be defined as follows:

Net Worth = Assets minus Liabilities.

In a limited company the net worth is generally presented in the following manner:
(i) Issued Share Capital, which means the funds raised from the owners.
(ii) Share Premium Account, which shows the premium — if any — paid by investors to purchase new shares in the business.
(iii) Reserves, which as a rule are divided into profits not paid out to shareholders and/or surpluses produced from revaluing the assets of the business.

THE PROFIT AND LOSS ACCOUNT (INCOME STATEMENT)

The Profit and Loss Account (Income Statement) measures the progress of a business over a period of time, most commonly twelve months. The Profit and Loss Account is usually made up of three distinct accounts. The Manufacturing Account estimates the total cost of manufacture during the period in question; the Trading Account deducts the cost of manufacture from sales revenue to establish a gross profit; the Profit and Loss Account deducts expenses to show the net profit or loss figure. Taken together the three statements are known as an Income Statement. The statements can be divided into five broad categories:
(1) Gross and net sales for the period. Any difference between the gross and net figures arises from discounts, allowances and returns.
(2) Cost of goods sold. Here, the cost of producing the sales is determined. The balancing figure between (1) and (2) is the Gross Profit.
(3) Selling and distribution expenses estimated and deducted.
(4) Itemised administrative, general and interest costs.
(5) Adjustments to profits, made for taxation and dividend purposes.

The undue concentration on net profit as a performance indicator and the use and abuse of extraordinary items in accounts led to the creation of the Financial Reporting Standard (FRS) 3 in 1992.

This standard stated as its objective the need 'to require reporting entities . . . to highlight a range of important components of financial performance to aid users in understanding the performance achieved by a reporting entity in a period and to assist them in forming a basis for their assessment of future results and cash flows'.

Auditors seek to achieve this objective by requiring a 'layered' format to the Profit and Loss Account. This is designed to disclose clearly various components of financial performance, by looking for the following information:
(1) — Results of continuing operations
  — results of discontinued operations
  — major exceptional items
  — extraordinary items (defined as being of 'a high degree of abnormality' and 'not expected to recur' — should be extremely rare).
The new approach to profit calculation and presentation should lead to the virtual

elimination of the use of the extraordinary item classification and its significant abuse by firms in their calculation of earnings per share (EPS).

The major exceptional items which the standard requires to be shown separately on the face of the Profit and Loss Account are:

    (a) gain or loss on sale or cessation of an operation.

    (b) costs of a fundamental reorganisation or restructuring.

    (c) gain or loss on the sale of a fixed asset.

These exceptional items should be disclosed after operating profit and labelled as referring to continuing or discontinued operations.

(2) A restatement by way of note of the historical profit or loss that would have arisen before asset revaluation and consequent depreciation adjustment.

(3) A statement of total recognised gains and losses to be added. This statement adjusts profit for other gains and losses not recognised in the Profit and Loss Account, such as changes in the valuation of assets and foreign currency movements, which previously were 'hidden' in the notes to the accounts. The objective is to help analysts better assess the return on investment of the firm.

(4) A note reconciling movements in shareholders' funds. This note draws together all changes in the various classes of reserves which, along with share capital, make up shareholders' funds.

Taken overall the above requirements should make it easier to analyse the Profit and Loss Account and should give a better view of the medium- to long-term underlying performance of the business.

The Profit and Loss Account or Income Statement is compiled on an accrual rather than a cash basis. This means that an attempt is made to match the firm's revenues for the period in question with the costs incurred in generating those revenues. This often gives rise to a difference between reported revenues and costs for the period and actual cash flows, due to the facts that:

    (a) revenues and costs recognised in the Income Statement reflect all transactions applicable to the period in question and not just cash transactions: that is, credit and cash sales, wages actually paid and owing;

    (b) certain expenses included in the Income Statement are non-cash items: that is, depreciation, goodwill.

THE CASH FLOW STATEMENT

The realisation that profit is a concept while cash is a reality gave rise to the need for a third statement reconciling the difference. This was done through the 'Statement of Sources and Applications of Funds', which became a requirement in 1976. This is now known as the Cash Flow Statement. It was deemed necessary to ensure more transparency and greater compliance in this area. Consequently, a new standard (FRSI) was introduced in 1991.

The objective was to highlight the importance of cash in the firm. This was done by improving the understanding of the firm's cash-generating and cash-absorbing mechanisms, thereby providing a basis for the assessment of future cash flows. The Cash Flow Statement is intended to answer questions relating to the cash position of an organisation, such as:

— Did the firm's profits generate sufficient funds for its continuing operations?

— How has the firm financed its increased fixed assets? Did it finance them from long-term sources or from operating activities?

— How did the firm meet its dividend and interest payments? Was it from operating activities, from increased borrowing or from sales of fixed assets?

The statement classifies inflows and outflows of cash and cash equivalents under five headings in this sequence:

- Operating activities
- Returns on investments and servicing of finance
- Taxation
- Investing activities
- Financing.

The contents of each category are generally clear from the heading. For example, the cash flow from operating activities may be shown on either a gross (direct method) or a net (indirect method) basis. Each method is summarised as follows:

Direct Method of Identifying Cash from Operating Activities

Operating Activities

—Cash received from customers	XXX
—Less cash payments to suppliers	(XXX)
—Less cash paid to and on behalf of employees	(XXX)
—Less other cash payments	(XXX)
Net cash in/(out) flow from operating activities	XXX

The direct method involves analysing the cash book to obtain the necessary breakdown of cash flow information.

Indirect Method of Identifying Cash from Operating Activities

Operating Activities

— Operating profit	XXX
— Depreciation charges	XXX
— Loss (profit) on sale of tangible assets	XXX
— Increase in stocks	(XXX)
— Decrease in debtors	XXX
— Increase in creditors	XXX
Net cash in/(out) flow from operating activities	XXX

The indirect method involves taking the operating profit from the Profit and Loss Account and adjusting for non-cash items, i.e. depreciation, loss/profit on sale of fixed assets and any movement in working capital items.

While either method is acceptable, accounting standards encourage use of the direct method and, as a minimum requirement, a reconciliation between the operating profit and the net cash flow. As this is effectively the same as the indirect method, firms choosing to use the direct method also have to show the indirect method in order to comply with the minimum requirement of the standard.

The limitations of a Profit and Loss Account and Balance Sheet are known to most practising accountants. Having discussed the year's results in detail, and told his client of the large net profit he has succeeded in making, the accountant will frequently be asked, 'Where has it gone?' It is not often that one can simply turn to the bank account and see the profit sitting there, waiting to be used. The introduction of the Cash Flow Statement goes a long way towards answering this question.

The description 'Cash Flow' is, unlike some accounting terms, purely factual. The statement shows the funds: that is, cash which has been introduced into the business during an accounting period, and how it has been applied or utilised. The clear focus is on cash, including demand deposits and cash equivalents defined as short-term (within three months' maturity) liquid investments.

THE ACCOUNTS OF ARDMORE LIMITED

The best way to illustrate the mechanics of financial statements is to work through an example. The accounts of Ardmore for 1994, with comparative figures for 1993, are presented in Table 2.1. Modern forms of presentation are used for both the Balance Sheet and Income Statement. The Balance Sheet is presented in columnar form instead of the more traditional listing of assets on the right-hand side and liabilities and net worth on the left. The Income Statement is presented in narrative form instead of the traditional listing of expenses on the left-hand side and sales and profit on the right. The Cash Flow Statement is shown to comply with modern accounting standards.

Table 2.1

Ardmore Limited
Balance Sheet as at 31 December 1994
(Amounts expressed as £'000)

	1994	1993
Fixed Assets (Note 7)		
Land and Buildings	310	310
Plant and Machinery	362	340
Fixtures and Fittings	71	68
Motor Vehicles	37	42
	780	760
Current Assets		
Inventory (Note 9)	390	310
Accounts Receivable	719	515
Cash	4	10
	1,113	835
Current Liabilities		
Accounts Payable (Trade)	386	334
Bank Overdraft	130	68
Short-Term Loan	180	220
Current Taxation	17	13
	713	635
Net Current Assets	400	200
	£1,180	£960
Financed by		
Authorised Ordinary £1 Shares		
Issued 600,000 Ordinary £1 Shares	600	600
Reserves:		
Share Premium a/c	25	25
Profit and Loss a/c	200	30
Government Grants (Note 6)	130	120
Debentures (Note 8)	225	185
	£1,180	£960

Ardmore Limited
Manufacturing, Trading and Profit and Loss Account
for the 12 Months Ended 31 December 1994
(Amounts expressed as £'000)

	1994		1993	
Net Sales		2,836		2,600
Stocks of Finished Goods: 1 January	238		220	
Cost of Manufacture (Note 1)	2,096		1,968	
	2,334		2,188	
Less Stocks of Finished Goods				
31 December	294		238	
Cost of Sales		2,040		1,950
Gross Profit		796		650
Less Expenses				
Selling and Distribution (Note 2)		324		302
Interest Charges (Note 3)		64		47
Administration (Note 4)		248		171
Add Profit on Sale of Asset		12		–
Government Grant (Note 6)		15		22
Net Profit Before Tax		187		152
Taxation (Note 5)		17		13
Net Profit After Tax		170		139
Balance in Profit and Loss c/fwd		30		(109)
Balance Carried Forward		£200		£30

Ardmore Limited Cash Flow Statement
for the 12 Months Ended 31 December 1994
(Amounts expressed as £'000)

• Net Cash Inflow from Operating Activities (note 10)		35
• Return on Investments and Servicing of Finance		
Interest Paid		(64)
Taxation		(13)
Investing Activities		
Purchase of Tangible Assets	(66)	
Proceeds of Sale of Tangible Assets	15	(51)
• Financing		
Short-Term Financing	(40)	
Debenture Loan	40	
Government Grants	25	25
Increase/(Decrease) in Cash and Cash Equivalents		(68)
• Movement in Cash		
Bank Overdraft	62	
Cash	6	£68

Notes Forming Part of the Accounts

Note 1 Cost of Manufacture. The details behind the cost of manufacture are provided here. All items directly connected with production are included: for example, wages, raw materials and direct costs associated with the factory. The movements in the value of inventory and work in progress are monitored to identify those costs, and only those costs, associated with sales during the calendar year 1994.

Ardmore Limited
Manufacturing Account for the Twelve Months Ended 31 December 1994
(Amounts expressed as £'000)

	1994	1993
Stocks of Raw Material 1 January	30	28
Purchases	1,343	1,302
Carriage Inwards	19	13
	1,392	1,343
Less Stocks of Raw Material		
31 December	46	30
Raw Materials Consumed	1,346	1,313
Factory Wages	620	559
Prime Cost of Manufacture	1,966	1,872
Works Overhead		
Repairs and Renewals	34	27
Rates	8	6
Light, Heat and Power	38	24
Laundry and Cleaning	15	11
Depreciation	43	36
	138	104
Works Cost of Manufacture	2,104	1,976
Add Opening Work in Progress		
1 January	42	34
Less Closing Work in Progress		
31 December	(50)	(42)
Cost of Manufacture	£2,096	£1,968

Note 2 Selling and Distribution Expenses. It is common to give details of the sums spent in obtaining sales. For many Irish companies, particularly those exporting, this is a very significant item. In the case of Ardmore one of the owners acts as sales manager.

	1994 £'000	1993 £'000
Salaries	114	103
Travel Expenses	142	126
Advertising	51	48
Discounts Allowed	17	25
	£324	£302

Note 3 Interest Charges. The company has a variety of loans on which interest is paid as follows:

	1994 £'000	1993 £'000
Debenture Interest	23	15
Term Loan Interest	22	22
Overdraft	19	10
	£64	£47

Note 4 Administration Expenses. Modern business has many overheads, such as rent, communications, etc. Such costs are often grouped as administration or establishment expenses.

	1994 £'000	1993 £'000
Directors' Fees	70	38
Office Salaries	91	64
Rates	5	4
Insurance	28	24
Telephone	26	21
Postage	7	4
Light and Heat	7	5
Miscellaneous	14	11
	£248	£171

Note 5 Taxation. Irish companies are liable to Corporation Tax, Capital Gains Tax and Value Added Tax on sales. The rate of Corporation Tax is 40 per cent for service industries and 10 per cent for manufacturing companies, and those licensed to operate in the Shannon Free Zone and the International Financial Services Centre in Dublin. The turnover figures in the accounts are net of VAT.

Value Added Tax (VAT) was introduced in 1972. Every taxable unit must be registered and must charge the proper amount of VAT. The taxable period is two months and returns must be filed with the Collector General of Taxes within nineteen days of the end of the taxable period.

In the case of Ardmore the taxation provisions have been estimated as follows:

	1994 £'000	1993 £'000
Corporation Tax	£17	£13

Taxable income is reduced in Ireland by capital allowances. These range from zero initial plant and machinery or industrial building allowances for all firms to 100 per cent for qualifying services companies in the Custom House Docks Area or in the Shannon Customs Free Area. Writing down and wear and tear allowances of 15 per cent for plant and machinery and 4 per cent for industrial building are allowed. Capital allowances are also available on commercial premises within designated Urban Renewal areas and in the Temple Bar area of Dublin. The 10 per cent rate of Corporation Tax for manufacturing was introduced on 1 January 1981 and expires on 31 December 2010. This applies to companies manufacturing in the state and certain non-manufacturing services conducted in the Shannon Customs Free Area. The relief also applies to fish farming activities and certain computer services carried on in the state in the course of a service undertaking which has obtained an employment grant. The 1987 Finance Bill extended the relief to the profits from:

(a) The carriage of cargo and passengers on seagoing ships which are Irish owned and registered.

(b) A trade which consists exclusively of the sale by wholesale on the export market of Irish-manufactured goods.

(c) Certain financial services carried on at the Custom House Docks site.

From April 1994 there are two rates of Capital Gains Tax on chargeable gains arising from the disposal of assets:

27 per cent on the disposal of certain shares

40 per cent on all other chargeable gains.

The 27 per cent rate was introduced to reward individual investors who provide venture capital funding for small to medium-sized companies. For disposals of certain shares on or after 6 April 1994 this rate applies, subject to a number of conditions being met. These include the requirements that the shares must be unquoted and the company resident in the state and that the market value of the issued share capital should not exceed £25 million. Furthermore, the individual must have held the shares for at least five years, and land dealing and financial services companies are excluded. In addition indexation applies, whereby the cost of any asset — including expenditure which enhances its value — is adjusted for inflation by reference to increases in the consumer price index.

Note 6 Grants. The state, through the IDA, is one of the largest providers of finance to manufacturing in Ireland, with up to 60 per cent of capital expenditure available from it. In exceptional circumstances the grant is repayable, so accounting conventions require it to be written into the Profit and Loss Account over the life of the asset to which it refers. In 1994 some £15,000 of grants were taken into the accounts. At the same time, additional grants of £25,000 were received so the Balance Sheet figures have risen by £10,000.

Note 7 Fixed Assets. The figures in the Balance Sheet for assets are net of depreciation. It is usual to give the gross cost figures and accumulated depreciation figures in a separate note.

	Cost £'000	Accumulated Depreciation	1994 Net Book Value	1993
Land and Buildings	310	–	310	310
Plant and Machinery	476	114	362	340
Fixtures and Fittings	93	22	71	68
Motor Vehicles	46	9	37	42
	£925	£145	£780	£760

It is important to be aware of what these figures tell and what they do not tell. There is no mention of the current realisable market value of the assets. In a period of inflation this can be particularly important. For instance, it has been estimated that the market value of the 10,000 square foot Ardmore premises was £465,000 in 1994. In like manner highly specialised plant may have only a break-up market value.

Note 8 Debentures. It is usual to explain the nature of debentures, especially if they are secured by mortgages. In this case Ardmore owes £185,000 to the Bank of Ireland on foot of a ten-year debenture which is secured by a floating charge over all of the assets of the business together with a specific charge on the premises. In addition a loan of £40,000 from the Industrial Credit Corporation is secured by mortgage ranking *pari passu*: that is, equally with that of the Bank of Ireland. These mortgages in effect restrict the business in that the assets cannot be disposed of, except within the terms of the mortgage agreements. For example, it is most unlikely that Ardmore Limited could sell its premises and distribute part or all of the proceeds to the owners. The banks would insist on first being repaid.

Note 9 Inventory. This is made up as follows:

	1994 £'000	1993 £'000
Raw Material	46	30
Work in Progress	50	42
Finished Goods	294	238
	£390	£310

Note 10 Reconciliation of Operating Income to Net Cash Inflow from Operating Activities.

	£'000
Operating income before interest and tax	251
Non-cash item — Depreciation	43
Profit/(loss) on sale of tangible assets	(12)
Inventory	(80)
Debtors	(204)
Creditors	52
Amortisation of Government Grants	(15)
Net Cash Inflow from Operating Activities	£35

CONCLUSION

Financial statements are a fundamental requirement in every business. The three basic statements presented here: the Balance Sheet, the Income Statement, and the Cash Flow Statement, represent only the most basic of statements. Modern financial and management accounting has developed a wide variety of statements designed to assist in controlling business. What you have here is only the bare bones.

A note of caution must be sounded. Accounting conventions and a circumspect approach to valuation means that a Balance Sheet rarely gives an accurate picture of the worth of the business. One must evaluate carefully the real worth of fixed, current and intangible assets. Likewise other methods of financing, such as project finance, may not be reflected on a Balance Sheet.

The Income Statement is often thought of as a better measure but it too suffers from serious defects. Frequently, profits arise from changes in the value of inventory. Such profits may never appear. Depreciation figures are notional and usually bear little relationship to the actual decline in the value of an asset or to the sum required to be set aside to enable replacement.

Once a businessman is aware of the limitations of financial statements, he can begin to use them. The uses to which financial data can be put are examined in the following chapter.

FURTHER READING

L.E. Rockley, *The Meaning of Balance Sheets and Company Reports* (London, Business Books, 1975).

F. Wood & T. Robinson, *Business Accounting*, Irish ed. (Pitman Publishing, 1994).

R. Hussey & M. Berhop, *Corporate Reports* (London, Woodhead Faulkner, 1993).

J. Blake, *Accounting Standards*, 4th ed. (Pitman Publishing, 1994).

N. Brennan, F.J. O'Brien & A. Pierce, *A Survey of Irish Published Accounts*, 2nd ed. (Oak Tree Press, 1992).

QUESTIONS

Question 2.1

Define or explain each of the following:

      (a) Balance Sheet
      (b) Profit and Loss Account
      (c) Cash Flow Statement
      (d) Assets
      (e) Liabilities

Question 2.2

Explain why notes to a firm's financial statements form an integral part of the financial statement.

Question 2.3
What distinguishes:
      (a) current assets from other asset classes on the Balance Sheet?
      (b) current liabilities from other classes of liabilities on the Balance Sheet?

Question 2.4
What are some of the limitations in using a Balance Sheet?

Question 2.5
A small business owner, selling and repairing cars, has received a copy of his financial statement for the current year. Certain entries seem incorrect in his opinion and he has asked your advice:
      (a) 'The house I own cost £40,000 three years ago and is now worth £55,000 but it isn't included in the financial statement. Why?'
      (b) 'Why do vehicles appear under both fixed and current assets?'

Question 2.6
Make the double entries for the following:

      (a) Paid rent by cash
      (b) Paid for goods by cash
      (c) Received by cheque a refund of rates already paid
      (d) Paid general expenses by cheque
      (e) Received commissions in cash
      (f) Goods returned by us to T. Jones
      (g) Goods sold for cash
      (h) Bought office fixtures by cheque
      (i) Paid wages in cash
      (j) Took cash out of business for private use.

3

Financial Analysis

Having received a set of financial statements, the next step is to elicit and interpret the information stored in them. The type of information being sought depends on the particular person or firm involved. A debenture holder wishes to know the long-term risk of the business not paying his interest or capital. A trade creditor or bank manager wants to know the availability of cash to meet short-term liabilities. An investor wants to know how profitable an investment in the company is likely to be. The financial *well-being* of the firm can be judged by answering some or all of the following:

(1) How liquid is the firm, i.e. can it pay bills when they are due?
(2) How does the firm's management finance its investments and/or capital expenditure?
(3) Is management generating sufficient profits from the firm's assets?
(4) Is cash being generated to meet interest and/or debt repayments?
(5) Are the common stockholders receiving sufficient returns on their investment?

The parties with interests in the health of the venture are shown in Figure 3.1.

Analysis of financial statements uses data in a relative sense. An absolute figure may have little value whereas a relationship between two or more figures can tell a story. Likewise, changes in a figure over time may be more important than the figure itself, i.e. the trend gives the information.

There are six methods of analysing financial statements:

(1) Comparative Analysis of financial statements from different periods. Each item in the Balance Sheet and Income Statement is compared across time and differences are then explained. This little-used and simple method of analysis shows whether a firm is making or losing money and highlights changes in the way in which money is invested in assets and the way in which the investments are financed.
(2) Working Capital Analysis examines changes in the current assets and liabilities of a business. Working capital management is examined in detail in Chapter 5.
(3) Internal Analysis is used mainly to assess credit risks. The relative size of each Balance Sheet item is examined and compared to some 'norm' or average. For example, if you know that a business has had increasing sales by means of easy credit terms then you would expect a large figure for accounts receivable. Should the figures be different from those expected, further investigation is required.

(4) Analysis by Sales compares data in the Income Statement with items in the Balance Sheet and develops a series of operating ratios.

(5) Ratio Analysis constructs a series of ratios which analyse trends and relationships in a business. They are then compared to 'norms' or averages either over time or by industry, company or sector.

(6) The Cash Flow Statement highlights the importance of cash in the business. It shows the significant components of cash flow under a number of headings and facilitates comparison within and across different businesses. Its application, which gained importance only in the 1990s, should lead to much greater transparency of the cash-generating and cash-absorbing capabilities of the firm. It is a significant improvement on the 'Statement of Sources and Applications of Funds' which it replaced.

Ratio Analysis and the interpretation of the Cash Flow Statement are the most common forms of financial analysis, and are applied to the Ardmore accounts.

Figure 3.1 Shareholders' Concerns

External Stakeholders

Bond/Debenture Holders
Ability of company to pay interest and capital promptly. Their security if the company gets into difficulty.

Accounts Payable
Current assets to pay current liabilities. Make-up of current assets. Earnings potential of possible expansion/contraction of the business. Priority of claim in event of company failure, if any.

Bankers
What is bank debt being used for? Prospects of firm — trend of profit as disclosed in past years' statements. Prior rights on liquidation.

Potential Investor
Trends of profit and sales over recent years. Forecasts of expansion in the industry. Yield on proposed investments.

Others
Revenue, Competitors, Customers, Finance Companies

Internal Stakeholders

Shareholders
Performance, dividends, expansion, future prospects.

Employees and Trade Unions
Profits/wage demands. Profit-sharing scheme.

Directors
Performance/survival. Earn optimum profits.

RATIO ANALYSIS

The financial health of a business is often measured by means of financial ratios. A ratio is a measure which relates two pieces of financial information. Financial ratios are used in two separate ways. Firstly, when compared across periods of time, changes in ratios will help to explain trends in areas such as the profitability and/or financial stability of a business. Secondly, inter-firm comparisons can be applied, either by comparing firms within the same industry or by comparing firms from different industries. In both the United States and the United Kingdom, firms such as Dun & Bradstreet publish financial ratios for different industries. These enable companies to compare their performances with those of other firms. In Ireland only the small number of publicly quoted firms publish financial data therefore comparisons are difficult.

The limitations of ratios must be stressed. Do not become a slave to figures. The mathematical nature of ratios frequently gives a precision to the analysis which is simply untrue. Often, the data on which ratios are based are estimates or are unrealistic valuations. In comparing ratios across companies the danger of false interpretations increases, so caution must be exercised.

Financial ratios fall into four broad categories: liquidity ratios; profitability ratios; activity ratios; debt ratios (also known as stability ratios).

Liquidity Ratios

Liquidity ratios rely on Balance Sheet data. The liquidity of a firm means the ability of the firm to meet its short-term liabilities without having to liquidate its long-term assets or cease operations. In short it means availability of cash to pay debts. The two principal liquidity ratios are:

    (a) Current Ratio.
    (b) Acid Test or Quick Ratio.

Current Ratio. This measures the relationship of current assets to current liabilities. For Ardmore Limited the ratios for 1994 and 1993 were

(Expressed as £'000)	1994	1993
$\dfrac{\text{Current Assets}}{\text{Current Liabilities}}$	$\dfrac{£1,113}{£713} = 1.6$	$\dfrac{£835}{£635} = 1.3$

The higher the current ratio, the greater the supposed ability of a firm to meet current payments.

Although it used to be held that a firm should aim for a current ratio of 2:1, it is now considered that the particular circumstances of each industry or company determine the optimum current ratio. Different industries have characteristics which seriously affect the current ratio. It is composed not only of cash but of assets such as inventory and accounts receivable, neither of which may be easily sold at prices close to their Balance Sheet value. There have been instances of firms going bankrupt with high current ratios: that is, many times more current assets than current liabilities. This could occur if the firm had a very low cash balance, a high proportion of unsaleable inventory and a large amount of bad debts. Despite these deficiencies, the ratio is widely used by managers, bankers and financial journalists, with its major strength being that it presents the analyst with an absolute yardstick for measuring the liquidity of the firm. In the case of Ardmore Limited there has been some change during 1994. The company appears to have been in a fairly tight current position in 1993, which has improved during 1994.

Acid Test or Quick Ratio. The current ratio includes the effect of inventory. This may not be readily realisable and so does not meet the liquidity criterion; that is, easily convertible into cash. The acid test ratio is a more severe and stringent test of the firm's ability to meet current obligations but it too has its critics. They point out that receivables may be stretching out in age and declining in quality of collectability, whereas inventory management might have ensured greater stability and control.

That being said, the Acid Test or Quick Ratio, like the current ratio, is of some significance provided it is subjected to qualitative as well as quantitative tests and is compared to the industry norm or standard. Applying the ratio to Ardmore Limited for 1993 and 1994, the following information was discovered:

(Expressed as £'000)	1994		1993	
Current Assets less Inventory	$\dfrac{£723}{£713}$	$= 1.0$	$\dfrac{£525}{£635}$	$= 0.8$
Current Liabilities				

In theory Ardmore Limited has just sufficient liquid assets to cover its obligations. If all of the current liabilities were immediately presented for payment, Ardmore would be just able to pay. A rule of thumb is a ratio of 1:1, though certain businesses — for example, supermarkets — would have a lower ratio. Ardmore is not in bad shape and has improved slightly in the year 1994.

A more accurate way to estimate cash sufficiency is to forecast expected payments and receipts month by month for the next twelve months (this topic is covered in Chapter 4). Internal management should do this as part of its ongoing budgeting process but will usually not make it available to the external analyst. Analysts have to rely on the published financial statements and keep an eye on trends and comparative data.

Profitability Ratios

These ratios use both the Balance Sheet and Income Statement. They are employed to discover how efficiently and effectively assets have contributed to the profits of the firm and can be divided into two groups: profitability in relation to sales and profitability in relation to investment. It is possible to examine only the most widely used ratios. They are:

(a) Gross profit margin.
(b) Net profit margin before and after tax.
(c) Total asset turnover.
(d) Return on investment.

Gross Profit Margin. The Gross Profit Margin is calculated by expressing gross profit as a percentage of net sales. It indicates the percentage of sales remaining after paying for the cost of goods sold. The higher the margin the better.

	1994	1993
Gross margin of Ardmore	28.1%	25.0%

The Ardmore gross margin is good and the increase year on year is a welcome development. It can also be seen as a satisfactory performance against the background of an increase in sales revenue of only 9 per cent on the previous year. The twin achievements of increased sales and improved gross margin are an indication of good management practice in regard to pricing policy and the control of manufacturing costs.

Net Profit Margin Before Tax. This is calculated by expressing net profit before tax as a percentage of net sales, and is the margin of profit remaining after all costs have been deducted.

For Ardmore,

	1994	**1993**
Net profit margin before tax	6.6%	5.8%

This level is not uncommon in Irish business.

The low ratio emphasises the difficulty of making profits in Irish manufacturing industry. The margin, though rising, is too low for comfort. For example, if one allowed a more realistic depreciation charge for the replacement of plant and equipment used during the year, then the profit percentage could be minimal.

Net Profit Margin After Tax. This is calculated by expressing net profit after tax as a percentage of net sales.

For Ardmore,

	1994	**1993**
Net profit margin after tax	6.0%	5.35%

Ardmore being manufacturing pays a 10 per cent corporate tax rate, reflecting the positive climate regarding the taxation of manufacturing profits in Ireland.

Total Asset Turnover. This examines the efficiency with which the resources of the business are being used. It is a measure of productivity as much as profitability. Extreme care must be taken in using this ratio for comparative purposes as issues such as depreciation policy, lease versus buy decisions, and the age and original value of the assets have to be taken into consideration. The performance of the firm in managing its working capital is also incorporated into this ratio and a review of the activity ratios may be helpful here. For Ardmore,

$$\text{Total Asset Turnover} = \frac{\text{Annual Sales}}{\text{Net Assets}} = \begin{array}{cc} \mathbf{1994} & \mathbf{1993} \\ \dfrac{£2,836}{£1,180} = 2.4 & \dfrac{£2,600}{£960} = 2.7 \end{array}$$

(£'000s)

The slight drop in the ratio means that more assets are having to be used to generate every unit of sales. Ardmore's overall asset turnover figures reflect the nature of the business — relatively labour-intensive engineering.

Asset turnover ratios range from a high in the 20s for supermarkets and most service industries to a low of about 0.5 for capital-intensive resource and manufacturing projects such as steel mills or mines.

Return on Investment (ROI). Ultimately, the success or failure of the business depends on whether the investment shows a sufficient profit. There are many methods of calculating ROI, the most common of which is

$$\text{Return on Investment} = \frac{\text{Net Profit After Taxes}}{\text{Net Assets}}$$

The ratio for Ardmore is (expressed as £'000)

$$\text{ROI} = \begin{array}{cc} \mathbf{1994} & \mathbf{1993} \\ \dfrac{£170}{£1,180} = 14.4\% & \dfrac{£139}{£960} = 14.4\% \end{array}$$

Basically, this states that Ardmore is making about 14 per cent on the money it has invested in the business.

The ratio by itself is of little value. A better version is the Return on Owner's Equity: that is, the return which an owner receives for investing his own funds (expressed as £'000):

$$\text{Return on Owner's Investment} = \frac{\text{Net Profit After Taxes}}{\text{Net Worth}}$$

The ratio for Ardmore is (expressed as £'000)

$$\begin{array}{cc} \mathbf{1994} & \mathbf{1993} \\ \dfrac{£170}{£955} = 17.8\% & \dfrac{£139}{£775} = 17.9\% \end{array}$$

An after-tax rate of return of nearly 18 per cent is high by Irish standards. It is important to know what it means. For giving up their money and investing it in a risky engineering venture, the owners see the book value of their investment grow by 18 per cent. That 18 per cent growth, which is still locked into the assets of the business, covers a payment for risk, inflation and time. The investors could have put their money into the Post Office or shares in the Bank of Ireland. The perils that go with investing in business demand an adequate and continuing reward in the form of profit, a small portion of which must be set aside for future growth. The firm cannot attract more or new investment funds without a substantial return to show for present and past investments, or at least the prospect of future profit attainment.

The 'Du Pont Formula' for calculating the Return on Investment is widely used. It breaks down ROI into two parts, net margin on sales and asset turnover. It is calculated as follows:

ROI = Net Profit Margin x Asset Turnover

$$= \frac{\text{Net Profit After Taxes}}{\text{Sales}} \quad \times \quad \frac{\text{Sales}}{\text{Total Net Assets}}$$

For Ardmore the figures are

	Margin		Asset Turnover		ROI
1994 ROI =	6.0%	×	2.4	=	14.4%
1993 ROI =	5.35%	×	2.7	=	14.4%

Though the ROI for both years is the same, the figures may hide what could be significant trends. In 1994 Ardmore management did get a reasonable increase in profits. At the same time it used more assets. It is possible that the increased profits in

39

1994 encouraged management to invest in more assets to take advantage of more opportunities. The increased sales revenue and margins must therefore be balanced against a slowing down in asset turnover. This could be due to a once-off adjustment in fixed assets or a slippage in the control of working capital. The latter is the more likely reason, as evidenced by the activity ratios below. Careful management is essential.

Activity Ratios

Activity ratios measure the speed with which money invested in current assets passes through the system and reappears as cash. The main activity ratios are:
(a) Inventory Turnover.
(b) Accounts Receivable Turnover.
(c) Accounts Payable Turnover.

Inventory Turnover. This is measured as follows:

$$\text{Inventory Turnover} = \frac{\text{Cost of Goods Sold}}{\text{Average Inventory}}$$

For Ardmore the ratio is:
(Expressed as £'000)

	1994		1993	
Inventory Turnover =	$\frac{£2,040}{(£310 + £390) \div 2}$	= 5.8	$\frac{£1,950}{(£282 + £310) \div 2}$	= 6.6

Average Inventory is defined as Opening plus Closing Inventory divided by two.

The opening figure for inventory on 1 January 1993 was £282,000. Clearly, there was a significant increase in inventory in 1994 not matched by a corresponding increase in sales activity. This resulted in a reduction in the number of times inventory was turned over, from 6.6 times in 1993 to 5.8 times in 1994. The slowdown in turnover is not welcome but to be meaningful the ratio should be compared with similar ratios in like businesses. In the light engineering business in Ireland a turnover of 5.8 would be low. Note that supermarkets might have a turnover of 30 or more while a shipbuilding business could have a turnover of less than 2. This ratio could serve as an early warning signal of a firm's financial difficulties, with a decline or slowing down in sales leading to a piling up of unsold and/or unsaleable inventory. There is some cause for concern in this regard for Ardmore Limited.

A derivation of inventory turnover is the average age of inventory in which the number of days in a year is divided by the turnover figures.

	1994		1993	
Age of Inventory	$\frac{365}{5.8}$	= 63 days	$\frac{365}{6.6}$	= 55 days

The shorter the days in inventory, the greater corporate liquidity is likely to be. In 1994 Ardmore held on average two months' stock.

Accounts Receivable Turnover. This ratio serves as the basis for determining how rapidly the firm's credit accounts are being collected and is defined as follows:

Accounts Receivable Turnover $=$ $\dfrac{\text{Annual Credit Sales}}{\text{Average Accounts Receivable}}$

For the sake of clarity, assume that all of the sales of Ardmore are on credit. The Accounts Receivable Turnover for Ardmore is as follows (expressed as £'000):

1994	1993
$\dfrac{£2,836}{(£515 + £719) \div 2} = 4.6$	$\dfrac{£2,600}{(£485 + £515) \div 2} = 5.2$

The figure for accounts receivable on 1 January 1993 was £485,000. The average age of receivables is normally then computed.

Average Age of Accounts Receivable $=$ $\dfrac{365}{\text{Accounts Receivable Turnover}}$

	1994	1993
Ardmore Age of Receivables	$\dfrac{365}{4.6} = 79$ days	$\dfrac{365}{5.2} = 70$ days

The above figure of seventy-nine days for Ardmore is the average period for collecting a debt. Many people may be surprised at the apparently long collection period. Unfortunately, Irish customers are notorious for taking extended credit. In periods of tight bank credit the collection period tends to extend. The collection period must be related to the credit terms offered by the firm. Ardmore nominally gives forty-five days' credit. Whatever the cause, the slippage in this ratio indicates greater risk, an increased chance of default or late payment by customers, with the resultant impact on the firm's cash flow. A 1994 study of Irish business revealed an average of eighty days for accounts receivable.

Accounts Payable Turnover. This ratio is defined in a manner similar to the accounts receivable turnover. It is:

Accounts Payable Turnover $=$ $\dfrac{\text{Annual Purchases}}{\text{Average Accounts Payable}}$

For Ardmore Limited this works out as (expressed as £'000):

1994	1993
$\dfrac{£1,343}{(£334 + £386) \div 2} = 3.7$	$\dfrac{£1,302}{(£290 + £334) \div 2} = 4.2$

The opening figure for accounts payable on 1 January 1993 was £290,000. Computing the payment period for payables produces the following:

	1994	1993
Average Payment Period $=$	$\dfrac{365}{3.7} = 99$ days	$\dfrac{365}{4.2} = 87$ days

Ardmore is 'stretching' its trade creditors. In 1994 Ardmore Limited has stretched the payable period by twelve days. This was accompanied by Ardmore allowing the collection period to rise by nine days and the inventory holding time to rise by eight days, giving rise to a slippage in the overall cash/liquidity position. The creditors have partly financed the build-up of inventory and the slippage in debtor collections. While credit from suppliers is a valuable source of finance, some concern could be noted at the possibility of 'stretching their goodwill' to an unacceptable level.

Debt Ratios (Leverage/Gearing Ratios)

Debt Ratios measure the ability of the firm to meet future obligations, such as interest and repayments on both debentures and term loans. A breach of these obligations is serious and may cause the business to close. Investors, suppliers and bankers pay close attention to the amount of debt owed by a business. Three ratios are commonly used to help evaluate the risk posed to the business by the level of debt:
(a) The Debt Ratio.
(b) Debt/Equity.
(c) Times Interest Earned.

These techniques measure the long-term financial stability of the business.

Debt Ratio. This ratio measures the extent to which the total assets of the firm have been financed using borrowed funds.

$$\text{Debt Ratio} = \frac{\text{Total Liabilities}}{\text{Total Assets}} = \frac{\text{Current Liabilities} + \text{Debentures}}{\text{Fixed} + \text{Current Assets}}$$

For Ardmore Limited the figures were:

(Expressed as £'000)	1994	1993
Debt Ratio =	$\dfrac{£938}{£1,893} = 50\%$	$\dfrac{£820}{£1,595} = 51\%$

Ardmore has managed to finance 50 per cent of its business by using borrowed funds. Using borrowed funds is known as financial leverage or gearing. Chapter 14 returns to the concept of leverage. The Ardmore figure is high by Irish standards.

Debt/Equity Ratio. This commonly used ratio measures the relationship between long-term debt and the owners' investment. It highlights the cushion of owners' funds available to the debt holders. For Ardmore Limited the ratios were:

(Expressed as £'000)		1994	1993
Debt/Equity Ratio =	$\dfrac{\text{Long-Term Debt}}{\text{Issued Capital} + \text{Reserves} + \text{Grants}}$	$=\dfrac{£225}{£955} = 24\%$	$\dfrac{£185}{£775} = 24\%$

The ratio is meaningful only when traced over time and/or when related to the business of the firm. Companies in capital-intensive stable businesses tend to have high ratios. The ratio for Ardmore Limited is well within the acceptable range for Irish engineering firms.

Times Interest Earned. This measures the ability of a firm to meet interest payments out of its annual operating earnings. The ratio is defined as follows:

$$\text{Times Interest Earned} = \frac{\text{Net Profit Before Interest and Taxes}}{\text{Interest Payments (including overdraft interest)}}$$

For Ardmore Limited the ratios were:

(Expressed as £'000)	**1994**		**1993**	
Times Interest Earned	$\dfrac{£251}{£64}$	= 3.9	$\dfrac{£199}{£47}$	= 4.2

The ratio enables one to see how far profits can fall before interest payments are not covered. For Ardmore, profits would need to decline by approximately 80 per cent before this would occur. A 'cushion' of five times is often put forward as a useful rule of thumb. Where there are specific repayment or sinking fund provisions attaching to long-term debt, a variant of this ratio is often computed: that is, Times Burden Covered. This measures the ability of the firm to fund both the interest and the capital repayments. Chapter 11 further examines this issue.

Comparative Ratio Analysis

So far, this chapter has identified and computed a number of ratios which cover a wide range of financial activities. It was pointed out that ratios must be handled with care. If comparisons are made, then be sure that apples are being matched with apples.

Users of financial statements should recognise that management can affect the timeliness and integrity of the information provided. For instance, minimal information about 'off balance sheet' financing may be disclosed in an attempt to have external parties underestimate the underlying risk of the firm.

There are a number of points worth noting. The Ardmore liquidity ratios are average to good. The debt ratio is a little high but this would not be unusual since Ardmore is small. As a result of the high debt ratio and low net margin on sales, Ardmore has a relatively poor interest cover. The activity ratios show that Ardmore Limited is much less capital-intensive than most publicly quoted firms. It appears that debt collection could be improved, as could profit margins.

Cash Flow Analysis

By tracing the flow of cash through a business over time, management can decide whether the policies followed were in the best interests of the firm. This is done by preparing a Cash Flow Statement which summarises how cash has come into and left the business during the period under review. It classifies the inflows and outflows of cash and cash equivalents under the following five headings.

(i) Operating Activities.
This can be shown on either a gross (direct method) or a net (indirect method) basis and shows the cash effect of transactions and other events relating to trading activities. The indirect method was used in the analysis of Ardmore Accounts by starting with the operating profit before interest and tax, adjusting for non-cash charges, such as depreciation, and highlighting profit on sale of assets and movements in current asset

and liability accounts. In this context an increase in an asset other than cash is a use of funds whereas an increase in a liability is a source of funds. The converse is also true in both instances. Depreciation is added back to the operating profit figure to reflect its non-cash status and account is taken of the amortisation treatment of government grants.

(ii) Return on Investment and Servicing of Finance.

This section reflects inflows resulting from the ownership of investments and payments to the providers of finance. It is usually classified under the headings of interest and dividend receipts or payments.

(iii) Taxation.

This heading shows cash flows to or from the taxation authorities in respect of the firm's taxes based on its revenue and/or capital profits. Sales or property taxes which are based on profits are not shown under this heading but are included in the operating activities section.

(iv) Investing Activities.

This reflects the cash flows from the purchase or sale of fixed assets. It could also include the cash flow from current asset investments such as short-term bank deposits or purchases of bonds, unless they are included elsewhere.

(v) Financing.

This section includes receipts and payments to external providers of finance in respect of principal amounts. The typical items comprise cash receipts from the issue of shares and debentures, with payment being the expenses associated with those transactions and repayment of loans.

The Cash Flow Statement for Ardmore Limited for the twelve months ended 31 December 1994 is repeated here (Table 3.2) and deserves the following comments.

Table 3.2

Ardmore Limited Cash Flow Statement
for the 12 Months Ended 31 December 1994
(Amounts expressed as £'000)

Net Cash Inflow from Operating Activities (Note)		35
Return on Investments and Servicing of Finance		
Interest Paid		(64)
Taxation		(13)
Investing Activities		
Purchase of Tangible Assets	(66)	
Proceeds of Sale of Tangible Assets	15	(51)
Financing		
Short-Term Financing	(40)	
Debenture Loan	40	
Government Grants	25	25
Increase/(Decrease) in Cash Equivalents		(68)
Movement in Cash		
Bank Overdraft	62	
Cash	6	68

Note forming part of the accounts	
Reconciliation of Operating Income to Net Cash Inflow from Operating Activities	
	£'000
Operating Income Before Interest and Tax	251
Non-Cash Item — Depreciation	43
Profit on Sale of Tangible Assets	(12)
Inventory	(80)
Debtors	(204)
Creditors	52
Amortisation of Government Grants	(15)
Net Cash Inflow from Operating Activities	£35

The year 1994 saw Ardmore use cash of £68,000, primarily by expanding its overdraft facility from £68,000 to £130,000. The application of this cash in paying interest of £64,000, taxation £13,000 and investing £51,000 in assets was partly offset by generating £35,000 from operating activities and receiving £25,000 in government grants.

While the expansion in sales and activity was welcome and required new investment in fixed assets, the management of working capital is the main reason for the firm's inability to be near self-financing. It started from a solid base of operating income but then allowed the increase in debtors and stocks to consume far too much of its cash flow. This is primarily evidenced by the increase in the age of receivables to seventy-nine days and the slowing down of inventory turnover to 5.8 times a year or average holding of sixty-three days. Assuming that the year-end figures are indicative of the operating pattern for the year and not just once-off peaks, then immediate corrective action may need to be put in place to bring both accounts receivable and inventories back into line.

The ultimate objective is to be at or near self-financing stage and raise long-term finance to cover investments in fixed assets as and when required. The benefits of the increased performance as measured by the profitability ratios has been offset by the slippage in working capital or activity ratio management. The net effect is that there is a neutral return on investment performance for the year, allied to a serious leakage of cash or cash equivalent not apparent from a review of the current or acid test ratios. The benefits of the Cash Flow Statement information can be clearly seen and it needs to be acted upon to ensure that Ardmore Limited remains a sound commercial entity.

CONCLUSION

This chapter has provided a framework for financial analysis. A series of ratios — liquidity, profitability, activity and debt — was presented and examined. The objective in selecting the ratios was to maximise the information obtained from the minimum of analysis.

While it is important to know what the above techniques can do, it is vital to be aware of what they cannot do. Ratio analysis is based on the assumption that the financial statements present a reasonable picture of what is happening in the business. This is not always the case. The information in the financial statements relates to one particular period of time only. Rarely do businesses stand still, so it is advisable when applying ratio analysis to examine the analysis in the light of developments which have occurred since the statements were drawn up. As well as the financial statements, there are many other sources of information which can be used to assess the performance of the firm. The chairperson's and director's statements would be a good starting-point. Employee newsletters, trade comment, independent analysis, personal/peer contacts, and production, demand and employment statistics are potential sources of information which can be used depending on the depth of the analysis required.

The significance of the results of any financial analysis lies in future action.

There is little point in carrying out the analysis if no action is to be taken. The difficulty here is that ratios are applied to past events and so may not truly represent the present or the future. In interpreting the trends or results in a business a skilled analyst will expect the analysis to provide a guide rather than a solution to present problems and future plans.

Users of financial statements over a long period of time have evolved rules of thumb for minimising the effect of the weaknesses of these statements. They may be summarised as follows:

(1) Analyse a time series of statements rather than those of one year.
(2) Study carefully the notes and explanations attached to the statements.
(3) Check the veracity of the items by comparing them with those of previous years and treating any sudden change with suspicion.
(4) Factor in the likely effects of any post-statement date information, e.g. changes in interest rates, new competition, etc.
(5) Adjust the data for inflation, if significant.

No attempt has been made to suggest absolute ratios for a firm. The most suitable ratio will depend on the industry, the competition, the financial resources of the firm, and company objectives. A firm would be inviting danger by attempting to apply rigid or inflexible rules to ratio analysis.

The second method of analysis, the Cash Flow Statement, is a simple but effective technique for identifying the flow of funds through a business during a particular period. The next chapter extends cash flow analysis into future projections.

FURTHER READING

G. Foster, *Financial Statement Analysis*, 5th ed. (New Jersey, Prentice-Hall, 1992).

C. Walsh, *Key Management Ratios* (London, Pitman Publishing, 1993).

N. Brennan, F.J. O'Brien & A. Pierce, *A Survey of Irish Published Accounts*, 2nd ed. (Oak Tree Press, 1992).

F. Wood & T. Robinson, *Business Accounting*, Irish ed. (Pitman Publishing, 1994).

J.K. Samuels, R.E. Brayshaw & J.M. Craner, *Financial Statement Analysis in Europe* (Chapman and Hall, 1995).

QUESTIONS
Question 3.1
Why is the current ratio sometimes referred to as the '2 to 1' ratio?

Question 3.2
On 31 December 1994 the following balances were extracted from the books of S. O'Neill:

	£'000		£'000
Sales	1,000	Current Assets:	
Cost of Sales	600	Stock	150
Gross Profit	400	Debtors	255
		Cash	195
		Total Current Assets	600

Current Liabilities:

Trade Creditors   200

Calculate:
  (a) Current Ratio
  (b) Acid Test Ratio
Comment briefly on the firm's liquidity position.

Question 3.3
Briefly categorise and describe the principal financial ratios.

Question 3.4
The following data apply to Nickett Products:

	£
Sales	1,000,000
Cost of Goods Sold	800,000
Gross Profit Margin	200,000
Overheads	150,000
Net Income	50,000
Long-Term Debt	40,000
Preferred Stock	50,000
Common Stock	50,000
Retained Earnings	50,000
Days' Sales Outstanding	40 days
Stock Turnover	4

From this information, determine:
  (a) Total Asset Turnover.
  (b) Return on Investment.
  (c) Net Profit Margin.
  (d) Gross Profit Margin.

Question 3.5
What are the limitations of ratio analysis?

Question 3.6
Given the following ratios, fill in the blanks on the Income Statement and Balance Sheet of Gekko Oil Company.

Ratios:

Current	2.0
Quick	1.75
Times Interest Earned	6
Net Equity	1
Gross Profit Margin	30%
Book Return on Equity	20%

Income Statement of Gekko Oil Company for the Year Ended 31 December 1994

Sales	600,000
Less: Cost of Sales	?
Gross Profit	?
Less: Fixed Costs	?
Net Operating Income	?
Interest	?
Taxes	20,000
Net Income	?

Balance Sheet of Gekko Oil Company as at 31 December 1994

Fixed Assets			
Net Plant and Equipment			?
Current Assets			
Stock	?		
Cash and Bank Balance	50,000		
Securities	25,000		
Accounts Receivable	?		
Less: Current Liabilities			
Accounts Payable	75,000		
Notes Payable	25,000	100,000	?
	100,000		400,000
Total Assets less Total Liabilities	400,000		
Financed by:			
Ordinary Shares			?
Debt			?
Retained Earnings			100,000
			?

Question 3.7

The following data relate to Modern Developments Limited as at 31 March 1995.

	£
Trade Creditors	60,000
Closing Stock	40,000
Plant and Machinery	185,000
Debtors	90,000
Land	105,000
Buildings	110,000
Share Capital	250,000
Debentures	200,000
Cash and Bank Balance	45,000
Sales (Credit)	350,000
Cost of Manufacturing	170,000
Interest Paid	25,000
Administration Costs	90,000

(a) Calculate the profit earned by the company and prepare a Balance Sheet.

(b) Calculate appropriate ratios which will explain the company's performance.

Financial Forecasting

[handwritten: LONG RUN - STRATEGIC. SHORT RUN - TACTICAL].

The analysis in Chapter 3 relied on historical data. Historical analysis can provide useful and valuable information to management but by itself it is insufficient. Business success lies in future outcomes. To assist the development of a strategic plan, most managers attempt to forecast the future. This is a normal and essential part of corporate planning. Financial planning is at the heart of such planning.

There are few firms operating today without a plan of some description. The plan may be in the mind of the owner or it may be an elaborate bound volume describing in detail the short- and long-run objectives of the business and of each section within it. Every plan and all the policies introduced to further the plan have financial implications. Every decision made will ultimately be reflected in the financial health of the firm.

Just as overall planning is divided into two distinct stages, long-run/strategic planning and short-run/tactical planning, so too is financial planning. Short-run or current financial planning deals primarily with the effect of plans on the liquidity position of the business. This is sometimes known as financial forecasting. Long-run financial planning examines the effect of proposed capital investments and is known as capital budgeting or investment appraisal. Methods of capital budgeting are examined in Chapter 6. As in corporate planning, there is no clear-cut distinction between the short and long term. Financial plans undertaken for the immediate future have long-term implications, while long-term planning has implications for every short-term projection.

In planning, a co-ordinated, integrated effort is required to ensure that the firm has the necessary resources to carry out the projected plan, and that the objectives of the plan are reached. A firm cannot plan any aspect of business in isolation. For instance, a marketing plan may have implications for both production and personnel departments, but it most certainly will have implications for the financial department. Likewise, production plans have cash and investment requirements. Planning is a dynamic process. It must respond quickly to outcomes different from those expected. Effective management cannot wait until the firm has experienced failure to take corrective action. Management must engage in continuous analysis for the earliest detection of outcomes which might cause targets to be missed.

A firm installing a financial management and control system will want to know the answers to the following questions: Why is financial planning necessary? What are the advantages of proper financial planning? What techniques should be used in financial planning?

If properly carried out, the financial plan should provide a number of benefits, such as:

(a) A readily available criterion for decision-making, i.e. easily understood figures, such as profit or return on investment, which help decision-makers.

(b) A communication link between the owners, managers and employees, i.e. figures which mean the same to all. *uniform*

(c) A motivatable device for the firm's employees.

(d) An invaluable tool in analysing the risk of the business and in identifying risks attaching to proposed policies.

It is the function of the financial manager to produce the financial plan based principally on company policy and on the forecasts of his marketing and production colleagues. In a small firm the general manager may undertake all these functions. It is his responsibility to co-ordinate the plans of each area. Once financial forecasts have been produced, management can review the projected plans and tailor them to match the resources of the firm. The plan should utilise in particular the financial resources available and should avoid placing the firm in the embarrassing position of making commitments which it cannot meet. The advantages of financial planning are clear-cut: it indicates to management the funds required, when, and for how long they will be required if specific plans and programmes are to be carried out. It demonstrates what financial outcome will result if certain paths are followed. It should provide a method of control whereby deviations from expected performance are quickly brought to light, thus allowing management to take corrective action in time.

Two basic methods are used in forecasting the short-term financial requirements of a firm:

(a) Cash flow forecasts.

(b) Projected Balance Sheets (Pro Forma Statements).

Cash is king. As long as a firm has cash, it can survive. The cash flow forecast takes account of expected cash receipts and payments over a period of time. It provides detailed information on the projected cash position for the period under examination. If a firm is preparing a cash forecast for the coming year, it may develop the forecast on a monthly or even on a weekly basis.

A projected Balance Sheet is a normal extension of a cash flow forecast since the information required to prepare a cash flow forecast provides the information necessary for the Balance Sheet.

The projected Balance Sheet method is used to give a broad picture of the firm's expected position at the end of a particular period — for example, every three or six months or at the end of the next financial year. This method has the disadvantage that it represents only one point in time and gives no indication of results or requirements within the period. A further disadvantage is that it does not indicate when the maximum amount of funds will be required or the size of the amount required. This disadvantage can be overcome by projecting a Balance Sheet for the date when the maximum demand for funds is expected. The advantage is the broad view it gives of the investments made by the firm and how they have been financed. It is like a photograph which shows how well or badly the subject looks.

CASH FLOW FORECASTING

Cash flow forecasting is also known as 'Cash Budgeting'. It allows a business to plan short-term cash requirements. It should provide a picture of the timing and amount of cash inflows and outflows. This method compares the expected cash receipts with the expected cash payments. Only cash flows are considered. No allowance is made for items such as depreciation which affect profitability but not cash. Cash received is generally known as cash inflow while cash paid out is called cash outflow.

Cash forecasting is usually done on a monthly basis. Receipts and payments are estimated and compared month by month over, say, a period of twelve months. For periods longer than a year ahead, forecasts are drawn up quarterly, semi-annually and finally annually. Inability to forecast cash flows accurately in the distant future is the major reason for broadening the forecast period. Some firms with large discrepancies between inflows and outflows of cash find it necessary to prepare weekly cash flow forecasts.

Preparation of a cash flow forecast has three elements:

(a) Preparing the cash inflow forecast.

(b) Preparing the cash outflow forecast.

(c) Comparing the two forecasts to discover whether there is a surplus or deficit of cash during each period.

Cash Inflow Forecast

The accuracy of the cash forecast depends on the reliability of the sales estimates and of the expected credit terms taken by customers. Sales forecasts are notoriously difficult to estimate accurately. They can be generated in two ways. An internal forecast builds a sales estimate from the bottom up: each salesperson is asked to give his estimate of sales for the relevant period. External forecasts are based on known relationships between sales and economic indicators — for example, a period of tight credit is known to have an adverse effect on car sales. Usually, a compromise must be reached between the two forecasts. The importance of an accurate sales forecast cannot be overstressed. The sales schedule is the cornerstone of all the remaining calculations. Sales estimates are the critical numbers for all other functions, particularly production and marketing, so a great deal of time and attention is given to this area.

Having estimated sales, the next step is to identify the percentage of credit sales and the likely credit terms.

The amount of cash required to fund sales is a function of the credit period taken by customers. Until recently, retail outlets had only cash sales so their money came in as they sold. Now, credit card sales mean that the owners may be waiting weeks for their money. At the other extreme, sellers of heavy equipment may get paid a small deposit up front and the balance over years.

Trends in credit terms are vital to monitor. Salespeople always want to give easier credit as it helps them sell. In periods of tight and expensive money customers are slower to pay. Note what happened in the 1994 Ardmore accounts. Also, in periods of high inflation slow payment means a serious loss of profits, as the goods made to replace those sold cost more yet the payment has not been received.

A factor of major importance in estimating cash inflows is the seasonality of sales. It is easy to see how sales of Christmas cards peak in one month but most businesses have seasonal sales. Fashion retailers in Ireland do 60 per cent of their total annual sales in the last twelve weeks of the year. Resort hotels in Ireland do 50 per cent of their business in July and August. A company such as Ardmore supplying an engineered product may have little seasonality. For the sake of clarity and simplicity, the example below assumes a constant level of sales each month.

The final item to be noted is non-trading cash inflows, such as sales of assets, grants, new issues of shares, etc. Ardmore does not expect any such inflows in 1995.

Cash Outflow Forecast

Given the cash inflow estimates, management can also produce a statement of all cash outflows. All cash payments must be included in the outflow statement — for example, payments for wages, supplies, interest, taxation and capital expenditure. The critical item is often the production schedule. Management must decide whether to produce in line with the estimates of sales or to produce for inventory, thereby facilitating a smooth production pattern. This decision is often the subject of friction between production, marketing and finance managers.

Once the production schedule is agreed, then estimates of supplies, materials and labour can be made. It should be noted that suppliers give credit and so the payment for purchases often occurs in a different period to that in which the goods are received. The amount of credit taken has a serious impact on month-to-month cash outflows.

ARDMORE FINANCIAL FORECAST

The rest of the chapter details the process by which Ardmore has set down its plans for 1995. It has done so with the objective of preparing a Pro Forma Income Statement, Balance Sheet and Cash Flow Statement. In addition it has prepared a detailed monthly cash flow budget in order to identify any cash flow problems arising from its operational or investment plans. Ardmore is fortunate in that it has a steady sales pattern. This is matched by an even flow production plan. It has achieved this over the past few years by successfully diversifying its product range and extending its distribution network. The company plans to build upon the sales strategies adopted in the year 1994 with a specific target of tighter cash flow management. The strategy of increased turnover has to be balanced against the obvious concern at the increase in its bank overdraft during 1994.

Given these overall objectives, the following issues were agreed as a basis for the preparation of the forecasted financial statements of Ardmore Limited for 1995.

Sales/Cash Inflows

— The marketing staff forecast a 12.5 per cent increase in sales revenue in 1995. This is based on an 8 per cent increase in sales volume and a 4.5 per cent increase in sales prices.
— Credit terms, though stated at forty-five days, were expected to remain at actual 1994 year-end levels of approximately ninety days. This is a significant change from the average age of receivables of seventy-nine days in 1994 and is seen as the worst case scenario. Special attention is to be given to improving on this target, if possible, without affecting the success of the increased sales effort. Note that the figure is the year-end figure, not the average for the year.
— There are no asset sales anticipated in 1995.
— Ardmore had no cash sales.

Cash Outflows

— The production schedule is based on the assumption that it will match the sales

requirements, thereby maintaining inventories at 1994 levels. This applies to all levels of inventory and will, if achieved, maintain the age of inventory at approximately sixty-three days or a turnover of 5.8 times per annum.
— Production is spread evenly throughout the year.
— Raw material input costs are targeted to reduce by approximately 1 per cent due to greater competition from suppliers. Costs fall from 47 per cent to 46 per cent of sales value.
— Trade purchases are all based on nominal credit terms of forty-five days. However, the reality is somewhat different. The actual days outstanding are planned to reduce to approximately ninety-six days. This is seen as a slight improvement on the average days outstanding of ninety-nine days in 1994 and is part of a deliberate policy initiated in late 1994 to restore some lost credibility with its trade creditors. As in the case of accounts receivable, special attention is being given to the achievement of this target.
— The number of employees is fixed at 1994 levels. An adjustment of 5 per cent is included for wage and salary increases to cover productivity agreements and nationally negotiated wage increases.
— Factory overheads and operating expenses are analysed in detail by cost classification and department. The factory overhead is expected to grow by 4 per cent in 1995, selling and distribution expenses by 7 per cent and administration costs by 6 per cent.
— Interest and other financing charges are based on the prevailing rates of interest and the mix of finance sources expected to be in place in 1995. It takes into account the scheduled repayment sums in respect of the short-term loan and debenture facilities.
— Scheduled repayments of £45,000 and £20,000 are due in 1995 as part of the debenture and short-term loan agreements.

Table 4.1 Pro Forma Income Statement Assumptions

	1994 £'000	Growth	1995 £'000	Monthly Average* £'000
Sales	2,836	12.5%	3,190	277
Purchases — Raw Material Consumed	1,343	9%	1,463	127
	(Approx. 47% of Sales)		(Approx. 46% of Sales)	
Wages	620	5%	651	54–57
Factory Overheads	138	4%	144	8–10k
	(Inc. Depreciation £43)		(Inc. Depreciation £46)	
Operating Expenses:				
— Selling and Distribution	324	7%	348	29
— Administration	248	6%	264	22

*Guide for cash flow purposes; reflects calendarisation due to plant holiday closure of two weeks in August.

Table 4.2 Pro Forma Balance Sheet Assumptions

	1994 £'000	Days	1995 £'000	Days
Accounts Receivable	719		831	
— Average Age (Days)		79		90
Accounts Payable	386		381	
— Average Age (Days)		99		96
Inventory	390		390	
— Average Age (Days)		63		63

— Taxation is estimated at 10 per cent of 1994 profits and is payable by June 1995.

— A specialised piece of machinery is required to upgrade the milling process. Tentative negotiations have taken place with the suppliers and the sum of £35,000 has been deemed reasonable and included in the second half of the year. Discussions have also taken place with Forbairt in regard to possible grant-aid. No clear decisions are forthcoming at this stage and consequently nothing is shown in the projected accounts.

The figures are rounded to the nearest thousand, as exact figures would imply spurious accuracy in the data. In summary the figures could be shown as follows and form the basis of the Pro Forma Statements shown in Tables 4.3 to 4.6.

Table 4.3

Ardmore Limited

Pro Forma Income Statement for the 12 Months Ended 31 December 1995

(Amounts expressed as £'000)

Sales		3,190
Raw Material Consumed	1,463	
Wages	651	
Factory Overheads	144	
Cost of Sales		2,258
Gross Profit		932
Less Expenses:		
— Selling & Distribution	348	
— Interest Charges	52	
— Administration	264	
Total Expenses		664
Net Profit Before Tax		268
Taxation		27
Net Profit After Tax		£241
(Amount Transferred to Profit and Loss Account)		

Table 4.4

Ardmore Limited

Pro Forma Balance Sheet for the 12 Months Ended 31 December 1995

(Amounts expressed as £'000)

Fixed Assets		
Land and Buildings		310
Plant and Machinery		378
Fixtures and Fittings		53
Motor Vehicles		28
		769
Current Assets		
Inventory	390	
Accounts Receivable	831	
Cash	4	
	1,225	

(continued overleaf)

Current Liabilities		
Accounts Payable	381	
Short-Term Loan	135	
Current Taxation	27	
Bank Overdraft	50	593
Net Current Assets (Working Capital)		632
		£1,401

Financed by
Authorised 1,000,000 £1 Ordinary Shares

Issued 600,000 £1 Ordinary Shares	600

Reserves

Share Premium Account	25
Profit and Loss Account	441
Government Grants	130
Debentures	205
	£1,401

Table 4.5

Pro Forma Cash Flow Statement for the 12 Months Ended 31 December 1995

	£'000	
• Net Cash Inflow from Operating Activities (Note 1)		249
• Interest Paid		(52)
• Taxation		(17)
• Investing Activities		
Purchase of Tangible Assets		(35)
• Financing		
Short-Term Financing	(45)	
Debenture Loan	(20)	(65)
• Increase/(Decrease) in Cash and Cash Equivalent		£80
• Movement in Cash		
Bank Overdraft £130 -> £50		£80

Note 1
Reconciliation of Operating Income to Net Cash Inflow from Operating Activities

	£'000
Operating Income Before Interest and Tax (i.e. 268 + 52)	320
— Non-Cash Item	
Depreciation	46
• Stocks	–
• Debtors	(112)
• Creditors	(5)
Net Cash Inflow from Operating Activities	£249

Table 4.6

Ardmore Limited
Cash Budget 1995 (Amounts expressed as £'000)

	1994 Oct.	Nov.	Dec.	1995 Jan.	Feb.	Mar.	Apr.	May	June	July	Aug.	Sept.	Oct.	Nov.	Dec.	Total 12 mths
Inflows																
1 Sales	240	240	239	277	277	277	277	277	277	277	143	277	277	277	277	3,190
2 Cash Inflow	–	–	–	240	240	239	277	277	277	277	277	277	277	143	277	3,078
3 Other Cash Receipts	–	–	–	–	–	–	–	–	–	–	–	–	–	–	–	–
4 Total Cash Inflows	–	–	–	240	240	239	277	277	277	277	277	277	277	143	277	3,078
Outflows																
5 Purchases	128	128	130	127	127	127	127	127	127	127	66	127	127	127	127	1,463
6 Payments to Suppliers	–	–	–	128	128	130	127	127	127	127	127	127	127	66	127	1,468
7 Wages	–	–	–	54	54	54	54	54	54	54	54	54	54	54	57	651
8 Factory Overheads (Net of Depreciation)	–	–	–	8	8	8	8	8	8	8	8	8	8	8	10	98
9 Expenses— Selling & Distribution	–	–	–	29	29	29	29	29	29	29	29	29	29	29	29	348
10 — Administration	–	–	–	22	22	22	22	22	22	22	22	22	22	22	22	264
11 Interest	–	–	–	–	–	13	–	–	13	–	–	13	–	–	13	52
12 Taxation	–	–	–	–	–	–	–	–	–	–	–	–	–	17	–	17
13 Loan Repayments	–	–	–	–	–	–	15	–	–	30	–	–	–	–	20	65
14 Fixed Asset Purchase	–	–	–	–	–	–	–	–	–	–	–	35	–	–	–	35
Total Cash Outflows	–	–	–	241	241	256	255	240	253	270	240	288	240	196	278	2,998
Net Cash	–	–	–	(1)	(1)	(17)	22	37	24	7	37	(11)	37	(53)	(1)	80
Closing Balance	–	–	–	(131)	(132)	(149)	(127)	(90)	(66)	(59)	(22)	(33)	(4)	(49)	(50)	–

Memo: Opening Balance 1 January 1994, £130.

57

The following should help in understanding the basis of the figures shown on the Pro Forma Statements.

— The fixed assets are calculated by taking the 1994 closing value of £780,000, increasing by £35,000 for the new machine purchased and deducting £46,000 depreciation in 1994. This gives a net book value of £769,000.
— Inventory is targeted to remain at the same level as 1994, i.e. £390,000.
— Accounts receivable at £831,000 is approximately ninety days' credit and represents sales in the last three months of the year at £277,000 per month.
— There is no change in the projected cash balance at £4,000.
— Accounts payable at £381,000 is approximately ninety-six days' credit and represents purchases in the last three months of the year at £127,000 per month.
— The short-term loan facility has been reduced by projected repayments of £15,000 and £30,000 in April and July of 1994.
— Taxation due represents the projected tax charge on the projected 1995 net profit which is still outstanding at the end of 1995.
— The bank overdraft is the net outcome of the cash inflows and cash outflows for 1995 together with the opening position on 1 January 1995. It shows a net increase in cash flow of £80,000, resulting in a significant reduction in the overdraft level to £50,000.
— The Profit and Loss Account is the accumulated profit to date and is the addition of the closing position in 1994 of £200,000 and the net after-tax profit of £241,000 in 1995.
— Debentures reflect a scheduled repayment of £20,000 in 1995.

The Pro Forma Statements highlight the possible effects of management policies in 1995.

The reduction in raw material input costs should increase the gross profit margin from 28 per cent to 29 per cent. This, allied to tight control of operating expenses, has resulted in an increase in the net profit margin after tax from 6 per cent to 7.6 per cent.

The slippage in working capital investment in regard to accounts receivable is offset by greater productivity out of the fixed assets, giving an almost neutral effect in all. This, when combined with the improved net profit after tax, gives a return on investment of over 17 per cent.

The repayment of both short-term and long-term debt will reduce the company's gearing significantly from 50 per cent to approximately 40 per cent, and the increased operating profits will improve the times interest earned cover from 3.9 times to more than 6 times.

Overall the projected position, if achieved, would restore the company to a strong financial position. The pro forma Cash Flow Statement shows the company's capability in generating cash and addressing the poor bank overdraft position of 1994. Some concerns still exist in regard to accounts receivable management and the ability of the company to achieve its operating targets. A detailed review of the cash budget shows that the company is more than capable of being self-financing and could support a heavier long-term debt burden. Some thought could be given to increasing the company's long-term leverage/gearing and reducing its dependency on bank overdraft and short-term loan facilities. A tentative view as to the company's plans for 1996 and 1997 may be useful in deciding on the proper course of action here. The historical and Pro Forma Statements support the view that Ardmore can generate reasonably acceptable levels of profit. This, allied to sound financial management, should also ensure that Ardmore has sufficient liquidity to meet its obligations and take advantage of both internal and external growth opportunities.

CONCLUSION

This chapter extended the financial analysis of a firm's operations into the short-term future. Two separate techniques, a cash budget and Pro Forma Statements, were developed to assist management in planning. The cash budget is an essential tool to forecast cash inflows and, more importantly, the net cash position on a monthly basis. Too many profitable firms go bankrupt because they lack cash. As managers become more expert in using cash budgets, they can change the many variables to allow for deviations from the expected outcomes.

The Pro Forma Statements provide incremental information to management. The Income Statement shows the effect on profits if projections prove accurate. The Balance Sheet shows the effect on assets and liabilities. Armed with the information provided by the above techniques, management can now decide what is to be done. The analysis here has raised question marks over Ardmore's accounts payable, inventory, accounts receivable and bank position. The following chapter examines in detail the issues raised.

FURTHER READING

J.A. Viscione & G.S. Roberts, *Contemporary Financial Management* (Ohio, Merrill, 1987).
J.W. Petty et al., *Basic Financial Management*, 6th ed. (New Jersey, Prentice-Hall, 1993).
L. Hopkins, *Cash Flow and How to Improve It* (London, Kogan Page, 1993).
P. Sneyd, *Principles of Accounting and Finance* (London, Routledge, 1994).

QUESTIONS

Question 4.1
What does a statement of cash flows show?

Question 4.2
What are the basic steps involved in financial forecasting?

Question 4.3
What is a pro forma financial statement?

Question 4.4
The following is a forecast of sales over three months for Leahy Motors Limited. Some additional information is included:

Forecasted Sales for July to September 1995

	£
July	400,000
August	500,000
September	450,000

Balance Sheet as at 30 June 1995

Fixed Assets	250,000	250,000
Current Assets		
Accounts Receivable	350,000	
Inventory	500,000	
Cash	30,000	
Total Current Assets	880,000	
Current Liabilities		
Accounts Payable	320,000	
Current Taxation	90,000	
Total Current Assets	410,000	
Net Current Assets	470,000	470,000
	720,000	£720,000
Financed by:		
Equity		440,000
Long-Term Debt		280,000
		£720,000

The assumptions include:
> (i) Sales made on thirty days' credit.
> (ii) Cost of goods sold has averaged 70 per cent of sales.
> (iii) Taxation is 20 per cent of profit.
> (iv) Depreciation is a set rate of £120,000 p.a.
> (v) Cash of £40,000 is to be maintained.
> (vi) On average, expenses are 10 per cent of sales.
> (vii) Inventory remains constant.

You are required to:
> (a) Prepare a monthly pro forma Income Statement for July, August and September and include a quarterly total.
> (b) Prepare a monthly pro forma Balance Sheet for July, August and September.

Question 4.5
What is the financial planning process? Compare long-term financial plans and short-run financial plans.

Question 4.6
John Grimes is a coffin maker who supplies funeral homes. Given the following information, you are asked to prepare a six-monthly Receipts and Payments Statement.
> (a) His permanent raw material stock value will be £10,000.
> (b) Machinery costing £10,000 will be installed and paid for in the first month.

(c) Equipment such as a van, forklifts, etc. will cost £25,000 and will be paid for in the first month.

(d) He has rented a warehouse at £300 per month.

(e) Credit terms on raw material, expenses and sales are net sixty days.

(f) He sells at raw material cost plus 25 per cent.

(g) Sales for the first three months are estimated at £10,000. Then it is expected that they will rise to £15,000 per month.

(h) His expenses are expected to be £4,000 per month.

5

Managing Working Capital

Working capital is an appropriate name for funds invested in the short-term assets of the business. All assets should work to produce a return on investment but it is easier to see capital at work in short-term assets — cash is used to buy raw materials which go into inventory until they are made into a product which is sold and transformed into an account receivable which becomes cash and so the cycle begins again. In some businesses capital invested in working capital works hard, maybe transforming itself into and out of cash twenty times a year. The food section of a supermarket is a prime example where orders placed one day are frequently delivered the next day, put straight on to the shelves and purchased almost immediately. The company would not have paid for the order before getting the cash from the sale. At the other end of the retail spectrum is speciality retailers such as upmarket jewellers, e.g. Weir's, which may hold a piece for years before selling it.

Think of the poor Irish shoe retailer who specialised in carrying a wide selection of sizes. Among his inventory was a pair of size 18 men's leather shoes. Over the years this item of stock became a talking point for a variety of reasons, not least of which was the cost of carrying a pair of shoes in stock for a decade. While he was attending to a customer buying size 15 shoes, talk turned to this unusually sized pair of shoes. The buyer, a foreign visitor, was very interested, requested a telephone and called his brother, who was also visiting the city. The brother took a size 18 shoe, arrived quickly, bought the pair and wanted to know if there were any others. Sure enough, at the back of the store room among other obsolete and forgotten stock was a second pair of size 18s. The original owner had a fear of being out of stock so when he got a request for something new or unusual he always bought at least two. Few companies could survive on such poor working capital management, but rest assured, in every company there are items of stock lying around for years and debtors who have not paid for years.

Managing working capital means deciding on a level of current assets and current liabilities. Working capital itself is defined as the excess of current assets over current liabilities. The adequacy of a firm's working capital has a direct bearing on the ability of a business to pay bills. The level of working capital and the relationship between current assets and liabilities provide measures of financial risk: that is, the probability that the business might become illiquid or what is known as technically insolvent. The purpose of working capital management is to control the level of investment in each current asset so

62

that an acceptable level of 'cover' is provided for the sources of current funds. Each individual source of short-term funds must be managed to minimise cost and risks. The easiest way to reduce the risk attaching to the working capital would be to finance all current assets with long-term equity funds. The possibility of lack of liquidity would be remote because there would be no short-term obligations. Many businesses do this, paying cash for purchases and having no bank borrowings. To use the vernacular, 'they owe no one'. No matter how long items remain in stock or how slow sales are, such businesses will not be pressurised by short-term obligations. Unfortunately, few in the modern world are afforded such luxury.

Therefore the answer to working capital management appears to be long-term equity finance and no current liabilities. Not so: as risk reduces, so too does profitability. Long-term money tends to be expensive. The cheapest sources of finance are often the shorter-term sources. The logic behind this is simple. The longer the period of the loan, the higher the payment to cover the various risks attaching to the investment. Banks charge people simply for the use of money. A debenture holder charges for the use of the money and also for the possibility that over a period of years something may go wrong and the money will not be repaid.

To understand the need for careful working capital management, consider once again the operation of a business. Owners and long-term lenders have provided funds to acquire fixed assets and to get the business operating through the purchase of supplies, the creation of inventory to meet the needs of sales, and the provision of credit to persuade customers to buy. One way the profitability of the business can be raised is by increasing sales. One method of doing this is to extend credit terms. Greater sales generally means more inventory of raw materials and work in progress. The cash to finance these expansions is often not available from profits. The extra sales will result in profits being made but they are tied up in the extra accounts receivable and inventory. To finance the expansion, bank overdraft and accounts payable are frequently the sources of finance used.

Many firms contrive to expand in this manner. Most survive but others discover the dreaded reality of '*Overtrading*' — having too small a base of long-term funds to finance an increase in operations. For example, suppose credit is restricted by government order. Business may slow up, leaving the firm with large inventories of unsold goods; customers slow up on payments; the bank insists on the overdraft being reduced; and suppliers threaten to cut off supplies unless they are paid. The crunch comes one Friday when management cannot pay the wage bill. Bankruptcy frequently follows. A credit crunch is only one of many factors which can cause illiquidity. Whatever the cause, the consequences are often dire.

WORKING CAPITAL POLICY

The primary consideration in developing an overall working capital policy is the risk/return trade-off associated with decisions about the appropriate mix of assets, current and fixed, and finance, short- and long-term. That policy requires that the level of working capital investment and the consequent financing decisions be analysed simultaneously so that their joint impact on the firm's expected profitability and risk can be evaluated. Therefore the precise level of investment in working capital is predicated on the management's attitude towards risk and the factors that influence the amount of cash, inventories, receivables and other current assets required to support a given volume of output. In determining the appropriate level of investment some basic principles can be used as a guide:

(i) If working capital is varied relative to sales, the amount of risk that a firm assumes is also varied and the opportunity for gain or loss is increased.

(ii) Capital should be invested in each component of working capital as long as the value of the firm increases.

(iii) The type of capital used to finance working capital directly affects the amount of risk that a firm assumes as well as the opportunity for gain or loss of capital.

(iv) The greater the disparity between the maturities of a firm's short-term debt instruments and its flow of internally generated funds, the greater the risk and vice versa.

The objective is therefore to maximise the value of the firm, and in so doing the management can choose to adopt either an aggressive, a conservative, a matching or a balanced working capital policy. The different policies are shown graphically in Figures 5.1 to 5.4 and described as follows.

An aggressive policy is where short-term finance is used to cover all the temporary and part of the permanent working capital investment. The increased risks of illiquidity associated with short-term finance are offset by the higher expected after-tax earnings resulting from the lower costs of finance. In summary a high risk — high required return strategy.

A conservative policy is where long-term finance is used to cover almost all asset investments, whether temporary or permanent. This reduces the risk of illiquidity and the firm's exposure to fluctuating interest rates. As long-term finance tends to have a high cost, the expected earnings will be less. In summary a low risk — low required return strategy.

A matching policy is where the cash flow generating characteristics of the assets are matched with the maturity of the financing. Temporary assets are financed by temporary financing and permanent assets are financed by permanent sources of financing. In practice the policy is difficult to implement due to the uncertainty in predicting cash flows, borrowing costs and its lack of flexibility in overall asset management. It is seen more as providing a benchmark that can be used to guide decisions. It is also called the hedging principle or self-liquidating policy.

A balanced policy is a compromise between the extremes of the aggressive and conservative policies. It involves using long-term finance to support permanent current assets and part of the temporary current assets. It calls for close management of fluctuations in cash flows to honour seasonal borrowings and get the best value for short-term surplus funds. It provides a margin of safety in terms of liquidity but has a cost implication partly offset by the investment income. It also allows the management a high degree of flexibility in funding increased activity or taking advantage of good raw material purchasing situations.

In formulating which policy to adopt, the management should also look at the firm's working capital cycle or operating cash conversion cycle. This measures the amount of time it takes for the initial cash outflow on goods and services to be realised as cash inflows from sales. Each component of working capital has its own life expectancy and liquidity features. The sum of the inventory conversion period and accounts receivable period is offset by the credit received on purchases to give the net time interval between the cash receipts and the cash outlays. It tells the management what additional non-spontaneous sources of finance are required to allow the firm carry out its operational activities.

Figure 5.1 Aggressive working capital policy

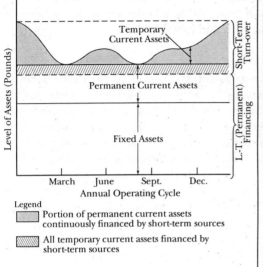

Legend

▨ Portion of permanent current assets continuously financed by short-term sources

▨ All temporary current assets financed by short-term sources

Figure 5.2 Conservative working capital policy

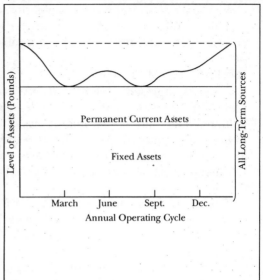

Figure 5.3 Matching working capital policy

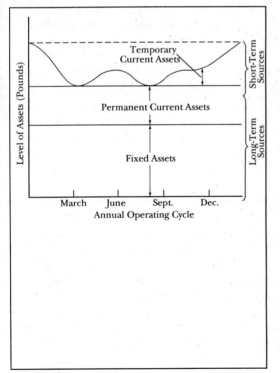

Figure 5.4 Balanced working capital policy

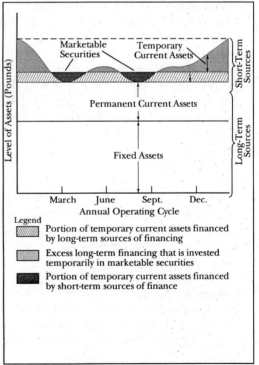

Legend

▨ Portion of temporary current assets financed by long-term sources of financing

▨ Excess long-term financing that is invested temporarily in marketable securities

■ Portion of temporary current assets financed by short-term sources of finance

Working capital management is a dynamic area. It involves managing the firm's liquidity and investment/financing decisions on a continuous basis. Each area involves risk and return trade-offs. The ability of the management to respond to changing circumstances is paramount to its objective of value maximisation for shareholders.

This chapter concentrates on methods of controlling investment in the following current assets: inventory; accounts receivable; cash and marketable securities.

INVENTORY MANAGEMENT

Inventories represent a significant investment for most firms. The Ardmore Balance Sheet for 1994 shows an investment in inventory equal to the total investment in land/buildings and fixtures and fittings. This is normal by Irish standards. The objective of inventory management should be to strike a proper balance between risk and return. The risk is seen in the form of production delays due to lack of material and stockouts of finished products as against the increased carrying and financing costs of holding higher inventory levels.

The general categories of inventory are raw material, work in progress and finished goods. Raw material consists of basic materials purchased from other firms to be used in the firm's production operations. Work in progress consists of partially completed goods requiring additional work before they become finished goods. Finished goods consist of goods on which the production has been completed but which are as yet unsold.

It is important to understand the role of inventory. It provides a coupling between production and sales. Only in very rare instances can a sales order be produced immediately. Usually, inventories of raw materials and parts are kept. Equally, most manufacturing firms have at any one time a range of products at various stages of manufacture, i.e. Work in Progress. Finally, management rarely produces to order. Instead, to minimise production costs and to facilitate efficient management, goods are produced for inventory. That means that products are produced and then stored until sold. Inventory allows flexibility.

The level of inventory maintained is often subject to significant conflict between the various functional managers. The marketing manager wishes to see a high level of finished goods inventory so that orders can be filled immediately. This is especially important in industries where competition is tough: for example, a buyer of whiskey in a supermarket might seek a particular brand but if it is not available then another brand will be chosen. From the viewpoint of profits, incremental sales can be very lucrative. Consider the effect on the profits of an ice cream company of having plenty of inventory during a long hot spell in August.

The production manager has different priorities to the marketing manager. He wants to minimise the unit cost of manufacture. He wants high raw materials inventories so that production is not disrupted by shortages, and long production runs to maximise efficiency. This can result in high levels of finished goods inventories but usually of only a few products.

The financial manager has yet another perspective: he regards inventory as an investment. He generally seeks to minimise levels of inventory at each particular level of sales — that is, he wants to maximise inventory turnover. Carrying inventory is expensive. Storage, handling, insurance, wastage, breakage, obsolescence and the cost of money tied up in inventory can result in annual carrying costs in excess of 30 per cent of inventory value.

The objective of inventory management is simple to state, but very complex to achieve. Inventory levels should be increased until the additional costs equal the profits resulting from higher levels.

Inventory Valuation

The overriding consideration is to give a true and fair view on the basis of the 'lower of cost or net realisable value'. The difficulty is that there is no precise definition of 'true and fair view' and the lower of cost or net realisable value can be open to judgment and conflicting views.

In arriving at gross profit, opening and closing inventory valuations are used with purchases in the case of a retail company and cost of goods manufactured in the case of a manufacturing company. This is to comply with the matching principle of comparing what was sold at sale price with what was sold at cost price. Consequently, inventory valuation policy can have a substantial impact on the gross profit of the firm. The general rule is that the higher the closing stock the higher the profit, and conversely, the lower the closing stock the lower the profit. Net realisable value is defined as the amount expected to be received for the sale of the product less any additional expenditure to be incurred on or before disposal. As the objective of most firms is to make a profit, one would normally expect the net realisable value of its product to be greater than the cost. The principal methods used to arrive at a value of inventory are **First In First Out** (FIFO) and **Last In First Out** (LIFO).

FIFO First In First Out. This assumes that materials purchased first are used first and approximates most closely to actual historical cost. Inventory is thus valued on the basis of the cost of the most recent purchases. This method has wide acceptability for both accounting and taxation purposes. In a period of rising prices inventory has a high value, and cost of goods is reduced. Therefore this method tends to produce high profits in periods of inflation. The deflation of the mid-1990s produced the opposite effect.

LIFO Last In First Out. This assumes that the most recently acquired goods are used first. Thus inventory is valued at the cost of the oldest goods held. The cost of goods sold is high and profits low when this method is used. While it tends to show a more realistic profit figure in times of rising prices, the LIFO method can give rise to an unrealistic and out-of-date Balance Sheet valuation.

Other methods, such as average cost, standard cost and adjusted selling price, are used. Standard cost is particularly relevant in medium to large manufacturing organisations with multiple raw material parts in each product.

In the final analysis the application of a consistent policy from one accounting period to the next and the exercise of prudence are the dominant considerations.

Other considerations, such as industry custom and practice, taxation, convenience and advice of the auditors, may be taken into account to varying degrees. Stock valuation is therefore a compromise between the various conflicting ends for which it is to be used.

The importance of knowing and understanding the inventory valuation method can be seen by looking at the inventory figure of £390,000 on the 1994 Ardmore Balance Sheet. This figure could vary by as much as 10 per cent depending on which method of

NB

valuation was used. In view of the fact that 1994 after-tax profits were only £170,000 it is evident that financial analysts must be aware of the method in use.

Inventory Control

The importance of effective inventory management is directly related to the size of the investment in inventory. As inventory is a reversible investment that fluctuates in size, inventory decisions usually concentrate on determining the optimal size. Also most businesses find themselves with an inventory composed of many thousands of items. It is economically impossible to have total control over all items, though the increasing employment of user-friendly computer programs improves the situation. Rather than attempt the impossible, managers often apply the '80/20' rule. This useful rule of thumb states that 80 per cent of inventory value is accounted for by 20 per cent of the items in store. Management concentrates effort on controlling the 20 per cent. To assist business, an inventory control system known as the Economic Order Quantity model (EOQ) has been developed. In addition Materials Requirements Planning (MRP) and 'Just in Time' (JIT) techniques have been devised.

The Economic Order Quantity Model (EOQ)

This model helps management to determine the optimal order size for an inventory item given its expected usage, carrying costs and ordering costs. The technique makes particular assumptions: that annual demand or usage is known with certainty and is uniform throughout the year, and that purchase orders are filled instantaneously with no need for safety stocks. The EOQ is therefore defined as the optimal inventory order size that minimises total cost, which is the sum of the ordering plus the carrying costs.

The simplest version of the EOQ model is written algebraically below and shown graphically in Figure 5.5.

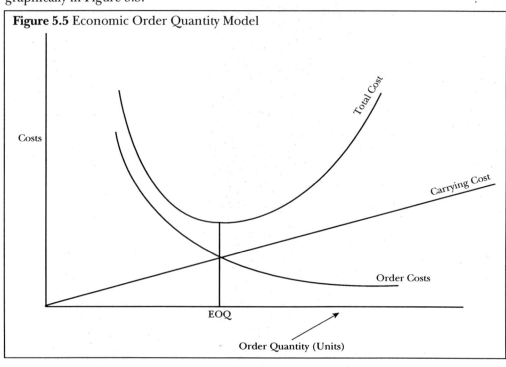

Figure 5.5 Economic Order Quantity Model

Costs

Total Cost

Carrying Cost

Order Costs

EOQ

Order Quantity (Units)

$$EOQ = \sqrt{\frac{2DS}{Ic}}$$

where

EOQ = order quantity
D = usage in units of the product per period
S = order cost per period
Ic = cost of placing an order *holding cost*

The formula and the logic involved can also be clearly seen in Figure 5.5.

The application of the EOQ model requires this information:

(a) The rate of usage of the product.
(b) The cost of ordering.
(c) The cost of carrying a unit in inventory. This is composed of interest plus storage plus an allowance for wastage, breakage and obsolescence.

An example will help. Ardmore Limited expects to use 8,000 steel plates (D) during 1995. The estimated costs of placing an order, verifying it and following up with written confirmation is £20 (S). The carrying cost of each plate costing £10 is 30 per cent per annum, that is, £3 (Ic). The economic order quantity for this item is:

$$EOQ = \sqrt{\frac{2 \times 8,000 \times 20}{3}}$$

$$= 327$$

This means that Ardmore Limited should place an order twenty-four times (8,000/327) a year for approximately 327 steel plates per order. Note that increasing the carrying cost means the EOQ declines, while it rises if the ordering cost declines.

There are many assumptions in this simple model noted above. The instantaneous delivery or zero lead time assumption is a critical weakness. If the lead time, i.e. the time from order to delivery, is constant and known with certainty, the optimal order quantity is not affected although the time when an order should be placed is. This is known as the reorder point or safety stock and is defined as:

Reorder point = Days from order to delivery: that is, lead time multiplied by daily usage.

In the case of Ardmore Limited it takes, on average, five days to obtain delivery. Daily usage is 22 (8,000 ÷ 365) so the following emerges:

Steel Plate Reorder Point = 5 × 22
                          = 110

When the number of steel plates in inventory falls to 110 an order for 327 is placed.

The second weakness, that of assuming constant usage, is also alleviated by the holding of buffer inventory or safety stock. The buffer inventory is held to allow for fluctuations in the demand for the product. Instead of waiting to order until inventory has fallen to 110, management may agree to hold a buffer of 50. In these circumstances an order is placed when the quantity in inventory falls to 160. This allows for variations in demand and also for delays in receipt of the reordered goods. Any uncertainty surrounding the delivery time and the daily usage will affect the level of safety stock required. The more certain the pattern of inventory movements, the less safety stock required and vice versa. Ultimately, the level of safety stock is a basic trade-off between the risk of running out of inventory with the consequent production disruption and customer dissatisfaction, and the increased costs associated with carrying additional inventory.

A further problem associated with the simple EOQ model is that it does not allow for quantity discounts. Suppose that Ardmore Limited could obtain a discount of 10 pence per plate for orders of 500 or more. The maximum saving to the firm is £800 (10 pence × 8,000). The costs would be the additional carrying costs less the lower ordering costs of increasing the order size to 500 from 327.

The additional carrying cost is calculated as follows:

$$\frac{(500 - 327) \; £3}{2} = \frac{£519}{2} = £259.5$$

where
      500 = minimum order size for discount
      327 = economic order quantity
      £3 = unit carrying cost.

The order cost savings are:

$$\frac{8,000 \times £20}{327} - \frac{8,000 \times £20}{500} = £489.3 - £320 = £169.3$$

The net effect on profits of taking a quantity discount is:

Cost savings + order cost savings − additional carrying costs
£800 + £169.3 − £259.5 = £709.8

Therefore the firm should move to an order quantity of 500.

Though the EOQ model has numerous weaknesses, it does provide useful information for management. Over time some of the weaknesses can be eliminated and the inputs into the model can be refined. There can be no doubt that this method of inventory control is far superior to subjective methods. Greater availability of computers and operations research techniques make the application of sophisticated techniques easier.

Effective inventory management also involves consideration of issues such as the potential marketing benefits from keeping a comprehensive inventory. This applies particularly to distribution firms. Inventory speculation, especially in inflationary periods or when supply lines are at risk for any number of reasons, should also be looked at within prudent limits. The risks of obsolescence, theft, breakage and possible fall in market value all form part of what should be a balanced management decision in line with the firm's objectives.

Materials Requirements Planning (MRP I and II)

Materials Requirements Planning was devised in the 1960s as a method of calculating the total quantities of materials required to manufacture the finished products. It did this by 'exploding' the build quantities through the bill of materials for each product and generating purchase orders based on inventory control criteria, i.e. safety stock levels, delivery lead times, etc. The upgrading of the basic concept led to the development and implementation of Manufacturing Resource Planning (MRP II) as a route to manufacturing excellence. This was seen as a natural evolution from manual to automated planning on a more sophisticated scale. The objective of MRP II was to integrate manufacturing material planning, capacity planning, shopfloor control and management accounting into a single, complete manufacturing control system. It built upon the planning strength of MRP I and augmented it with the reporting of achievement against plan. It closed the loop in the planning or replanning process by enabling management to monitor production and take corrective action, where necessary. It also allowed integration with the distribution process and the firm's accounting records.

MRP II has not been without its critics. The primary objection is that by being modelled on the reality of the manufacturing process, it builds in all the faults, such as long lead times, large batch sizes, scrap and quality problems. It allows current productivity levels to be built into the system rather than working towards their elimination. It is also criticised for being too complex and administratively demanding. Despite the criticisms MRP II is a tried and tested planning and control system and is being used successfully by many firms. Its introduction and application has to be carefully prepared to suit each firm's specific circumstances and be supported by proper training and education. Otherwise it can be a very expensive and bad investment decision. The development of inventory control systems from manual to automated is now complemented by the 'Just in Time' philosophy.

'Just in Time' Inventory Control

This control system originated in Japan with Taiichi Okno, a vice-president of Toyota, and is, in effect, a production and management system. The concept is that a firm should keep a minimum level of inventory on hand, thereby relying on suppliers to furnish parts 'just in time' for them to be assembled. This is in direct contrast with the traditional inventory philosophy of most firms, sometimes referred to as a 'just in case' system, where healthy levels of safety stocks are kept to ensure that production will not be interrupted. When interest rates are high, this philosophy can become costly.

JIT is seen primarily as a daily shopfloor control system working to the theme of simplicity, quality and the elimination of waste. It should be seen as complementary to MRP II in concentrating on the systematic improvement of the production process and thereby ensuring adherence to plan and continuous improvements year on year.

JIT is seen as very suitable for firms with high-volume repetitive manufacturing processes where demand is smooth and predictable and there is a high percentage of common parts.

While the 'just in time' inventory system is intuitively appealing, it has not proven an easy system to implement. Strong and close relationships with suitable suppliers located in the same geographical area take time to develop, and ease of access and handling systems need to be installed. This is especially true for Irish firms, many of whom import materials and/or have a very limited choice of local suppliers. Yet in spite of the difficulties of implementation, many firms are committed to moving towards a 'just in time' inventory system. In doing so they are effectively adapting a new approach to the EOQ model by reducing and/or eliminating the need for safety stock and recognising the need to reduce the cost of ordering inventory.

ACCOUNTS RECEIVABLE MANAGEMENT

In order to obtain sales it is normal to offer credit to customers. Credit sales lead to the establishment of accounts receivable, usually on terms which require payment within a number of weeks. Credit terms are an important element in marketing. A firm offering tighter credit terms than those available from competitors will find sales more difficult to obtain. Accounts receivable represent a major investment for most business. For Irish business in particular, the taking of extended credit by customers means that accounts receivable may represent the largest single investment on the part of the business.

As is the case with most business decisions, accounts receivable management involves consideration of the risk versus return trade-off. The need to stimulate sales has to be balanced against the illiquidity and risk of default in payment. Good accounts receivable management involves establishing a clear credit policy backed up by collection procedures and monitoring reports.

Credit Policy

Management has the power to decide on the level of accounts receivable. Economic conditions do have an effect on payments but by lowering or tightening standards management can either increase or decrease the level of accounts receivable. A lowering of credit standards assists the marketing effort and should increase sales. Offsetting the good effects are higher debt collection costs, increased working capital needs and a greater probability of bad debts.

Credit policy is based on a set of standards that determine which customers will be granted credit and how much. The framework for making that decision involves marketing and manufacturing considerations, the bad debt level that the firm is comfortable with, and the need continually to update that policy to reflect seasonality and general economic conditions. Like almost all financial decisions, credit policy involves a strong element of judgment and an awareness that the quantitative analysis is only part of the information. Nevertheless a professional approach should be adopted in protecting the firm's accounts receivable investment by using some or all of the techniques available. They include:

(a) Financial Statement Analysis
    — applying the financial analysis techniques shown in Chapter 3 to assess the potential customer's financial strength and ability to pay.

(b) Comprehensive Analysis Involving the 'Four Cs':
    — character: customer's willingness to pay.
    — capacity: customer's ability to generate cash flow.
    — capital: customer's overall financial resources including collateral.
    — conditions: current economic or business conditions.

(c) Numerical Credit Scoring
    — the use of simple default rate indexes up to sophisticated multiple discriminate analysis.

In using the above techniques the firm can liaise with banking institutions, specialist credit agencies, trade associations and other business firms. It should also take into account generally published information and any previous experience of dealing with the potential customer, and give due weight to the sales representative's report.

Dun & Bradstreet is the largest provider of business information in Ireland, with a database holding information on over 30,000 businesses. Customers may gain access to this service by having a direct computer link from their own desks or by phoning in to the DunsTel Centre in Dublin. The type of information available includes company identification information; business principals, their background and functional responsibilities; financial and banking information; bill-paying histories; legal information, such as judgments or bankruptcies; business history and operations and special events such as ownership changes, moves or disasters. Customers also have direct access to Dun and Bradstreet's databases in Europe, US, Canada and Australia, and to an international network of offices.

An additional source of credit information is the Irish Trade Protection Association Limited (ITPA). The ITPA has been in existence since 1882 and is a non-profit company formed to protect the interests of traders. It provides full credit reporting and debt recovery services nationally and internationally, including on-line credit information, to its members. The ITPA publishes a weekly gazette containing particulars of registered court judgments, bankruptcies, statements of affairs, mortgages, charges, satisfactions and business names.

The information having been obtained, a credit decision must be made. In most instances the answer is clear from an assessment of the references, credit ratings or reports as applicable. In some others the information may be contradictory and require a compromise decision between the relevant managers involved. While much emphasis is placed on the character and reputation of the management, the size of the order and the probable future potential business tend to be the dominant issues.

Varying Credit Policy

On many occasions management will be under pressure to relax credit terms. The temptation to do this is especially strong in those cases where a significant sales increase can result, giving rise to increased profits. However, easing credit policy can lead to an increase in bad debts, higher costs due to increased working capital and possibly higher costs for the credit control department. The test is to use incremental or marginal analysis to see if the potential increased sales generate enough profit to more than offset the increased costs. In so doing, it is possible to make a quantitative assessment of the effects of changes in sales credit policy.

The marketing department has informed the general manager of Ardmore Limited that it can increase sales by £200,000 during 1995 if it is allowed to offer more liberal credit (Table 5.6). It has estimated that the effect on accounts receivable will be an increase by four weeks or approximately thirty days. Note that the credit period is on sales of £3,390,000, i.e. £3,190,000 plus the incremental £200,000 sales. An increase of £8,000 in administrative costs is expected while bad debts of £20,000 might occur.

The first question to be answered is the availability of additional production capacity. Having confirmed that it does exist, the next step is to estimate if the additional profit which will arise from the proposal is offset by the finance costs associated with the proposed credit policy change. Apart from the profit and loss effect, there will be a major increase in cash required to fund the additional sales. Is the cash available? In this case Ardmore can borrow the increased working capital at a rate of 12 per cent annually.

The answer is clear. The marketing department proposal will be rejected. Indeed, given the existing high level of accounts receivable, management might calculate the effect on the company of tightening up credit standards. Credit policy is not just about determining the creditworthiness of the potential customer. It also involves establishing the terms on which credit is granted. These include issues such as the type and length of credit sought, discount policy, reservation of title clause and insurance cover available.

Table 5.6

	£
Incremental Sales	200,000
Variable Cost of Production (71% of Sales)	
(This comes from the Pro Forma	
Income Statement: 2,258 ÷ 3,190)	142,000
Contribution	58,000
Less Bad Debts and Clerical Costs	28,000
Increased Profits	30,000
Incremental Accounts Receivable (4 Weeks)	260,000 approx.
Increased Interest Cost at 12% per Annum	31,200
(£260,000 @ 12%)	
Net Effect on Profits	(£1,200)

Credit Terms

There are basically three types of credit agreement: open book, instalment credit and revolving credit. Open book is the most common type and is where goods are sold on credit without a contract. Instalment credit is where payment is made by a series of regular or monthly instalments. This type of agreement is used for the purchase of once-off capital goods. Revolving credit is a combination of open book and instalment credit. The agreement is based on paying a regular minimum amount and is a particular feature of credit facilities offered by the financial institutions to personal clients.

Apart from widely used methods of providing credit, a number of commercial credit instruments (bills of exchange) can be used. They include a sight draft, time draft and banker's acceptance. A sight draft is where the customer has to pay the amount on presentation before receiving title to the goods. It is effectively a bill of exchange containing an immediate order to pay. A time draft is where the customer has to pay a number of days after presentation and is effectively a bill of exchange with a delayed order to pay. A banker's acceptance is a time draft on which the customer has secured a bank's guarantee of payment.

The length of the credit period is usually determined by the custom of the trade as similar terms are generally adopted by firms within the same industry. Other issues, such as the shelf life of the product, typical order size and delivery destination, can affect the decision. The credit terms are written to include discount for early payment in the following way: '2/10, net 30'. This means that the customer can deduct 2 per cent of the invoice amount if payment is made within ten days of the invoice date.

Table 5.7 gives some details on credit terms which have existed over a long period in a number of Irish industries.

CWO
COD.   CIA.

Table 5.7 Irish Credit Terms

Industry	Terms
Hosiery	Net 30 days, 3 per cent for payment within 7 days of invoice.
Clothing	2 ½ per cent discount 30 days; 3 ¾ per cent 7 days.
Footwear	Cash 5 per cent discount. Net 15th of the month following delivery.
Confectionery	Net 30 days, 2 per cent discount 10 days.
Grain Merchants	Net 30 days from date of invoice.
Textiles	Net 30 days, 1 ½ per cent discount 10 days.
Engineering Suppliers	Net 30 days.

Selling terms should state clearly the period of credit, the cash discount if any, and the length of time allowed for making the deduction from the invoice. The costs of offering cash discounts must be noted. Take, for example, the terms granted in the confectionery trade, 2/10 net 30 days: that is, a 2 per cent cash discount if paid within ten days, otherwise the full amount within 30 days. The cost of offering this discount is 2 per cent to obtain money twenty days before it is due. On an annual basis this works out to be

$$\text{Annual Cost of Discount} = 2\% \times \frac{365}{20} = 36.5\%$$

The cost looks prohibitive and indeed it would be. However, as was stated earlier, the average credit period taken in Ireland in 1994 was eighty days. Therefore the cost for the average customer is now

$$\text{Annual Cost of Discount} = 2\% \times \frac{365}{70} = 10.4\%$$

The seventy-day period is the eighty-day average less the ten days in which the discount can be taken. It can be seen that, relative to the average payment period, a 2 per cent discount for prompt payment is not unduly expensive. What must be very carefully monitored is a tendency among Irish customers to pay after a few weeks while still deducting the cash discount.

In specific industries particular credit terms may be granted. This is done to encourage sales to customers who are unable to finance the building of inventories in advance of their peak selling period because of a weak working capital position, limited borrowing capacity or both. It can also be used to reduce a manufacturer's inventory storage costs and assist in even flow production control in highly seasonal-type industries. Agricultural suppliers operate a system of *seasonal dating,* whereby customers agree to pay their bills on a date in autumn when their crops have been harvested.

Cash terms are used in some trades. They may be Cash with Order (CWO), Cash on Delivery (COD) or Cash in Advance (CIA). The timber importing industry uses Cash on Arrival (COA), where payment is due when the timber arrives at the Irish port. International trade uses Letters of Credit, where a specific date of payment is stipulated. As this is usually guaranteed by a bank, there is no danger of bad debts.

Reservation of Title

This powerful legal process has entered the area of accounts receivable management. Now, by means of a clear statement on an invoice, the vendor of products reserves the ownership of these goods until they are paid for. In the event of delayed or non-payment the vendor *may be* able to retrieve the goods in question. Of more value, perhaps, is the fact that in the event of bankruptcy, goods on which title has been reserved must be returned to the vendor. Where a manager has doubts about the creditworthiness of a particular client, he should insist on a title retention clause on each invoice.

Reservation of title also affects lenders and investors. Inventory values may not be what they appear to be. Title retention clauses do not have to be filed for public inspection; hence there is no way of knowing the effect, if any, on the inventory of a specific firm.

It was believed in the 1980s that reservation of title would revolutionise credit management and greatly reduce bad debts. The 1990s have proven otherwise. Where businesses have gone into liquidation without paying creditors, it has been difficult in many cases to obtain the return of the goods. Liquidators and receivers have questioned in detail the rights of creditors to recover goods. The Irish courts have frequently supported the power of the liquidator or receiver. Reservation of title is a powerful tool, but the documentation and the wording involved must be exact.

Credit Insurance

It is possible to insure against bad debts. The risks insured by a standard policy are insolvency and protracted default. On being asked to provide cover, an insurer will first satisfy himself that the credit control arrangements in operation are sensible and are adhered to.

There are a number of different styles of cover available, including:
   (a) Whole Turnover Basis
   (b) Specific Customers Only
   (c) Datum Line Policy.

Where at least 50 per cent of annual sales are to a small portion of the total customers, insurers may well be prepared to insure only sales to these specified buyers. This can be an attractive proposition for both insurer and client in view of the much reduced administration involved and the fact that the client will have concentrated the available resources on being covered against the collapse of substantial customers whose demise would otherwise have been even more painful.

Datum Line Policies apply to all customers with balances above an agreed minimum outstanding. Cover for each customer must be specifically requested. There is no facility for automatic cover in respect of customers already being traded with as there can be with the Whole Turnover Basis.

As for other insurances, the insured pays a deposit premium at the beginning of each period of insurance. This deposit premium is based on the anticipated turnover for the year, applying the agreed rate. At the end of the period a declaration is completed by the proposer, showing the actual insured turnover which has taken place. An adjustment is then calculated, with an additional or return premium due to the insured as the case may be.

Among the problems in acquiring credit cover at an acceptable price are the following:

(a) While quite a few insurance companies are licensed to transact this class of business, only two or three do so and, finding themselves in a seller's market, they are under no pressure to price keenly.

(b) In some sectors suppliers compete so fiercely that credit terms being afforded would not be considered prudent by an impartial underwriter.

Credit insurance is intended to complement good credit management. The basic principle is that the risk be shared, thereby giving both insurer and insured a clear interest in good credit management. The insurer will normally pay 90 per cent of a loss up to 90 per cent of the customer's established credit limit.

In Ireland the government, in its attempt to promote specific industries and build up new export markets, operates a system of export credit insurance. As normal insurance criteria would not allow cover to high-risk markets, the government filled that void through specific firm and contract export insurance cover. The pitfalls of this approach were shown in the débâcle of beef exports to Iraq, where over £180 million appears to have been lost.

Managing Existing Accounts Receivable

A later section deals with credit policy towards new customers but the efficient management of existing accounts receivable is at least as important to the success of the business. Managers often consider their job done when they have approved the initial credit application. This is not so. Continuous review of existing accounts is essential to ensure that they do not turn bad. This involves putting in place the necessary administrative procedures to ensure strict adherence to the credit policy decisions already taken. This involves written and oral communication with the customer in default and the initiation of legal action at the appropriate time. An early warning system is also required to cut off imminent or future shipments to a customer in default and alert the relevant sales force personnel to assume greater responsibility in bringing the problem to a satisfactory conclusion. At this stage the firm's objective is to limit the financial exposure without antagonising the customer and to create a climate of conciliation in the best interests of all concerned. Too much aggression can have long-term negative consequences, as can indecision and weak management.

Another valuable method of controlling debtors is the construction of an ageing schedule. This schedule tells the management the proportion of accounts outstanding for particular periods (Table 5.8).

Table 5.8

Ardmore Limited
Ageing Schedule of Accounts Receivable
as of 31 December 1994

Period Outstanding	£	% of Total
30 days or less	185,500	25.8
31–45 days	106,410	14.8
46–60 days	80,000	11.1
61–90 days	212,800	29.6
Over 90 days	134,290	18.7
	719,000	100.0

The terms granted by Ardmore are net forty-five days. Only 40.6 per cent of Ardmore customers are abiding by the credit terms. Of more concern is the fact that 18.7 per cent of the debtors are over ninety days. The Ardmore credit policy appears to be in a shambles. Yet prior to making this decision consider the following:

(a) Sales seasonality. It may mean that in certain periods more is sold than the average, thus distorting the percentages. This does not apply in this instance.

(b) The general trend of credit. In the 1990s credit was tight in Ireland. However, there is evidence that Ardmore Limited is average. The seventy-nine-day collection period is in line with the eighty-day average for Irish business discovered in a 1994 survey of 400 Irish businesses by Deloitte & Touche. The customers taking the extended credit need to be examined. It is likely that some bad debts exist in that figure of £134,290. A substantial bad debt could endanger the safety of the business.

One way for Ardmore to reduce the age of accounts receivable is to improve the collection procedures. An increasing number of Irish businesses are finding it necessary to allocate an employee to collect accounts receivable. Among the steps which can be followed to obtain payment are letters, telephone calls, personal visits, use of collection agencies and legal action.

Far too many Irish firms baulk at the use of tough collection policies. As a result there is a general lack of discipline in credit matters. Customers who will not pay should be taken to court. The excuse put forward for not taking legal action is that you will lose the customer. The answer is that you do not want such a customer. It is possible to calculate the value of an increased collection effort. Ardmore Limited is considering hiring a credit control clerk at a salary of £15,000 in 1995. It is expected that letters, calls and visits to customers by the employee will cost a further £6,000. It is thought that the accounts receivable period would decline by two weeks with the addition of this employee. More important perhaps is the likelihood of a reduced level of bad debts. The impact of this potential action can be analysed as in Table 5.9.

Table 5.9 Impact of Extra Debt Collector

	Value*	Days on Hand
Expected 1995 Accounts Receivable Level	£831,000	95
Accounts Receivable Level with New Clerk	£708,537	81
Savings	£122,463	14
Interest Saving at 12%	£14,696	
Cost of Clerk	(£21,000)	
Savings (Loss)	(£6,304)	

* Year-end figures are used in the interests of clarity.

This shows that hiring the employee is not worth while. If the investment in accounts receivable can be reduced by up to three weeks then the effort may pay off.

THE MANAGEMENT OF CASH

Cash management is the maintenance of liquidity in the business and is based on due consideration of the risk and return trade-off. This involves having enough liquidity to meet all obligations and not holding excess cash since investment in long-term assets generally provides higher returns than short-term investments. Cash means not only the actual cash held by a business but the availability of cash from bank accounts and 'near cash': that is, assets which are readily realisable for cash. Near cash assets are known as marketable securities.

A business holds cash for three main reasons, i.e. trading, as a hedge against uncertainty and for potential speculation. Trading cash, or the transactions motive, is money used in the course of day-to-day business activities. This is the money to pay the wages, fuel, light, heat suppliers, taxation and dividends. Precautionary cash is the name given to money required to meet unexpected demands, therefore providing a hedge against uncertainty. Such demands arise in many ways — for example, a machinery breakdown, strikes, a credit squeeze. No business activity is certain, so variations in the expected outcomes are always likely. To allow for the unexpected, businesses keep a 'cash cushion' over and above the sums required for trading. This cushion does not have to be actual cash but usually consists of marketable securities and/or borrowing facilities at a bank. Availability is more important than size.

The speculative motive in holding cash or 'near cash' is to allow the firm to take advantage of potential profit-making situations. As the raising of cash is neither instantaneous nor costless, this motive — while the least important generally — may be of direct interest to some firms on an occasional opportunistic basis. This could allow them to take advantage of raw material prices or discounts, exchange rate movements or market share values, or to complete an acquisition or merger project.

Defining Cash Needs/Optimal Cash Levels

How much cash should a business hold? As previously noted, a firm should hold as little cash as possible, as it is a non-productive asset, but must also be conscious of the risk of illiquidity. The answer depends on the following:

(1) The expected pattern of cash flows as shown in the cash budget (Table 4.6, Chapter 4).
(2) The certainty of cash flows. Some businesses, such as electricity suppliers, can predict revenues with a high level of certainty. At the other extreme are firms operating in competitive markets and selling products with high obsolescence possibilities. The greater the level of uncertainty attaching to cash flows, the larger the cash amount required.
(3) General monetary climate. In periods of tight credit customers can be very slow in paying; therefore cash inflows can be reduced. As credit gets tighter a firm needs to monitor cash levels continuously.
(4) Borrowing capacity. A firm with agreed borrowing capacity can afford to maintain very low cash levels.
(5) The efficiency of cash usage. This means the speed with which cash is utilised. Two ratios are used to measure cash usage.

$$\text{(a) cash in current assets} = \frac{\text{cash balance}}{\text{current assets}}$$

(b) cash turnover $= \dfrac{\text{sales}}{\text{cash balance}}$

In Ireland the above ratios are rarely used, as most businesses have bank overdrafts and so minimal cash balances. The ratios can be made more meaningful by including the bank overdraft in the cash balance figure. Management should aim, over a period of time, to reduce the first ratio and increase the second.

In addition to the above simple rules of thumb a number of models have been developed to help determine the optimal cash balance. These include the Baumol inventory model and the Miller-Orr stochastic model. They are based on the principle that the optimal cash balance is determined by a trade-off between interest income and transaction costs.

The Baumol model is based on the simple inventory (optimum order size) model and involves merely redefining the variables. It is defined as

$$C = \sqrt{\dfrac{2Ds}{Ic}}$$

Where
    C = optimal transaction size
    D = annual cash disbursements
    S = fixed cost of a transaction
    Ic = interest rate

An example will help.

Suppose that the interest rate on government securities is 8 per cent, each transaction costs £20 and the firm pays out an average of £100,000 per month or £1,200,000 per year. Therefore the optimal transaction size (c) is as follows:

$$C = \sqrt{\dfrac{2 \times £1,200,000 \times £20}{.08}}$$

$$= £24,500$$

Thus the firm should sell approximately £24,500 of government securities, four times a year and carry an average cash balance of £24,500/2 or £12,250. In general when interest rates are high you want to hold small average cash balances. However, if you have a high rate of cash disbursements or high transaction costs in selling securities you will want to hold large average cash balances.

Baumol's model is based on the assumption that the size and timing of cash flows are known with certainty. Consequently, it has limited use in times of uncertainty and for firms whose cash flows are discontinuous or bumpy. In addition it can be difficult to calculate the full transaction cost. Nevertheless it does offer a conceptual framework that can be used with caution as a benchmark.

The Miller-Orr model can be used in times of uncertainty and random cash flows. It is based on the principle that control limits can be set which when reached trigger off a transaction. The control limits are based on the day-to-day variability in cash flows and the fixed costs of buying and selling government securities. The formula for calculating the spread between the control limits is

$$3 \left(\frac{\text{¾} \times \text{transaction cost} \times \text{variance of cash flows}}{\text{interest rate}} \right)^{\text{⅓}}$$

The higher the variability in cash flows and transaction cost, the wider and higher the control limits will be. Conversely, the higher the interest rate, the lower and closer they will become. Within the control limits, the cash balance meanders unpredictably. When it hits an upper or lower limit, action is taken by buying or selling securities to restore the balance to its normal level within the control points.

The return point is calculated using the formula

$$\text{Return point} = \text{lower limit} + \frac{\text{spread}}{3}$$

In applying the Miller-Orr model one must set the lower limit for the cash balance. This could be zero or some minimum safety margin above zero.

It is presented graphically in Figure 5.10. An example will help.

Assumptions	
Interest rate per day/annum	.03%/10.95%
Transaction cost per sale	£20
Variance of cash flows per day/annum	£3,000/£9,000,000
Cash balance lower limit	£20,000

$$\text{Spread (between control limits)} = 3 \left(\frac{\text{¾} \times 20 \times 9,000,000}{.0003} \right)^{\text{⅓}}$$

$$= \text{£22,990 or about £23,000}$$

Therefore the upper limit is equal to the lower limit of £20,000 plus the spread of £23,000, i.e. £43,000.

The return point is equal to the lower limit of £20,000 plus the spread of £23,000/3, i.e. £20,000 + £23,000/3 = £27,667.

In summary, therefore, the firm's cash management policy should be based on lower and upper control limits of £20,000 and £43,000 respectively and the need to initiate action to keep within those limits should it move outside this band.

Like the Baumol model, the Miller-Orr model does provide a starting-point for determining optimal cash levels. The intuition and experience of the financial manager, allied to the firm's own particular requirements, needs to be considered in finalising decisions on optimal cash levels.

Cash Management Policy

The correct policy for managing cash is easy to state but difficult to implement. The following is advisable:

(a) Stretch payables as long as possible without damaging the credit rating of the firm. This means delaying payment to suppliers. If very favourable cash discounts are offered then they should be taken.

(b) Reduce levels of inventory to the minimum required to meet sales projections and to enable efficient production.

(c) Have a tight credit control on accounts receivable. Do not, as Ardmore Limited has done, allow control to slip over time.

Figure 5.10 Miller-Orr Cash Management Model

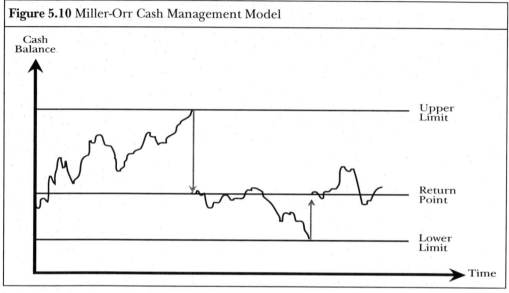

(d) Improve the collection and deposit of cash receipts.

(e) Invest surplus cash balances.

Stretching accounts payable can ease cash problems, at least in the short term, but may damage the reputation of the firm. Where a supplier is dependent on the firm, there is little danger in slowing up payments. Irish firms have become adept at stretching payables. As a result, suppliers often include interest provisions in their invoices and/or charge higher prices. One method of stretching accounts payable is to offer Bills of Exchange. Instead of paying suppliers on the due date the firm offers to accept a Bill of Exchange for a period of 60, 90, 120 or 180 days. The supplier can usually discount the Bill and receive cash. Through the use of more efficient management controls in purchasing, production and marketing levels, the amount of cash invested in inventory can be reduced. It is possible to release the cash tied up in inventory by borrowing. Specific financial instruments using inventory as collateral are available in Ireland. Together with other sources of finance, they are discussed in later chapters.

Speeding up debt collection has been dealt with at some length. Careful credit control can release large sums of cash. It is also possible to reduce the capital invested in accounts receivable by selling them. This method of raising cash is known as factoring. It is examined in Chapter 9.

A number of techniques exist to speed up the technical process of collecting, depositing and clearing cheques. Technology can now support and ensure virtually instantaneous transfer of funds from both banking and customer sources. Efficient cash collection and disbursement management can have a significant effect on the firm's overall profitability and can also play an important public relations role. Many firms still lodge receipts irregularly. The cost per day of holding cheques should be noted. At 12 per cent interest this is .033 per cent (12 ÷ 365). Of course the additional administrative cost of daily banking must be offset against interest saved. If a firm has many sales outlets throughout the country, it can make use of concentration banking, whereby accounts are paid into the local branches of a bank. This method reduces the time between cheque mailing and receipt.

Another means of managing cash is the 'float': that is, the money tied up in cheques written but not yet paid. Using the float involves 'cheque kiting' — writing a cheque on an account knowing that the funds are not there but intending to lodge the funds before the cheque is presented. Some firms write their cheques on distant banks knowing that it will take much longer to clear this cheque. 'Kiting' is illegal. Care must be taken to preserve the good name of the business.

Investing surplus cash balances, which is the last step in efficient cash management, is the subject of the following section.

Investing in Marketable Securities

Marketable securities are short-term near cash investments. Though many firms suffer from cash shortages, other firms have excess cash. Some Irish companies such as Woodchester and Fyffes have substantial cash deposits. It is undesirable to leave cash unused. Excess cash usually means temporary cash surpluses which are available for short-term investment. Firms with cash not needed for trading or emergency purposes should seek long-term investment opportunities in their own business or in diversifications. If no worthwhile investment opportunities can be discovered, consideration should be given to paying out excess funds to the shareholders by means of dividends or by a repayment of capital.

Caution should be exercised when investing in short-term securities. Risk, either to income or to capital value, should be minimised. In addition marketability, maturity, taxation and the interest (coupon) rate are important factors. The need to get professional advice and diversify the portfolio may also be worthy of consideration. The main outlets for cash are:

(a) Exchequer Bonds. These are short-term, ninety-day, securities of the Irish government. The bonds are sold at a discount from their face value. They are readily saleable.

(b) Commercial paper. This is an unsecured promissory note issued by top-quality businesses. Chapter 9 discusses this financial instrument in more detail.

(c) Term deposits with financial institutions. Banks will negotiate a rate of interest for a deposit left with them for a specific period.

(d) Government loans. These are long-term loans to the state. They are quoted on the Irish Stock Exchange. There is, however, a risk that should interest rates rise there will be a loss in the capital value of the investment. Since an active market exists in government loans there is little difficulty in obtaining cash when required.

CONCLUSION

This chapter on the management of working capital has concentrated on asset management. The techniques of handling short-term liabilities are considered in Chapter 9, which deals with short-term sources of finance. The essence of working capital management is liquidity, the ability to provide cash when it is required. Liquidity can be measured by the time it takes to turn an asset into cash, as evidenced by the working capital cycle and by the certainty of the value contained in the asset. The management of liquidity involves decision-making on the types of investment and on the level of commitment to each investment. Business profitability and risk are affected by the decisions made.

FURTHER READING

D. Mehta, *Working Capital Management* (New Jersey, Prentice-Hall, 1984).
L.J. Gilman, *Principles of Managerial Finance*, 6th ed. (New York, Harpur, 1991).
R. Dixon & L. McAuley, *Management Finance* (London, ACCA 1995).
J.W. Petty et al., *Basic Financial Management*, 6th ed. (New Jersey, Prentice-Hall, 1993).

QUESTIONS

Question 5.1
What is working capital?

Question 5.2
Explain the role of safety stocks in the management of inventory.

Question 5.3
In Moriarty's department store one of their best-selling items is a brand of perfume. Buying costs are £30 per order. Sales average 100,000 bottles per year with storage costs of £1,500 per annum per 1,000 bottles. Orders are delivered after five weeks. Assume a fifty-week year.

Calculate:
(a) The economic order quantity.
(b) The reorder stock level.

Question 5.4
Micro Electronics Corporation uses 300,000 microchips in the production of its computers. The cost of each chip is £1. Order costs are £250 per order and carrying costs 40 per cent of cost price. Deliveries take eight weeks. Assume a forty-eight-week year.

Calculate:
(a) The economic order quantity.
(b) The reorder level.

Question 5.5
A company orders walkmans in batches of 1,000. Each order costs £20 to place. Demand from stores is 20,000 per month with a carrying cost of £2 per walkman.

    (a) What is the optimal order quantity?
    (b) What would it be if carrying costs were £1 per walkman?
    (c) What would it be if ordering costs were £10 and carrying costs £2 per unit?

Question 5.6
What are the different sources that exist for credit analysis?

Capital Budgeting and Fixed Asset Management

Previous chapters have concentrated on the financial effects of short-term plans. Managing operations in the short term is only one side of the financial management coin. The ultimate profitability of a business depends on the success or failure of the long-term investments made by that business. Part of the process of selecting these investments is known as capital budgeting, with the primary motive being to increase the value of the firm. This means choosing investments that have a positive net present value and managing them well. The capital budgeting techniques discussed in this chapter can help managers perform this task. Capital investments create jobs and promote economic growth, hence increasing the wealth of society, so governments have a keen interest in long-term investment decisions and frequently produce policies to assist and encourage such investment.

Long-term investments are an integral part of the corporate strategy followed by the firm. Corporate strategy can be defined as follows:

'Given the resources available to a firm and the environment facing the business, corporate strategy is that set of policies followed to achieve the objectives of the owners.'

Corporate strategy is decided on by the owners, who are usually represented by the board of directors. To assist decision-making it is common to find that the effects of various policy decisions are all reduced to a common denominator — money. Examples would be a board of directors considering such projects as an overseas investment, a new domestic factory and/or the introduction of new product lines. To arrive at the decision it helps to have the potential outcomes of proposed investments reduced to cash flows, profit and loss statements and financial returns on the investment.

To place the role of capital investment decision-making in context look at the structure outlined in Figure 6.1. An ongoing business operates in an ever-changing environment. Such changes may offer opportunities or present threats. For example, consider the dangers facing tobacco companies in the Western world yet opportunities are opening up for them in the East.

The political environment often poses more threats than opportunities. War, civil disturbance and the possibility of nationalisation all militate against investment. Yet here too opportunities emerge. The fall of the Berlin Wall opened up many new markets while political changes in China could provide a significant boost to world growth.

Economic changes such as in oil prices, interest rates, currencies and government policy have an impact on business.

Possibly the area of greatest challenge is technology. To the optimist new technology offers only opportunities while to the pessimist threats abound. Consider some of the effects of technology. Many of the world's largest businesses of the 1950s are struggling today. The businesses which will lead the world into the twenty-first century, such as Microsoft, Mc Caw, Walmart, came into being only in the last quarter of the twentieth century.

The resources which a firm has or can gain access to play a major role in deciding long-term strategy and the investment needed to implement that strategy. Irish firms facing a small home market, relatively underdeveloped capital markets and a limited technological background find it difficult to compete on world markets. To succeed they must find a niche where their available resources can be effectively used.

Figure 6.1 Corporate Strategy

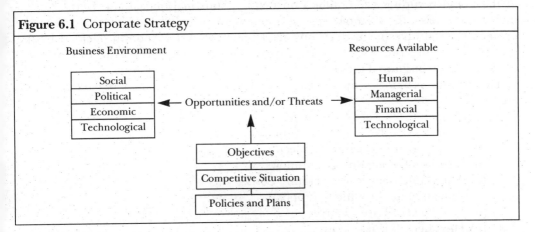

Generally, there are a number of alternative investment opportunities open while resources are limited. Techniques have been developed which assist decision-making in allocating funds to prospective investments. These techniques are known collectively as capital budgeting. Investment projects are evaluated to see which best meets the objectives of the business and for this reason capital budgeting is known also as project appraisal. This title can be somewhat misleading, however, in that capital budgeting is in fact a complex process comprising a number of stages. They can be summarised as
— the search and identification stage
— the assessment stage
— the acceptance or rejection stage
— the implementation stage
— the control and post-completion audit stage. The process is dynamic, ongoing and involves consideration of the types of finance to be used and the appropriate finance mix to be adopted. It is based on the economic principle that the firm's wealth is maximised at the point where marginal revenue is equal to marginal cost. Marginal revenue is the rates of return earned on succeeding investments, while marginal cost is the cost of successive increments of capital required by the firm. The risk return trade-off involving higher returns for higher risk has also to be considered, as does the opportunity cost of capital, before arriving at a final decision. When the decision has

been reached, implementation and control procedures are just as important to ensure success and protect the asset base of the firm. In addition a post-completion audit programme can provide valuable information for corrective action and future decision-making. While most investment decisions are financially based and have quantifiable benefits, some investments are undertaken for regulatory or compliance reasons. These provide no direct cash benefit to the firm but are necessary to allow the firm continue in operation. They could include compliance with fire and safety regulations, environmental improvements or the provision of minimum working conditions.

The types of decision which require the application of capital budgeting techniques include the replacement of assets, modernisation, new fixed asset acquisitions and the purchase of other businesses. The size of capital investments ranges from the purchase of inexpensive equipment to outlays which may dwarf the existing assets invested. Examples are Arcon PLC spending £65 million to develop the Galmoy mine, and Fruit of the Loom spending $200 million on textile plants in Donegal and Derry. On an international level, the Channel Tunnel company spent £11,000 million to develop one project. Capital investment decisions are almost without exception decided by the owner/board of directors. Often the commitments are so large as to threaten the existence of the business if they go wrong.

This chapter examines some of the critical areas involved in capital budgeting. These are:

    (a) Estimating the Total Investment.
    (b) Analysing the Timing of Expenditures.
    (c) Estimating the Life of the Project.
    (d) Forecasting Long-Run Cash Inflows.
    (e) Forecasting Long-Run Operating Costs.
    (f) Evaluating the Investment Proposal.
    (g) The Effect of Price Changes.
    (h) The Effect of Uncertainty.

After an examination of the theoretical aspects of the process, a worked example is presented. This example analyses the long-run return to Ardmore Limited of replacing some existing machinery with new high-speed equipment.

THE TOTAL INVESTMENT REQUIRED

The first task facing management is the estimation of the total investment required. Total investment covers not only the costs of equipment and buildings, but installation expenses, taxes, pre-production costs and working capital requirements. For many projects it is very difficult to estimate the total, particularly where lengthy construction periods are involved. Conservative managers usually provide a contingency allowance. The Electricity Supply Board's allowance for contingency is typically in the order of 10 per cent. Other significant costs which are frequently ignored are architects' and engineering consultants' fees. These costs average 6 per cent of total investment in fixed assets. Interest during the construction period must also be provided for. Inflation in construction costs can seriously affect the ability of management to predict costs, as can delays in construction. Figure 6.2 provides a framework for estimating the total capital investment in a project.

In many cases new investments are designed to replace existing assets. This means that the old assets can be sold. The salvage value less the removal costs is deducted from the cost of the new investment. Depending on the price received for the old asset there may be a tax charge. Frequently, assets are fully written off against profits and have no value in the books of the business. If these assets are sold for a price greater than the book value then a 'balancing charge' of corporation tax may arise. If land or buildings are involved there may be a capital gains tax liability. In estimating the total capital investment one should focus only on 'incremental cost', i.e. cash outflows that exist only if the decision is adopted.

Figure 6.2 Estimating Capital Investment	
Item	£
1. Site, Costs and Preparation	
2. Plant and Equipment Cost, plus Installation	
3. Ancillary Equipment, e.g. offices, canteen, hygiene, estimated cost at date of expenditure	———
Total Fixed Cost	
4. Consulting Fees (6%)	
5. Contingency Allowance (10%)	
6. Pre-Production Interest/Costs	
7. Working Capital Required (Inventory, Accounts Receivable)	———
8. Training Expenses	
Total Cost	
9. Less Proceeds from Sale of Surplus Assets (if any)	———
Total Incremental Cost	

TIMING OF CAPITAL EXPENDITURE

Often capital projects have expenditure spread over a long period of time; the Channel Tunnel project, for example, took about eight years to construct but it was in the planning stage for at least an equal number of years. The Arcon zinc mine was discovered in 1986 but will not come onstream before 1997. Having estimated the total investment involved, the timing of expenditures must be calculated. Rarely will the entire cost be payable at one time. 'Overnight' projects do not exist. In reality most, if not all, projects involve a sequential stream of expenditures over a finite period of time. For instance, payments for buildings are usually made over a period of months or years — so-called 'progress payments'. Working capital will not be required until close to production start-up and then it will increase as output grows.

A chart should be drawn up covering the pre-operational life of the project — that is, from decision time to full output time — showing the outflow of costs. Figure 6.3 indicates a pattern of expenditure found in many capital projects. This **S Curve** can be explained by the low outflow during the early days of a project. Large payments as equipment arrives are followed by a slowdown as the project goes into operation. The bump at the top of the curve is caused by final payments to a wide variety of interested parties — often known as completion payments — paid when the project achieves certain levels of production efficiency.

THE ESTIMATED LIFE OF THE PROJECT

How long will the project under analysis be economically viable? This simple question is frequently ignored in project appraisal but the profitability of many projects is determined primarily by the revenue-earning life. This is difficult to determine because it is usually quite different from the physical life. A zinc refinery may have an indefinite physical life but a finite economic existence. The major uncertainties are technological obsolescence, currency changes and inflation, uncertain operating costs and output prices. A change in technology could result in a new process which would render existing facilities unprofitable. Technological forecasting is notoriously inexact but management should at least scan the business environment to see if innovations are on the horizon.

Figure 6.3 Cumulative Expenditure Pattern Over Time in a Capital Investment Project

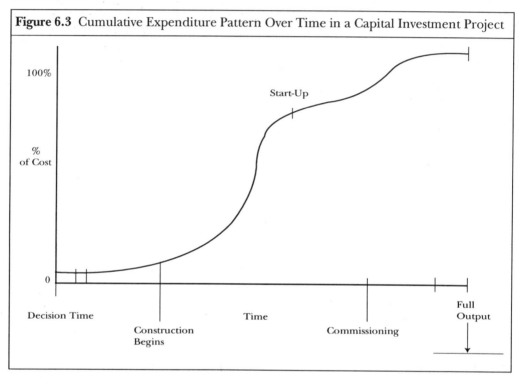

Inflation attacks the economic lives of projects in an insidious way. At the time of planning, the process used represents the best obtainable mixture of capital and labour. Inflation results in increasing labour costs. Over time labour-saving devices become available but are not used so that within a period of years existing facilities are relatively high-cost because they are labour-intensive. The effects of sustained currency changes must be evaluated. It is possible that long-term currency changes will render a location totally uneconomic. For example, a hardening US dollar value against most developing country currencies has rendered uneconomic in the US many mining- and metal-related projects. The gradual appreciation of the Japanese yen against the US dollar has meant a flight of labour-intensive clothing and textile investments from Japan to lower-cost countries while the dearer yen finally resulted in US and Japanese car companies competing on a fairer basis. Apart from technology, inflation and currency, other variables act to reduce the economic lives of projects. Tastes change, leading to a decline in demand for certain products, sources of raw materials dry up, the taxation environment changes or political attitudes change.

There is no easy way to estimate the economic life of a project. Many companies simply take fifteen years as their planning horizon. During a period of great economic uncertainty in the 1970s and 1980s, the planning horizon dropped to ten years. Though it is difficult, attempts must be made to evaluate the expected economic life.

FORECASTING LONG-RUN CASH INFLOWS

Estimating the likely revenue for a period of ten or fifteen years is a daunting yet vital task. There is no way in which profitability can be assessed unless sales revenue figures are forecast. Chapter 4 dealt with the problems and difficulties of forecasting one year in advance. Now the exercise must be pushed a decade or more into the future. Business operates in an uncertain environment. Uncertainties multiply as prediction is extended. It is hard enough to place a value on the various risks faced by a project but virtually impossible to estimate uncertainties. Uncertainty can be defined as not knowing what you do not know.

All revenues from a project are measured on an incremental cash flow basis. This means that non-cash items are ignored and that the only revenues counted are additional ones arising from the particular project.

In attempting to forecast future revenue management needs to predict two variables: price and quantity. It is possible to get estimates of the likely price from market research studies and marketing department estimates. Estimating the likely level of sales is more uncertain. Guidelines may be obtained from the sales levels of substitutes or competing products. If the product in question is replacing existing products then forecasting is easier. Often future estimates are projections of past sales.

As the forecasts stretch two, five, ten and fifteen years into the future, other assumptions need to be made. Factors such as the growth of the economy and the relationship between the economy and the particular product become important.

An examination of the factors affecting sales will allow management to make estimates of the most likely cash inflows in a given year. But note that the word used is 'estimates'. It is probable that by changing some assumptions the sales estimates will vary. Therefore a risk is attached to the selection of a best estimate cash flow. To handle the risk and uncertainties attaching to cash flows, the techniques of Sensitivity Analysis and Probability Distributions have evolved, and these are addressed in the next section.

Note that in addition to sales cash flow, three other types of cash flows can influence the investment decision. They are the salvage value of the assets, the recovery of net working capital when the project's useful life ends, and any exit costs, e.g. cleaning up a site, laying off workers. These are generally described as the terminal cash flows.

Sensitivity Analysis

This provides a simple way of treating risk and helps to give an indication of the 'economic robustness' of a project. Management is asked to furnish a range of sales estimates for each year. Generally, a group of 'expert' individuals is asked to give three estimates: worst, best and most likely. Very little additional work is required to produce these estimates as most individuals tend to operate within a certain range when forecasting. Figure 6.4 demonstrates the outcome of a sensitivity analysis.

This illustration shows that management is being reasonably conservative: that is, the most likely estimate is closer to the pessimistic than to the optimistic. Using this data, management can now provide three rates of return. This method, which is simple to use, is appropriate in most situations where management is uncertain about the future.

Figure 6.4 Sensitivity Analysis of Projected Revenues for Project X

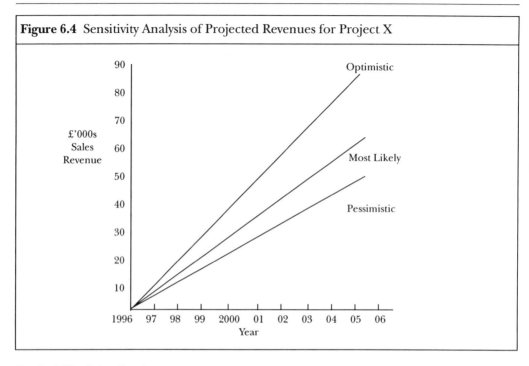

Probability Distributions

The application of probabilities to outcomes is a refinement of the sensitivity method outlined above. A probability is the percentage chance of a particular outcome occurring. The example below (Table 6.5) shows the technique applied to the estimates for the third year of a project being considered by Ardmore Limited.

Table 6.5 Range of Possible Outcomes in Year 3 for Project X

	Ardmore Limited	
Cash Inflows	Possibility of Occurrence	Expected Value
(1)	(2)	(1 × 2)
£20,000	05	£1,000
17,000	.15	2,550
15,000	.20	3,000
12,000	.35	4,200
10,000	.15	1,500
8,000	.10	800
	1.00	£13,050

Management, in conjunction with marketing and production staff, has estimated that the net results in year three for Project X could be any of the six outcomes in Table 6.5, column 1. The top outcome would normally correspond with the 'optimistic' estimate of the previous approach, while the bottom estimate is the equivalent of the 'pessimistic' in Figure 6.4. The next step is to decide the possibility of each of these estimates being the actual result. Probabilities must add up to one, meaning that the entire range of possibilities is covered. It is decided that there is only a 5 per cent chance of a net cash inflow of £20,000 but a 35 per cent chance of a cash inflow of £12,000. At the other end of the scale, cash inflows are not expected to be much less than £8,000 and in fact it is considered that there is only a 10 per cent chance of an £8,000 cash inflow. Multiplying columns 1 by 2 gives the expected value of the various estimates. The sum of this column is the expected value of cash inflows for the particular year being examined. The expected value of £13,050 can then be incorporated into the project appraisal. The figure can be put in context by realising that the cash inflow may range from £20,000 to £8,000 but considering the possibilities within this range the expected value or most likely inflow is £13,050.

The above method becomes simple to apply with experience. It should be applied to the cash flows of each projected period, thus giving management some estimate of the risk attaching to the project, and an idea of the likely range of benefits or losses.

Further extension of the analysis of uncertainty through probability distributions and their means and standard deviations is useful, but beyond the scope of this text.

In applying sophisticated techniques remember that the results obtained are only as good as the data. If the original forecasts on which the analysis was based were poor then the final output will also be poor.

Management, using all available data, produces a long-run forecast of cash inflows. In the last year of the project's economic life two non-revenue cash inflows are likely: (a) a salvage value for the plant and equipment and (b) a release of the capital tied up in inventory and debtors. Estimating the salvage value of machinery is difficult, and a low figure is usually taken. The recovery of working capital is often forgotten but since this can be a substantial item care should be taken to include an appropriate figure.

Increasingly, there is a cash outflow at the end of a project. Workers being laid off with years of service frequently obtain heavy redundancy payments while planning permissions often require site clean-ups, land reclamation and other expensive cash outlays. Mining, metal and chemical companies face major capital expenditures to close down a project.

FORECASTING LONG-RUN OPERATING COSTS

Capital budgeting is concerned only with incremental costs. Incremental costs are those which vary with alternative courses of action. Costs are relevant only if they arise specifically from an investment decision. If a cost will remain the same whether or not a proposed investment is undertaken, it should not be considered in the analysis. The following, though not comprehensive, provides a useful checklist for costs that are likely to be affected by a new proposal (Figure 6.6).

Figure 6.6 Incremental Cost Checklist

Direct Labour	Material Costs	Inspection Costs
Indirect Labour	Other Supplies	Set-Up Time
Fringe Benefits	Insurance	Down Time
Maintenance and Repairs	Tools	Power and Fuel Costs
Materials Handling	Tool Repair	Floor Space
Marketing Costs	Scrap and Rework	Subcontract Costs

Management must attempt to measure the extra or incremental costs attaching to each of the above which would arise if a new investment is made. Costs such as direct labour, materials and power may be easily estimated, but others — such as the costs attached to the sales representatives carrying an extra line, fringe benefits, extra maintenance, etc. — may be difficult to compute.

It is easier to predict costs than revenues, as management has experience of costs and their trends. Of course costs are a function of sales volume so it is necessary to undertake an exercise to provide a range of costs suitable for the sales estimates generated by the sensitivity analysis or probability distribution analysis. It is important to note that many costs will be fixed across large ranges of output. Three cost items deserve special comment. They are Sunk costs, Capital (Financing) costs and Closure costs.

Sunk Costs

The concept of sunk costs can be of vital importance in capital expenditure decisions. A sunk cost is one resulting from a past decision which cannot now be reversed. Once an investment is made, it is completely irrelevant to any future decision unless it can be recovered in whole or part. Suppose £40,000 has already been irrevocably invested in the development of a new product, but a further £10,000 is necessary to get it off the ground. Here, all the future benefits must be measured against the incremental outlay of £10,000 and not the original £40,000 or the combined £50,000. This concept applies particularly to situations involving replacement of machinery, buildings, etc. It is not correct to consider either the original cost or depreciated value of existing assets. The only figure of 'cost' to be considered is the market value of the assets.

Capital (Financing) Costs

The cost of capital is mentioned here because it is most certainly a cost relevant to investment proposals. Estimating the cost of capital is one of the most difficult problems in business finance, and one that may be approached in various ways. For the smaller private firm, an approximation of the cost of capital is the rate paid by the firm on borrowed funds. For larger firms with different sources of long-term funds, the cost can be approximated by the weighted average cost of the various sources used.

The cost of capital as used in capital budgeting is either the required rate of return or a cut-off/hurdle rate. Business people examine a project to see if it costs more than it yields: that is, will the cost of the funds raised to finance the proposed investment be greater than the profits from the investment itself. In many instances the return which a project must offer should equal or better a target rate. This target rate must be higher than the cost of the money if any real profit is to result from the project.

Chapter 14 examines the cost of capital.

Closure Costs

Modern social legislation places a high cost on people losing jobs. Therefore redundancy payments must be provided for in the final year of operation. Increasingly, environmental controls are forcing businesses to clean up projects before leaving an area. This can be costly, particularly in heavy industries.

The total costs attaching to revenues having been estimated, the net cash position is worked out in a manner identical to that used in the cash budget shown in Chapter 4 (Table 4.6). The net difference between cash generated from sales and that paid out to cover costs is the money available to repay the investment made.

EVALUATING INVESTMENT PROPOSALS
Having gathered together all of the information required on investment, timing, inflows and outflows, management must now combine the data into a framework which produces a measure of investment worth. There are four methods commonly used to evaluate investments:
(i) Payback.
(ii) Simple Rate of Return (ROI).
(iii) Internal Rate of Return (IRR).
(iv) Net Present Value (NPV).
   The first two methods are relatively simple to apply and are used widely. Unfortunately, they each have a major theoretical weakness. The latter two methods of evaluation are more sophisticated and incorporate the time value of money.

Payback
The payback is the period of time required to recover the initial cost of the investment. Two methods are used in calculating the payback.

$$\text{The Average Payback Period} \quad = \quad \frac{\text{Initial Investment}}{\text{Average Annual Net Cash Flow}}$$

$$\text{The Actual Payback Period} \quad = \quad \text{The actual time required for net cash inflow to equal the initial investment.}$$

   Generally, the payback period is compared with some maximum acceptable standard. If the payback on the project is less than the reference period, the project is accepted; if not, it is rejected. Studies have shown that the payback method is by far the most widely used project appraisal technique. Most businesses use a reference payback period of five years or less. The popularity of the payback method arises from its simplicity of application. To a limited extent the payback period measures risk — that is, the longer the payback then the greater the risk. It is also a rough measure of liquidity. Payback is commonly used even by large companies in projects where risks and uncertainties are very high.
   There are two weaknesses inherent in the payback method. Consider the following two proposals before the board of a company. Each proposal requires a £30,000 investment (Table 6.7).

Table 6.7 Proposed Investments Payback Period

Outflows				Inflows				
Year	0	1	2	3	4	5	6	7
A —	£30,000	£6,000	£12,000	£12,000	£18,000	£18,000	£18,000	£18,000
B —	£30,000			£30,000				
Projects A and B rank equally.								

In both cases the payback is three years, but the method ignores all cash flows after that period. It also ignores the magnitude and timing of cash flows within the payback period. In the above example Proposal A provides a cash inflow two years before B, yet both are equally ranked and give the same percentage rate of return in payback terms.

Of course no management would simply calculate the payback period and ignore all other data. As a screening device this method of capital budgeting is useful.

Simple Rate of Return (ROI)

There are many different ways of calculating this measure. A common definition is as follows:

$$\text{Simple Rate of Return} = \frac{\text{Average Profit After Tax and Depreciation}}{\text{Average Investment}}$$

This method is used primarily because the data required are available from the normal accounting statements, and is often known as the Accounting Rate of Return. Average profits are found by adding up the total after-tax profits of the project over its life and then dividing the total by the life of the project. The average investment is simply total investment divided by two. The logic behind this is that annual depreciation returns part of the capital to the original investors. Therefore over the life of the investment, on average only half of the original investment is committed.

In using this method it must be compared to some standard cut-off rate. Frequently, standards for comparison are estimates of the cost of capital invested in the project. If the rate of return on the project under appraisal is greater than the cut-off rate, the project should be accepted. It is an improvement on the payback method in that it allows for differences in the useful lives of the projects being compared but it does have numerous shortcomings, including the following:

(a) It is based on accounting income rather than on cash flows.
(b) It ignores the time value of money. £1,000 received in year fifteen is as valuable as £1,000 received in year one. It ignores the power of compound interest, which is taken into account when calculating the internal (true) rate of return. Consequently, the simple rate of return by using average figures can give rise to dangerous inaccuracies and is in effect a statistical illusion.
(c) It is biased by the method of depreciation used.

It is difficult to find anything good to say about the Simple Rate of Return. It is a hazardous but widely used method of evaluating a capital investment. If it is to be used at all it should be as one of a number of methods.

Internal Rate of Return (IRR)

This is also known as the Discounted Cash Flow (DCF) rate of return. The two appraisal methods outlined above totally ignore the timing of cash receipts. Yet few people, if given the choice, would prefer to accept £1,000 next year to £1,000 today. However, change the offer to £1,000 received a year from today or £920 today and some people will choose the future income. Change the offer to £1,000 next year or £850 today and an even greater number will accept the future cash flow. This simple example points out a fact of life: there is a time value attached to money. An individual with cash today can invest it, spend it, bank it or simply look at it but he is better off having the cash now than having to wait for it. The time value of money is the equivalent of the risk-free rate of interest. It is that payment which is made for the use of money for a particular period. Numerous experts, among them Keynes and Fisher, have attempted to define the true rate of interest. Inflation and risk mean that no existing interest rates are true cost of money rates. The nearest rate would be the rate on government bonds, because it is virtually without risk. To that an allowance for inflation should be added. Fisher thought that 5 per cent was a good estimate of the long-run risk-free true rate of interest.

The time value which attaches to money plays a very important role in capital budgeting. Most projects have cash inflows spread over a number of years. Frequently, annual cash receipts differ substantially in size across years. Table 6.8 shows cash inflows for three separate projects.

Table 6.8 Annual Projected Net Cash Flows for Projects A, B and C

Project Outflow	Net Inflows (£)										Total Inflows
	Years										
	1	2	3	4	5	6	7	8	9	10	
A (£30,000)	6,000	12,000	12,000	12,000	12,000	12,000	12,000	12,000	12,000	12,000	£114,000
B (£60,000)	–	12,000	48,000	165,000	–	–	–	–	–	9,000	£234,000
C (£30,000)	–	–	30,000	–	–	–	–	–	–	84,000	£114,000

Each of these hypothetical projects would have the same payback period and a similar Simple Rate of Return; yet quite clearly the projects are not equally acceptable.

Two methods of project evaluation have been developed which use the time value of money concept. The concept is known as Discounted Cash Flow or DCF. The methods are the Internal Rate of Return (IRR), discussed in this section, and the Net Present Value (NPV), analysed below. The advantage of using DCF techniques is that they consider all cash flows and their timing. Further, they are based on a cash flow basis rather than a profit basis, give a clear accept/reject decision and allow risk to be incorporated by adjusting the discount rate accordingly. Their strength lies in the fact that they facilitate comparison between the true return on an investment and the opportunity cost of capital.

The Internal Rate of Return is that rate of return which equates the present value of all cash outflows with the present value of all cash inflows. The relationship is as follows:

$$TI = \frac{NCI}{(1+r)^1} + \frac{NCI}{(1+r)^2} + \frac{\dots \ NCI}{\dots (1+r)^n}$$

where

TI = total investment
NCI = net cash inflows each period
r = the time value of money or, as it is more commonly known, the discount rate for the period

In this instance r is the unknown. A trial and error method is used to identify the rate of discount which equates the two sides. A closer examination of the formula will show that it is the opposite of compound interest. Compounding is the future value of present value cash flows. Discounting is the present value of future cash flows. A series of discount tables is readily available to assist the financial analyst. Appendix A at the back of the book gives a selection of these tables.

To make the Internal Rate of Return meaningful it must be compared with some cut-off rate. The cut-off rate, generally an estimate of the cost of capital, is known as the *Acceptance Criterion* or *Hurdle Rate*. If the Internal Rate of Return exceeds the cut-off rate, the project is accepted; if not, then it is rejected. The method of trial and error outlined above must seem ponderous to many. Indeed it is, but computer models have done away with much of the drudgery. Where annual cash flows are constant there is a simple and quick method to arrive at the present value of a series of inflows. Tables have been prepared which give the present value of £1 received for a specific number of periods; see Appendix B at the back of the book.

Consider the following simple example. A young man is in receipt of a trust fund which will provide him with the annual sum of £4,000 net for the next five years. However, he wants to buy a car costing £13,600. A friendly financier has offered him £13,600 in return for all rights to receive the flow of £4,000 at the end of each of the next five years. The young man wants to know the rate of interest that equates the two flows. The sum is as follows:

$$£13,600 = \frac{£4,000}{(1+r)^1} + \frac{£4,000}{(1+r)^2} + \frac{£4,000}{(1+r)^3} + \frac{£4,000}{(1+r)^4} + \frac{£4,000}{(1+r)^5}$$

At a 10 per cent rate of discount the figures are

$-£13,600 = £4,000(.909) + £4,000(.826) + £4,000(.751) + £4,000(.683) + £4,000(.621)$

$-£13,600 = £3,636 + £3,304 + £3,004 + £2,732 + £2,484$

$-£13,600 = £15,160$

$\quad$ NPV $= £1,560$

Check the discount factors in Appendix A using a discount rate of 10 per cent. Obviously, the True Rate of interest is higher. At a 15 per cent rate the figures are

$-£13,600 = £4,000(.870) + £4,000(.756) + £4,000(.658) + £4,000(.572) + £4,000(.497)$

$-£13,600 = £3,480 + £3,024 + £2,632 + £2,288 + £1,988$

$-£13,600 = £13,412$

$\quad$ NPV $= -£188$

A 10 per cent rate is too low and a 15 per cent rate too high.
Summary

	Discount Rate	Discount Rate	Present Value	NPV
A		10%	£15,160	£1,560
B		15%	£13,412	-£188
Difference		5%		£ 1,748

The process of interpolation can be used to approximate the true return. This can be done either graphically or by using the equation:

$$\text{Internal Rate of Return (IRR)} = A + \frac{P}{P+N} \times (B-A)$$

where

IRR = true rate of return
A = lower rate of return with positive net present value (NPV)
B = higher rate of return with negative net present value (NPV)
P = amount of positive net present value at discount rate A
N = amount of negative net present value at discount rate B.

$$\text{IRR} = 10\% + \frac{1,560}{1,560 + 188} \times (15\% - 10\%)$$

$$= 14.5\%$$

The above process assumes that the relationship between the two discount rates is linear and this is reasonable in most instances. For absolute accuracy it *may be* necessary to carry out a further calculation, using the discount rate at or near that arrived at through the process of interpolation.

Instead of having to work out individually the present values for each year, it is possible because of the constant cash flows to use the cumulative tables (see Appendix B). Using these tables the present value of £4,000 received each year for five years at 10 and 15 per cent discount rates is as follows:

Discount Rate	Cumulative Rate of 5 Years	Cash Flow Each Year £		Present Value of the Stream
10%	3.791	4,000	=	£15,164
15%	3.352	4,000	=	£13,408

The young man now knows that to accept the £13,600 at this point will cost him an annual rate of 14.5 per cent. It is up to him to accept or reject the deal.

In summary, therefore, assuming the firm wishes to maximise the wealth of its shareholders, the decision rules that can be derived for the IRR method are:

— if IRR exceeds the discount rate, accept the project.
— if IRR is less than the discount rate, reject the project.

The use of the IRR method has some limitations. In certain rare cases it can give rise to multiple rates of return, particularly if the project has a non-conventional cash flow format, i.e. positive and negative flows in succeeding years. It assumes that cash flows can be reinvested at the internal rate of return, which will seldom be the same as the cost of capital. This can cause problems in the ranking of mutually exclusive projects. It also ignores the magnitude or scale of the investment. While the use of the IRR method has intuitive appeal and its popularity is part-psychological, the fact remains that when one has to decide between mutually exclusive proposals, the decision should be dictated by differences between the net present values of the respective proposals and not by their internal rates of return.

Net Present Value (NPV)

Mkcant rate.

The Net Present Value method of capital budgeting is similar to the internal rate of return except that the discount factor is given. All cash flows are discounted to the present value using the required rate of return. The net difference between the inflows and outflows is examined. The decision rules that can be derived for the NPV method are:

   — when NPV is positive, accept the project.
   — when NPV is negative, reject the project.

Sector Specific.

Returning to the simple example outlined above, the young man has decided that money is worth 12 per cent per annum to him. He can have £13,600 now or £20,000 spread over five years. The formula required is:

$$\text{Net Present Value} = -£13,600 + \frac{£4,000}{(1.12)^1} + \frac{£4,000}{(1.12)^2} + \frac{£4,000}{(1.12)^3} + \frac{£4,000}{(1.12)^4} + \frac{£4,000}{(1.12)^5}$$

$$= -£13,600 + £3,572 + £3,188 + £2,848 + £2,544 + £2,268$$

$$= +£820$$

The positive present value means that the young man prefers to take the £20,000 spread over five years. If the financier increases his offer to £14,421 then the young man should accept.

The NPV method of discounting is easy to apply and to understand. It is seen as theoretically superior to the IRR method with important technical advantages. It properly reflects the absolute magnitude of the projects, it implicitly assumes reinvestment of the cash flows at the cost of capital and it can give a clear accept/reject decision when dealing with non-conventional cash flows. The NPV criterion is always consistent with the goal of shareholders' wealth maximisation and allows the financial manager to make decisions that increase the firm's market value. It is an absolute measure of profitability but it has its faults. It does not provide a relative measure of profitability and treats risk as being fixed when in reality it evolves over time. The absolute figure of £820 is the only guide that management has and therefore it can be difficult to compare projects.

To enable comparison a *Profitability Index* can be constructed which enables management to rank projects on the basis of desirability. The Index is defined as follows:

$$\text{Profitability Index} = \frac{\text{Present Value of Inflows}}{\text{Present Value of Outflows}}$$

The decision rules associated with the profitability index are:

   — if the index is greater than 1, accept the project.
   — if the index is less than 1, reject the project.

The higher the index the more desirable the project. Where capital is scarce and management has more investment opportunities than cash, the projects should be ranked by the profitability index, as the example in Table 6.9 demonstrates.

Table 6.9 Projects Presented to the Board of Directors of Ardmore Limited

Project	Investment	Profitability Index
X	£9,000	1.40
P	£50,000	1.20
R	£15,000	1.12
A	£25,000	1.07
C	£21,000	1.05
M	£15,000	.99
T	£18,000	.75

The capital available for investment is £100,000.

Projects M and T are not profitable and so will be rejected. Projects X, P, R, and A are accepted. Project C, though profitable, is held back due to lack of funds or capital rationing. However, because the profitability index is a relative measure of profitability it can lead to problems when mutually exclusive projects are being considered and when capital rationing exists. It does not reflect differences in the scale of the investment and re-creates this disadvantage associated with the IRR method. Nevertheless in a capital rationing situation a less than strict application of the profitability index can give rise to the optimum result and overcome this disadvantage. This involves considering all possible combinations of projects and establishing those that are clearly divisible, i.e. capable of being altered in scale, from those that are indivisible, i.e. must be implemented in full or not at all. The issue is further complicated by the question of whether capital is rationed on a single- or multi-period basis. Single-period rationing is generally taken to mean one year whereas multi-period can mean any number of years.

PRICE CHANGES AND CAPITAL BUDGETING

It has been said that inflation makes all capital projects profitable. This occurs simply because over time the profits of a project grow in current terms. If the inflated profits are compared with historical costs, then the project looks extremely profitable. However, on the other hand the presence of inflation results in lower real after-tax cash flows and acts as a disincentive for firms to undertake capital investments. The increased income is offset against depreciation based on original rather than replacement cost value, thereby giving rise to an increasing tax charge. The specific use of tax incentives in this area can have a significant impact on the real rate of return.

The treatment of price changes in capital budgeting techniques is particularly thorny and not fully resolved. Two principal methods are used to handle the problem. Before deciding on what approach to adopt it is useful to distinguish between the 'real' rate of return on a project and the 'nominal' rate of return. The 'real' rate of return represents the rate of interest that would be required in the absence of inflation, whereas the 'nominal' rate is the money or market rate of interest. The relationship between them was summarised by Fisher in the following equation:

Nominal Rate of Interest = Real Rate of Interest + Expected Rate of Inflation.

This formed the conceptual basis for the two approaches that can be adopted:

(a) Discount 'real' cash flows with the 'real' required rate of return, or
(b) Discount 'nominal' cash flows with the 'nominal' required rate of return.

The adoption of either method should lead to the same answer. A preference could be shown for using the second method, due to the difficulty in estimating 'real' cash flows given that capital allowances generally remain constant.

There would be little difficulty in dealing with inflation if the rate were low, but double-digit inflation tends, over time, to overshadow all other costs. Remember that in the twenty-year period 1970–90 prices rose by 600 per cent and average wages by 500 per cent. These high rates make a mockery of long-term forecasting. This trend was reversed in the early 1990s as the nominal rates of interest exceeded the rate of inflation by a number of percentage points, giving investors a positive real return.

In practice the average project will allow for inflation up to the time of commissioning; thereafter it will ignore it. This approach is both conservative and acceptable. Where management does expect significant differences to arise between the rates of revenue inflation and cost inflation it may be essential to predict each year separately. It may be necessary in such cases to increase the discount factor by an appropriate inflation rate. Alternatively, management can turn the problem around by testing how sensitive the discounted return is to various inflation rates. This will then highlight at what inflation rate the project is no longer viable and allow management to use its judgment as to whether such rates are likely to occur.

The 1990s have seen the appearance of deflation, which means that fixed assets decline in price. This can lead to the terminal value of assets being lower than expected. The fall in the price of raw materials and energy led to a fall in the price of many products. Indeed in countries such as Switzerland and Germany the consumer price index has declined.

Deflation can be good for a project in that there may be a lag between falling input prices and the price of the finished products. However, deflation can affect the value of inventory, particularly in competitive industries. The result is inventory losses as stock is sold at the new lower prices. Careful budgeting tends to ignore deflation as well as inflation, but management needs to be aware of the possible impact on its business.

CAPITAL BUDGETING AND UNCERTAINTY

An earlier section of this chapter examined the effects of uncertainty on cash receipts and disbursements. It was suggested that a series of estimates be obtained for receipts and outflows. At the simplest level three estimates, Optimistic, Most Likely and Pessimistic, for both Inflows and Outflows were suggested. Figure 6.10 shows the matrix of Net Cash Flows arising from this approach to uncertainty estimation.

Nine potential returns are evident, ranging from the 'Worst', which would be Pessimistic estimates of both costs and revenues, to the 'Best', which would be Optimistic estimates of both. Unfortunately, this basic analysis allows for very little variation. In the cost estimates, variations can occur in labour, power and materials, to name only three important elements. To examine changes in these three variables together with three revenue estimates requires eighty-one sets of calculations ($3 \times 3 \times 3 \times 3$). Remember this analysis covers only one year. It must be done for each year.

Figure 6.10 Potential Net Cash Flows to Project X for Year 1

		Cash Inflows		
Cash		Optimistic	Most Likely	Pessimistic
Outflows	Optimistic			
	Most Likely			
	Pessimistic			

If, as is more advisable, a probability distribution of estimates for each variable is produced then manual manipulation becomes virtually impossible. In recent years simple computer programs have been devised to do all of the work. Now the analyst will be asked to supply a list of variables, a range of probable outcomes and the probabilities attaching to each outcome.

At the push of a button the computer will produce a distribution of expected Internal Rates of Return together with estimates of the most likely outcome and the potential deviations from this outcome. Figure 6.11 shows the likely outcome. A distribution of Profitability Indices is usually produced. A popular approach in dealing with risk is to recognise that different investments carry different degrees of risk and therefore should earn different target rates of return. This involves adding an extra discount rate, called a 'risk premium', to the basic cost of capital. The risk premium is based on the subjective assessment of the risks involved and ultimately leads to the view that high risk projects demand high returns and conversely with low risk projects. The process can be taken a step further by incorporating the idea that it is not the individual project risk that matters but its effect on the overall collection of projects. This is the basis of portfolio theory and is best seen through the application of the capital asset pricing model. A review of this concept appears in Chapter 14.

References at the end of this chapter provide additional information on this area.

Figure 6.11 Distribution of Internal Rate of Return to Project X

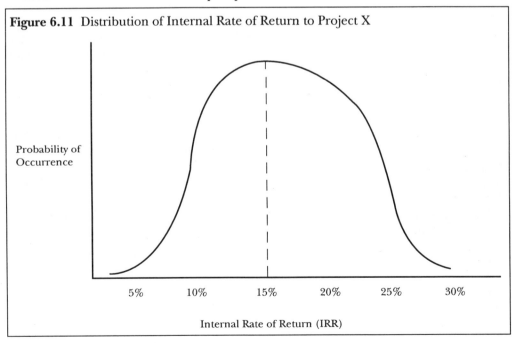

Probability of Occurrence

5%   10%   15%   20%   25%   30%

Internal Rate of Return (IRR)

TAXATION AND CAPITAL BUDGETING

The tax policies applying to investment can seriously affect the return on investment. Taxation normally reduces the cash available to a project. In Ireland an extensive system of tax incentives existed for many years. When examining the return to the shareholders, after-tax cash flows must be used and the effect of incentives taken into account. The incentives available in Ireland were:

    (a) Depreciation allowances.
    (b) Deductibility of interest.
    (c) Offsetting allowances against other income.
    (d) Low overall tax rates.

Depreciation Allowances

Ireland had a tradition of liberal depreciation allowances for manufacturing investment whereby the full cost of an investment could be written off against tax in the year in which it occurred. The passing of the 1988 and subsequent Finance Acts amended this and effectively eliminated the practice altogether. Liberal depreciation has a cash flow timing effect — taxes are deferred.

Interest Deductions

All business interest charges can be offset against business incomes. This reduces the cost of borrowed funds.

Offsetting Allowances or the Tax Shield

A company investing in new machinery can usually offset the depreciation on that machine against the general profits of the business. This provides a 'tax shield' and means that many firms can fully utilise depreciation allowances in the year in which expenditure occurs. This has a timing effect — it defers taxes.

Low Corporation Tax Rate for Manufacturing

To encourage manufacturing investment in Ireland a low rate of 10 per cent is charged on company profits arising from manufacture. It should be noted that the low tax rate reduces the benefit of tax shields but does encourage investment overall.

CAPITAL BUDGETING EXERCISE ON ARDMORE LIMITED

The following is a worked example of a capital investment appraisal. For some time now Ardmore Limited has been pursuing investigations into the possibility of expanding operations into a totally new product area — stainless steel tanks which would be used in the rapidly growing dairy and chemical sectors in Ireland. Eolas (formerly the Institute for Industrial Research and Standards) has assisted with technical information, the Irish Productivity Council has offered a financial appraisal and Forbairt has indicated that grants might be available. The following data have been presented to the general manager of Ardmore Limited. He wishes to examine the project before submitting it to the board.

Capital Cost. No new work space is required. The expected expenditure is as follows:

Expenditure

Plant and Equipment Installed	£100,000
Increased Working Capital	£88,000
Total Investment	£188,000
Financed by:	£48,000
State Grants	£40,000
Term Loan	£100,000
Total	£188,000

There is little uncertainty here as the machinery prices have been quoted. The estimate of working capital was arrived at by assuming an inventory turnover of 5.8 times, allowing a twelve-week credit period to debtors and receiving approximately ninety days' credit from suppliers. These figures are consistent with forecasted 1995 Ardmore operations.

Grants. Traditionally, the state has grant-assisted Irish business on the basis of a percentage of capital investment, usually 40 per cent. The trend in the mid-1990s is to give a grant based on the levels of employment, training needs, etc.

For the sake of this exercise assume that Forbairt has approved a once-off grant of £40,000, which is against the purchase of plant. As a consequence of this approach the level of depreciation available is lower, i.e. £100,000 less £40,000 grant. If the grant had been to reduce operating costs then a higher 'profit' would be made in the start-up year.

Investment Timing. The machines can be delivered and installed during January 1996. Full production should be achieved by June 1996.

Economic Life. The physical life of the machines is twenty years or more. The economic life is much more difficult to ascertain. The management of Ardmore Limited has little knowledge about technological developments but it does know that foreign competition is likely in the future. Based on its assessment of the market it decides on an eight-year life.

Salvage Value. Management finds it difficult to estimate salvage value. A figure of £10,000 has been selected. Approximately 40 per cent of the working capital will be recovered. A figure of £35,000 is taken as recovered working capital.

Revenues. The market for stainless steel tanks in Ireland grew from virtually nothing in 1970 to £5 million annually by 1995. Modernisation of dairy farming and a rise in chemical/pharmaceutical production has led to the increased demand. Forbairt has identified stainless steel tanks as an excellent import substitution product: that is, a product currently imported but suitable for local production. Studies have produced annual growth figures of 20 per cent for the late 1990s.

Ardmore expects to sell to a local ready-made market. Within a ten-mile radius of the plant there are a number of agricultural equipment suppliers. The company has also held discussions with a large Dublin-based engineering products distributor who has agreed to carry the new product line.

The sales estimates are as follows:

Year	1996	1997 onward
Sales Levels (£'000)	£230	£300

No sensitivity analysis was performed.

Costs. A detailed analysis of the costs attaching to the above levels of sales is as follows:

	1996	1997 onward
Operating Costs of New Project (£'000)		
Raw Materials	£88	£108
Wages	£57	£67
Factory Overheads	£26	£31
Marketing and Administration	£52	£44
Total Cost	£223	£250

Depreciation is not included in the above figures. The operating costs in 1996 are disproportionately high due to training costs, extra materials, wastage and general start-up costs. Marketing costs in 1996 reflect expenditure on literature, trade fairs, etc.

Capital Structure. Apart from a grant of £40,000, Ardmore Limited plans to take up a £100,000 seven-year term loan costing 15 per cent interest. The loan has a moratorium on capital repayments for one year. The owners of Ardmore will have to put up the balance of the investment, £48,000, as equity.

Cost of Capital. The equity investment of £48,000 is a strain on the owners of Ardmore Limited. They are very concerned about the investment for two reasons: (a) loss of the money might bankrupt both Ardmore Limited and its owners and (b) the owners have many alternative uses for the money. In addition since no sensitivity analysis was undertaken on costs or on revenues, they wish to incorporate a risk factor into the analysis. They estimate that their cost of making the investment is

Time Value	=	15 per cent per annum
Risk Factor	=	10 per cent per annum
Required Rate of Return	=	25 per cent per annum

This might on first sight appear very high but considering the fact that the revenue figures are based on selling the full production capacity of the machinery, the risk factor is not excessive. Therefore the decision criterion is an Internal Rate of Return equal to or greater than 25 per cent or a positive Net Present Value using a 25 per cent discount rate.

Table 6.12 shows the cash flow estimates. It is assumed that the loan is repaid in six instalments of £15,000 each plus one of £10,000. All are paid at the end of the year. The taxation position is as follows:

The net fixed asset investment of £60,000 is allowable in full against taxable profits as a wear and tear allowance up to a maximum of 15 per cent per annum. This amounts to an effective tax shield of £9,000 per annum for six years and £6,000 for one year. The tax calculations, 10 per cent of the net cash flow after interest, are rounded off for presentation purposes.

Financial Appraisal. The data in Table 6.12 has been analysed as follows:
Payback Period to Equity. The payback period is the length of time taken to recover the owners' investment. The equity investment is £48,000. The net inflows to equity are:

	Annual Cash Flow to Equity (£'000s)	Cumulative Cash Flow to Equity (£'000s)
Year 1	(6)	(6)
Year 2	17	11
Year 3	19	30
Year 4	22	52

The full equity investment of £48,000 is recovered towards the end of year four. Specifically, £18,000 of the £22,000 year four net inflows is required to give a cumulative net inflow of £48,000. The payback period is therefore 3.8 years (i.e. 18/22 = .8 year).

Simple Rate of Return. The example here is dealing with cash flow but a working approximation of net profit can be found.

Remember the formula for the Simple Rate of Return is:

$$\frac{\text{Average Profit After Tax and Depreciation}}{\text{Average Investment}}$$

The average investment in the project can be taken either including or excluding any capital grant.

The cumulative after-tax cash flow to the project can be found in Table 6.12.

Cumulative Cash Inflow	£357,000
Less Tax	23,000
Less Depreciation	60,000
Net Proceeds	274,000
Life of Project	8 years
Average Annual Proceeds	34,250
Average Investment	94,000

$$\text{Simple Return} \quad = \quad \frac{34,250}{94,000} \quad = \quad 36.4\%$$

Table 6.12 Ardmore Limited: Cash Flows Arising from the Stainless Steel Project (£'000s)

	1996	1997	1998	1999	2000	2001	2002	2003	Cum.
Revenues	230	300	300	300	300	300	300	300	
Less Operating Costs	223	250	250	250	250	250	250	250	
Net Cash Flows from Revenues	7	50	50	50	50	50	50	50	357
Salvage Value								10	10
Working Capital Recovered								35	35
Net Cash Inflows Before Interest and Tax	7	50	50	50	50	50	50	95	402
Interest (figures rounded to nearest 1,000)	15	15	13	10	8	6	4	2	73
Net Cash Inflows After Interest and Before Tax	(8)	35	37	40	42	44	46	93	329
Taxes [Note 1]	2	(3)	(3)	(3)	(3)	(3)	(4)	(6)	23
Net Cash Flow After Tax	(6)	32	34	37	39	41	42	87	306
Capital Repayments	–	15	15	15	15	15	15	10	100
Cash Flow to Equity	(6)	17	19	22	24	26	27	77	206
Cumulative Cash (Outflow) / Inflow	(6)	11	30	52	76	102	129	206	

Note 1 The depreciation shield of £9,000 per year will reduce tax liabilities by £1,000 each year in the first six years. Since Ardmore has taxable income already, the losses in year seven plus the depreciation could be used to save tax. A loss of £8,000 plus depreciation of £9,000 will reduce the tax charge in 1996 by £2,000.

Internal Rate of Return (IRR). To estimate the IRR three rates of discount were tried: 15 per cent, 25 per cent and 30 per cent. The calculations are shown below.

Discount Rates

Year	Cash Flows (£'000)	15%	PV	25%	PV	30%	PV
1	(6)	.870 =	(5.2)	.800 =	(4.8)	.769 =	(4.6)
2	17	.756 =	12.9	.640 =	10.9	.592 =	10.1
3	19	.658 =	12.5	.512 =	9.7	.455 =	8.6
4	22	.572 =	12.6	.410 =	9.0	.350 =	7.7
5	24	.497 =	11.9	.328 =	7.8	.269 =	6.5
6	26	.432 =	11.2	.262 =	6.8	.207 =	5.4
7	27	.376 =	10.2	.210 =	5.7	.159 =	4.3
8	77	.327 =	25.2	.168 =	12.9	.123 =	9.5
Present Value of Cash Flows			£91.3		£58.0		£47.5

The present values of inflows must be compared with the equity outflow of £48,000. Clearly, the IRR is higher than 15 per cent and 25 per cent but slightly lower than 30 per cent. Using interpolation the rate has been estimated as

Discount Rate		Present Value (£'000)
25%	=	£58.0
30%	=	£47.5
Difference 5%	=	£10.5

The rate is £10.0 (£'000) above the 25 per cent rate so using the formula outlined above

$$\text{Internal Rate of Return} = 25\% + \frac{£10.0}{£10.5} \, (5\%)$$

$$= 29\% \text{ (approx.)}$$

Net Present Value (NPV). Using the required discount rate of 25 per cent the net present value is as follows:

$$\text{Net Present Value at } 25\% = -£48,000 + £58,000$$

$$= £10,000$$

The Profitability Index on this project is

$$\text{Profitability Index} = \frac{£58.0}{£48.0}$$

$$= 1.2$$

Recommendation. Relying on the information provided and on the results of the analysis the project should be accepted. All of the techniques point to the same answer.

CONCLUSION

This chapter has examined capital budgeting decisions in the context of overall corporate strategies. The examination of total cost, economic life and particularly projected cash flows requires all the skill and experience at the command of management. A mistake in capital budgeting can ruin a firm. The methods of appraisal presented are designed to lower the possibility of this occurring. No one method provides all the answers. Though four methods of analysis were presented, two were stressed. These are the so-called discounted cash flow methods of capital budgeting. These techniques are being increasingly applied, especially to large projects. Despite their apparent complexity they become easy to apply with practice. It must be remembered that they are only techniques and do not of themselves furnish correct information for decision-making. If the information regarding cash flow projections, economic life, etc. is not correct then the techniques will not provide the correct answers. The methods themselves are not perfect and are criticised on the basis of reinvestment rate assumptions and on the fact that they ignore the need of management to supply a constant or increasing stream of earnings per share.

The use of capital budgeting techniques depends very much on the human, financial and time resources available to the individual firm. Some firms will not have skilled personnel to gather the information and analyse it fully. Others may consider that the expenditure of time and money is not justified by the results.

If possible, it is recommended that all four methods of appraisal be used. The extra work necessary to apply discounting methods may well be worth the effort. Much of the drudgery associated with this work has been removed by the availability of cheap, straightforward computer software and easy-to-use personal computers. For the smaller firm, the use of the firm's auditors as financial analysts may be both advisable and fruitful.

FURTHER READING

J.C. Van Horne, *Financial Management & Policy*, 9th ed. (New Jersey, Prentice-Hall, 1992).
R.H. Pike & M. Wolfe, *Capital Budgeting for the 1990s* (London, CIMA, 1988).
R. Butler, L. Daws, R. Pike & J. Stamp, *Strategic Investment Decisions* (London, Routledge, 1993).
R. Dixon, *Investment Appraisal* (London, CIMA, 1994).
S. Lumby, *Investment Appraisal and Financial Decisions*, 5th ed. (Chapman and Hall, 1994).
H. Levy & M. Sarnat, *Capital Investment & Financial Decisions*, 5th ed. (UK, Prentice-Hall, 1994).

QUESTIONS

Question 6.1
What is capital budgeting?

Question 6.2
How do the payback and the accounting rate of return methods differ from discounted cash flow methods?

Question 6.3
A certain project is expected to yield the returns given below for the next five years. An initial investment of £15,000 is required. Calculate the Internal Rate of Return (IRR).

Year	Returns £
1	3,000
2	2,000
3	5,000
4	6,000
5	4,000

Question 6.4
Each of two mutually exclusive projects involves an investment of £120,000. The estimated cash flows are as follows:

Year	Project X	Project Y
1	£70,000	£10,000
2	£40,000	£20,000
3	£30,000	£30,000
4	£10,000	£50,000
5	£10,000	£90,000

The firm's required Weighted Average Cost of Capital (WACC) is 11 per cent. Calculate the Net Present Value (NPV) and Internal Rate of Return (IRR) for both projects. Should either or both projects be accepted?

Question 6.5
Calculate the expected value of the following cash inflow given the associated probabilities.

Cash Inflow	Probability
£30,000	.10
£20,000	.20
£15,000	.21
£16,000	.06
£8,000	.08
£12,000	.15
£14,000	.05
£20,000	.15

Question 6.6
If the discount rate is 8 per cent, find the NPV of the following set of cash flows:

(a) £200 three years from now.
(b) £100 two years from now and £200 three years from now.
(c) £150 a year for five years.

7

Irish Financial Institutions

An earlier chapter pointed out that financial management involved not only the management and control of investments, but the efficient raising of the funds required to undertake the investments. Money is raised from a variety of sources. It is the purpose of this and the following chapter to examine the various institutions which provide finance to Irish business. Chapters 9 to 13 analyse the types of finance supplied. To understand the role played by financial institutions it is useful to be familiar with the market for capital. The availability of funds which can be invested depends on the level of savings. Individuals and corporations save for a multiplicity of purposes: a holiday, a house, to protect against the 'rainy day' or to provide security. There are many ways of saving. Table 7.1 gives some idea of the level of savings and the relative share of the various financial institutions in the market for deposits in September 1994.

Table 7.1 Savings in Ireland		
Institution	*£m*	*%*
Associated Banks (Current and Deposit Accounts)	11,008	42
Non-Associated Banks (Current and Deposit Accounts)	4,490	17
Building Societies	5,545	21
Other Credit Institutions (ACC Bank, ICC Bank and TSB Bank)	2,019	8
Government Savings Schemes	3,287	12
Total	£26,349	100
Source: Central Bank of Ireland, September 1994.		

In addition to the above the Irish Stock Exchange, insurance companies, credit unions and charities actively solicit savings and ensure a very competitive environment.

This competitiveness has resulted in a significant shift in market share, with the building societies gaining at the expense of the associated banks. This was primarily due to the increased demand for housing. The banks' response was to enter that market and compete head-on with some success against the building societies. Recently, building societies have entered the banking market, e.g. the purchase of Guinness & Mahon Ltd by the Irish Permanent.

The Irish savings/income ratio at 12–15 per cent of gross national product is high by international standards and provides the funds necessary for the efficient operation of the capital market. Savings are liquid in that they can be easily realised. The application of savings to productive investment can play an important role in assisting economic growth as part of overall fiscal policy.

The various financial institutions in which the funds are lodged know from experience what their inflows and outflows are likely to be. Funds not likely to be withdrawn by savers can be loaned to borrowers who need money for investment purposes. The length of time for which savings are likely to be held ranges from hours to decades; so too does the pay-off on the various investment opportunities which exist. The financial institutions which hold the savings have developed special financial products which best market their funds. These products are known as financial instruments.

Business is a major, but by no means the only, participant in the demand for capital. Money is also provided for private mortgages, personal credit and state borrowing. Indeed, one of the main problems in Ireland in the 1980s was that the demand for capital far outstripped the supply. The state in particular was a big borrower, often at the expense of the private business sector. Late in the decade demand for funds declined dramatically as investment opportunities were limited and the economic climate was depressed. The Irish government took serious steps at that stage to control its public expenditure. The turbulence on the world financial markets in the early 1990s forced interest rates beyond the reach of many borrowers. By mid-1993 some stability had been restored, and with excess inflows and weak demand intense competition between the financial institutions brought sophisticated products and innovative marketing to the fore. In 1995 interest rates began to move upward once again in response to trends internationally.

HISTORICAL BACKGROUND

Financial institutions have a long and chequered history. Saving is a method of reducing future uncertainty, so historically people have saved. The concept of saving money on which interest could be paid is one which taxed many brains during the Middle Ages. In the Christian world usury — that is, a payment for the use of money — was frowned upon, but it did exist. Paying interest is still illegal in most Muslim countries. Institutions in which money in the form of metals could be deposited have existed for millennia, but it was not until the growth of trade in the seventeenth and eighteenth centuries that modern financial institutions appeared.

Ireland lagged behind the United Kingdom in the development of banking. Though the Bank of Ireland was chartered in 1783 it was not until after the passing of the 1821 Banking Act that modern banking evolved. The 1821 Act permitted branch banking. It was passed in the aftermath of the financial crash of 1820, which saw many Irish financial institutions go bankrupt. Between 1825 and 1836 the ancestors of Allied Irish Banks, the

National Irish Bank and Ulster Bank were formed.

Remember that at this time Ireland was part of the United Kingdom and the UK financial system existed locally. This had one unusual effect — the institutions which evolved in Ireland did so as part of an advanced United Kingdom economy.

Independence saw the country with over 950 bank branches, a well-developed Post Office Savings Bank network, insurance offices and building societies. Though it was a poor country, there were some savings. These were generally channelled from Ireland to the United Kingdom. This was not a political decision: the demand in Ireland was low and the period between the two world wars was a time of financial confusion in the country. In 1927 the Currency Act provided for an indigenous currency and in 1942 the Central Bank Act established the Central Bank. Yet, until 1979, the Irish financial system was tied closely to that of the United Kingdom due to the link with sterling. Since the establishment of the state the Irish punt had been on a parity with sterling. This, in effect, provided for a free capital market in the British Isles and it meant that Irish financial policy was dominated by events on the London capital markets. In March 1979, when Ireland joined the European Monetary System, the link with sterling was broken. Chapter 16 returns to this topic.

Irish financial institutions developed slowly during the first half of the twentieth century. As economic growth rates improved here, the demands on the financial institutions grew. Older institutions adapted and new ones appeared. Merchant banks, industrial banks, North American banks and European banks opened offices here. Many of these institutions introduced new financial instruments into the country. Ireland, for her level of economic development, has a highly sophisticated set of financial institutions. Table 7.2 shows the main categories of financial institutions here.

Table 7.2 Irish Financial Institutions	
Category	Number
Central Bank	1
Associated Banks	4
Non-Associated Banks	
• Merchant and Commercial	29
• Industrial Banks	6
Other Credit Institutions	
• ACC Bank, ICC Bank, ICC Investment Bank and TSB Bank	4
Post Office Savings Bank	1
Building Societies	6
Hire Purchase Finance Companies	32
Insurance Companies	49
Stock Exchange	1

Source: Central Bank of Ireland Winter Report 1994.

Recent developments in electronic banking have added to that sophistication. Virtually all the Irish clearing banks and the major non-associated banks have an electronic link to their clients for balance reporting, transaction information and to receive electronic fund transfer requests. These systems are now regarded as an essential part of the bank's product range and can be an important factor in its gaining a competitive advantage over rivals. The rapid growth of computerised banking is a response to the needs of international trade and management information requirements. The question of transfers to third parties and overall security versus convenience is open to some debate, but one thing is certain: the current state of electronic banking is an early step on a path which will revolutionise financial services.

Each of the categories in Table 7.2 is dealt with below, with the exception of the Stock Exchange, which is discussed in Chapter 8.

THE CENTRAL BANK

The function of a central bank is to safeguard the integrity of the currency of the country. The primary function is subdivided into six major tasks.

(1) Controlling the level of credit. This is one way of controlling the growth of an economy. By forcing banks to increase interest rates and/or reduce the amount of credit outstanding, the Central Bank reduces inflationary pressures. If economic growth is sluggish then credit can be relaxed and investment encouraged. By selling government loans, the Central Bank drives up interest rates and reduces the amount of cash available. This dampens down the growth in credit. When it purchases bonds, interest rates decline and credit is relaxed. These latter two methods of controlling credit are known as 'Open Market Operations'.

(2) Acting as state banker. A modern state has very many complex cash flows, such as tax, loans, salaries, social welfare. The Central Bank acts as banker to the state, monitoring and co-ordinating the finances. As an example, consider the work involved in controlling the many state loans. As of 1995 the state has total borrowings in excess of £28,000 million.

(3) Issuing currency. Imagine the situation whereby a state finances expenditure simply by printing more money. The currency becomes debased and worthless. It is the function of the Central Bank to issue and control currency. As of mid-1995 there was almost £1,700 million in currency outstanding.

(4) Acting as lender of last resort. Financial institutions should maintain adequate liquidity. Should they get into difficulties they can borrow from the Central Bank. In practice this function is used to control credit.

(5) Acting as banker to banks. This function is similar to (4) above. The Central Bank may require the commercial banks to deposit certain sums in the Central Bank on special terms.

(6) Holding the external reserves of the country. Many countries, including Ireland, have very strict controls on the movement of funds across borders. This is largely due to the weak level of external reserves. At the beginning of 1995 the external reserves of Ireland amounted to almost £4,500 million. By controlling all reserves, the Central Bank is in a better position to defend the currency against undesired devaluations. It also plays a very active role in deciding Irish economic policy.

The passing of the Central Bank Act 1989 resulted in much greater powers being extended to the Central Bank. These included supervision of money brokers, financial futures traders and companies associated with the International Financial Services

Centre. It also brought under its control commercial bank charges and a deposit protection scheme to guard the savings of small depositors. In essence the Act set out the legislative structure for the prudent management of the commercial banking sector and gave the Central Bank the powers necessary to carry out an overseeing brief. The Central Bank audits internally the institutions over which it has responsibility and receives monthly reports from them to ensure that they are complying with the prudential limits set down, i.e. credit limits, reserve asset ratios, etc. Finally, under the Building Society Act 1989 and the Trustee Savings Bank (TSB) Act 1989 it also assumed responsibility for their supervision. A 1995 Act extended Central Bank control to include the Stock Exchange.

The pivotal role of the Central Bank in supervising the operation of the financial system has been recognised in the recent legislation. The legislation assists in the harmonisation of financial services in a European Community context.

REGULATORY CONTROL OF THE IRISH FINANCIAL SYSTEM

The Irish regulatory environment was uncertain up to the passing of the Central Bank Act 1989. This was due in part to the lack of a single regulator responsible for all deposit-taking institutions. Despite the small size of the Irish financial system, there were multiple government agencies involved. There were other regulatory agencies besides the Central Bank: the Department of Finance was responsible for the control of the state banks and the TSBs; the Department of the Environment was responsible for the building societies; the Department of Industry and Commerce was responsible for the insurance companies as well as those lending under exemptions from Moneylenders Acts. The consequence was a fragmented regulatory environment which needed to be revamped.

It would appear that, with the exception of the building society regulators, the tendency in regulation in Ireland is mainly to copy trends in the UK.

Historically, the Irish regulatory environment has discriminated against the associated banks in favour of the non-associated banks and against the Irish-based banks as opposed to the non-Irish-based banks. Asset constraints were imposed at a higher level on the associated than on the non-associated banks. Equally, the high level of primary reserve requirements imposes a substantial cost on Irish-based institutions. The net effect of these impositions is to direct business towards the least-cost supplier of funds: that is, those lending from outside the Irish market. The high level of secondary liquidity imposed on the associated banks is currently not a binding constraint on either group of banks, largely because of the lack of loan demand. However, in the event of loan demand increasing in the late 1990s the associated banks may once again be restricted by the secondary reserve requirement.

Similar and additional problems exist for the building societies. A substantial portion of their growth has been due to tax advantages and their dominant position in the mortgage market. Historically, they have been less subject to competition.

The initial thrust of regulatory change for the building societies was not aimed at allowing them more freedom to compete. Its objective was to remove tiered interest rates and other practices which were deemed to be non-competitive. However, the consequence of the legislation was to reduce their profit levels. Building societies, because they were traditionally mutual societies, did not have ready access to capital. In addition, because of the small size of the domestic Irish market, the Irish societies had a much lower capital base than their potential foreign competitors.

With the passing of the Building Society Act 1989 and the trend towards an open EU market process, the building societies are now competing head-on with the banks and gearing themselves up to deal with international competition. The Act gave them the freedom to compete fully in the financial services market and brought them under the regulatory control of the Central Bank. These developments have forced the building societies to move from providing a narrow range of products to marketing a broader range of financial services. The aim was initially to recover market share in its core mortgage business and increase market share across its range of products. The building societies have aggressively targeted the traditional banking domain of current chequing accounts by not charging transaction fees and have gone after a bigger slice of the corporate deposit and lending market. They have been innovative in raising finance by introducing a Note Issuance Facility (NIF) for commercial investors and tax-efficient unit-linked savings products. Building societies are now fully-fledged financial institutions and ready to meet the challenge of the banking sector and international competition. Developments in this sector are discussed below.

Both nationally and internationally the financial services industry has undergone a radical transformation. The elements contributing to this process are familiar: financial innovation, increased use of complex technology involving almost instantaneous communication, the removal of exchange controls, abandonment of interest rate ceilings or quantitative credit controls in favour of more market-based instruments of monetary policy, and the removal of traditional barriers to competition between different types of financial institution.

The passing of the Central Bank Act 1989 was part of the process to provide the framework for the Single European Market in Financial Services. The introduction of this 'European Passport' in January 1993 allowed EU credit institutions to establish branches or to provide financial services directly into any of the member states without having to establish themselves there. The underlying principle is the concept of home country control. This means that we must look to the member state where legal and commercial control of a credit institution is based to provide the prudent supervision for all its activities in other member states. This concept, which is at the heart of the Second Banking Co-Ordination Directive of the EU, is the cornerstone of the Single European Market in Financial Services and formalises and consolidates a movement which has been developing for a number of years. We now have a common market. This market stability requires co-ordination between all the relevant supervisory authorities.

Under legislation enacted in 1995 the Stock Exchange was placed under the control of the Central Bank. Under this Act the Exchange authorities were delegated the role of day-to-day compliance monitoring in line with the spirit of self-regulation. This legislation was required to implement EU Directives.

In summary, therefore, the Central Bank is the supervisory body in charge of our banks, building societies, hire purchase and finance companies, foreign exchange markets, money brokers, and companies operating in the International Financial Services Centre (IFSC).

THE ASSOCIATED BANKS

The term 'associated banks' comes from the Central Bank Act 1942, which defined a special relationship between the four associated banks and the Central Bank. These four banks, two Irish-owned, one UK-owned and one Australian-owned, dominate Irish finance with total assets of over £18,000 million or 60 per cent of total bank assets.

The four associated banks, together with Guinness & Mahon, an Irish merchant bank, provide a clearing house for cheques. The four associated banks are Bank of Ireland, Allied Irish Banks, Ulster Bank — which is owned by National Westminster Bank (UK) — and National Irish Bank — a subsidiary of the Australian National Bank. Bank of Ireland and Allied Irish Banks control the bulk of business in the Irish Republic.

For the first forty years of the existence of the state there was little demand for loans in Ireland. Excess funds were invested in the London money market. Industrialisation in the 1960s and agricultural growth in the 1970s increased demand and placed severe financial and organisational strains on the banks. Growing demands for credit were met by improved lending procedures. The difficulties of understanding the needs of new industries and technologies were handled by hiring experts. In the 1970s and 1980s the two Irish-owned associated banks expanded overseas.

In the mid-1960s, at the time the two major banking groups were formed, the associated banks controlled about 70 per cent of the domestic resources with deposit-taking institutions. By 1995, this high level of concentration had stabilised at around 65 per cent after going as low as 40 per cent over the previous decade. Table 7.3 compares the pattern of lending by the associated banks with that of the non-associated banks. During the 1980s there was increasing fragmentation of the savings and lending market, spurred by uneven tax policies and the entry and growth of new competitors in the market.

Table 7.3 Pattern of Lending by Irish Banks, August 1994

Categories of Borrowers	Associated Banks		Non-Associated Banks		Total	
	£m	%	£m	%	£m	%
Agriculture, Forestry and Fishing	1,278	12	88	2	1,366	9
Energy	51	70	2	121	1	
Manufacturing	753	7	672	13	1,425	9
Building and Construction	254	2	80	2	334	2
Distribution, Garages, Hotels and Catering	1,164	11	614	12	1,778	11
Transport	96	1	245	5	341	2
Postage Services and Telecommunications	15	–	17	–	32	–
Financial	1,718	16	2,015	40	3,733	24
Business and Other Services	1,181	11	711	14	1,892	12
Personal	4,270	40	501	10	4,771	30
Total	10,780	100	5,013	100	15,793	100

Source: Central Bank of Ireland Winter Report 1994.

The associated banks, conscious of the need to address the diversion of resources away from them and in response to the requirements of a growing Irish economy, transformed themselves, with each setting up merchant and other banking subsidiaries. They began to participate actively in the life insurance market through the management and/or marketing of investments with a tax-efficient life insurance dimension. In the 1980s they expanded into the home mortgage business. Not all their investments have been successful. Three of the major groups bought control of large stockbroking firms: Bank of Ireland bought Davy's, Ulster Bank bought NCB while AIB bought Goodbody's.

With a network of over 800 branches and more than 20,000 employees, the four associated banks play an important role in Irish business. As 'full service banks' they provide services ranging from personal services such as cheque cashing to funding multinational investments. Many of their services are labour-intensive and so more and more costly. Modern technology such as ATMs (Automatic Teller Machines) and electronic movements of money between accounts are being used to increase efficiency. Changes in ownership of the two smaller groups, Ulster Bank and National Irish Bank, gave rise to concerns that the relatively small size of the Bank of Ireland and the AIB would, with the freedom to establish Directives of the EU, lead to their takeover by European banks. This at least partially explains the movement by AIB and Bank of Ireland into the UK and USA. The overseas investments have been troublesome for each bank.

Figure 7.4 below gives some statistics on the role played by the main banks in Ireland.

Figure 7.4 Selected Statistics on Irish Clearing Banks

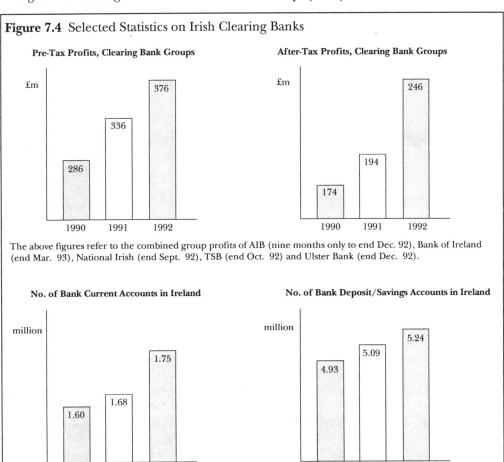

The above figures refer to the combined group profits of AIB (nine months only to end Dec. 92), Bank of Ireland (end Mar. 93), National Irish (end Sept. 92), TSB (end Oct. 92) and Ulster Bank (end Dec. 92).

The number of both current accounts and deposit/savings accounts held with banks in the Republic has grown since 1990, by 9.3% in the case of the former and 6.3% in the latter.

The number of both current accounts and deposit/savings accounts held with banks in the Republic has grown since 1990, by 9.3 per cent in the case of the former and 6.3 per cent in the latter.

Competition and changing technology are the two areas of greatest concern to the four main banks. Large international banking groups are continuing their slow incursion into Irish banking. The two smaller banks, owned by powerful international parents, pose a threat to the two Irish-owned banks.

Technology offers threats and opportunities. The threat comes from two sides. Technology enables smaller banks to provide a wide range of services without the need for branches. Technology makes redundant the skills of many hundreds if not thousands of bank staff. The associated banks are heavily unionised, and the union members have resisted change. The high staffing levels increase the cost base of the banks.

The opportunities arise from an ability to offer more and better products to customers. The main banks have developed currency dealing rooms of international standard.

THE NON-ASSOCIATED BANKS

There are basically two categories of non-associated bank, merchant/commercial and industrial banks. Table 7.5 gives a profile of the number and size of the different categories of banks, and for comparative information the associated banks in summary form.

Table 7.5 Non-Associated Banks, 1994 — Profile			
Category	No. Banks	Total Assets £m	Non-Government Lending £m
Total Merchant and Commercial	29	7,233 (24%)	3,253 (20%)
Total Industrial	6	4,636 (16%)	1,717 (11%)
Total Non-Associated Banks	35	11,869 (40%)	4,970 (31%)
Total Associated Banks	4	18,163 (60%)	11,098 (61%)
Total Irish Banks	39	30,032	16,068

Source: Central Bank of Ireland Winter Report 1994.

MERCHANT BANKS

Merchant banks specialise in financing business. More wholesale than retail, they deal in large financings, in the placing of shares and in public flotations. They can be termed wholesale banks in that they deal in very big sums. As of September 1994 the twenty-nine merchant/commercial banks had total assets of £7,233 million or 24 per cent of total bank assets. Their non-government lending, manufacturing being the largest category of borrower, amounted to £3,253 million or 20 per cent of all lending in the state.

Merchant banking grew rapidly in the 1970s both in numbers of banks and in extent of lending. The expansion in numbers began with the entry of North American banks in response to US and Canadian firms investing in Ireland, initially in the mining industry and later in the chemical and electronic industries. This development was followed by the entry of a number of powerful European banks after Ireland's accession to the EU.

The major strength of these institutions is their international expertise and extensive networks throughout the world. In addition, through their parents, they have close links with most of the multinational corporate clients. Within Ireland, they have a small geographic base and a small, but premier-quality, corporate customer base. Because of their instantaneous access to world-wide expertise, these banks tend to be product innovators within the Irish market. They have a less rigid regulatory environment and are not subject to Irish capital adequacy requirements. They are given the flexibility to get into new activities for which the associated banks would require permission from the Central Bank. The branches operating in Ireland are subject to minimal Irish control, as they are presumed to be adequately controlled by the authorities in the country where the parent is located. While historically they have had a competitive disadvantage relative to the associated banks in certain areas, recent legislative changes have greatly reduced the disadvantage and consequently eroded the competitive strength of the associated banks.

With the equalising of lending facilities and the expertise in these merchant banks, one might have expected them to continue to increase their share of the corporate market. Surprisingly, the overseas banks have found it difficult to make profits in Ireland. A number have closed (Chase Manhattan, Bank of America and First National Bank of Chicago), while others have moved into different financial sectors, such as leasing.

Four of the merchant banks are owned by the associated banks; one, Guinness & Mahon, is now a subsidiary of a building society while most of the others are subsidiaries of non-Irish-owned banks. Appendix 7.1 (page 137) lists all the financial institutions operating in Ireland in 1994, and Appendix 7.2 (page 139) ranks the top fifty in terms of gross assets.

In former times the so-called merchant banks offered a service to prized customers which the associated banks found hard to match. They were quick to respond to requests, they could offer customised loans to big customers and specialised investment advice to large investors while many had top-quality foreign currency facilities. These advantages have been eroded as the main banks have built up formidable competencies in most financial areas.

INDUSTRIAL BANKS

A group of six banks provides instalment credit in the form of hire purchase and leasing. The smaller banks provide loans to consumers on durables while the larger banks offer services such as block discounting, bridging loans and export finance. Some of the bigger industrial banks have a small number of branches. Total assets amounted to £4,636 million in September 1994. Their non-government lending amounted to £1,717 million. Property, construction, car and household durables comprise much of their lending.

Three of the six banks are subsidiaries of the associated banks. Another — Woodchester — is a subsidiary of Credit Lyonnais, the large French bank, while Anglo Irish is a publicly owned Irish company. Woodchester evolved in Ireland as a leasing company and expanded into banking by the acquisition of Trinity Bank. Though strongly backed by the financial resources of the parent, Woodchester has found it difficult to expand profitably. Anglo Irish grew in a decade from a small industrial bank into a medium-sized financial institution providing a range of financial services to many companies in Ireland.

Not examined

HIRE PURCHASE FINANCE COMPANIES

Hire purchase finance companies are not licensed banks but in common with the industrial banks their principal business is the extension of instalment credit. These companies derive their main resources from loans made to them by their own banking affiliates or from the non-associated banks, and are prohibited from accepting deposits from the public. There are over thirty of such companies and in September 1994 total instalment credit extended by them amounted to £47 million.

The bulk of the business done by hire purchase companies is in financing private and commercial motor vehicles. The chief business users are small companies and individuals. The dominant hire purchase companies are Allied Finance, ICC Finance and Woodchester.

Not examined

POST OFFICE SAVINGS BANKS (AN POST)

An Post, established by the state over 100 years ago, operates the national postal service and the Post Office Savings Bank as agent for the Minister for Finance through the National Treasury Management Agency. It directly employs almost 8,000 people, with 3,000 more involved in sub-offices throughout the country. The Post Office Savings Bank was originally established to encourage small individual savers, with no sum being too small. Many diligent savers learned thrift by purchasing savings stamps at a couple of pence each. These stamps could be redeemed at any post office. Today An Post offers numerous options to savers, big and small, young and old. It can provide a wide range of financial services, is state-guaranteed and there is no charge for handling accounts. Its deposit accounts give tax-free returns and can start as low as 50p. It also offers money transmission instruments, i.e. postal/money orders, prize bonds for £5 each, and in some of the larger offices the facility to buy and sell foreign currencies and get travellers' cheques.

The freedom from Deposit Interest Retention Tax (DIRT) liability strongly benefits the savings schemes administered by An Post. In the twelve-month period ended September 1994 there was a net inflow of almost £600 million. The total amount invested in Post Office savings schemes stood at £3,287 million in September 1994, an increase of approximately 22 per cent on the previous year.

Table 7.6 Amount on Deposit at 30 September 1994	
	(£m)
Savings Certificates	2,495
Savings Bonds	470
National Instalment Savings	209
Prize Bonds	113
	3,287

Not examined

TRUSTEE SAVINGS BANK

The Trustee Savings Bank (TSB) can be traced back over 100 years to a number of small banks in Dublin, Cork, Waterford and Limerick. Their position was similar to that of the Post Office Savings Bank in targeting small but regular savers. They provided a narrow range of services and because of a low overhead structure could afford to pay higher interest on deposits than the associated banks. In line with other financial institutions they recognised the need to broaden their range of services and capitalised on several long-drawn-out strikes in the associated banks. This allowed them to increase market share significantly and necessitated a rationalisation of their resources through a series of mergers with each other. The final merger of Cork and Limerick Savings Bank and the TSB Dublin took effect in mid-1992, bringing into existence the fourth largest branch banking network in Ireland.

The TSB positions itself as an alternative to the associated banks, with the personal sector its natural market.

In 1994 the TSB had an asset base of over £1,200 million and reported a profit growth of 15 per cent.

It appears that the days of the TSB as an independent banking force are numbered. In mid-1995 it was being examined by at least three major banking groups with a view to a merger. The front runner was National Irish Bank, though Ulster Bank and Credit Lyonnais were also involved in talks. The interest in acquiring the TSB stems from a need to grow to a minimum size which would enable the potential acquirers to compete with AIB and Bank of Ireland.

The ACC Bank and ICC Bank, given their status as state-owned institutions, will be dealt with in Chapter 13. Like the TSB they went through significant change in their ownership structure in 1992. They too are candidates for being sold off.

BUILDING SOCIETIES

The building societies are an important and growing part of the financial sector. They are the largest single providers of mortgage finance for housing in Ireland, accounting for approximately 70 per cent of such finance. Although the building societies have primarily long-term assets, they solicit and incur short-term liabilities in the form of shares and deposits.

Major rationalisation has taken place in this sector with the result that there are half the number of societies operating today that there were in 1987. This is primarily due to increased competition from the main banks and sluggish demand for home loans. Building societies had to become more professional and cost-conscious and to broaden their range of products and services to survive. They lost to the banks and then recovered their share of their core business, i.e. home loans. In addition they attacked the banks by being very aggressive in the resident deposit market and capturing a high percentage of the growth in that area. In 1994 the societies had total assets of £8,180 million.

The building societies have seen major changes in legislation affecting their business, and like all other financial institutions have been part of the revolution in the financial services area.

In the late 1980s the government passed legislation in relation to the building societies which permitted unsecured lending by them for specific purposes. Unsecured lending, allowed for bridging finance and home improvement purposes only, is limited to 4 per cent of the total assets of a society and can be engaged in only by societies that have a minimum cash reserve to total assets ratio of 4 per cent.

In 1987 the Minister for the Environment introduced additional regulations governing certain society activities. The new regulations outlawed the charging of tiered mortgage rates and redemption fees, provided for choice of insurance company and access to valuation reports by borrowers, obliged societies to pay their own legal fees and brought changes in the way society directors are elected. These changes met with strong resistance from the societies, some of which were slow to comply fully with them.

In 1989 building societies were brought under the control of the Central Bank. From being founded as mutual societies helping savers to acquire finance for house purchase against the security of the property, building societies are now more in line with ordinary banks. They are governed by the Central Bank, which sets limitations on their operations and ensures full implementation of their rules, regulations and procedures.

The EU Mortgage Credit Directive came into effect in 1988 and impinged in a major way on the Irish building societies. The Directive facilitated barrier-free trade for credit institutions offering mortgage credit within the EU and gave rise to serious competitive pressures on the Irish societies. The increasing sophistication of available technology encouraged cross-border developments and made it easier for foreign institutions to transact lending business with a minimal physical presence in Ireland.

Given the strong impetus for change from the market, the government and the societies themselves, the nature of the building society movement has evolved rapidly in the 1990s and will continue to do so. It is inevitable that the present level of competition between the societies and the banks will intensify as the range of services offered by the societies is extended. Any new activities undertaken by societies are likely to encroach on the traditional realms of the banks. The growing overlap between the two groups will eventually create a conflict between the mutual nature of the societies and the need to maximise profits in an increasingly competitive market. The need for change is highlighted by the fluctuating profitability of building societies in recent years, mainly due to a heightened level of competition in the savings market. If building societies are to survive further increases in competition, they will need to respond with greater flexibility in raising funds and in adapting to changes in the marketplace.

Building societies have moved quickly from the periphery of the financial markets towards centre stage, with their operations being more and more integrated into the financial system generally. Their financial services are widening to the extent that they are competing across the full range of retail banking services with the commercial banks. This evolution will continue to the point where banks and building societies will be virtually indistinguishable across a variety of markets. Changes in the regulatory system through the Central Bank Act 1989 and others have provided the framework to allow that process develop to its full potential.

Traditionally, building societies were 'mutuals'. That meant that the objective of the society was the mutual benefit of investors and borrowers; there were no shareholders seeking profit.

A major step away from the mutual nature of building societies took place with the conversion of the Irish Permanent Building Society (IPBS) into a Public Limited Company in mid-1994 and the subsequent launch of the new company on the Stock Exchange in October 1994.

The transformation of the IPBS into a private enterprise publicly quoted company brought over 160,000 new shareholders into the Stock Exchange and made the IPBS the company with the largest number of shareholders.

Other building societies have chosen to go a different route. The ICS was taken over by the Bank of Ireland while the Norwich is a subsidiary of an insurance company.

INSURANCE COMPANIES

The insurance industry is closely related to banking in that it takes money from the public and invests it so that it can make payments if certain events occur. It therefore provides essential protection for both the individual and the business sector and plays a significant role in the long-term savings and investment market. The Department of Enterprise and Employment is responsible for the industry and carries this function out primarily through the process of self-regulation. Self-regulation was introduced by the Insurance Act 1989, whereby specific responsibility for brokers was assigned to the Irish Brokers Association (IBA) and for insurance companies to the Irish Insurance Federation (IIF). In support of this process the Insurance Intermediaries Compliance Bureau (IICB), part of the IIF, was set up and later an ombudsman was appointed to the industry. The Act of 1989 and the acceptance of European Community regulations effectively replaced the Insurance Act of 1936 and ensured that the concept of 'home market regulation' could be achieved prior to the Single European Market of 1992. Home market regulation means that a company which is regulated in its home state and meets the requirements of that state is not required to be regulated in another EU state for the purposes of operating or marketing its services there. These initiatives were taken to ensure an EU-wide set of standard rules and regulations and were to promote a strong international and competitive marketplace. They were also seen as necessary to provide a degree of protection for the consumer or investor in the wake of a number of investment fraud cases and to restore lost credibility in the industry generally. Investment advisors have to show that they are financially sound, have appropriate bonding, are properly registered and are competent to offer investment advice.

The coming into effect on 1 July 1994 of the Third Life EU Directive was a further consolidation of that process. If you are buying a life assurance product you are now entitled to considerably more information about your contract than has hitherto been offered. This Directive means that the life assurance company you deal with must, for example, define the nature of your particular policy, the benefits and the length of time you should hold on to it, how the premiums are calculated, where those premiums are invested, the surrender and paid-up values of the contract for at least five years, how to cancel the policy (as well as including an initial cooling-off period when you first buy the product) and any subsequent effects on the investment, give you general information about tax and let you know the arrangements the company has made for taking complaints.

The introduction of this Directive is no guarantee against misselling of products by intermediaries: with substantial premium and commission income at stake, high pressure sales techniques continue. But the compulsory inclusion of this kind of information should mean that the sensible buyer of a life assurance-related product (especially savings- and investment-related ones) has a better chance of finding out exactly what it is he is buying and whether it is appropriate for his needs. Certainly, no one should sign any life contract without first being satisfied that his policy document clearly conforms to the terms of the Directives.

The insurance industry has changed dramatically in the past decade. From hitherto being perceived as old-fashioned, slow-moving and conservative, it is now a significant part of the dynamic financial services industry. The most striking factors are the global nature, the range and sophistication of products which are available and the intense competition for new business. Irish companies now realise that alternative markets for purchasing insurance exist and that buyers are no longer limited to the traditional Irish market and Lloyds. The range of contemporary insurance products is wide. While covers for property, liability and motor still form the bedrock of most insurance programmes, they are being increasingly augmented by a variety of niche products catering for specialist needs. Some examples include malicious product tamper/product recall cover for food and drink producers, environmental damage cover for the chemical and pharmaceutical sector, key man insurance and company directors and officers liability cover.

Along with the development of new products, the industry has come up with different methods of structuring an insurance programme. These include self-insurance and the establishment of a subsidiary captive insurance company. Self-insurance is where the company retains a predetermined layer of risk and thereby encourages in-house risk management to improve safety and quality control. Captive insurance companies have been defined as insurance companies set up by industrial or commercial groups primarily to insure the risks of their parent or parents. They were first formed to counteract the restriction or elimination of coverage and resulting price increases within the commercial insurance market. Seen to be stabilising elements in self-insurance programmes, they have developed from a very basic concept to one which embraces a total risk management philosophy.

The creation of the Single European Market and the establishment of the International Financial Services Centre (IFSC) in Dublin in 1987 have been a major impetus to the growth of the insurance market in Ireland. An insurance company with its head office in the IFSC and freedom of services throughout Europe can benefit from the low 10 per cent corporate tax rate, which applies to both its investment income and its underwriting profits. This should allow insurance companies build up their reserves at a much faster rate than in most European jurisdictions and accelerate that momentum by offering more competitive premium rates and investment returns.

The insurance industry in Ireland is a key sector of the economy. Collectively, insurance companies in Ireland employ over 10,000 people and many thousands more jobs are created in spin-off areas such as insurance broking and loss adjusting. The combined turnover of Life and General insurance companies in Ireland in 1995 was in excess of £2,600 million. The market value of assets held by them in 1995 was nearly £16,000 million, 75 per cent of which is invested in Ireland to the benefit of the Irish economy.

There are forty-nine insurance companies in Ireland. Many are British-owned and have been in Ireland since the nineteenth century. The process of European integration will have a profound effect on the structure and competitive operation of the Irish insurance market. It will allow Irish-owned firms to invest abroad while at the same time allowing foreign-based firms to enter the Irish market. In addition the market has seen the entry of new home-based companies such as the Allied Irish Banks Group through Ark and Bank of Ireland Group through Lifetime Assurance. It has been suggested that competition from the EU will halve the number of insurance companies in Ireland by the year 2000.

The overall insurance market is divided into two main segments, Life Assurance and General. Life Assurance is concerned with long-term risk and includes such items as permanent health insurance. The leading companies in terms of market share are Irish Life, Norwich Union, New Ireland, Scottish Provident and Standard Life. General insurance is concerned primarily with short-term risk, such as house and car insurance. In this section the leading companies in terms of market share are Hibernian, New

PMPA, Guardian Royal Exchange, Sun Alliance and Insurance Corporation of Ireland.

The largest company by far is Irish Life. It has a pre-eminent position in the life assurance market and is the dominant investment force on the Irish Stock Exchange. It changed its status from a state-owned company to one of public ownership in 1991. In so doing it generated £374 million for the Irish Exchequer and gave itself the freedom and flexibility to trade on a full commercial and international basis.

LEASING COMPANIES

The most spectacular growth among financial institutions in the 1980s was in leasing companies. These companies — which, not having banking licences, were not subject to stringent control — grew at exponential rates during the 1980s only for some to crash in the 1990s.

Such companies use their own equity and bank borrowings to lease assets to users. Most leases are simply financial leases, in that at the end of the lease period, for a small payment, the user will take over ownership of the asset. Anomalies in taxation laws relating to depreciation allowances and differing tax rates between service and manufacturing companies meant that leasing companies could offer cost-efficient funds to manufacturing companies. Other leasing companies used the taxation allowances available in the state and the tax haven status of the Shannon Free Zone and Dublin Custom House Docks site to offer cheaper capital to domestic and international customers.

By far the best example of tax haven-based leasing was the growth of Guinness Peat Aviation (GPA). During the 1980s GPA, based in Shannon, developed into the world's largest aircraft leasing company with turnover of hundreds of millions of pounds and profits greater than those of the Bank of Ireland. Originally Irish-owned, GPA was bought into by Japanese, US and Canadian companies. The world-wide recession had a profound impact on the airline industry and this, allied to deregulation and bad timing in regard to a public flotation, brought GPA to earth. It was resurrected in part by the intervention of General Electric in 1993. It continues in a much slimmed-down state.

In the 1980s the growth of domestic leasing saw the emergence of a number of publicly quoted leasing companies. Woodchester grew into the dominant force in leasing. In the early 1990s it was acquired by Credit Lyonnais. Other publicly quoted leasing companies were not so successful. Reflex was established to lease computers. After rapid growth it incurred heavy losses and withdrew from leasing. Capital Leasing grew quickly, ran into financing problems and was acquired by a French bank. Anglo Irish Bank entered the Irish and UK leasing market only to retire with heavy losses. But the most spectacular rise and fall was Cambridge. Formed in the late 1980s it grew organically and by acquisition to be valued at over £50 million by the early 1990s. Difficulties in a UK subsidiary and problems with the confirming section of the Irish business led to a loss of confidence by lenders, resulting in the failure of the group in 1993.

Leasing remains a primary source of finance for domestic Irish business. Woodchester and Smurfit are the main domestic suppliers while there is a resurgence in tax-based leasing companies located at Shannon and the Custom House Docks area in Dublin.

CREDIT UNIONS Not examined

Credit unions play an active part in promoting small savings. This modern movement prospered in Canada and the USA, from where in the 1950s it eventually spread to Ireland. Dramatic expansion took place and has been maintained over the last four decades, so that today, the credit union is recognised in Ireland as a unique and practical expression of self-help through co-operative endeavour. The essential element of any credit union is that all members and potential members should have something in common. The law provides for a number of different common bonds. Two types generally exist: community bonds and industrial or associational bonds.

There are 523 credit unions in Ireland; 103 in Northern Ireland and 420 in the Republic. These credit unions are directed by over 8,000 volunteers and employ over 500 full-time staff. Total credit union membership is almost 1,400,000. Total savings in 1994 were in the order of £1,250 million with a slightly smaller amount advanced by way of loans.

Each credit union is separate, autonomous and completely in control of its own affairs. Credit unions are regulated by the state and the government official responsible is the Registrar of Friendly Societies. By law a credit union may charge not more than 1 per cent per month on the unpaid balance of a loan. This represents an Annual Percentage Rate (APR) of 12.68 per cent.

A Credit Union Bill is proposed which would afford more consumer protection and remove the shackles which at present limit the introduction of new services by credit unions. Among the expected key proposals are increased powers for the Registrar of Friendly Societies. The Registrar will be able to impose on individual societies a limit on shares, deposits, interest charged, and the size and period of loans where it is felt that the society may be unduly influenced by a small number of people in terms of their savings or indebtedness.

The Registrar will be able to appoint an accountant to inspect the books of a credit union upon application being made by twenty of the union's members and also may keep a file on each credit union, available for public inspection.

In addition credit unions will have to be insured against loss or liability incurred through 'fraud or dishonesty'. There will be restrictions on where and how a credit union can invest surpluses — savings not given out in loans — to avoid 'unwise and uncoordinated investment decisions by individual credit unions'.

There will also be curbs on any speculative property transactions and finally a reminder that credit unions need to distinguish themselves from other institutions by emphasising their differences: namely, the common bond; the facts that they are member-owned, are run by volunteers and are not-for-profit co-operative financial organisations.

THE DUBLIN MONEY MARKET

A money market deals in short-term funds, and until the 1970s there was no such market in Ireland. It acts like any other market: buyers and sellers attempt to match each other's needs. Prices, in this case interest rates, are a function of supply and demand.

Today a small but thriving money market exists in Dublin. It is made up of two main segments — the market for Exchequer Bills and Central Bank deposits and the interbank market.

The Central Bank controls credit to some extent by imposing certain liquidity requirements on the licensed banks. The banks can meet the requirements by holding non-interest-bearing cash or by depositing funds with the Central Bank for agreed periods at agreed rates. Banks unable to meet the liquidity requirements can borrow from the Central Bank at high rates.

The Central Bank also curbs credit by controlling the issue of Exchequer Bills, which are ninety-day loans. Through the purchase of such bills money is released into the economy; through their sale funds are tightened. Exchequer Bills are negotiable and an active market exists in them. Banks selling cash can sell or rediscount Exchequer Bills at the Central Bank.

The interbank market is based in Dublin. It developed during the 1970s, primarily in response to the needs of the non-associated banks, which — while the associated banks deal in this market — remain its main participants. They do not enjoy the same degree of continuity as the asociated banks in the flow of domestic savings to them or in their domestic lending. Some banks draw temporarily on the interbank market to mobilise the necessary funds for lending to customers, while some find that their liquidity becomes excessive at times and they lend to other banks in Dublin or place deposits with the Central Bank. Deposits in the interbank market are repayable at call, two and seven days' notice, and are also placed for fixed periods ranging from seven days to twelve months. Most activity is centred in the call to one-month range. The growth in the market has been rapid and because it is competing with other investment outlets, the rates offered reflect conditions in London and in other money markets abroad.

Since the break with sterling, access to the London money market has been somewhat restricted, so activity increased in Dublin. This resulted in a series of new instruments being developed, such as:

(1) Financial Futures Contracts;
(2) Interest Rate Hedges;
(3) Interest Rate Swaps;
(4) Interest Rate Options.

Financial futures contracts are binding agreements to buy or sell through an established exchange, at a definite date and at a specified price, a standard amount of financial paper of predetermined quality under fixed conditions of delivery. In principle actual or anticipated risks in money and bond markets (cash markets) can be minimised by taking an equal and opposite position in a futures market. Any cash market loss resulting from adverse interest rate movements should be offset by profits on futures contracts.

Interest rate hedges are similar to financial futures contracts in that they also allow a customer to enter into a future late agreement. However, unlike a financial futures contract, which is provided by a bank that then lays off the risk in a traded futures market, the risk in a future rate agreement is taken on by the bank itself.

Interest rate swaps consist of sets of forward exchanges of interest payments between two companies. Interest rate swaps allow a corporate treasurer to change the nature of the interest rate payments on the company's debt. The swap does not involve any exchange of principal amounts. It consists only of an agreement to exchange interest flows. The only payment that is made is the difference between the fixed and floating interest rate calculations on the amount stated in the agreement.

Interest rate options allow corporate treasurers to insure against adverse interest rate movements on anticipated drawdowns of new debt or on rollovers of existing floating rate funds. They also allow treasurers the potential for upside gains should interest rates move favourably.

Banks offering an interest rate option essentially sell their customer the right, but not the obligation, to borrow a specified amount at any time during the option period at a fixed rate for the stated period of the option. The option gives the corporate treasurer a combination of a pre-set fixed borrowing rate and the flexibility of choosing the drawdown date or choosing not to draw down at all. For that right the treasurer pays a premium. The premium cost will depend on the degree of interest rate volatility, the intrinsic value (the difference between the current borrowing rate and the exercise rate) and the time value (the longer the option period, the more the option costs). Interest rate options can also be tied to a futures instrument to lock in a fixed rate for some point in the future: that is, an option on a future rate agreement.

The most common use of interest rate options by corporate treasurers is to provide an 'interest rate cap' on floating rate debt through an option on a future rate agreement. Chapter 16 shows the relevance of these instruments in the task of managing currency and interest risks.

THE CAPITAL MARKET

Apart from a short-term money market a capital market for longer-term funds exists in Dublin and is located at the Stock Exchange. The Irish Stock Exchange (ISE) link with the London Stock Exchange was broken in 1994 after 200 years. The Central Bank is now responsible for the authorisation of the ISE and member firms, approval of the ISE rules and financial regulation of member firms. The regulation of brokers' conduct of business and the market is done by the ISE board, which includes representatives of the wider industry. The new rules have been directly modelled on the UK rules and will possibly include a contract with the UK securities and futures authority under which it will provide a surveillance support service in Ireland. The biggest challenge facing the ISE is exchange control deregulation and the need to attract enough buyers, both national and international. Liquidity is the lifeblood of any market and competition is intense. The introduction of special savings accounts taxed at 15 per cent has distorted the market and overturned the fundamental tenet that the highest reward should be given to those taking the highest risk. Their introduction has further alienated the personal investor from unit-linked funds at a time when they were already unpopular following three years of disappointing returns. However, all is not doom and gloom. Positive signs have been evident in the Irish market, with an increasing number of international buyers and rising values on the back of the world-wide bullish market trends. Chapter 8 deals with the operation of the Stock Exchange in more detail.

The capital markets are composed of two elements, an equity market and a bond market. The latter market is often the larger and includes, in addition to the inevitable government bonds, a substantial corporate element. In Ireland a thriving government bond market exists with outstandings of over £14 billion, yet there is no market for corporate debt. Apart from some scattered issues for state companies, one or two convertibles, and latterly some Euro-Irish issues for non-resident financial institutions, there has been no corporate activity in the Irish bond market.

Many reasons have been advanced for the failure of the local corporate bond market to develop. Some argue that the dominant position of the government has frozen out other potential issuers. It has been argued also that no alternative issuers exist who could provide sufficiently liquid issues to be attractive to institutional investors. Others cite the unfavourable taxation environment, still others the barriers posed by the listing requirements of the ISE and the information requirements in a prospectus. Investor demand for corporate bonds is said to be low, while some consider the absence of any recognised rating system a deterrent to investors.

It is worth examining at the outset the question of the government's dominant position in the market. Its direct influence as regards entry to the bond market has been restricted to the regulation of state companies. While at times there has been no great enthusiasm exhibited towards prospective issues from semi-states, there has never been a prohibition on such issues. Indeed, semi-state issuers have found at various times investor indifference more of an obstacle than regulatory restrictions. In any case the government's activity in the market has led to its present size and depth. The Irish bond market grew steadily in the seventies and early eighties and over the past ten years has generated returns for investors exceeding either the US or UK bond markets.

It is arguable that the role of the government has been positive in regard to the development of the market, firstly through its increasing use of the market, and latterly through creating the stable low inflation conditions that have provided attractive returns to investors in Irish bonds.

Why then has there been no demand to issue corporate bonds from this source? One reason is that there has been little necessity for funding from this source. A combination of grants, leasing and what was known as Section 84 lending (see below) has been used in the past to meet the medium-term financing requirements of the larger Irish corporates. There has also been a tradition of using bank debt to meet general financing requirements, partly because of existing relationships and partly because the information required for a bank loan is less than that for a public securities issue. A further factor to explain the concentration on bank debt is that some of the largest and most active entities in recent years were private companies which would not have been able to issue publicly quoted or traded securities.

For the publicly quoted companies which have potential access to the domestic institutional market an explanation is harder to find. Very probably their absence is due to a combination of factors. Many will have found their local requirements met by bank finance and will have raised finance for foreign acquisitions off shore in foreign currency, thus matching foreign currency assets with foreign currency liabilities. Others will have been deterred by the numerous apparent obstacles to an issue. For many years one of the main deterrents was the exchange control system, which required finance for overseas investments to be raised in foreign currency. A further deterrent is the disparity in tax treatment between government and corporate bonds. Government issues and guaranteed bonds benefit from a range of exemptions relating to income tax, capital gains tax and stamp duty. These make government paper more attractive for investors to hold and consequently increase the price at which corporate bonds must be issued to meet investor yield expectations. At least as important has been a reluctance by investors to take a long-term view on Irish companies. The distortions caused by a 10 per cent corporate tax rate have also affected financial decisions.

The greatest impediment is in the area of stamp duty, where current regulations make an initial issue of bonds very expensive and subsequent trading prohibitively so.

Another impediment commonly cited is the costs of listing securities on the Dublin market, compared with other centres, such as Luxemburg.

Beyond that, however, there are discernible changes in progress that give added impetus to the creation of this market. The most profound change, world-wide, is the transfer of prime corporate credit from the banking to the bond markets. This is occurring as on the one hand companies continue to expand their search for cost-effective funding and on the other hand banks beset by bad debt problems and capital adequacy restraints seek to limit the growth of their Balance Sheets and extract higher returns from corporate debt. Within the domestic market two of the main sources of finance for Irish companies, leasing and Section 84 loans, have to all intents and purposes disappeared. With bank credit becoming scarcer and costlier there is now more pressure on the larger companies to seek alternative sources.

A welcome development is the greater involvement of overseas investors in the domestic bond market, a trend which has been reinforced by the final abolition of exchange controls. Foreign investors have had mixed experiences in the equity market and the bigger Irish companies have by and large not yet developed an extensive non-resident investor base. However, the experiences to date of foreign investors in the gilt market have been better, and provided the conditions in the basic market remain stable and yields favourable, there is good potential for corporate issuance into this market.

A significant barrier to external investors is the general lack of rated issuers in the market. This obstacle could be removed either by the establishment of a domestic rating agency or by the larger companies' obtaining ratings from one of the international rating agencies.

Surmounting the barriers requires some initiative and imagination and the answer may lie in the expansion of the main existing corporate securities market, the commercial paper market. This is proof that in the right circumstances a local market in corporate debt can be developed. It could be done through the medium-term note structure. This facility offers issuers the ability to issue fixed or floating rate securities in maturities greater than one year. Reasonably large and liquid issues can be created quite rapidly, which is an attraction for investors. Since medium-term note facilities can be structured in a similar way to commercial paper issuance and are targeted at a similar investor base, the cost of issue to companies that already participate in the commercial paper market is relatively low. Also, since medium-term notes can be placed flexibly and privately, such an issue can be made without listing and without the information overhead of the public issue.

THE FOREIGN EXCHANGE MARKET

Ireland has an open economy. That means that a large part of the Gross National Product is accounted for by foreign trade. Foreign trade must be financed; exporters must receive foreign currencies and bills of exchange which they need to convert into punts. Importers seek foreign currencies to pay their suppliers.

Up to 1970 most foreign exchange business was done in London. In 1970 the Central Bank commenced dealings in the major foreign currencies. Buying and selling rates for foreign currencies are quoted throughout the day by the Central Bank. Until March 1979 the task was simple. Parity with sterling meant that Irish and British exchange rates against other currencies were identical; otherwise arbitrage took place. Breaking of the link with sterling resulted in a significant expansion of the Dublin foreign exchange market. Now the Irish punt has a quotation against every major currency. But since more than 30 per cent of all foreign trade is with the United Kingdom, the punt/sterling rate is the critical foreign exchange rate.

To protect the punt, the Central Bank instituted a series of restrictions on overseas investments. This enabled it to exercise limited control over movements in the punt and saw the emergence of a forward foreign exchange market, with the Central Bank bearing some of the risk involved initially. This support and the development of local expertise saw the Dublin market integrate into the international foreign exchange market in the context of membership of the European Exchange Rate Mechanism (ERM). It operated until January 1993 within the constraints of the remaining exchange controls on short-term capital movements that were introduced in 1978 when Ireland decided to join the European Monetary System (EMS).

Now that forward cover is allowed for known and specific financial outflows, the need to use the currency hedge market has disappeared. Previously, under hedge contracts, banks matched customers with opposite currency flows and contracts were negotiated outside the realms of exchange controls. With the winding down of this market those particular requirements obviously no longer exist. A further implication for the investor is the convergence of the offshore with the domestic markets. Ireland has been the only ERM country to apply rigid exchange controls, resulting in over 50 per cent of Irish pound foreign exchange dealings being transacted off shore, creating the Euro-Irish pound market. The existence of this market has historically distorted pricing and illiquidity in domestic forward markets. The convergence of these markets should mean less distortion of pricing, a reduction in interest rate volatility and keener pricing of long-dated forward transactions.

For domestic banks which traded in short-term derivative instruments, such as forward rate agreements, interest rate swaps and cross-currency swaps, the now redundant control dictated that the basis of the deal had to be as a hedge for a non-speculative transaction. However, in the present environment, which allows freer and easier movement of capital, domestic banks are experiencing increased volumes in this area, thus allowing them to develop new relationships with foreign banks and investors and thereby strengthen and widen their revenue bases. This is a further positive impact resulting from the removal of exchange controls which most participants had anticipated and are currently benefiting from.

Special savings accounts and special investment accounts have been introduced to counteract the offshore investment opportunities now available. The unique characteristics of these accounts mean that investors can avail of premium interest rates with considerable flexibility while limiting the amount of withholding tax due. In fact, as successive governments have tended to structure a more equitable income tax regime, they have encouraged a certain type of investor to look for investment opportunities in the domestic market. Previously, due to a particular tax profile this investor had looked for and availed of cross-border opportunities.

Another area of corporate investment which had concerns about its continued viability, due to more favourable tax regimes in a post-exchange control era, was the Commercial Paper (CP) market. CP is usually issued as a promissory note or acceptance credit at a discount and in time horizons of less than one year. For the domestic borrower (issuer) his cost of funds is more competitive, saving on Reserve Asset Cost (RAC). Where the absolute level of withholding tax reduces, the attractiveness of cash market rates can be compared more favourably. However, while the removal of certain exchange controls has coincided with a reduced withholding tax, as long as this tax remains in some shape or form the CP market should continue to shade the investment decision.

The foreign exchange market is maintained by telephone and telex links and is confined almost exclusively to banks. Financial innovation in international banking is being stimulated by a wide range of factors, such as:

(1) The changing regulatory environment, which relaxed structural rigidities world-wide and increased financial competition. The increased competition reduced the profitability of traditional banking services and forced the development of new specialised products to compensate.

(2) Regulatory pressure in the form of a demand for a strong capital base in financial institutions. This led to the development of off balance sheet hedging and liquidity management techniques such as futures, swaps, options and Note Issuing Facilities (NIFs).

(3) Technology improvements which reduced the costs of telecommunications and information processing, while also encouraging greater competition in traditional standardised services.

(4) The increased volatility of interest rates and exchange rates. This higher volatility has increased the risk in financial institutions which do not exactly match the term structure of their assets and liabilities. Consequently, there has been an incentive to develop effective hedging devices to deal with these higher risks. The new financial instruments have largely focused on this risk shifting.

(5) Fundamental shifts in the allocation of international funds.
    (a) Sharp fall in investable surpluses in many countries.
    (b) Reduced access to credit by major borrowers from less developed countries.
    (c) Switch in the role of the US from large net provider of funds to large net taker.
    (d) Growth in current account surpluses in Europe and Japan.

The key changes which have resulted from these forces for innovation have been:

(1) The emergence of new financial instruments — mainly focusing on off balance sheet commitments: for example, futures, options and other so-called derivatives.

(2) Securitisation of the capital markets. Large international loans have shifted to the direct credit market rather than using the banks as intermediaries. This shift has been helped by some of the new instruments, such as NIFs.

(3) Closer integration of world-wide financial markets — partially because of communications.

(4) Increased volume of transactions.

(5) Increased mobility of capital.

Financial innovations have offered a broad range of products for borrowing, deposits, and for managing interest rate and exchange rate exposures.

CONCLUSION

The coming years will see further major changes in Irish financial institutions.

Deregulation will lead to a scramble to lend. Established policies and patterns will become blurred. New lenders and new lending instruments will appear.

The challenge facing the associated banks is severe. They are large traditional labour-intensive institutions used to operating in a cartel, which ensured that interest rates charged were high enough to cover all costs and leave a profit.

Bank opening hours will have to adapt to the needs of the customer. The merchant and industrial banks will struggle to find a profitable role in the new environment. Some US banks have already decided that they are not equal to the task and have withdrawn. The associated banks are merging many of the activities of their merchant bank subsidiaries into their main banking activities. The building societies will become more aggressive lenders.

It is likely that the number of banking licences will decline through mergers and acquisitions.

Finance is the lifeblood of business. As a business grows and develops, it will find that contacts with financial institutions also develop. The credit union, local bank or building society which provided the second mortgage to get the business started will become less relevant with growth. Greater financial needs result in contacts with industrial banks and merchant banks. Overseas deals may require the permission of the Central Bank and the assistance of the North American or European banks. Larger ventures may result in loans from insurance companies or a quotation on the Stock Exchange. In general Ireland is very well served by the range of financial institutions and products available. Competition will ensure that the price paid by Irish business for finance is competitive.

Ireland has a variety of well-developed financial institutions which have a selection of financial products, one or more of which can suit practically every financial need.

FURTHER READING
A. Molloy, *The Irish Investment Market* (Oak Tree Press, 1993).
Central Bank Annual & Quarterly Report.
Annual Reports of financial institutions.

QUESTIONS
Question 7.1
Why do commercial banks mainly supply short-term finance while insurance companies supply long-term finance?

Question 7.2
Explain the role of the investment banker (merchant and commercial banks) in helping industries raise necessary long-term debt and equity funds. Why has there been an increase in the number of banks providing investment advice in Ireland?

Question 7.3
To finance investment projects, which would be more desirable: a bank overdraft or long-term debt?

Question 7.4
Distinguish between money markets and capital markets. What types of asset are traded in each?

Question 7.5
What reasons have been given for the growth in international banking?

Question 7.6
What changes in legislation, both at home and abroad, have affected the building societies in Ireland?

Appendix 7.1 Financial Institutions Reporting to the Central Bank

---

Associated Banks
Allied Irish Banks PLC
The Governor and Company of the Bank of Ireland
National Irish Bank Limited
Ulster Bank Limited

Non-Associated Banks
Merchant and Commercial Banks
ABN-AMRO Bank NV
AIB Capital Markets PLC
Ansbacher Bankers Limited
Bank of America National Trust and Savings Association
The Bank of Nova Scotia
Banque Nationale de Paris SA
Barclays Bank PLC
Chase Manhattan Bank (Ireland) PLC
Citibank NA
Codan Bank
Daiwa Europe Bank PLC
DePfa-Bank Europe PLC
Deutsche Bau-und Bodenbank Ag (Bauboden Bank)
Ford Credit Europe PLC
Guinness & Mahon Limited
Helaba Dublin Landesbank Hessen-Thüringen International
Hill Samuel Bank Limited
Internationale Nederlanden Bank NV (ING Bank)
The Investment Bank of Ireland Limited
Irish Bank of Commerce Limited
Irish Business Bank
Irish Intercontinental Bank Limited
Kredietbank NV
National Irish Investment Bank Limited
Pfizer International Bank Europe
Rabobank Ireland Limited
Scotiabank (Ireland) Limited
Smurfit Paribas Bank Limited
Ulster Investment Bank Limited
Westdeutsche Landesbank (Ireland) Limited

Industrial Banks
AIB Finance Limited
Anglo Irish Bank Corporation PLC
Bank of Ireland Finance Limited
Equity Bank Limited
Lombard and Ulster Banking Limited
Woodchester Credit Lyonnais Bank Limited
Building Societies
EBS Building Society
First National Building Society
ICS Building Society
Irish Nationwide Building Society
Irish Permanent PLC*
The Norwich Irish Building Society

* Irish Permanent Building Society became Irish Permanent PLC on 21 September 1994. For statistical purposes it remains classified with building societies.

Other Credit Institutions
ACC Bank PLC
ICC Bank PLC
ICC Investment Bank Limited
TSB Bank

Post Office Savings Bank

Hire Purchase Finance Companies
Advance Finance Limited
Allied Finance Limited
Annesley Leasing Limited
Arrow Trust Limited
Cambridge Financial Services Limited
The Commercial Trust Company Limited
Cresington Finance Limited
Euro Finance Limited
Everyday Finance Limited
Exchange Finance Limited
Fiat Auto Finance Limited
M.J. Flood (Leasing) Limited
Henry Ford & Son (Finance) Limited
Gaeleas Teoranta
General Finance Trust Limited
Highland Finance Ireland Limited
ICC Finance Limited
Irish Permanent Finance Limited
Kimberley Finance Limited
Livestock Credit Corporation Limited
Montbrison Limited
National Carways Limited
National Carways Investment Society
National Credit Finance Limited
Raasay Limited
Shannon International Leasing and Financial Services Limited
Smurfit Finance Limited
Smurfit Leasing Limited
Woodchester Leaseline Limited
West European Credit Finance Limited
Western Finance Company Limited
Woodchester Finance Limited

Source: Central Bank of Ireland, September 1994.

Appendix 7.2 Gross Assets of Lending Financial Institutions in Ireland (£000s)

Company	Assets	Profit	Shareholders' Funds	Year End	Employees
1 AIB	18,252.0	171.6	995.8	31/12/92	15,500
2 Bank of Ireland	15,288.0	124.3	743.0	31/03/93	12,130
3 Ulster Bank	5,504.3	61.3	294.6	31/12/92	3,900
4 GPA	5,186.0	(678.0)	161.3	31/03/93	250
5 Central Bank of Ireland	4,647.8	190.6	710.0	31/12/92	626
6 Irish Permanent Building Society	2,235.5	19.7	134.3	31/12/92	917
7 First National Building Society	1,439.5	15.6	74.7	31/12/92	523
8 Woodchester Investments	1,398.3	35.4	232.5	31/12/92	713
9 Educational Building Society	1,225.3	15.0	90.0	31/12/92	478
10 Irish Intercontinental Bank	1,164.4	12.2	46.1	31/12/92	145
11 TSB Bank	1,129.0	15.1	57.4	31/10/93	995
12 ICC Bank	1,080.6	8.4	58.1	31/10/92	332
13 National Irish Bank	1,075.0	14.6	72.0	30/09/93	840
14 Anglo Irish Bankcorp	1,073.1	9.3	92.2	30/09/93	215
15 Post Office Savings Bank	1,000.0	1.6	n/a	31/12/92	211
16 Norwich Union Group	880.0	n/a	n/a	31/12/92	612
17 ACC Bank	860.1	8.5	38.8	31/12/92	440
18 Barclays Bank PLC	830.0	n/a	n/a	31/12/93	65
19 Bank of Nova Scotia Group	752.1	n/a	n/a	31/10/90	48
20 Standard Life Assurance Company	735.7	n/a	n/a	15/11/92	150
21 New Ireland Holdings	698.1	4.0	39.8	31/12/92	823
22 Hibernian Group	608.7	15.6	72.4	31/12/92	780
23 Irish Nationwide Building Society	589.3	16.5	76.9	31/12/92	250
24 Canada Life Ireland	562.0	n/a	n/a	31/12/92	670
25 GRE/PMPA Group Ltd	527.9	26.7	63.2	31/12/92	907
26 Eagle Star Life Assurance Co. of Ireland	515.6	4.5	n/a	31/12/92	234
27 Friends Provident Life Office	395.6	n/a	n/a	31/12/92	206
28 AGF — Irish Life Holdings PLC	392.1	8.2	48.0	31/12/92	729
29 Scottish Provident	386.5	n/a	n/a	31/12/92	101
30 Citibank	369.0	n/a	n/a	31/12/92	100
31 Housing Finance Agency	361.3	(6.5)	n/a	30/06/93	9
32 Royal Liver Friendly Society	321.8	0.0	n/a	31/12/92	n/a
33 Prudential Life of Ireland	304.6	0.0	n/a	31/12/92	185
34 FBD Holdings PLC	244.9	11.5	39.7	31/12/92	393
35 Westdeutsche Landesbank (Ireland)	215.5	0.0	4.7	31/12/92	28
36 Eagle Star Insurance	198.0	33.5	n/a	31/12/92	280
37 Ansbacher & Co.	176.7	0.0	11.4	31/12/92	55
38 General Accident	174.7	0.0	n/a	31/12/92	270
39 Irish Public Bodies Mutual Insurances	149.2	0.3	n/a	31/12/92	45
40 Hill Samuel Bank (Ireland)	142.5	0.0	24.8	31/10/92	49
41 Bank of America	140.0	0.0	n/a	31/12/93	26
42 Irish Life Building Society	135.0	1.5	5.3	31/12/92	60
43 Sun Alliance Ireland	132.9	0.0	n/a	31/12/92	274
44 Smurfit Paribas Bank	131.7	0.0	13.9	31/12/92	25
45 Royal Insurance	105.3	0.0	n/a	31/12/92	210
46 Yeoman International Group	82.8	4.5	(43.4)	31/02/93	18
47 Guinness & Mahon	72.4	0.0	7.8	30/09/92	42
48 Sun Life of Canada	63.3	n/a	n/a	31/12/92	n/a
49 National Mutual Life (Irl.)	58.3	0.0	n/a	30/09/92	80
50 AIG Europe (Ireland)	49.4	3.4	n/a	31/11/92	74
51 Gandon Holdings	39.2	1.9	25.9	31/12/92	52
52 Cornhill Insurance Co.	38.5	0.0	n/a	31/12/92	40
53 Voluntary Health Insurance Board	36.9	5.8	n/a	28/02/93	369
54 Celtic International	36.7	1.2	n/a	31/12/92	160
55 QBE Insurance & Reinsurance	27.1	0.5	n/a	30/06/92	45

8

The Stock Exchange

The capital or funding which is invested to create businesses is usually invested in the form of shares if it is owners' risk capital or debentures if it is loan capital. Investors owning shares or debentures in businesses of various types may need to liquidate their investment. Companies, on the other hand, may wish to raise new capital from the public at large. The solution to both problems lies in the Stock Exchange — a market where shares and debentures may be bought and sold. By virtue of there being a market, individuals and companies can change wealth freely, consume wealth and accumulate wealth without having to acquire tangible assets directly. Over eight million people in Britain and Ireland invest in more than 9,000 different shares and bonds on the Stock Exchange.

The buying and selling of shares has gone on for hundreds or even thousands of years. In the eighteenth century business activity grew rapidly, with a consequent growth in the amount of capital invested. Specialists, who bought and sold shares, developed in business centres such as Amsterdam, Stockholm and London. These specialists would meet daily to do business. At first, they had no formal meeting place so they used coffee houses or restaurants. Amsterdam was the first city to have a formal location. By 1772 the London Stock Exchange occupied premises in Sweeting Alley in the City of London. Business at that time was confined mainly to shares and debentures in trading companies, mining companies and canal building companies. Government loans were traded too.

Wealthy people living in Ireland also wished to participate in the buying and selling of shares and debentures. A number of stockbrokers opened up for business. In 1793 twelve Dublin stockbrokers thought that they were doing sufficient business to organise a Dublin-based market. The market consisted largely of shares in canal companies, mining companies and government stocks. An Act of Parliament in Dublin in 1799 firmly established the Dublin Stock Exchange. The rules of the Dublin Exchange were similar to those of its London counterpart. The Cork Stock Exchange opened for business on the South Mall in 1886.

At the same time as the Irish exchanges were developing, regional exchanges were growing throughout England. By 1960 it was realised that this multitude of local exchanges was not offering the best service to the investing public. Developments in communications meant that anyone in the British Isles using a telephone could be in instantaneous contact with a central exchange. A series of mergers took place in the United Kingdom, and also in Ireland, which culminated in the Irish Exchange merging with the London Exchange in 1973. The Irish Exchange operated in Anglesea Street in Dublin as a unit of the London Stock Exchange until 1995, when legislation passed in Ireland set up the Stock Exchange as an independent unit regulated by the Central Bank.

Table 8.1 Level of Activity on the Irish Stock Exchange

Money Raised (£m)	1992	1991	1990	1989
Irish Gilts	(685)	583	529	234
Irish Equities	234	817	736	681
(All Markets)*				
	(451)	1,400	1,265	915

*Note: 1991 figure includes money raised by privatisations of £312.5m

Turnover (£m)				
Gilts	47,902	42,215	36,097	41,016
Equities	3,266	3,460	3,346	3,783
(Official List and USM)				
Other*	3,731	1,936	2,443	1,952
	54,899	47,611	41,886	46,751

Bargains				
Equities	124,826	172,001	198,310	267,680
(Official List and USM)				
Other*	44,591	44,716	37,709	46,279
	169,417	216,717	236,019	313,959

Market Capitalisations (£m)				
Irish Gilts	12,782	13,545	12,289	10,900
Irish Equities (All Markets)	7,466	8,074	6,472	8,741

*Others = UK government stock; Irish and foreign corporation and local authority stock; fixed interest and preference stock; non-Irish equity.

FUNCTIONS OF A STOCK EXCHANGE

The Stock Exchange performs many functions in a modern economy. Its primary functions are:

(1) To channel savings into investment. In 1993 alone a total of £466 million in new equity was raised on the Irish Stock Exchange. This excludes £312 million raised by the government through the sale of shares in Greencore. In addition over £400 million was raised from corporate bonds, the first time this type of instrument took such a strong hold in Dublin.

(2) To provide a market for existing shares and debentures. In 1993 on the Irish Stock Exchange over £6 billion worth of shares were traded and the gilt market had a

turnover of £83 billion. These figures were 84 per cent and 73 per cent respectively up on 1992, and though some caution is suggested as regards double counting of deals, 1993 was a bumper year for the Irish equity market.

(3) To act as an indicator of the economic health of the country. Trends in the prices of shares and debentures reflect the business confidence in the country. Governments keep a close eye on the Stock Exchange as trends there are reflected later in the economy. Against the background of London, New York and many European markets trading at all-time highs, the Irish market by mid-1995 had recovered to be about 2 per cent short of its previous high, achieved in January 1990.

(4) To provide safeguards for investors. The Stock Exchange carefully examines and regulates the activities of those businesses which are quoted on the Exchange. In addition its members, the stockbrokers, have to abide by stringent rules which are designed to protect the investing public. A special Stock Exchange Compensation Fund exists to pay in full investors who lose money because of actions by stockbrokers.

(5) To advise investors. The Stock Exchange, through the stockbroking members, provides a pool of competent advisors to assist the public.

ORGANISATION OF THE STOCK EXCHANGE (LONDON/DUBLIN)

Only Stock Exchange members may deal on the Exchange. The general public buys and sells shares and other securities through agents, known as stockbrokers, who are members of the Stock Exchange. Membership is very tightly controlled and at present numbers 3,300. Traditionally, the members were split into two distinct groups: stockbrokers and jobbers.

Stockbroker

A stockbroker is an agent who buys and/or sells on behalf of clients. Apart from acting on behalf of clients, they often act as financial advisors. For their services stockbrokers receive a commission, usually 1.5 per cent of the value of the business carried out. They occasionally specialise in certain groups of shares or securities. There are fewer than ten stockbroking firms in Ireland.

Stock Jobber

This form of specialist no longer exists. A jobber was a principal in that he bought or sold for his own account. He dealt only with stockbrokers. A jobber was a wholesale buyer and seller of shares. He operated by quoting two prices when approached by a broker or another jobber. The party approaching the jobber simply named the share of interest without stating whether he was buying or selling. Thus a jobber would quote two prices, say, 100–105. The higher quote, 105, represented the price at which the jobber would sell the share, and the lower quote, 100, the price at which he was prepared to purchase the share. The difference between the two quotes, 5, was known as the jobber's turn. Because a number of jobbers were active in any given type of share, providing scope for shopping around, the prices quoted tended to be competitive and to give an accurate reflection of the worth of a share. Jobbers usually specialised in certain categories of share — for example, mining, oil, banks, stores, rubber. Rapid changes in technology, which turned the market into a screen-based one, and new regulations led to the demise of the jobber in the late 1980s.

Deregulation of the Stock Exchange

The traditional 200-year-old system of dealing on the Stock Exchange came to an end in 1986 in an event known as the 'Big Bang'. 'Big Bang' is often referred to as the deregulation of the financial markets. In the London context the major changes were:

(1) The amalgamation of the roles of stockbroker and jobber. Since the 'Big Bang' brokers and jobbers do the same work.
(2) Deregulation of commissions. Companies were allowed to compete when they were offering commissions on deals. Until the Big Bang the commissions were strictly set. Theoretically, since the changes, investors are able to shop around not only for the best price for a share from position takers in the market but for the best commission from a market maker.
(3) Other changes include allowing outside companies to buy into existing Stock Exchange member companies and the buying of brokerages by banks.
(4) New types of gilt-edged dealer.
(5) New screen-based dealing systems.
(6) New investor protection legislation.

The Big Bang affected Dublin. In the last half of the 1980s the very traditional atmosphere of the Irish Stock Exchange was enlivened by a series of mergers, takeovers and new entrants. A number of smaller firms were unable to compete in the new environment and merged with larger entities. Four big stockbroking firms emerged to dominate the sector, Goodbody's, J. & E. Davy, Riada and National City Brokers. These firms developed research capabilities, gilt dealing rooms, corporate finance departments and a full range of modern dealing technologies. Business premises which for 200 years had been oases of wealth and tranquillity were transformed into high technology areas with rows of flickering screens and batteries of telephones. The number of firms halved from twenty to ten.

Since deregulation, stockbrokers 'make markets' in certain shares. That is, they offer buy and sell prices for agreed lot sizes. Their buy and sell prices are on screens to which every broker has access. Market makers are often large prestigious well-financed companies though smaller firms can specialise in certain stocks.

The companies quoted on the London Exchange are divided into four groups: Alpha, Beta, Gamma and Delta. The Alpha group comprises the biggest and most secure companies, such as Shell, ICI, Hanson, General Electric. There are numerous market makers in the shares of these companies. Quotations are competitive and lot sizes large — 100,000 shares and up. Beta, Gamma and Delta companies have fewer market makers. In the case of Delta companies there may be no active market. As a consequence the share prices have a wider spread between bid and offer (buy and sell) and lot sizes are much smaller.

Some Irish companies trading in London are Beta but most are Delta. Active shares such as CRH and Smurfit's may have up to four market makers but many Irish companies have at most two market makers.

In Dublin shares are still traded between brokers though most deals are now done by telephone. In London the changes are greater. Among them is a new type of Gilt-Edged dealer. These primary dealers, being the market makers in government stock, play a vital role in the smooth operation of the whole bond market. They provide the market with its liquidity by being willing to quote two-way prices in government stocks. To do so they need access to large amounts of capital. The Bank of England recognises the service they provide and assists them in several ways, by dealing only through them and also by allowing them both stock and cash borrowing facilities. A second line of dealers, called inter dealer brokers, act as agents for transactions between the primary dealers and thereby facilitate the market by enabling transactions to be carried out by market makers without disclosing their positions. The National Treasury Management Agency (NTMA) in 1995 proposed to introduce Gilt Edged market makers in Dublin.

From the viewpoint of the ordinary investor the main change has been in how ordinary shares are traded. The introduction of an electronic screen-based dealing and pricing system — called SEAQ — for the equity market was overdue. The millions of new investors created in the UK by the privatisation of UK state companies necessitated a 'real time' dealing and pricing system which could keep the market fully informed.

Now brokers throughout the British Isles can deal almost instantaneously in practically every company which is listed on the Exchange. Each company has a Stock Exchange code. This code is in fact a page on a computer program. By keying in the code a broker immediately obtains

   — the last price at which the stock dealt,
   — the market makers who are offering to buy and/or sell shares,
   — the prices at which they are willing to deal,
   — the quantities in which they are willing to deal.

The final area of change is in relation to the introduction of legislation designed to regulate the activities of the participants and to protect investors. The legislation tries to combine the US method of pure statutory regulation with the British tradition of self-regulation.

Since 1973, as part of the International Stock Exchange of Great Britain and the Republic of Ireland, an anomaly existed whereby the Irish Exchange was subject to Irish law but effectively controlled and regulated from London. This was particularly apparent in regard to takeover situations involving Irish companies. The panel on Takeovers and Mergers in London would make judgments based on their principles, rules and UK law while in Ireland the then Department of Industry and Commerce had a statutory role within the state for such matters. This situation caused obvious confusion and uncertainty. The process of regulation was carried out by the Securities Association, later to be called the Securities and Futures Association (SFA), and under the terms of the Financial Services Act 1986.

In order to rectify this situation and comply with EU requirements to implement EU-wide harmonisation, the ISE was granted powers of self-regulation under the Companies Act (Part 5) 1990. This Act also made insider dealing a criminal offence. Insider dealing prohibits someone termed an 'insider' who has price-sensitive information on a company from dealing in that company's shares or passing on inside information which is used to make a profit. Advisory groups on 'insider trading' were set up under the Irish Association of Investment Managers. They have issued a code of best practice for all those involved in the Stock Exchange. In addition the Capital Markets Advisory Group (CMAG) was set up so that users of the Exchange could share views on its operation and deal with issues arising out of the provisions within the Companies Act of 1990.

The ISE also began at that time the process of establishing a separate regulatory structure for Ireland in the light of the proposed EU Investment Services Directive. This required that each member state have a statutory basis for regulation and appoint a national authority to supervise the market. In March 1993 this Directive was adopted by the Council of Ministers.

The Stock Exchange Bill 1995 transferred the power of self-regulating the Irish Stock Exchange from London to the Irish Central Bank. The Bill consolidated and updated Acts stretching back 200 years. The principal reason for it was an EU Directive which stipulates that domestic exchanges within the EU must be regulated by a national authority. The key features of the legislation are:

— members and member firms must be approved by the Central Bank,
— firms, both foreign and Irish, will be able to operate in other EU member states,
— the Central Bank can object to acquisitions or disposals of significant stakes in member firms,
— rule breaches will be investigated by a Stock Exchange committee but the report must be made available to the Central Bank,
— a Stock Exchange board will control day-to-day operations. This board will include non-broker members and will be chaired by a non-broker.

The *de facto* position is that the Irish Stock Exchange will continue to implement and operate the rules and incentives established in London. Dublin will have access to technical and information support services from London.

London plays a pre-eminent position in the whole Euroequity market and lives up to its title of the International Stock Exchange. While it ranks third in size to Tokyo and New York, it trades a greater value of foreign shares than any other market and has a greater number of foreign companies listed. It also has a larger number of companies, domestic- and foreign-listed, than any other exchange except the electronic over-the-counter market in the USA known as the NASDAQ (National Association of Securities Dealers Automatic Quotation System).

REGULATIONS ON THE STOCK EXCHANGE

The ISE is very careful to avoid, where possible, any suspicion that share prices are manipulated or that the small investor is getting less than a fair deal.

Each company quoted on the Exchange abides by a listing agreement which controls information of such things as notification of profits, changes in the directors, issuance of accounts and share transfers. One aspect of Stock Exchange activity which is now strictly regulated is that of takeovers. To protect investors a Panel on Takeovers and Mergers was established. This panel issued a series of rules, which is known as the 'City Code on Takeovers and Mergers' and contained in the 'Blue Book'. The principal rules refer to (a) the need for secrecy, (b) the behaviour of the bidders and (c) the behaviour of the directors on both sides.

GETTING A STOCK EXCHANGE QUOTATION OR 'GOING PUBLIC'

There are ninety-six companies quoted on the ISE. The number was much higher but mergers, takeovers and closures have reduced the total. For many years, the gaining of a Stock Exchange quotation was regarded as the pinnacle of success for a business. Recently, many companies have questioned the value of being quoted. Private companies such as Clery's, Dunnes Stores and Bell Ferries are larger than most of the quoted companies but for many reasons they have decided to remain unquoted.

The advantages of a Stock Exchange quotation are as follows:
(1) Access to a wider source of funds. A quotation on the Exchange enables a company

to raise larger sums from the public and, more importantly, from the big financial institutions. These institutions — insurance companies, unit trusts, investment trusts and pension funds — may not be allowed to invest in private companies.

(2) The creation of an efficient market in the company's shares. This provides an opportunity for the original owners of the company to realise some or all of their reward for building up the company.

(3) Because the shares are marketable and have a value, the possibility of using them as a means of paying for the takeover of another company. The share quotation reflects the fact that the company is a true entity distinct from its owners and that it has continuity apart from the original founders.

(4) The prestige attaching to having a Stock Exchange quotation. Greater publicity is possible, which results in benefits such as better credit ratings, consumer and government confidence, higher employee morale, better management. Scope exists for using share option schemes as a carrot to attract top managers and workers.

Before the public can be approached to buy shares, the Stock Exchange itself must be satisfied that the company can be given a quotation. This initial procedure, prior to quotation, can be quite rigorous. The company usually appoints financial advisors to prepare the documentation and reports required to satisfy the Stock Exchange. This may include a long form report, a pathfinder prospectus and a full prospectus. The Exchange will deal officially only with one of its own members, so a stockbroker must be appointed to represent the company in negotiations. The advisors and the sponsoring broker will carry out a considerable amount of investigation into the business prospects and financial position of the company before a formal approach is made to the Stock Exchange. The detailed procedure for applying for a quotation is given in the 'Yellow Book' published by the Exchange. Apart from taking time, the process is very costly. The 1994 flotation of the Irish Permanent had costs which ran to millions of pounds.

Once a company has been accepted by the Exchange a decision must be made on the method whereby the public will be asked to buy shares. A company can 'go public' using one of the following five methods.

(1) Issue by Prospectus. A company offers shares to the public at a given price. The advisors to the company prepare a prospectus which gives details of the firm's assets, earnings and management. It also gives details of the number of shares offered and their unit price. Strict regulations on drafting a prospectus are enforced by the Stock Exchange. A broker or merchant bank agrees to underwrite the issue: that is, agrees to buy any shares not applied for at the price stated in the prospectus. This method of issuing shares is rare in Ireland. It is also very expensive, costing up to 5 per cent of the proceeds.

(2) Offer for Sale. Often a merchant bank will buy a large block of shares in a private company. Over time, it will prepare the company to go public. When ready, the bank will offer its block of shares for sale to the public. This method is the most common form of going public in Ireland.

(3) Stock Exchange Placing. Raising new equity money is very expensive. A cheap way to 'go public' is to get a stockbroking firm to sell blocks of shares to various clients. The shares are 'placed' before the price is quoted on the Exchange. The Exchange expects at least 25 per cent of the shares to be sold to other stockbrokers. Money is saved by not having to issue a prospectus and by not having the operation underwritten.

(4) A Stock Exchange Introduction. The Stock Exchange will allow an 'introduction' only when the security in question is already quoted on another Stock Exchange or when it is widely distributed among the investing public. Usually, an introduction is suitable only when the company is fairly well known. A sufficient number of shares must be made available to make a quotation meaningful. Normally, this method is not a means of raising new finance for a company.

(5) An Offer by Tender. An unusual method of raising money is to issue a prospectus but no price. Bids are accepted at or above a stated price. Individuals can then decide how much a share in the company is worth and submit a tender. On a certain day the issue is closed, the tender bids are examined and a price accepted. All tenders above this price are accepted. People who tender at very high prices pay only the accepted price.

Often companies wish to raise new capital but do not want to affect the ownership or control of the company. They raise capital by means of a '*Rights Issue*'. This means that existing shareholders are given the right to subscribe for new shares. The shares are priced attractively. Owners not wishing to take up their right to subscribe can sell the rights to other investors.

It is common practice for companies not to pay out all the profits earned by way of dividends. Over time the retained profits per share can grow very large. One effect may be a high share price. The psychology of the market is such that investors prefer a low price per share so that their investment purchases a big block of shares. Companies reduce their share prices by a '*Bonus Issue*' of shares: that is, they capitalise earnings by turning the reserves of retained profit into issued share capital. Bonus issues are 'free' shares. In theory there is no net effect on the worth of the company but it is not unusual to see the share price after a bonus issue at a premium to the consolidated pre-bonus issue price.

CATEGORIES OF LISTING ON THE EXCHANGE

There are five levels of Stock Exchange listing as shown in Table 8.2:

Table 8.2	
Category	No. Listed in 1993 in Dublin
Official List	61
Unlisted Securities Market (USM)	18
Rule 4.2	–
Smaller Companies Market (SCM)	4
Exploration Securities Market	13
	96

The USM and Rule 4.2 markets are due to disappear in 1995/6 to be replaced by a new market modelled on the Alternative Investment Market (AIM) introduced in London in 1995.

Source: Irish Stock Exchange.

Official List

This has the most stringent set of listing requirements. Companies must have:
(a) A clean audited record for at least three years.

(b) A market capitalisation of £15 million when quoted.

(c) Profits of £750,000 per annum.

(d) At least 25 per cent of shares in the hands of the public.

An official or full listing is important for prestige, and because certain institutions have restrictions on their investment rules which confine them to investing only in shares of fully listed companies.

During the 1980s and 1990s the rules and costs attaching to a full listing became severe obstacles to most companies. As a consequence new listings declined. To combat this and to implement EU Directives, regulations were relaxed in 1994.

In 1994 Irish Permanent Building Society was the largest company to gain a full listing on the Irish Exchange.

To accommodate the needs of companies which wished to have their shares quoted but did not meet the requirements for a full listing, new categories of listings evolved in the 1980s.

Unlisted Securities Market (USM)

The USM was launched in November 1980 with a twofold purpose. Principally, it was to provide a formal, regulated market designed to meet the needs of smaller, less mature companies unlikely or unable to apply for a full official listing. Secondly, the USM brought under formal regulatory control of the Stock Exchange many of those unlisted companies whose securities were being freely traded under the provisions of Rule 4.2 (formerly 163.2) of the Stock Exchange. That rule permitted occasional bargains, subject to the permission of the Council, in the shares of unlisted public and private companies. The USM was therefore designed as a separate, distinct market within the Stock Exchange, standing between official listing, on the one hand, and the restricted dealing facility of Rule 4.2 on the other. The rules governing USM entry were contained in the 'Green Book'.

Entry to the USM required a three-year profit record, reduced to two in 1993, and a capitalisation of £7 million. The detail and expense of the prospectus required was less than that required for the official list market.

To encourage privately owned companies to go public without losing control, only 10 per cent of the issued capital had to be in public hands.

There is a significant advantage in being on the USM compared to a full listing insofar as continuing obligations are concerned. The requirements for circulating shareholders with information are not as stringent on the USM as on the official market. Under a full listing a company is obliged to send a circular to its shareholders in the event that it makes an acquisition or disposal, where the profits or assets acquired or disposed of are greater than 15 per cent of its own profits or assets. Where such profits or assets are greater than 25 per cent, the company must obtain its shareholders' approval for the transaction. In the case of USM companies the level at which a circular must be sent to shareholders is 25 per cent and not 15 per cent, and there is no specific obligation to obtain shareholders' approval if a transaction is above a certain size.

A USM company, however, must notify the Stock Exchange where the above test shows a figure of 100 per cent or more, and it is felt that in these circumstances the Stock Exchange would generally require the transaction to be conditional on shareholders' approval.

The USM is a most versatile market in that it can accommodate quite small companies and ones with a large market capitalisation, such as Fyffes PLC, valued in excess of £350 million in early 1995.

In 1980, the first year of the USM, some twenty-three companies joined. This grew to one hundred and three in 1988, when £308 million in new equity was raised. However, by 1992 the USM was virtually defunct, with only seven new issues.

In Ireland only sixteen companies were members of the USM in 1995. A review of the USM by the Exchange in London concluded that there was very little future for the market. Consequently, it was decided to close it as of December 1995. Companies on the USM were offered an easy passage to a full listing. Those not taking the option would revert to a Rule 4.2 listing, i.e. trading on a matched bargain basis. It was expected that the Irish Exchange would follow the UK pattern.

Rule 4.2/Formerly the Third Market

This matched bargain market is designed to make it easier for companies to raise equity finance than would be the case if they had to meet the requirements of a USM quote. It is a follow-up to the initiative taken by the London Stock Exchange in providing an accessible marketplace with a suitable standard of investor protection for many of the shares which were being traded outside the Stock Exchange. The market is characterised by simplified, unexacting admission procedures, and disclosure requirements which, while formal, are not onerous.

Companies must have a stockbroking firm as a sponsor. Audited accounts and projections must be submitted to the Stock Exchange in time to permit adequate examination. Audited accounts cannot be qualified. Dealing will be carried out only in the open market. In other words no after hours dealings. In addition the Stock Exchange will make it clear that the companies listed under Rule 4.2 are not officially listed on the Exchange and are not subject to scrutiny by the quotations department of the Stock Exchange.

Investors in companies traded on a matched bargain basis should be appraised of the nature and extent of the risk which they are accepting in making such investments. Broker dealers are, however, required under the new financial services regime to demonstrate that any investment is a suitable investment for the individual client for whom it is purchased and be able to show a customer agreement letter in which Rule 4.2 stocks are explicitly mentioned before they may recommend or, if they have discretion, buy such stocks for a client. The Stock Exchange for its part has specified the wording of a 'risk warning' for inclusion in advertisements, circulars and contract notes.

All investors in Rule 4.2 stocks enjoy the full protection of the Stock Exchange Compensation Fund. This is designed to meet costs suffered by investors as a consequence of any failure of a member firm of the Stock Exchange.

In the early 1990s there was rapid growth in Rule 4.2 listed companies. Two UK stockbroking firms, Winterflood's and John Jenkins, made a market in over 700 such companies, ranging from the well-known — such as Tottenham Hotspur — to high risk exploration companies — such as African Gold.

Smaller Companies Market (SCM)

This is available only in Ireland. In March 1986 the ISE, in response to the government's concern about the limited flow of Irish private funds into small Irish companies, set up a new market called the Smaller Companies Market. It was specifically designed to attract:

(a) Existing small Irish companies whose shareholders require a market quotation for their shares and the facility of disposing of all or part of their holdings.

(b) Small growth-oriented companies wishing to finance their expansion through additional equity capital and reduce their reliance on borrowings.

(c) Companies approved for grant aid by the Industrial Development Authority.

(d) Companies approved under the Business Expansion Scheme.

Entry requirements are less onerous than for the Unlisted Securities Market (USM) and on the other hand there is less regulation by the ISE. There is a greater reliance on the professional advisors to the company to ensure compliance with legal stipulations.

Provided a company has a sufficient spread of shareholders to enable a market to operate, has a trading record of at least one year and has the support of a sponsor (stockbroker/bank) then application can be made for quotation on the SCM. Costs are kept to a minimum by this way of entry. If there is a marketing operation — that is, if an SCM entrant wants to raise capital through the issue of securities to the public — it must produce a prospectus which will need an accountant's report, in compliance with the Companies Acts 1963 to 1986.

The principal ongoing disclosure requirement for a company on the SCM is to disclose to the ISE any information necessary to enable shareholders to appraise the trading and financial position of the company and to avoid the establishment of a false market in the securities of the company.

In 1987 eight companies went public on the SCM. These were: Sportsfield Equipment, Castletown Press, Oglesby and Butler, Superwood Holdings, Sunday Tribune, Classic Thoroughbred, Printech International and Reflex Investments. It was expected that a continuous stream of companies would come to this market. This did not happen and today just four companies remain.

A significant advantage of the SCM is the range of taxation reliefs which can apply to companies quoted on that market. Companies benefiting from the reliefs given to investment in certain corporate trades, commonly known as Business Expansion Scheme companies, and in research and development, retain those advantages on the SCM.

In addition ownership of shares quoted on the SCM gives the shareholders a considerable advantage in terms of any capital gains tax payable on the sale of the shares. There is some doubt as to whether institutional investors would be interested in acquiring shares in companies listed on the SCM, due to the lack of regulation compared to the USM or official list, the likely size of the companies involved, lack of liquidity, and investment rules in relation to certain investors.

Exploration Securities Market

In the 1970s and 1980s over twenty mineral and oil exploration companies were formed in Ireland. These companies had virtually none of the requirements necessary to get a listing on any market — no revenue, no track record and little capital. It was agreed that such companies could be listed under special dispensation. Each company had to find a stockbroker to act as sponsor, produce a document listing essential particulars and agree to abide by the rules which applied to the former third market.

By the end of 1994 mergers and takeovers had reduced the number of companies to twelve. In September 1994 the first new listing in three years, Petroceltic, joined the market.

Table 8.3 gives an indication of the capital raised by each method in the early 1990s.

Table 8.3 Funds Raised on the Irish Stock Market				
Money Raised: By Market (£m)	**1992**	**1991**	**1990**	**1989**
Government Funds (Net)	(685.0)	582.5	529.0	234.0
Other Official List	192.6	473.0	648.7	576.8
Unlisted Securities Market	29.5	20.6	79.5	88.4
Exploration Securities Market	10.3	9.57	5.1	10.4
Smaller Companies Market	1.2	1.06	2.2	5.0
	(451.4)	1,086.7	1,264.5	914.6
Money Raised: Method (£m)	**1992**	**1991**	**1990**	**1989**
Options	10.4	8.2	56.8	31.0
Placing	132.2	156.2	109.4	96.1
Acquisition/Vendor Consideration	51.2	37.4	105.2	99.3
Offer	14.6	197.1	157.3	70.7
Rights Issues	25.2	105.4	306.8	383.6
	233.6	504.2	735.5	680.6

DEALING ON THE EXCHANGE

For over 200 years dealing on the Exchange followed a fixed pattern. A year was divided into twenty-three accounts, each of two weeks' working duration, and two three-week accounts. The account began on a Monday morning and ended the following Friday week. During the long history of the Exchange a number of unusual and indeed rare practices grew up, many of which derived from the slow communications of earlier times.

The traditional procedure for dealing on the London Stock Exchange was as follows:

(1) An investor, having read an article on North Sea Oil, decided to buy some shares in British Petroleum (BP). He telephoned his stockbroker on a Tuesday morning, discussed the potential of BP and finally decided to buy 500 shares. The price of BP at the close of business on the previous day was £2.40 per share. The investor was willing to pay up to £2.50 for each share.

(2) His stockbroker telephoned the order to a partner who was working in the Stock Exchange, that is, he was 'trading on the floor'.

(3) The partner would go to the section of the Exchange where the oil jobbers were. He would approach a jobber and state 'BP'. The jobber would answer '240–260'. Since the price at which the jobber would sell was outside the investor's limits the stockbroker had to do one of three things: go to another jobber seeking other quotations; challenge the jobber by offering £2.50 for shares in BP; ask the jobber to reconsider his quotes.

(4) The stockbroker decided to move to another jobber, who quoted '240–250'. The stockbroker struck a 'bargain' for 500 BP shares at £2.50 each. He then transmitted the information to his home office.

(5) Within forty-eight hours the investor received a contract note which informed him of the purchase, gave the total sum due and the date of settlement — that is, the day on which the jobber must be paid. Additional information on the note related to stamp duty, commission, the date of the bargain and the type of share bought.

(6) Should the investor have decided to sell his BP shares before the end of the account he could have done so without paying any additional commission and without having to pay the stamp duty. Assume, for example, that the price of BP went to £3.10 in the week following the original purchase. The investor might have decided to sell at £3.10, thus realising £1,550. Since his purchase price was £1,250 for the shares plus £20.63 commission for a total of £1,270.63, the profit for the venture was £279.37.

(7) For those holding onto their shares the next important day was Ticket Day. Ticket Day was the Wednesday following the end of the account. On Ticket Day the process of linking the original seller and the final buyer began. The buying broker issued a name ticket to the jobber from whom he bought the shares. The name ticket gave the full name and address of the buyer, and the name and number of shares bought. From the jobber, it was sent to the seller's broker. If the shares had been dealt in more than once during the account, it would pass through several hands before reaching the seller's broker. From the same ticket, the selling broker then prepared a transfer form, giving the name and address of his client and the buyer, and the details of the shares sold.

(8) On the Monday week following the end of the account, Settlement Day was reached. On Settlement Day, cash changed hands, as did share certificates and share transfer forms. The share certificate was then sent to the registration department of BP. The company registrar in time issued a new certificate in the buyer's name.

Figure 8.4 gives a visual description of the workings of the old Stock Exchange account system.

The development of communications technology meant that brokers did not need to have a presence in a physical market. Screen-based trading has become the norm. Now every broker can check on his computer screen the buy/sell prices and the dealing quantities for every stock listed on the market. By direct telephone line he too can deal in it. The computer system which tracks the stocks is called TOPIC. Dealers also provide a 'Newstrack' service.

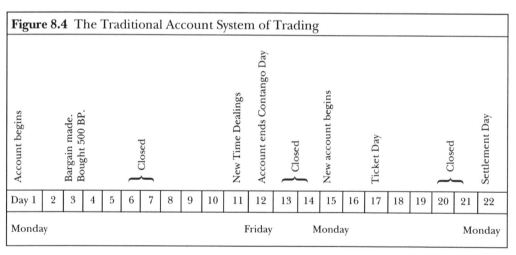

Figure 8.4 The Traditional Account System of Trading

Two unusual items appear in Figure 8.4, *Contango Day* and *New Time Dealings*. Contango Day was the day on which buyers could persuade sellers to postpone seeking payment for a further account period. If the seller agreed, the buyer received a further twenty-two days' credit — that is, until the next Settlement Day. Contango was the fee charged by the seller to the buyer. It was a rate of interest usually higher than that charged on overdrafts. In certain circumstances the seller could not deliver the shares to the buyer and asked for a postponement. If this were granted, the buyer was paid a fee known as backwardation.

New Time Dealings were transactions completed for the new account during the last two days of the old account. Buyers using new time dealings effectively got an extra fourteen days' credit. They paid a charge, often one penny extra per share, for this privilege.

The trading system changed in July 1994 with the introduction of the 'rolling settlement' for share transactions. The primary reason for change was to shorten the period between dealing and settlement and reduce the risk of investors' defaulting on their transactions. All transactions were due for settlement ten business days after dealing. What this in effect means is that every business day has become a Settlement Day. In July 1995 the settlement time was reduced to five business days.

Thus, stockbrokers or other professional advisors now work within a five-day trading period, unless other terms are agreed. Therefore all paperwork, payments, etc. must be implemented within the period. It is unlikely that private investors will benefit greatly from the new change.

The new system has some disadvantages. These include the need for tighter control on the administrative aspects of share transactions. In the past investors had two or three weeks to look after the administrative side of things. Under the new system, they will have only five days to complete their deals. While investors could previously trade within the account and have up to three weeks before parting with any money, the new system places a greater burden on cash flow in that each deal must be completed.

Investors who are worried about possible cash flow problems may be able to agree an arrangement with their stockbroker including terms that allow them up to sixty days to repay their broker for dealings carried out on their behalf. This type of arrangement is called margin trading. For the investor who is particularly active in the market, the best course of action is to ask his stockbroker to set up a special settlement account which tracks his trades. This sort of account will eliminate some of the administration work.

The increased burden of administration should reduce the risk of investors running up losses on their accounts. In addition the fact that every day will now be Settlement Day eliminates the excess buying at the end of an account which could often be a characteristic of the old system.

It is important to note that the investor is not involved in the complicated dealing pattern outlined above. He simply gives the order to the stockbroker and pays cash within five days.

The principal impact of the new rolling settlement method of Stock Exchange dealings is the elimination of speculation within the account. This may mean the end of the ability to avoid paying for purchases by paying a contango.

However, speculation is at the heart of Stock Exchange dealings. Arrangements can be made to borrow stock if a speculator has sold stock which he cannot deliver on Settlement Day. The price for this facility is essentially the same as backwardation.

Dealing on the Irish Stock Exchange
Dealing in Dublin follows the same system as in London, the only difference being that

there is little market making in Dublin. There would be insufficient business to support big market makers since there are fewer than 200 quoted securities in Dublin compared to 9,000 plus in London.

The ten stockbroking firms in Ireland make up a broker-to-broker market. They are Davy, BCP, Bloxham, Riada, NCB, Campbell O'Connor, Butler and Briscoe, MMI, Goodbody and W. & R. Morrogh. Once an Irish stockbroker receives an order to buy an Irish share he will attempt to find a seller. Stockbrokers in Ireland operate in two ways.

(1) They meet twice daily in Dublin to fix prices. At these meetings each security is called out by name. If there are buyers and sellers, attempts are made to match, buy and sell orders. If a deal is struck the price is marked on a large board which contains the names of all of the securities with Irish quotations. It is expected that this ancient method of marking deals will disappear in coming years.

(2) Outside the Exchange, stockbrokers are in constant contact, attempting to match, buy and sell orders. If a deal is done outside the Exchange it is marked in the Exchange at the next meeting of brokers. This system uses computers to give instant dealing information to brokers.

Using modern technology, the Irish Stock Exchange operates in a similar fashion to the London Exchange. If an Irish investor wishes to purchase shares quoted in London he can do so through Irish stockbrokers, who will approach a market maker on the floor of the London Exchange. Irish brokers operate open telephone lines to brokers in London.

STOCK EXCHANGE INVESTMENT THROUGH A FUND

To invest in the Stock Exchange, an individual can either buy shares in selected companies or buy into funds which hold numerous shares and are managed by professionals, i.e. managed funds. For example, Irish Life manages over sixty unit-linked funds, some of which are in cash and property but most of which are in equities. Through these funds an investor can gain exposure to stock markets all over the world and practise some degree of risk management through portfolio diversification. In order to cater for this process the industry has been subdivided into headings such as cautiously managed, managed growth and aggressively managed funds.

Significant innovation has taken place in this area over the years as companies compete for new business. The tracker bond was developed for the small investor who wants to combine a capital guarantee with a risk-proof opportunity to cash in on equity gains. Irish Life pioneered this investment vehicle in 1990 and in late 1993 launched its seventh tracker product, called World Investment Bond II. This bond tracks the performance of four equity markets — Europe, the US, the UK and Japan. Features include a capital guarantee (less a 3 per cent entry charge) and 100 per cent of the average growth in these four markets. The proceeds will be free of capital gains tax, income tax and deposit interest retention tax (DIRT) and are totally confidential. There are some downsides that need to be considered, such as the facts that lump sum funds are committed for the full investment period, i.e. three to five years, no dividend payments accrue to the individual and it is not usual to have any income stream. A number of other financial institutions have launched similar investment products.

Further innovation in this area included the introduction of Special Investment Accounts (SIAs). These were introduced in an attempt 'to level the playing field' as regards the advantages given to the banks in relation to Special Savings Accounts (SSAs).

These accounts incur DIRT at 15 per cent instead of the standard 27 per cent and have a maximum investment ceiling of £50,000 or £100,000 for a married couple. The SIA must place at least 40 per cent of the investor's funds in Irish equities in the first year rising to 55 per cent by year five. Part of this sum, rising to a maximum of 15 per cent after five years, must be invested in smaller companies with a market capitalisation of under £100 million. Investment in BES companies attracts a further incentive in that the 10 per cent tax charge will not apply to dividends or gains on such shares. The introduction of these accounts was an attempt to encourage equity investment in Irish industry on a somewhat similar basis as unit-linked funds.

TYPES OF SECURITY LISTED ON THE STOCK EXCHANGE — IRISH
The range of securities quoted in Ireland is as follows:

— Government Bonds
— Corporation, Semi-State and Transport Bonds
— Undertakings for Collective Investment in Transferable Securities (UCITS)
— Ordinary Shares
— Preference Shares
— Industrial and Financial Bonds

Government Bonds
These are divided between Government Funds and Land Bonds. They are securities issued by the government and represent its borrowings from the public to meet capital expenditure on such items as roads, hospitals and defence. They are gilt-edged securities with no risks attached. They bear a fixed rate of interest guaranteed by the government, and in most cases are repayable at their face value on some future date.

Corporation, Semi-State and Transport Bonds
These are identical to government bonds except that they are indirectly guaranteed by the state. They are gilt-edged securities and are generally used to finance major capital investment projects. The principal borrowers include the Dublin and Cork Corporations, Córas Iompair Éireann and the Electricity Supply Board.

Undertakings for Collective Investment in Transferable Securities (UCITS)
A number of EU Directives and Regulations were issued and passed in the 1980s. One of these provided for the free transfer of capital between member states. Investment trusts established in one member state could market their securities in and accept investment from other member states.

Over eighty investment trusts have established in Ireland and had their shares listed on the Dublin Exchange. To do this they needed to be licensed by the Central Bank, have an Irish trustee — often the Bank of Ireland — and a local management company.

The real effect on Ireland and Irish investors is minimal. The country receives income in the form of fees but there is little or no trading by Irish investors in the shares.

Figure 8.5 gives a selection of the funds listed in 1994 together with the managers and trustees.

Figure 8.5 Undertakings for Collective Investment in Transferable Securities (UCITS)

Fund	Manager	Trustee
UBZ Euro-Optimizer Fund	AIG Fund Management Ltd	Investment Bank of Ireland Ltd
GAM Universal D.Mark Fund	GAM Fund Management Ltd	Chase Manhattan Bank (Ireland) PLC
High Life Fund	AIG Fund Management Ltd	Investment Bank of Ireland Ltd
Summit Investment Funds PLC	EBS Asset Managers Ltd	ABN AMRO Bank NV
Scottish Value Portfolio Fund	Scottish Value Management (Ireland) Ltd	Chemical Ireland Custody and Trustee Services Ltd
Federated International Funds PLC	Federated International Management Ltd	Ulster Bank Custodial Services
UBZ Liquidity Fund — Deutschmark	AIG Fund Management Ltd	The Governor and Company of the Bank of Ireland

Ordinary Shares

The holders of these shares are the owners of the company. All remaining profits, after loan interest and preference dividends are paid, belong to these ordinary shareholders. However, it is both customary and prudent to provide for the replacement of existing assets and future expansion (purchase of new assets) and so companies tend to retain some of the profits that in theory the ordinary shareholders can claim in full. Those profits not retained are then distributed to the ordinary shareholders in the form of dividends. Dividends on ordinary shares can fluctuate in line with profits; sometimes dividends are not paid in bad times. Ordinary shares, while carrying the greatest risks, also hold the best prospects of future growth, particularly as regards capital appreciation: that is, an increase in the market price of the share. The market price of ordinary shares is determined not so much by past results as by expected future results.

Shares in the best companies are known as 'blue chip'. This denotes low risk and stable earnings.

There are two quite distinct markets in Dublin, one in government stocks and the other in ordinary shares. The gilt market is by far the more important, accounting for around 80 per cent of the total market value. The person who makes the market in government stocks is the Government Broker (GB). He works for the Department of Finance and the Central Bank, buying and selling gilts.

In theory the market happens in this way. In the morning the gilt dealers, who work for the stockbroking firms, take a market overview. They look at money market interest rates, international rates, foreign exchange rates and other factors such as political issues which could affect a market. Having done this they take a position on the market and then ring their customers — who are mainly the pension funds — and advise them on a course of action. When the funds work out what they should do they give a sell or buy order to the gilt dealers, who in turn go to the GB and offer to buy or sell stock. Depending on the amounts of stock to be dealt with, the GB can make a rapid or a very slow decision on what he plans to do. The decision can take up to two hours to be reached. These decisions have to be made twice a day and the system is known as 'call over'.

As can be seen, it is a slow and inefficient system and one with which many if not all of the principal players are dissatisfied. Fund managers are often left not knowing what direction the market is going. It is also very unsatisfactory for those concerned with interest rate directions since the yields on the various government stocks determine, to an extent, the money market rates or at least mirror them. Money market rates can move around if the GB effectively does not want to deal, while for days on end the yield on the gilts does not move at all.

It is estimated that the gilt market in Ireland is worth roughly £14 billion. This pales when compared with the size of the British gilt market, which is worth well over £100 billion. The number of players in the market is also very small, with only ten main institutions making up the bulk of the market and three of those, Irish Life, AIB and the Bank of Ireland, accounting for over 40 per cent of the market.

There are four leading stockbroking firms in the gilt market. Figures are never released but it is estimated that there would not be a huge difference between Davy's, Riada, NCB and Goodbody. Davy's is owned by Bank of Ireland, Riada is owned by a Dutch bank (ABN), NCB is owned by the Ulster Bank while Goodbody is a subsidiary of AIB.

The National Treasury Management Agency (NTMA), which is responsible for the management of the national debt, has for about four years wanted to make a radical change in the way gilts are traded. The NTMA wants brokers to facilitate those who wish to buy and sell gilts by operating a 'market making' system rather than merely matching buyers and sellers as they do at the moment. The NTMA believes that such a system would make our gilts more attractive to foreigners and save money as they could be offered at lower interest rates. The Competition Authority, which is supporting the NTMA position, adds that it is unrealistic to continue the current risk-free commission system in the face of international trends and efficient operation. The Irish Stock Exchange, brokers and fund managers are opposed to the proposed change, saying it is too risky and could backfire due to the small number of potential players in the market. Foreign institutions would have to be licensed to enter the market, they add, and this would transfer profits and jobs abroad.

In predicting what might happen it is worth looking at the UK experience. A similar change was introduced in the UK in 1986. Within two years the twenty-nine brokers who applied to operate in the new environment had lost stg£190 million between them. It was four years before they started to make a profit, by which time one-third of them had pulled out. Irish brokers are unlikely to suffer the same fate because their numbers are so few that the competition will not be as intense.

Right now Ireland has £14 billion worth of loans or IOUs in the hands of banks, insurance companies, pension funds and other investors. Around 27 per cent of those are in the hands of foreign investors and at the moment any new issue is taken up almost entirely by foreigners.

The IOUs are issued by the NTMA, which is entrusted with borrowing as cheaply as possible the money the government needs to make up the shortfall between its spending and its tax revenue (the Exchequer borrowing requirement). Hundreds of years ago state IOUs came in the form of a certificate with a gilt or gold edge, hence the name 'gilts'. Around half of the government's gilts are due for redemption in less than five years, 40 per cent in five to fifteen years and 10 per cent in more than fifteen years. The interest rates they bear range from 6.25 per cent to 14.75 per cent.

The vast majority of those who buy gilts have no intention of holding them to maturity but are looking to make a profit in the secondary market. If they believe that, once bought, Irish gilts will be more difficult to sell than, say, German or UK gilts, the Irish stock will be less popular and will need to offer a higher interest rate to persuade investors to buy.

That is the crux of the argument. The NTMA argues that Irish gilts are difficult to sell because the Stock Exchange's rules prevent a highly active market from developing. Only brokers who are members of the Exchange, and subject to its rules, have quick access to the necessary information on which gilts are for sale or are in demand and at what prices. But the Exchange's rules prevent brokers from ever owning gilts themselves. As a result, an investor who wants to deal must wait until a broker has found a buyer or seller on the other side. The broker will charge a commission ranging from 0.013 per cent to 0.52 per cent of the deal. For most gilts, the commission is fixed by the Stock Exchange so brokers cannot compete on price.

Under a market making system, however, an investor can ring the broker and ask him to quote a price at which the broker himself will buy and sell a specified amount of a certain gilt. The investor can instantly agree to buy or sell and the broker is obliged to accept. For the investor, there is no waiting around. If the broker has sold gilts that he doesn't have, he must then buy them in the market and to make a profit must do so at a lower price. If he can't, he will have to buy at a higher price and will lose money.

The rules prevent the 'spread', the difference between the price quoted for buying and for selling, from being too high. Thus, the broker cannot avoid doing any deal by both quoting a buying price which is unacceptably low and a selling price which is unacceptably high. So, market making is a risky game which requires a shrewd reading of the markets. Under the system, those who are prepared to take the risk would be licensed and only they could make markets.

According to the NTMA, the present system slows down the market and means Ireland has to offer higher interest rates on its gilts. Now that almost all new Irish gilts are bought by foreigners, our gilts are increasingly competing for buyers with those of other countries. The NTMA argues that without the Stock Exchange's ban, a market making system would inevitably develop. It says the ban is there purely to prevent this, because the Exchange is controlled by brokers who don't want the present risk-free system disturbed. It also says that without commissions, Irish gilts would be less costly for investors.

The Stock Exchange, however, has responded that in reality only the brokers owned by large banks would have the money to take the risk of market making, and that because of the smaller number of players, gilts could actually be more difficult to trade under the new system.

Market makers in gilts are expected by the end of 1995.

STOCK EXCHANGE CYCLES

The period 1955–79 was not good to the Stock Exchange. Rampant inflation proved disastrous for investors. For generations it was believed that share prices were a hedge against inflation. The 1960s and 1970s demonstrated otherwise. Private investors became disenchanted with low returns and moved their funds to other areas, such as property, art and stamps. Gradually, the large institutional investors, like pension funds, insurance companies and unit trusts, came to dominate the market (Table 8.6). Such investors had income with the prospect of some capital gain as their objective and so they concentrated on low risk, blue chip shares and government loans. Towards the end of the 1970s life began to reappear in Stock Exchanges. Many shares were simply cheap. They had good earnings or alternatively high assets. Inflation during the 1970s made many companies asset-rich. Shrewd investors found it cheaper to buy rather than build: that is, it was cheaper to take over an existing business than to build a new one from scratch. New terminology evolved to define unacceptable bidders as 'grey knights', rapid takeovers as 'Saturday night specials' and acceptable purchasers as 'white knights'.

Table 8.6 Share Ownership on the Stock Exchange

Sector of Beneficial Owner	% Distribution by Sector						
	1963	1969	1975	1981	1989	1990	1992
Individuals and Unincorporated Businesses	54.0	47.4	37.5	28.2	20.8	20.5	20.0
Non-Profit-Making Bodies	2.1	2.1	2.3	2.2	2.1	1.6	2.2
Public Sector	1.5	2.6	3.6	3.0	2.0	2.0	1.2
Banks	1.3	1.7	0.7	0.3	0.7	0.7	0.2
Insurance Companies	10.0	12.2	15.9	20.5	18.5	20.4	20.7
Pension Funds	6.4	9.0	16.8	26.7	30.5	31.4	31.1
Unit Trusts	1.3	2.9	4.1	3.6	5.9	6.1	5.7
Other Financial Institutions	11.3	10.1	10.5	6.8	3.1	2.7	2.8
Industrial and Commercial Companies	5.1	5.4	3.0	5.1	3.8	2.8	3.3
Overseas	7.0	6.6	5.6	3.6	12.7	11.8	12.8
	100	100	100	100	100	100	100

Source: Fact Book London Stock Exchange 1993.

The Irish Stock Exchange experienced a pattern of evolution similar to that experienced in the United Kingdom and the United States.

The 'Great Bull Market' began in 1982 and lasted for over five years — a record length of time for a bull market. Substantial rises in share prices took place in each of the years 1982–6. The US Dow Jones Index rose by 350 per cent in this period. The *Financial Times* Index did even better, rising over four times. The good times also visited Ireland. The few shares available, exchange restrictions and increasing institutional cash inflows combined to produce a strongly rising market. This despite a weak and declining economic performance in the country.

As happens in most bull markets, prosperity led to growing confidence. Confidence fed on itself to produce euphoria. In 1987 world-wide stock markets boomed at a rapid rate. Despite the huge rises of the previous five years the markets grew by a further 40 per cent between January and October 1987. Fundamental values and negative economic signals were ignored. Markets operated on the 'Greater Fool Theory' — that is, that there would always be a buyer available at even higher prices.

Certain companies' share prices were selling at values which anticipated almost impossible outcomes. Gold mining shares were selling at up to 100 years' earnings though the companies had gold reserves for only twenty years. The expectation was of a swiftly rising gold price.

Blue chip companies such as Smurfit were selling on dividend yields of 1 per cent thus anticipating high rises in capital values.

When the fall came it was unique in the level of severity. 'Meltdown Monday' or 'Black Monday' in the United States, 19 October 1987, saw 25 per cent of the entire value of Wall Street wiped out in one day. This compares with 12 per cent on the worst day of the 1929 crash. Around the world panic replaced euphoria. Almost without exception Stock Exchanges crashed by 40 per cent and more in the last three months of 1987.

The greatest bull market of the twentieth century crashed in the greatest fall in the long history of Exchanges. Overnight, pessimism replaced confidence and fears of a substantial recession in the United States economy became a reality in 1988. World stock markets entered a bear market phase where weak rallies in share prices were snuffed out by precipitous falls. After 'Meltdown Monday' subsequent peaks were below previous highs while lows plumbed new depths. By 1988 a classic bear market was in progress.

In Ireland the crash occurred on Tuesday, 20 October 1987 as the real panic hit Wall Street late on Monday after the Irish Exchange had closed. Many people, knowing from late news on Monday that their wealth would evaporate before their eyes on Tuesday morning, did not sleep well.

The opening of the Dublin market was anti-climactic. There were almost no buyers. For many shares there were no buyers in the succeeding weeks and even months. When a price was finally struck in most cases it was a fraction of the price prior to 19 October. The few blue chip shares in Dublin did trade at prices up to 20 per cent below their previous night's closing.

This bear market resulted in a fall of up to 25 per cent in the value of the Irish market by the end of 1988 and this pattern continued until a new low was reached in October 1992. By that stage the market was stripped of any worthwhile investor confidence. Interest rates were at an all-time high, the currency crisis arising out of sterling's exit from the ERM and other international factors was in full flow and the introduction of 15 per cent DIRT SSA accounts had accounted for any liquidity in the savings market.

By early 1993 a new bull market was well under way all over the world. The principal causes were

— a reduction in inflation rates to levels not seen since the 1960s
— rapidly declining interest rates
— evidence that the basic economy in many countries was ready to expand.

Bond prices were the first to rise as lower interest rates meant that the high coupons on debt issued by governments in preceding years now appeared attractive. Following the rise in bonds, prices of blue chip shares rose as did those benefiting from lower interest rates, e.g. property companies, and/or higher consumer spending, e.g. supermarkets. 1994 saw a slowdown in the bull run, as inflation fears returned and interest rates rose once more. During early 1995 the US and UK markets raced ahead to new all-time highs. Experienced investors thought this to be the first leg of the 1993 bull market.

The bull market was slower to take off in Dublin but low interest rates on savings combined with other factors to lead to a sharp rise, with gains of up to 70 per cent on the index achieved by the end of 1993. A big disappointment was the failure of any new company to come to the market during that time. In fact seven names vanished from the list, through a combination of mergers and acquisitions and in one case a receivership. In 1994 Irish Permanent became the first full listing in years and Petroceltic joined the

Exploration sector. Overall in 1994 share prices marked time despite a strong performance in the domestic economy. During the first half of 1995 blue chip stocks began to move in Dublin but the upward trend was weak and lagged behind those in the US and UK.

The outlook for the remainder of the decade is cautiously optimistic. In charting the way forward an understanding of how the market has reached a healthy state in 1995 is important. Firstly, the portfolio diversification by Irish fund managers abroad which contributed to the domestic bear market of 1990–92 came to a natural end. Secondly, the punt devaluation in early 1993 focused the attention of international investors on Irish equities and their clear undervaluation. Thirdly, Ireland's entry into the Morgan Stanley Capital International indices attracted index-based funds from overseas. Fourthly, after a gap of several years, earnings growth resumed for several leading Irish companies, such as the banks and CRH. Finally, the rerating of Irish shares and equities in general on the back of a structural decline in inflation and the sharp fall in Irish long bond yields has been the most significant factor.

The new low inflation environment of the 1990s has been brought about by a number of factors, including the effects of too much 1980s debt, increased labour market flexibility, corporate restructuring, plant overcapacity and greater global competition. It is possible to be optimistic about the future valuation of the Irish market as future liquidity flows should favour equities and not gilts.

SPECULATION

At the beginning of the nineteenth century a French observer of Stock Exchange movements categorised buying and selling activity into the following cycle.

Period	*Relevance to Recent Stock Exchange Activity*
Quiescence	— 1975–9
Confidence	— 1980–81
Prosperity	— 1982–6
Euphoria	— 1987
Convulsion	— 19 October 1987
Panic	— October 1987–Early 1988
Quiescence	— Early 1988–Late 1991
Confidence (Slow-burning)	— 1992–1994
Prosperity	— 1995–

Every share price represents hope — a price is the present value of the sum of all future expectations. In good times hopes are high, in bad times expectations are low, hence the large swings in share prices between 'bull' and 'bear' phases.

The 1988–91 bear market ceased when the panic and forced selling was over and investors refused to sell because they believed the prices to be too low.

Ever since time began people have speculated. They have been prepared to invest capital in the hope that their reading of the situation is better than that of the market as a whole.

The Stock Exchange is a good medium of speculation. Speculators on the Stock Exchange are referred to by different names, depending on the nature of their speculative activities. The major types of speculator are bulls, bears, stags and pigs. Lame ducks also exist.

Bulls

A bull is a speculator who buys now, expecting an immediate increase in price. Bulls buy shares in the hope that they will quickly rise in price so that they can be sold at a profit.

Bears

A bear is a speculator who sells shares he does not own, anticipating that he can buy them at a lower price before he has to pay for them. If such a fall does not materialise, the bear either buys at a higher price and suffers a loss, or settles with the help of a broker who lends him shares to complete the deal he has made with the original buyer. The speculator pays a fee called 'backwardation' for this service.

Stags

A stag is a speculator who applies for a large quantity of a new issue expecting that the initial price of the share when quoted on the Stock Exchange will be higher than the issue price. He can then sell his shares at a profit.

Prior to the 1970s a successful stagging operation was easier, as new issues often required only part-payment on application and allotment. Now, however, almost all new issues require payment in full on application. Irish issues of recent times have tended to be oversubscribed, causing the initial Stock Exchange price quotation to be in excess of the issue price. The stag's problem, then, is to be allotted enough shares. Stagging declined in the mid-1970s but recently it has reappeared in the United Kingdom. In general, new share issues are priced to cause a premium when quotation begins so the stag is usually successful.

Pigs

A legendary United States speculator was once asked to account for his great success. 'I always bought and sold at the wrong time,' he declared. The pig is a speculator who does not know when to take a profit. He is determined to make every last penny, forgetting that speculative changes in share prices are volatile and can easily reverse themselves. Stock Exchange lore has a saying, 'Pigs never make profit.'

Lame Ducks

A 'lame duck' is one who cannot meet his commitments. One early account of the London Stock Exchange recalls how in 1787 on one account day, 'twenty-five lame ducks waddled out of the Alley' — that is, the location of the exchange. A lame duck is a very rare bird on the modern Exchange though rampant speculation in oil stocks in the 1980s produced a small number.

OPTIONS

A sophisticated form of speculation is by means of options. These are rights to buy, sell or buy/sell at previously agreed prices.

An option is a contract between a buyer, known as a 'holder', and a seller, known as a 'writer'. Options may be of three types: call options, put options or put and call options.

A call option entitles the buyer to purchase shares from the writer at a fixed price called the 'striking' price. The buyer of a call option expects the price to rise. The price paid for this right is known as an 'option premium'. It is usually a price per share.

A put option is a right to sell a certain share at an agreed price. The purchaser of a put option expects the price of the share to fall.

Sometimes, an individual expects a swing in the price of a share though he is unsure of the direction. For example, an investor expects that the price of Aran Energy will be subject to a heavy movement up or down depending on the results of exploration drilling. In such a situation one buys the right either to buy or sell the shares at an agreed striking price. This is a 'put and call' option or 'double' option.

Options are normally for periods of three months. At any time during the ninety-day period the option can be exercised. Options are expensive; a price of 10 per cent for each put or call and 20 per cent for a double is normal. An option is a way of gearing up or levering one's investment while at the same time hedging one's risk. An example will illustrate.

An investor with £3,000 is interested in purchasing shares in Blue Sky PLC. He can purchase 3,000 shares at £1 each or he can:

Buy £3,000 worth of options giving him the right to buy 30,000 Blue Sky shares at £1 each for an option price of 10p each share.

$$\text{That is } \frac{£3,000}{10 \text{ pence}} = 30,000 \text{ shares}$$

Assume that the share stands at £1.20 at the end of the option period. The option that the investor paid £3,000 for is now worth £6,000, i.e. the investor can buy 30,000 shares at £1 each and sell them at £1.20 each. The investor in options has a profit of £3,000.

A more conservative investor might simply use the £3,000 to buy 3,000 shares at £1 each. After he sells them for £3,600, i.e. 3,000 × £1.20, he has a profit of £600. If the price of the above rises to £1.10 then the option holder makes no profit while the direct investment in the shares makes £300.

After a tentative introduction in 1980 Option Trading has grown dramatically on the Exchange. It is now possible to write options on many shares for periods of three, six and nine months.

FUTURES

A recent development is the growth of 'futures'. A future is simply a bet on a price at a future date. While futures trading has become one of the largest sectors of financial activity, there has been only a small impact on Stock Exchanges. Most futures cover expected trends in interest rates and currencies. Such contracts are traded on special exchanges. In Ireland IFOX — the Irish Futures and Options Exchange — opened in the late 1980s.

The main futures product applicable to the exchange is an index future, i.e. a three-month contract setting out the expected level of a Stock Exchange index.

UNDERSTANDING THE FINANCIAL PAGES OF THE NEWSPAPERS

Movements on the Stock Exchange have long held a fascination for the ordinary man in the street. Newspapers and periodicals report trends in share prices in great detail. In Ireland the morning newspapers carry at least one full page of financial news, much of which is devoted to activity on the Stock Exchange. In addition the national dailies carry occasional reviews of quoted companies. The papers also give the current market prices and provide information which will assist investors in deciding whether a share is a worthwhile investment. There is a lot of jargon used and it is helpful to understand the basic words and phrases. Set out below are explanations of some of the most commonly used terms.

(a) Earnings per share.
(b) Earnings yield.
(c) Price earnings or P/E ratio.
(d) Dividend yield.
(e) Dividend cover.
(f) Ex and cum dividend.
(g) NAV
(h) Redemption yield.
(i) Blue chips or 'first line' shares.
(j) 'The Index'.

Earnings Per Share (EPS)

This is the annual profit (earnings) of the business divided by the number of shares outstanding. It is that portion of the annual profit attributable to one share. In 1994 Grafton Group PLC had a pre-tax profit of £4.1 million, a tax rate of 21.1 per cent and 15.6 million shares issued. The EPS was 20.7 pence per share.

Earnings Yield

This is the earnings per share divided by the current market price. For example, in early 1995 Grafton Group PLC had earnings per share of 20.7 pence and a then price per share in the market of 365 pence. The earnings yield is as follows:

$$\text{Earnings yield} = \frac{20.7}{365} = 5.7\%$$

This percentage figure is a rough measure of the return on the investment: that is, every 365-pence investment earned profits of 20.7 pence. This yield is an historical yield in that it divides the present market price into the reported profits of the company. Remember that profits are reported months after the end of the financial year, so it is possible that major changes in earnings will have taken place. Goodbody stockbrokers in 1994 forecast that Grafton would earn £7.2 million the coming year or 34.2 pence per share.

Price/Earnings Ratio

This widely used measure of investment worth is defined as follows:

$$\text{P/E Ratio} = \frac{\text{Market Price of the Share}}{\text{Earnings Per Share}}$$

This represents the period of time required to recover the purchase price assuming that earnings per share remain constant. It is the inverse of the earnings yield.

In the case of Grafton the ratio was:

$$\frac{\text{Market Price}}{\text{Earnings Per Share}} = \frac{365}{20.7} = 17.6$$

The P/E ratios for all shares quoted in Dublin are published in newspapers each Monday morning. An investor can cast his eye along the list, picking out anomalies. In 1994 the average P/E ratio was between 11 and 15, so Grafton was rated above the average because a large increase in profits was anticipated.

Dividend Yield

Typically, a company pays out a proportion of its profits to the shareholders. The cash payout is known as a dividend. The dividend yield is defined as follows:

$$\frac{\text{Dividend Per Share}}{\text{Market Price Per Share}}$$

In 1994 Grafton paid a gross dividend of 9.7 pence on each share. Therefore the dividend yield for Grafton was:

$$\frac{9.7}{365} = 2.66\%$$

Comparative P/E Ratio and Dividend Yields are shown in Table 8.7.

Table 8.7 Comparative Price Earnings Ratios and Dividend Yields in the Period 1972–1994

	P/E Ratio				Dividend Yield (%)			
	Current	High	Low	Average	Current	High	Low	Average
US	19.2	22.8	6.7	12.4	2.61	6.79	2.24	4.09
Japan	57.3	71.0	12.6	32.2	0.82	3.12	0.44	1.44
Germany	24.6	25.0	7.8	12.2	1.74	4.98	1.52	2.94
France	21.0	30.8	5.7	11.4	2.76	9.17	2.05	4.38
Netherlands	16.1	16.6	3.8	9.2	3.20	8.51	3.15	5.15
UK	19.2	20.1	3.1	11.9	3.55	11.93	2.89	4.97
Ireland	25.1	25.1	4.4	10.1	2.73	11.41	2.29	5.12

Source: Goodbody Stock Investment Strategy 1994, p. 61.

Dividend Cover

Total profits are rarely paid out as dividends because the directors usually decide to retain some to assist investment. The 'cover' is the relationship of earnings to dividends. In the case of Grafton the cover is as follows:

$$\frac{\text{Earnings Per Share}}{\text{Dividends Per Share}} = \frac{20.7}{9.7} = 2.13$$

A high cover means that the dividend can continue to be paid even if earnings drop. It may also mean that there are many investment opportunities open to the business so there is the possibility of rapid growth in future earnings. A cover of less than 1 means that the business is paying dividends out of reserves.

Ex and Cum Dividend

Shares which are sold with the right to collect an imminent dividend are sold 'Cum Div'. If the seller retains the right to the dividend the shares are sold 'Ex Div'. In theory the share price should reflect the value of the dividend.

NAV = Net Asset Value

This is the total assets of the company at the last Balance Sheet date less all loans and creditors, divided by the number of issued shares. The Grafton NAV in mid-1994 was 231 pence per share — compared to a 365 pence per share price on the markets. Investors were prepared to pay more than the asset value per share to buy the flow of earnings and dividends.

Redemption Yield

This measure applies to loan stocks. Loan stocks are repaid or redeemed at some future date. Usually, the market price differs from the repayment or redemption price. Therefore an investor obtains the right not only to the interest payments but to the premium or discount on redemption. Loans are rarely priced above the redemption price but they are frequently at a major discount. For example, in late 1994 an ESB loan paying 8.25 per cent annual interest and repaying £100 per unit of stock, in 2003 could be purchased at £89.90. The redemption yield is the annual earnings yield plus the capital profit. This equals:

$$\frac{8.25 \times 100}{89.9} + \frac{10.1\%}{9 \text{ years}}$$

$$= 9.18\% + 1.12\%$$

$$= 10.3\%$$

where

$$
\begin{aligned}
8.25 &= \text{annual interest} \\
100 &= \text{issue and redemption price} \\
89.90 &= \text{market price October 1994} \\
10.10 &= \text{discount between market and redemption price} \\
9 &= \text{length of time in years until redemption}
\end{aligned}
$$

This overestimates the redemption yield because £100 in five years' time will have less value than £100 now. The exact formula for redemption yield is

$$\text{Redemption Yield} = \text{Flat Yield} + \left(\frac{[RP - MP] \frac{r}{100}}{\left[1 + \frac{r}{100} \right]^n - 1} \right) \%$$

where

$$
\begin{aligned}
RP &= \text{redemption price} \\
MP &= \text{market price} \\
r &= \text{annual interest rate} \\
n &= \text{number of years to redemption} \\
\text{Flat Yield} &= \frac{\text{annual interest rate}}{\text{current market price}}
\end{aligned}
$$

Luckily, stockbrokers issue daily lists of the redemption yields on loan stocks so it is rarely necessary to work out the above formula.

Blue Chips

Blue chips are the strongest and most reputable shares on the market. These are shares with a history of top-class financial performance. In Dublin shares such as AIB, Bank of Ireland, CRH and Smurfit's rank as blue chip. Such shares are also known as first line shares in that they are the first to rise at the outset of a bull market.

Second line shares are regarded as being of a lower quality in that they may have less stable earnings patterns, be in a poorer-quality industry, have suspect management or simply be relatively unknown or closely held, thus providing a poor market in the shares. At the opposite end of the spectrum from blue chip are blue-sky shares. These are highly speculative issues where there is no pattern of earnings or management. Small speculative exploration stocks epitomise this term.

The Index

There are a number of Stock Exchange indices in use. In the United States the Dow Jones index is the most important while in the United Kingdom movements in the *Financial Times* index are carefully monitored. In Ireland *The Irish Times* and *Irish Independent* each produces an index.

The Dow Jones index is composed of thirty blue chip shares. Every company in the index is valued at the number of shares times the market price per share. The index is the arithmetic average of the sum of the market value of all shares in the index. A change in a share price will change the total and thus change the index.

The two Irish indices were developed in the mid-1970s. Each is an aggregate index, which means that it is the sum of the market value of all quoted shares. In theory the movements of an index reflect general investor sentiment. An upward movement suggests more buyers than sellers while a downward trend suggests an excess of sellers.

A glossary of Stock Exchange terms is presented in the final section of this chapter.

PORTFOLIO SELECTION

Ultimately, an investor must decide what shares and loan stocks to purchase. The combination of shares purchased is known as a 'portfolio'. An investor selects a portfolio of shares whose risk, expected income and expected capital gains best meet his needs. This apparently simple statement is fraught with complexity. Every investor dreams of shares such as Poseidon, which in 1968 rose from 50 pence to £139 in one year, or Eglinton (now Aminex), an Irish oil exploration stock which in the early 1970s rose from 20 pence to £12.70. Attaching to the Poseidons of this world is a huge risk. Many investors, while seeking the return, will not understand the risk. In fact investors in Poseidon and Aminex saw the share price crash back to virtually nothing. Investors have different preferences and needs; some want little risk of loss, others want income, while others wish to speculate in the hope of significant capital gain. Determining the mix of shares that an investor should purchase is known as portfolio composition or selection. A simple approach to the problem involves two steps: (a) decide on investment objectives; (b) select shares to meet the objectives.

Investment Objectives

Investors' objectives can be broken into four categories: (a) straight income; (b) mainly income and some capital gain; (c) mainly capital gain and some income; (d) capital gain. The length of time an investor is willing to invest funds is also part of the policy. Examples of investors at either end of the investment spectrum would be a retired couple with school-going children and a capital sum to invest. Compare this to a wealthy individual paying the top rate of income tax seeking to speculate a sum which he can easily afford to lose. The chief determinant is the degree of risk which the investor is willing to take.

Selecting Shares to Meet Objectives

Once the objectives are known, a portfolio of shares must be selected and a decision made on how much to invest in each. The retired investor seeking secure income might look no further than government loans. The wealthy speculator might split his investment between exploration shares such as Aran Energy and Kenmare Resources, recovering companies such as Seafield, and maybe a takeover prospect such as Heiton's.

Not surprisingly, a great deal of research has gone into portfolio selection. A body of principles called portfolio theory now exists. Much of the seminal work was done by Harry Markowitz, who developed a model of investor behaviour. Markowitz assumed that investors sought the highest return at the lowest possible risk. His model became known as the Mean-Variance Portfolio Composition Model. Those interested in pursuing the topic are referred to the reading list at the end of this chapter.

At a more basic level a number of steps can assist an investor in selecting a portfolio which meets his objectives. Such an investor should:

(a) Identify objectives in investing and select a strategy to fit the objectives.
(b) Decide on industries and/or business sectors with risk profiles suited to the objectives.
(c) Gather information on the industries, trends over time, relationship to the economy, structure, competitive advantages, future threats or opportunities.
(d) Examine the companies in each sector to identify those likely to perform in a way most suited to the objective of the portfolio.
(e) Analyse the past performance of the company using the tools and techniques presented above and those in Chapter 3.
(f) Identify the availability and marketability of shares in selected companies.
(g) Discuss potential purchases with a stockbroker.
(h) Purchase shares in round figure lots.
(i) Monitor the performance of the portfolio on a regular basis.

The following is a simple summary of portfolio selection.

Object	*Portfolio Strategy*
Major requirement, income with no risk.	Invest in government bonds.
Income a requirement but want some opportunity for capital appreciation.	Mixture of gilt-edged bonds and blue chip shares.
Want investment to keep up with inflation.	Blue chip shares assuming a medium-term investment period.
Capital appreciation more important than income, willing to take some risk.	Mixture of first and second line securities.
Want high returns, willing to take high risk.	Look for speculative shares.

CONCLUSION

For hundreds of years the Stock Exchange has played two vital roles in economic development: it provides access to capital to entrepreneurs, who are the creators of wealth, and it provides a means whereby holders of assets can liquidate their investments to obtain cash.

The level and direction of trading on the Exchange are among the most important leading economic indicators available. If investors are buying in numbers then they expect the future to be better than the past, if they are selling then the economic future may be clouded.

GLOSSARY OF STOCK EXCHANGE TERMS

This is only a partial list of frequently used terms.

Account Day
This was the day on which payment was made, or received, for business done in the previous account. It was normally the Monday of the week following the end of the account. The account ceased to exist in July 1994 and was replaced by rolling settlement.

Allotment Letter
A person who applies for a new issue of shares is informed by allotment letter of the number of shares which he has been allotted.

Application Form
This is a special form on which application for share issues must be made. The forms are printed in the daily press and are available from stockbrokers and banks.

Backwardation
A bear who cannot deliver shares which he has sold can postpone delivery by borrowing shares to deliver. The fee paid to borrow the shares is known as backwardation.

Bargain
Any transaction on the Stock Exchange.

Bear
A person who has sold shares which he does not own, in the hope of buying the shares at a lower price before he has to deliver them.

Bearer Shares
Shares which have no central register. Whoever holds the share certificate owns the shares. Such issues of shares have almost died out.

Big Bang
September 1986, when deregulation was introduced to the Stock Exchange. The principal effect was the replacement of jobbers by market makers.

Blue Chips
Top-quality shares, usually in large stable industrial or financial firms. Irish blue chips include Bank of Ireland, CRH, Allied Irish Banks and Smurfit's.

Broker
An intermediary who matches buyers and sellers.

Bull
A person who buys shares, hoping to sell them at a profit before he has to pay for them.

Call

Certain shares are only partly paid up. Demands by the company for some or all of the unpaid amount is a 'call'. There are no partly paid shares on the Irish Stock Exchange.

Call Option

The right to buy a share at an agreed price for an agreed period.

Capitalisation Issue

Where a company has reserves of undistributed profit, it may capitalise part or all of the reserves by issuing additional shares to existing shareholders. This is also known as a Scrip or Bonus Issue.

Commission

The fee charged by a stockbroker. It is also known as 'brokerage'. There is a flat fee for small transactions, often £20. Thereafter a rate of 1 to 1.5 per cent is common.

Consideration

The price paid to purchase shares exclusive of commission and stamp duty.

Contango

This was the price paid by a bull to postpone paying for shares which he had bought. The contango was a rate of interest charged to 'carry over' the deal for one account.

Contango Day

The last day of the old account.

Coupon Rate

The annual interest rate on debentures.

Cover

This is the ratio of the earnings to the dividend paid. The higher the cover the more conservative the dividend policy.

Cum Dividend

A share is cum dividend when the price paid includes the dividend which is due. Shares may also be 'cum capitalisation' or 'cum rights'.

Debenture

Loan stock issued to the public.

Discount

Occasionally, shares, when they are first quoted on the Exchange, are priced lower than the issue price. The difference between the issue price and the market price is the discount.

Dividend

The amount of profit paid to shareholders. Usually, dividends are declared as a percentage of the par (face) value of the share.

Ex Dividend

A share may be bought without the right to receive a dividend which is due to be paid. In such cases the seller receives the dividends.

Ex Rights

New shares may be issued to existing shareholders at a preferential price. When the new shares arc issued the old shares become 'ex rights', which means that the price adjusts downwards to take account of the new shares.

Gilt
An IOU issued by the government and 'bought' by an investor who earns interest by lending the money.

Interim Dividend
Many companies pay two dividends each year: an 'interim' and a 'final'. The dividend must be approved by the shareholders at the Annual General Meeting.

Issue of Shares
This term covers the mechanism of moving new shares from the company to the new owners.

Jobber
Jobbers made a market in certain shares. They were called share wholesalers in that they never dealt with the final customers but only with stockbrokers.

Letter of Indemnity
Share certificates get lost. Before issuing new certificates the company must be indemnified by the shareholder against any legal claims. Banks and/or insurance companies may have to sign the indemnity.

Letter of Regret
Applicants who are not allotted shares in an issue are sent a 'letter of regret'.

Limit
This is the price above which a stockbroker cannot buy for a client or below which he cannot sell.

Mark
This is the price at which a bargain was completed. It is the price quoted in the papers for shares dealt in on the Stock Exchange — Irish.

Market Guide Prices
A set of 'bid' and 'offer' prices for shares quoted on the Stock Exchange — Irish. Some prices may be out of date.

Market Makers
Stockbroking firms which offer to buy or sell certain shares at published prices.

Middle Price
London share prices quoted in British newspapers are usually the mid-price between the bid and offer price of two market makers.

Nominal Value
The par value of a share.

Offer
This is the price at which a market maker offers to sell shares. In Ireland it is the price at which a stockbroker is willing to sell.

Option
A right to do business with a broker at an agreed price for an agreed period in an agreed share.

Passed
If a company decides to miss a dividend payment it is said to have 'passed the dividend'.

Pig
Someone who holds on to make the last few pence profit on a share. Often the market turns and the pig loses.

Pink Slips

In new issues certain individuals are offered preference in buying the shares. The application form issued to preferential buyers is coloured pink.

Premium

New issues whose first quoted price is above the issue price are quoted at a premium. Issues are priced to open at a 'premium'.

Price/Earnings Ratio (P/E)

This is the ratio of the current market price to existing earnings per share (EPS).

Put Option

A right to sell a share at an agreed price for an agreed period.

Put and Call

An option to buy or sell at an agreed price for an agreed period. This is also known as a 'double option'.

Put Through

A stockbroker may be able to match buy and sell orders among his own clients. He announces the deal on his screen. It is known as a put through. It is noted in the papers with a small 'p' after the price.

Redemption

The repayment of a loan.

Redemption Yield

Government bonds which are redeemed at par often sell at a discount. The redemption yield is the rate of interest received on purchasing the bond plus the additional payment received by holding on until the bond is redeemed divided by the number of years to redemption.

Rights

Existing shareholders may be offered the right to subscribe for new shares. Rights issues rarely affect the control of the company. Shareholders not wishing to subscribe for new shares can sell the rights.

Rolling Settlement

Under rolling settlement the account period ceased. Every business day is now a Settlement Day, with transactions due for completion five days after the transaction was dealt.

Secondary Market

A subsequent sale of a security by the investor to another investor for a higher or lower price than it originally cost.

Securities

An American name for bonds and shares quoted on a Stock Exchange.

Squeeze

Sometimes investors realise that bears will have to buy stock to meet their commitments. In such cases prices rise and the bears are 'squeezed' as they have to pay the price to acquire the necessary shares.

Stag

New issues are a source of speculation to individuals who apply for shares hoping to sell them to individuals who want the shares but were unlucky in the allotment.

Stale Bull
A person who has bought shares expecting a price rise which has not occurred.

Stamp Duty
Payable at the rate of 1.00 per cent on the transfer of shares.

Stock
Historically, money was raised by issuing stocks in lots of £100. Stock could be sold in fractions. Now all issues are of shares, and 'stock' is interchangeable with 'shares'.

Stock Exchange Official List
This is a daily listing of every share on the Exchange. It includes details of dividends, the ex-dividend date and the date of dividend payment.

Tap
A sale by the government of new stock of an existing gilt.

Turn
The difference between the bid and offer price. The larger the turn, the greater the uncertainty about the market for the share.

Underwriter
A bank which agrees to buy any shares not purchased by the public. There is a fee for this service.

Warrant
Cheques sent to shareholders in payment of dividends are known as 'dividend warrants'.

XD
An abbreviated form of 'ex dividend'.

Yield
This may be the earnings per share divided by the market price of the share, which is the earnings yield, or the dividend per share divided by market price, which is the dividend yield.

FURTHER READING
Business and Finance, weekly journal.
Investor's Chronicle, weekly journal.
Business Week, weekly journal.
The Economist, weekly journal.
The Irish Stock Market Annual, J. D. O'Neill Dublin, annual.
B. Grey, *Beginner's Guide to Investment* (London, Century Business Press, 1991).
J. Andrew, *How to Understand the Financial Press,* 2nd ed. (London, Kogan Page, 1993).
The Stock Exchange, *Facts and Figures 1994* (London).
M. Brelb, *How to Read the Financial Pages* (London, Hutchinson, 1991).
S. Lofthouse, *Equity Investment Management* (John Wiley & Sons, 1994).

QUESTIONS
Question 8.1
What is the function of the Stock Exchange?

Question 8.2
Explain the stock market terms 'bull' and 'bear'.

Question 8.3
What are the advantages and disadvantages of 'going public'?

Question 8.4
What types of market were there on the Stock Exchange before and after 'Meltdown Monday' on 19 October 1987? Briefly describe them.

Question 8.5
Describe the type of market set up for companies unable to apply for a full listing.

Question 8.6
How would an investor go about selecting a portfolio of shares?

9

Short-Term Sources of Finance

The introduction to this text defined one function of the financial manager as that of fund raiser. This requires having the right type of money in the right place at the right time. It is easier said than done. Money can be raised in many different ways, from overnight funds which must be repaid within twelve hours to permanent finance. In this and following chapters many different sources of finance will be examined. Each source affects a business in three distinct ways — risk, income and control.

Every source of finance has a risk attaching to it. The *risk* is that the business will not be capable of meeting the financial commitments relating to the source. A business generally uses a multiplicity of sources. The total risk of the mix of capital sources is known as the 'financial' risk of the business. The financial risk is very different from the commercial or business risk of the enterprise. The business risk relates to the possibility that the commodities produced by the venture will result in losses. The financial risk is the risk arising from a mismatch, often deliberate, between the sources of funds and the uses to which such funds are put. Chapter 14 examines this area in more detail.

The *income* effect of financial sources relates to the cost of funds. Each source of finance has a cost attaching to it. Reducing the cost of funds should increase the income of the owners. Examples of the income effect include the cost of accounts payable, which have no explicit cost but are included in the supplier's price, government grants, which appear costless but may have to be repaid given certain conditions, and raising new equity by an issue of shares on which dividends may have to be paid during the lifetime of the business. Note that using one particular source may affect the cost of others, i.e. using too much debt may increase the cost of equity.

The *control* effect of financial sources refers to the possibility of new sources of finance affecting management or ownership control. New shares usually have voting rights, thus diluting the control of each existing share. Loans often have covenants which restrict the activities of management in areas such as dividends and directors' salaries. Bank overdrafts normally require collateral, which restricts the freedom of management to sell the assets.

It is the job of the financial manager to provide the required finance at minimum risk and loss of control while at the same time maximising the income to the owners. The task is exceptionally difficult if for no other reason than the wide range of financial sources on offer. Table 9.1 provides a listing of the major sources of finance available to Irish business. It should be noted that not all sources are available to every business. As a rule of thumb, the larger the business the greater the number of sources which tend to be available.

This chapter covers the many short-term sources of capital available to Irish business. Smaller businesses tend to make extensive, and often excessive, use of short-term funds. Chapter 10 examines medium-term sources of finance. Two medium-term sources, leasing and term loans, are highly developed in Ireland. Chapter 11 extends the analysis of funds into long-term sources.

Table 9.1 Sources of Finance

	Short-Term Period Up to 1 Year	*Medium-Term* 1–7 Years	*Long-Term* Longer than 7 Years
			Debt Capital
Sources	1. Trade Credit	1. Leasing	1. Mortgage/Debentures, Bonds
	2. Accrued Expenses and Deferred Income	2. Hire Purchase	2. Sale and Leaseback
		3. Term Loans	3. Section 84 Loans
	3. Taxation		4. Project Financing
	4. Bills of Exchange		
	5. Acceptance Credits		**Ownership Capital**
	6. Commercial Paper		1. Preference Share Capital
	7. Bank Overdraft/Short-Term Loan		2. Ordinary (Equity) Share Capital
	8. Inventory Financing		3. Retained Earnings
	9. Accounts Receivable Loans		
	10. Factoring		**Capital Grants**
	11. Confirming		
	12. Insurance Premium Loans		

Uses	Seasonal Fluctuations
	    in Trade
		Plant and
		Equipment
			Fixed Assets such as
			    Buildings

As Irish business grows and develops, greater use is being made of sophisticated forms of long-term financing. The thorny problem of ownership funds is tackled in Chapter 12. Giving away control to obtain money is always difficult, never more so than in small firms. In recent years in Ireland a number of 'seed' capital and 'venture' capital sources have appeared. The role of the state in providing financial assistance is highlighted in Chapter 13 which deals with the range of capital grants available.

Short-term financing can be categorised as spontaneous or negotiated.

SPONTANEOUS SOURCES OF FINANCE
Spontaneous sources of finance refer to those sources which arise through the normal course of business. They are also known as 'non-negotiated' in that the user as a rule has to do nothing to obtain the use of the funds. They are also 'self-adjusting' in that when the business expands, sources such as trade credit or payables tend to increase; conversely, when sales decline, payables tend also to decline. These sources are

unsecured and are generally 'free' insofar as no interest is charged for their use.

The three principal spontaneous sources of finance are (1) trade credit, (2) accrued expenses and (3) taxation.

1. Trade Credit (Accounts Payable)

Trade credit arises spontaneously with the firm's purchases. A firm sends a purchase order to a supplier who then evaluates the firm's creditworthiness, using various sources of information and decision criteria. If the supplier decides to extend credit, the goods ordered are shipped and the accompanying invoice describes the contents of the shipment, the total amount due and the terms and conditions of sale. When the purchaser accepts the goods, he is committed to pay the amount due as specified by the terms of sale on the invoice.

Trade credit has two main advantages:

(a) It is available to almost all buyers who purchase on a regular basis — once it has been established it becomes almost automatic and is subject to only periodic reviews.

(b) Most trade credit is made on 'open book' and is not secured by a pledge of any specific asset as collateral.

The importance of trade credit can be seen from an examination of the accounts payable figure on a Balance Sheet. Studies have found that trade credit accounted for as much as 15 per cent of all sources of finance. The very existence of many small firms often depends upon the availability of trade credit. In general very large firms tend to be net suppliers of credit and small firms net receivers. Note that the accounts of Ardmore (Chapter 2) show a heavy reliance on this source of finance.

At first glance trade credit appears to be a free source of finance but obviously someone has to bear the cost. In granting credit the supplier incurs the cost of the funds invested, plus the cost of any cash discounts that are taken. Normally, the supplier passes on all or part of these costs to its customers implicitly as part of the price, depending on market supply and demand conditions. Chapter 5 looked at trade credit from the viewpoint of the issuer. The cost of giving cash discounts was examined. The analysis applies equally well to not taking cash discounts offered on purchases. The trade terms 2/10 net 30 mean in theory that a company gets a 2 per cent discount for paying within ten days; otherwise the full amount is due in thirty days. The company not taking the discount loses 2 per cent for twenty days' use of the money. This is an annual interest rate of 36.5 per cent. However, few people observe the normal credit terms. If a company, instead of paying after thirty days, waits until eighty days have elapsed, the cost of foregoing the discount is,

$$2\% \times \frac{365}{70} = 10.4\%$$

The figure of an eighty-day average credit period is supported by a 1994 study of European terms of credit taken (Figure 9.2), as well as by the Irish study cited earlier (see Chapter 5).

This may be an attractive rate of interest. Two general rules apply:
- (a) always take advantage of the full discount period.
- (b) forego the cash discount only when the implicit cost of the trade credit is lower than alternative sources of short-term finance.

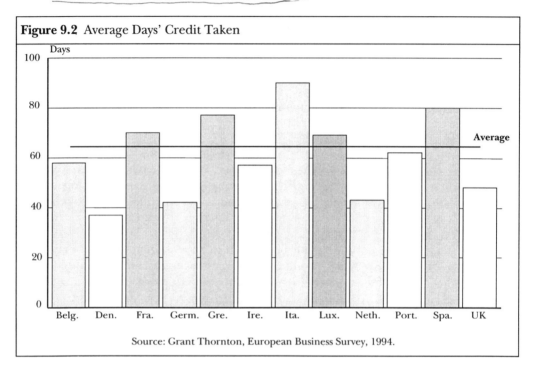

Figure 9.2 Average Days' Credit Taken

Source: Grant Thornton, European Business Survey, 1994.

Trade credit has another important characteristic. In times of crisis it can be 'stretched'. Very often suppliers will continue to supply goods though the payment record of the purchaser is disimproving. There are many reasons for this; it takes time for the payment record to filter through the suppliers' organisation, and suppliers usually want to hold customers and so are lenient. Trade credit can act as a 'buffer' in bad times. The practice of stretching accounts payable is known as 'leaning on the trade'.

It is commonly believed that the cost of trade credit is zero. Even where discounts do not exist trade credit may not be free. A slow-paying customer may be paying more for his goods than a cash- or fast-paying client. Apart from paying more it is possible that slow payers will be refused supplies or else made to pay cash. This latter requirement can have a traumatic effect on a business.

The amount of trade credit available to a firm depends on (a) the proportion of raw materials in the product, (b) the terms of credit offered by the supplier and (c) the payment policies of the purchaser. In addition variations in trade credit are very much in evidence due:
- to the nature of the commodity being sold, i.e. perishable or low shelf-life products carry short credit terms.
- to the risk of failure inherent in the industry, e.g. retail clothing outlets.
- to the nature of competition among suppliers, i.e. new entrants to the market trying

to gain a foothold or older firms trying to consolidate or increase their market share.

— to the financial strength of the supplier relative to that of the buyer and their dependency on each other for continuity of sales and profit.

— the cost and availability of bank credit. If money is cheap and available easier terms apply.

The objective of trade credit management should be to stretch the payment period as far as it can go without affecting the credit rating of the business.

2. Accrued Expenses and Deferred Income

The average business obtains services and inputs from a wide variety of sources. The expenses of these sources are usually paid in arrears and classified as accrued expenses. Wages are weekly in arrears, salaries monthly, electricity bi-monthly. These sources are spontaneous and costless if bills are paid when due. Though the sources are costless to the individual firms it is likely that the price of the service is higher because money is not received immediately. Consider the case of the Electricity Supply Board (ESB), providing power as and when required but not receiving payment for a number of weeks. While awaiting payment the ESB must pay its bills for gas, wages and other expenses. It must finance the period of credit by borrowing or by issuing new equity. Borrowing increases costs, which in turn are passed on to the customer in the form of higher power prices.

Accrued expenses are normally a small but useful source of finance.

Deferred income is an accepted practice in some industries whereby customers are required to make advance payments or deposits for goods and services to be delivered at a future date. These amounts increase the firm's liquidity and appear on the Balance Sheet as deferred income or customer advances/deposits. They have no explicit or implicit cost and in exceptional instances may be interest-bearing. In that case they are considered a negotiated source of finance.

3. Taxation

Taxation can be a very large spontaneous source of finance. Under current legislation businesses act as tax collectors for the state. The two principal taxes collected by business are Value Added Tax and income tax.

Value Added Tax (VAT) is charged on all invoices but is returned to the state only every two months. In fact the tax due is payable within nineteen days of the end of the two-month tax period. VAT can be a very important cash item, amounting to 21 per cent of an invoice. Should a business not remit the tax in the permitted time, it may be guilty of an offence and liable to interest on sums due. The lax credit policies of Irish business can cause havoc with VAT. VAT is payable on all invoices sent out on a two-month period — that includes invoices sent out on the last day of the period. Therefore, assuming that invoices are sent out on a regular basis over the period, the average time before VAT is due is one month plus nineteen days. The average period of credit taken in Ireland is longer than fifty days so it is likely that in many cases VAT is a use of finance rather than a source.

Income tax and Pay Related Social Insurance are other major cost items in business. The Pay As You Earn (PAYE) system of income tax requires a business to deduct tax from wages and salaries. This is then remitted to the Revenue Commissioners. Since 1979 social welfare contributions have been handled in a similar manner. Many businesses, particularly small firms, are slow in remitting payments to the state. This practice is illegal and unethical.

Corporation tax is yet another spontaneous source of finance, albeit for a very short time. The profits of a business are liable for tax, with the normal payment date being halfway through the accounting period. It should be noted that as a spontaneous source of finance corporation tax is very sensitive to any changes in the fortunes of a business and is further affected by the decision of the Minister for Finance to eliminate entirely the system of accelerated capital allowances. Arrears of taxation incur interest at a rate of 1.5 per cent per month. This interest is not tax-deductible.

Excise duties are a major factor in the sale price of alcoholic drink, tobacco and motor vehicles. For example, the excise duty on a twelve-bottle case of whiskey is £73.00. Excise duties can be paid forty-five days after the goods are removed from a bonded warehouse. If a seller can get paid cash or grant only a short period of credit then duties can be an important source of finance.

In reality most customers take more than forty-five days' credit so the vendor has to provide additional finance.

NEGOTIATED SOURCES OF FINANCE

4. Bills of Exchange

Not examined

A bill of exchange is an unconditional order in writing addressed by one person to another, signed by the person giving it, requiring the person to whom it is addressed to pay on demand or at an agreed future time a certain sum of money to, or to the order of, a specified person or to bearer. It is in effect a financial contract which enables the buyer with the agreement of the seller to delay payment, usually for a period of thirty, sixty, ninety or one hundred and eighty days. The buyer 'accepts' a bill of exchange by writing 'accepted' across it and by signing it. The seller can either hold the bill to maturity or he can discount it at a bank and get immediate cash. The bank will pay the face value of the bill less a rate of discount.

Bills of exchange are common in foreign trade but have virtually died out in domestic commerce. In the 1980s they made a short reappearance, mainly as 'trade bills': that is, an agreement between seller and buyer. An alternative form is a 'bank bill' where a bank issues a letter of credit to a buyer. This is discussed below under 'Acceptance Credits'.

The growth in trade bills in Ireland was partly a reflection of tight credit. By offering sellers bills of exchange, buyers were extending the period of credit which they would normally obtain from the seller. Often the seller was happy to obtain a bill, in that he had a fixed payment date and it was possible to discount the bill with a bank.

5. Acceptance Credits

Acceptance credits are a form of 'Bank Bill of Exchange'. A bank issues a letter of credit to a business. The management of the business can draw bills of exchange on the bank for specific amounts and specific periods. These bills can be discounted by another bank. The market for acceptance credits was, until recently, confined to big Irish firms and to the subsidiaries of overseas firms. Restrictions on other forms of bank credit led to a rapid expansion in acceptance credits.

Acceptance credits are an excellent supplement to other short-term sources of finance.

6. Commercial Paper

Large businesses often wish to borrow substantial sums for periods up to six months. Such companies have a variety of short-term sources open to them, including commercial paper. Commercial paper means the IOUs or promissory notes of big firms. These notes are sold in the money market. Sometimes other substantial businesses with excess liquid funds are the purchasers of these notes. The commercial paper market in Ireland evolved some years after an explosive growth in the United States market. There, many finance companies found it cheaper and easier to borrow direct from the money market than from the banks. The industrial banks are large users of the Irish commercial paper market. The advantages of commercial paper are: (a) an interest cost below overdraft rate; (b) a simple and cheap negotiating procedure; (c) the status and prestige connected with the ability to borrow by this method.

The main disadvantage of using commercial paper stems from the impersonal nature of the paper market. If a firm encounters financial difficulties and cannot redeem its paper, it will find it hard to get extensions of time from the investors who hold the firm's paper. Banks are more inclined to help the firm work things out in times of distress. The introduction of Deposit Interest Retention Tax caused a movement out of the interbank market into commercial paper. While the Finance Act of 1993 eliminated this tax on commercial deposits and introduced Special Savings Accounts for sums up to £50,000, commercial paper still offers many benefits to investors.

The two most common types of commercial paper are Government-Guaranteed Notes issued by semi-state bodies and Bank-Guaranteed Notes issued by major Irish companies. What are the main attractions of such notes for the parties involved? Top-quality issuers of notes can normally issue such paper at the Dublin Interbank Offered Rate (DIBOR) + 0.15 per cent whereas a term loan for a similar period could be as high as DIBOR + 1.0 per cent or more, a significant difference. Issuers can borrow cheaply in this way as a result of the growth in demand for commercial paper from depositors seeking to invest in a negotiable instrument and/or to avoid Deposit Interest Retention Tax (DIRT). Depositors are willing to accept lower returns to avoid DIRT, which causes cash flow problems for many companies as the tax is deducted at source. In cases where tax would otherwise not be payable, DIRT can reduce the overall return by 27 per cent if it is not recoverable.

While government-guaranteed paper has proven most popular with investors, many are now willing to accept the paper of other issuers, provided in most instances that the placing bank adds its name to the note by way of endorsement. Such bank guarantees are off balance sheet contingent liabilities and therefore require a lower capital allocation than the more traditional form of bank lending. This allows the bank to offer cheaper funding to the corporate borrower and a better return for the depositor while reducing pressure on the bank's scarce capital resources. The bank can achieve the same return on equity as a deposit/term loan structure although halving its margin, with the benefit being passed on to the borrower and lender. Merchant banks are the major providers of this form of commercial paper.

The principal products in this market are Note Issuance Facilities (NIFs) and Promissory Notes (PNs) and it is currently estimated to be of the order of £750 million. PNs comprise by far the bigger portion of the market.

The move towards commercial paper or 'securitisation of assets' as bankers convert illiquid loans into marketable securities has been a world-wide phenomenon. The advantage for the bankers was that it helped free up Balance Sheets and eased capital adequacy demands while it offered cheaper credit to borrowers. However, the banker continues to fulfil the role of the risk underwriter. While NIFs have been in the market for a number of years, the PNs really burst into life with the introduction of DIRT. At its simplest a PN is a DIRT-free instrument. A borrower arranges with his bank to issue a PN with a duration of up to six months. The banker then finds an investor who discounts the paper and through the bank remits the net proceeds to the issuer. On maturity the issuer pays the face value through the bank to the investor. Under taxation legislation in force in the mid-1990s discount does not equate with interest and hence the PN is DIRT-free.

The attraction of PNs for issuer, banker and investor is that all make money. The issuer raises cheaper finance, primarily through avoiding the RAC. The bank gets a spread between the issuer and investor. The investor, if it is a corporation, avoids paying DIRT up front, which would be the case if it had made a conventional deposit. For the pension fund an investment in a DIRT-free instrument is exceptionally attractive as it cannot reclaim any DIRT which it incurs on a conventional deposit; these funds are the first port of call for any bank with PNs to sell.

In the case of corporate investors in PNs the DIRT is merely delayed for a period between the time of the interest payment and the agreement of accounts with the Revenue Commissioners.

The main issuers of PNs are the state-sponsored bodies and the major Irish and multinational companies.

The growth in PNs, which are off balance sheet for the banks, has caused headaches for the regulatory authorities world-wide. In assessing a bank's capital adequacy the Central Bank of Ireland gives a weighting of 50 per cent to PNs, which of course adds to their appeal for the bank (that is, a margin of 0.25 per cent on a PN is the equivalent of 0.5 per cent on a conventional loan from a capital adequacy point of view, while no asset is created on the Balance Sheet).

7. Bank Overdraft/Short-Term Loan

Bank overdraft facilities are widely used by business. Though not as large a source of finance as trade credit, this source is more important in that many firms use the bank overdraft as their cash cushion — that is, if for some reason the firm is caught short of cash, it relies on bank overdraft to cover the situation. Bank overdraft facilities are intended to meet specific short-term capital needs. Ideally, banks prefer a STISL — a short-term inherently self-liquidating loan. An example of this is a retailer using his bank overdraft to finance stocks of Christmas toys. He should be in a position to repay the loan after Christmas.

The bank overdraft is a negotiated source of finance in that consultation with bank officials is necessary to gain sanction to use the facilities. Generally, a credit line is set: that is, an overdraft up to a fixed amount. Once the credit line is agreed the firm may borrow and repay money within that limit. This flexibility is one of the advantages of bank overdraft. Another advantage is that it tends to be one of the cheapest sources of finance available. Interest charges are usually tied to current interest rates; interest is charged only on the outstanding daily balance; furthermore, bank interest is an allowable charge against profits for tax purposes. A disadvantage of bank overdraft facilities is that they can be called in at any time.

In granting an overdraft banks often require security for the loan in the form of a mortgage or lien. This can be restrictive on business, particularly if the mortgage 'floats' over all of the assets: that is, every asset is part of the mortgage. The difficulty here is that management may not pledge any of its assets for further finance without first clearing the bank overdraft or renegotiating the security provisions. In many instances banks do not require the security of a mortgage but instead accept either formal or informal guarantees from management. Such practices undermine the concept of limited liability. This aspect of bank lending highlights the benefits of a sound relationship with local bank officials. If the bank knows the management of the firm, the history of the firm and has had previous dealings with the principals, it is inclined to look more favourably on requests for overdraft facilities. A sound relationship with a bank can be built in the following manner:

(1) By keeping the firm's bank accounts with one bank. In this way the bank can profitably use any of the firm's deposits and can build a case history of its 'financial record'.
(2) By supplying the bank with all pertinent information. This includes not only annual accounts but quarterly or other accounts, cash flow forecasts, marketing plans and staffing plans. By doing this a firm will provide the bank with the necessary information on which to base decisions. A bank will look favourably on a client who furnishes information showing that he has a logical objective in business and is planning and organising to attain this objective. It is advisable to present adverse reports along with optimistic reports as there is little advantage in attempting to hide what a good analyst will undoubtedly find. 'No surprises' should be the policy.
(3) By preparing and presenting well-thought-out proposals showing the reasons for the loans, the collateral offered and repayment schedules.

It has long been an article of faith among small businesses that the banks exact too high a collateral price for loans. A survey in the early 1990s (Table 9.3) showed that the security and collateral requirements in Ireland were similar to those in the US, UK and Canada.

Table 9.3 Collateral Requirements Sought or Pledged (% of respondents)				
	Ireland	UK	US	Canada
No Collateral/Security Sought	20	29	30	15
Business Collateral Required	36	24	34	34
Personal Collateral Required	19	26	12	16
Business and Personal Required	25	21	24	35
	100	100	100	100

Source: A. Foley and B. Griffith, 'Irish Banks and the Development of Small and Medium Sized Enterprises' in *The Irish Banking Review*, Autumn 1994, p. 35.

Historically, Irish firms have regarded the bank overdraft as a source of permanent capital. As long as the banks had surplus deposits requiring profitable outlets, they were content to have them invested. Theoretically, bank overdraft was, and is, recallable at short notice, but this feature has rarely been employed by banks. In recent years, as the Irish economy has expanded, demands on all sources of finance have increased. Banks have found their deposits insufficient to meet the total demands. The ability of banks to create credit became subject to government policy. In times of credit restrictions, where banks were expected to curb lending, they discovered that it was difficult, if not impossible, to call in bank overdrafts. This was due to the fact that the borrowers had invested short-term bank money in medium- and/or long-term assets. Had the banks insisted on being repaid, many firms would have been unable to comply with the demand and may have closed.

In order to bring discipline into bank lending and to relate investment opportunities both to the risk involved and to the money supply available, banks have replaced many overdrafts or parts of overdrafts by term loans. This approach requires firms to present to the banks a reasonable application for the provision of a loan. Among the requirements is a timetable of repayments. Bank loans are tailored to individual requirements as regards interest rates applied and repayment terms allowed. Where the term of borrowing exceeds seven years or cannot be determined, a custom-made loan account may be established.

The purpose of the revised approach is to avoid short-term bank deposits being invested in long-term business assets, with the result that the bank can recover only by foreclosing on the firm — something that no lender wishes to do. The replacement of the 'permanent' form of bank overdraft enables the banks to use their own scarce resources more efficiently while at the same time it forces the business to plan its financial requirements better. From this point of view, the change in bank policy appears beneficial to both sides, though many business people find that the cost of bank money has risen.

NEGOTIATING A BANK OVERDRAFT/SHORT-TERM LOAN

The most important source of bank overdrafts and short-term loans are the associated banks. In 1995 the associated banks had over £6 billion in loans to business. As lenders banks are mainly concerned with three factors: safety, suitability and profitability. A good financial manager should be aware of this and be able to address these issues as part of his application. In addition the financial manager in choosing a bank should appraise himself of its loan policy, in the interests of establishing an ongoing relationship. There are a number of other criteria to be considered in choosing a bank, such as size, specialisation, loyalty, general attitude towards risk, and other services which may be available.

Remember that a bank overdraft is meant to be a short-term loan. In practice banks require the borrower's account to be in credit for a period of thirty days in a year. In presenting a request for bank facilities borrowers should have a cash budget drawn up along lines similar to that developed for Ardmore in Chapter 4. A cash budget shows the peak needs of the firm and it is this maximum figure that the company should seek to borrow.

The rate of interest charged on a bank overdraft depends on the risk category of the borrowers. In 1995 the following were the categories used and the typical overdraft rates charged by the associated banks.

Table 9.4 Overdraft Rates Mid-1995	
Prime Rate	
AAA — Typical rates charged to large commercial borrowers for short-term borrowings	6.25%
AA Rate (Borrowers in industry and services)	10.45%
A Rate (Personal and small private companies)	11.5%

The amount of the overdraft facility may be called a 'line of credit'. The borrower may borrow up to this amount. It is important that borrowers stay within their agreed limits. If the overdraft limit is exceeded then 'penalty rates' are charged, as well as banking fees for referral and consultation. The penalty rates are high — upwards of 6 per cent above the overdraft rate.

The interest rates outlined above are those charged by the associated banks. All banks base their charges on the cost of money plus a premium.

8. Inventory Financing

Earlier chapters highlighted the importance of the investment in inventory. Irish firms often have high levels of raw materials, work in progress and finished goods. In theory inventory is a liquid asset and as such it is suitable as collateral for short-term loans. Inventory financing or 'stock loans' have recently become popular in Ireland. The lender examines the inventory and decides to provide loans up to a certain percentage of the market value of the inventory. The more marketable the inventory, the higher the percentage. An example in Ireland is the grain trade. Farmers sell their grain to merchants in September. These merchants dry and store the grain until the spring, when it is sold. Grain, with a fixed Common Market price, is a liquid asset and so certain Irish financial institutions will advance up to 80 per cent of the purchase price to the merchant.

On the other hand, there are items which are so specialised that there is little or no market for them. These items would not qualify for an inventory loan. The size of the loan as a percentage of the market value of inventory is decided by the bank on the basis of marketability and perishability. When accepting inventory as collateral, the lender is also concerned with its ability to control its use. This factor will determine the risk of loss to the lender if the borrower defaults on the loan.

Resale value is affected by the inventory's perishability, risk of obsolescence and marketability. Control is affected by the nature of the collateral agreement drawn up. The three methods of achieving lender control are floating liens, trust receipts and warehouse receipts.

A floating lien is where the lender has a general claim on all the borrower's inventory, both present and future. There is no administration expense because the lender does not monitor specific units of inventory. The borrowing firm maintains full control of the inventories and continues to sell and replace them as it sees fit. Obviously, this lack of control greatly dilutes the value of the security and the percentage funds advanced against the book value. This type of financing is restricted to commercial finance companies which have long experience in this specialised form of lending.

A trust receipt (chattel mortgage agreement) is a security agreement under which the lender has control over specific units of the inventory and retains legal title to the pledged inventory. All inventory items must be readily identifiable by serial number or code and can be sold only with the lender's consent. This type of agreement is costly to implement and is used only for major items of inventory, i.e. Cooley Distillery in financing immature whiskey maturing in numbered barrels.

A warehouse receipt agreement is where the inventory is placed under the lender's physical as well as legal possession. This overcomes the disadvantage of the trust receipt agreement where the goods remain in the hands of the borrower. The lender's control can be exercised by using an independent third party to manage the inventory on its premises (terminal warehouse agreement) or on the borrower's premises (field warehouse agreement). The third party will release the stored inventory only when authorised to do so by the lender. As the borrower repays the loan, the lender authorises the third party to release the appropriate amount of inventory held.

This type of agreement is expensive, as the services of the third party have to be paid for by the borrower. It is particularly useful for large bulky items and for firms which have built up significant inventories for sale. The disadvantage of the physical separation of the inventory from the borrower's premises under the terminal warehouse method can be overcome by using the field warehouse method. In this case the inventory is located in a fenced-off designated area of the borrower's warehouse and remains under the control of the independent third party.

An example of inventory financing is the whiskey business. Whiskey when distilled must be matured in bonded warehouses for up to five years. Few if any businesses could survive for five years without sales unless specialised financing were available. Luckily, whiskey has a ready market and an international price for a unit of stock is easily established. In addition Customs and Excise requirements mean that each unit must be recorded and then warehoused in a tightly controlled bonded warehouse. These characteristics mean that lenders are willing to advance money against the security of individual barrels of whiskey which are held under the control of the Customs and Excise authorities.

9. Accounts Receivable Loans

Frequently, a firm's receivables are among its most liquid assets. Consequently, they are considered by many lenders to be prime collateral for a secured loan. Upon default of the loan agreement, the lender has first claim on the pledged assets in addition to its claim as a general creditor of the firm. Offsetting these advantages are potential difficulties. The borrower may attempt to defraud the lender by pledging non-existent accounts. The recovery process in the event of insolvency may be hampered by counter-claims, and administration costs can be high.

Notwithstanding these drawbacks, many firms use accounts receivable as a short-term source of finance by either pledging their receivables or factoring them. This is done by means of a loan agreement whereby a bank or financial institution grants a short-term loan to the firm and holds the receivables as security. The firm collects the receivables itself and honours the conditions of the loan agreement. The borrower assumes the default risk, with the lender having recourse to him even if he is unable to collect the pledged receivables.

Because it is very difficult to assess the worth of accounts receivable, the loan is rarely for more than half the total book value. Where a borrower submits a list of debtors and the lender accepts only the best-quality accounts then the loan may go as high as 80 per cent of the face value of the accounts. Lenders are usually interested in only a few large accounts, as the monitoring cost on a collection of small accounts would be too high.

A development of accounts receivable financing is where a potential borrower submits individual invoices to a lender. If the customer is an acceptable risk, the lender will advance to the borrower up to 80 per cent of the face value of invoices. This is known as invoice discounting.

Invoice discounting has been designed to release funds tied up in debtors without running the risk of losing creditworthiness by having accounts paid directly to a factor. Using this facility involves an examination of the debtor's ledger. Once credit levels are agreed on selected accounts, all future sales invoices are assigned to the factor. An agreed proportion of the gross invoices is paid to the client firm. When the invoices are paid, the client passes the proceeds to the factor. This facility is aimed at companies which are growing, well managed, providing credit terms to customers and which can profitably deploy additional working capital finance. Ideally, they should have a minimum of five active customers with a reasonable spread without an overreliance on any one particular customer. Sales should be free from any future contractual obligations on the part of the company in relation to any individual sale.

The facility can be negotiated to apply to export sales on an open account basis. This eliminates the need for bills of exchange or letters of credit and provides automatic exchange risk cover and full protection against bad debts. It is an ideal service for exporters with no overseas staff.

The facility involves a cost similar to prevailing commercial finance interest rates on the funds drawn down by the company, and an administrative fee. An example is shown below.

TECHSTAFF LTD IS A FAST-GROWING SERVICE COMPANY DEALING WITH A RANGE OF NATIONAL COMPANIES. TURNOVER IS EXPECTED TO DOUBLE IN THREE YEARS TO £6.7 MILLION.

The company provides technical staff to industry (that is, labour hire). The nature of the business requires a sizeable workforce which is paid on a weekly or monthly basis, dependent on individual contracts, and which therefore calls heavily on the cash flow of the business.

Nevertheless, during years 1 and 2 the company showed considerable growth despite a competitive marketplace. A significant element in this achievement was the investment in a computer system to streamline the company's administrative functions. In a competitive market this had a positive effect on margins by reducing the cost of administration thereby allowing the handling of a greater volume of work, which ultimately meant offering a higher level of service while maintaining competitive prices.

The company's principal method of funding at this stage was a bank overdraft facility secured by a fixed and floating charge on the company's assets and the personal guarantees of the directors, together with periodic loans from the directors.

In order to strengthen the company's position and improve liquidity, under pressure due to the nature of the business, an approach was made to their bankers for an additional increase in facility. Despite support from the local bank manager, this request was turned down at regional level on the grounds of an insufficient asset base.

Reluctant to offer their own personal property as security, the directors were recommended to investigate the possibility of invoice discounting as a means of providing additional working capital, while allowing full control of the sale ledger to remain with the company.

Year three saw the commencement of an invoice discounting arrangement providing a 75 per cent prepayment facility. This allowed a reduction in the company's overdraft, the release of the directors' personal guarantees and a revolving facility geared to the turnover of the company, thus allowing a ready cash flow despite the company's obligation to pay its staff promptly.

Table 9.5

Financial Record (£'000)	Year 1	Year 2	Year 3
Sales	£3,491	£5,003	£6,704
Retained Profit (Loss)	69	80	244
Simplified Balance Sheet			
Current Assets:			
Debtors	583	808	320
Stock and WIP	56	93	116
Total Current Assets	639	901	436
Current Liabilities			
Overdraft	250	472	70
Creditors	349	501	357
Total Current Liabilities	599	973	427
Net Current Assets	40	(72)	9
Fixed Assets	174	366	560
Long-Term Liabilities	(75)	(75)	(106)
Net Assets	£139	£219	£463
Issued Share Capital	55	55	55
Profit & Loss a/c	84	164	408
Net Worth	£139	£219	£463

10. Factoring

This involves the outright sale of a firm's accounts receivable to a financial institution called a factor. The origins of modern factoring are rooted in the old colonial practice of using mercantile agents. Because of the risks, great distances and slow communications involved when dealing in colonial markets from the sixteenth century onwards, European producers would appoint such agents or factors to receive, sell, distribute and collect payment for their goods.

This method of doing business ensured that producers could sell their goods abroad without fear of non-payment. It developed strongly on the east coast of Northern America, especially in the textile, clothing and related industries. Factors gradually began not only to hold stocks and sell goods on behalf of principals, but to guarantee payment as *del credere* agents.

In time it was this role of guaranteeing payment for goods which began to supersede the factor's selling functions. In tandem with this change the burgeoning domestic cotton and textile trade of the United States was increasingly using factors to ensure payment for goods.

By the middle of this century factoring had matured to its modern state and in the 1960s it was imported to Ireland via textile-associated businesses.

Factoring is another method for reducing the investment of long-term funds in current assets. It generally involves a combination of provision of finance, insurance against bad debts, sales accounting service and a cash advance.

Factors offer four main services:

(a) They take over the debt collecting function of the client.
(b) They may offer insurance against bad debts.
(c) They pay the client agreed percentages of invoices on agreed dates.
(d) They may pay cash to the client in advance of invoice payment.

The factor begins dealing with a client by examining the client's accounts receivables. A list of approved customers is prepared. The factor agrees to provide complete protection against bad debts on all subsequent sales to these customers provided certain limits are maintained. Naturally, the customers selected by the factor tend to be those on which there would be, in any event, no credit risk. If the client company wants to introduce new accounts or to increase the limits on approved accounts, the factor must first be consulted.

Having established the service, the factor agrees to pay the invoice on an agreed maturity date. For example, a medium-sized textile company began factoring accounts receivable. The factor examined the accounts receivable ledger and discovered that the average credit granted by the firm was fifty-five days. The factor agreed to pay the firm fifty-five days after receipt of invoice. The advantage to the firm was that instead of a varying, somewhat uncertain, cash flow from customers, it now had guaranteed receipts.

A prepayment facility exists in most factoring agreements. An agreed percentage of the debtor balance, usually 70 per cent, is advanced to the client on the day the invoice is issued. Factoring may be 'with recourse', which means that in the event of bad debts the factor must be reimbursed by the client. More commonly, the service is 'without recourse'. This means that the customer pays an insurance premium against bad debts.

The firm's customers are informed by a notation on the original invoice that the debt is due to, and should be paid to, the factor. To avoid public knowledge of the use of factoring, the factor may establish a wholly owned subsidiary with a name similar to that of the client firm — for example, Ardmore (Sales) Limited. Invoices can then be made payable to this company.

The cost of factoring depends on the amount of work involved and the firm's industry, product and customers. The total cost is made up of three segments: (a) interest charges, which are about 4 per cent above DIBOR, i.e. the rate at which banks borrow in Dublin; (b) a charge for insuring bad debts; (c) a service charge to cover debt collection, accounting records, etc. Generally, the insurance and service charges together will not exceed 2 per cent of the net sum factored.

Factoring is considered worth while, from both the firm's and the factor's points of view, only if total credit sales are in excess of £250,000 per annum and the average invoice value in excess of £500.

Companies using a factor have immediate access to cash that they would not normally receive for up to two, three or more months. The facility can stabilise the timing of cash flows and make accurate cash flow planning a reality.

The factor's financial facility enables businesses to:

(1) Pay suppliers more promptly, giving enhanced credit reputation.
(2) Obtain cash and quantity discounts on supplies, thus improving profit margins.
(3) Cope with seasonal and other peak demands for cash.
(4) Make future purchasing and other plans knowing the working capital that will be available.
(5) Finance a higher level of sales.
(6) Obtain off balance sheet finance.
(7) Improve the return on their capital without giving up equity or control.
(8) Save on the cost of maintaining own sales administration.
(9) Save on management time previously spent supervising sales accounts or chasing slow-paying customers.
(10) Obtain swifter payment by customers, giving cash flow improvement and interest savings.
(11) Avoid sales relationships with customers being damaged by sales staff and management repeatedly requesting payment.
(12) Spend more time on sales and business development.

Offsetting the advantages are the costs and a disturbing image problem. In many countries, but especially in Ireland, factoring accounts receivable is seen as a sign of financial weakness. This misconception of the role of factoring is prevalent among Irish financial institutions. The logic behind the setting up of a like-named firm should now be clear. A customer paying invoices to Ardmore (Sales) Limited may not realise that Ardmore has factored its debtors. It is important to note that fewer than 40 per cent of UK companies using factoring are manufacturers, some 35 per cent are distributors — often engineering and metal distributors, while printing and publishing, catering and other business services make up 25 per cent.

Export factoring is a fast-growing area. Using a world-wide network of offices and contacts, international factoring firms can advise Irish exporters on the creditworthiness of foreign customers. Where overseas customers are accepted by the factor, cash collection is improved due to the local contacts with the customer. Export financing also guarantees the Irish exporter an agreed price in punts; the factor assumes the currency exchange risk. Removal of both the credit and currency risks makes exporting more attractive to Irish business.

11. Confirming

An ancient method of financing working capital which has recently gained new life is 'confirming'. Confirming is a technique whereby a finance house agrees to guarantee payment to either a supplier or a bank in return for a fee. An example will best explain the procedure.

An Irish importer of electrical goods wishes to expand his business. His UK supplier is reluctant to give additional credit. His Irish bank does not want to increase its exposure. The importer applies for a facility to a confirming house. Having examined the importer's business, the inventory and the accounts receivable, the confirming house agrees to guarantee the debts of the importer to an agreed limit. In return it charges a guarantee fee of up to 4 per cent plus an administration fee. The confirming house holds title to the inventory and the accounts receivable until the sums guaranteed have been paid. The importer goes to the supplier with a confirming house guarantee. The supplier can now discount the importer's invoice. In this way the importer can expand his business.

After growing very rapidly in the late 1980s, confirming suffered a setback as the world-wide economic recession caused the collapse of many firms. Confirming houses discovered that their reservation of title was often queried. Where they did get control they frequently found that forced sale of inventory yielded a low percentage of the Balance Sheet values.

12. Insurance Premium Loans

For many Irish companies the annual insurance payment has become a heavy burden. Insurance in Ireland is expensive, particularly employer's liability, public liability, theft and motor cover. It would not be unusual for a company with fifty employees to pay £50,000 a year. Insurance must be paid; delays can void the policies.

To this end a number of institutions have developed insurance premium loans whereby the lender pays the insurance premium on the due date, and the borrower repays the loan, usually in six payments at two-monthly intervals. The security for the loan is often weak, but the lender can reserve the right to cancel the policies and recoup some of the funds.

CONCLUSION

One point to be taken from this chapter is that the raising of finance is a complex and sophisticated job. The short-term sources of finance alone involve many different combinations of risk, income and control. The objective in raising short-term money is to minimise risk and possible loss of control at the lowest cost. Very often this means stretching short-term sources to the limit beyond which the image and/or reputation of the company becomes damaged. A generation ago bank overdraft and trade credit were the only short-term sources of note. A decade ago the range had expanded to include some factoring. Now the short-term money market offers even wider opportunities, and inventory financing and accounts receivable financing are common.

In the final analysis the borrowing and payment schedule for short-term financing should be arranged to correspond to the expected swings in current assets. In this way financing would be employed only when it was needed, a similar approach to hedging in the commodities futures market.

FURTHER READING

J.C. Van Horne, *Financial Management & Policy*, 9th ed. (New Jersey, Prentice-Hall, 1992).

A.N. Cox & J.A. MacKenzie, *International Factoring* (London, Euromoney, 1986).

S. Crichton & C. Ferrier, *Understanding Factoring and Trade Credit* (London, Waterlow, 1986).

R.C. Moyer et al., *Contemporary Financial Management*, 5th ed. (New York, West Publishing, 1992).

B. Edwards (ed.), *Credit Management Handbook*, 3rd ed. (Aldershot, Gower Publishing Company Ltd, 1990).

QUESTIONS

Question 9.1

What determines the amount of trade credit available to a firm?

Question 9.2

How would sources of finance affect a business?

Question 9.3

Describe the most important taxes collected by a firm.

Question 9.4

Would you consider accounts receivable to be a better source of collateral than inventories? Why?

Question 9.5

What are the advantages and disadvantages of commercial paper? Why have bankers moved towards commercial paper in recent times?

Question 9.6

What is the difference between a bank loan and a bank overdraft?

Question 9.7

Examine and describe the method of 'factoring'.

Question 9.8

What are the advantages and disadvantages to companies using factoring?

10

Medium-Term Sources of Finance

The sources of finance identified in the previous chapter are best suited to investments in current assets. This means that the assets liquidate themselves in time to repay the funds raised. But not all investments are short-term; some, such as land or buildings, are long-term and are best financed by permanent or long-term sources of capital. Other investments have intermediate lives. Plant and machinery often have economic lives of between three and five years. A great many projects have paybacks of less than five years. To fund these intermediate-term investments a series of medium-term financial instruments has been developed. The principal instruments are leasing, hire purchase and term loans.

1. LEASING

A lease is a contractual agreement whereby the owner of the property (lessor) allows another party (lessee) economic use of an asset for a specified period of time without his obtaining an ownership interest in the asset. In essence the lessee has borrowed an asset and in so doing taken on a contractual obligation to make periodic payments for the use of that asset.

Leasing can be traced back many years. It is reputed to have originated in the United States, where in 1832 the firm of Cottrell and Leonard leased academic gowns, caps and hoods. In the twentieth century some firms specialised in leasing. Hertz pioneered car leasing, IBM leased computers while Xerox for many years would only lease copiers. Today leased assets range from specialised heavy industrial equipment to bathroom fittings, paintings and furnishings. From financing a narrow range of products, such as office equipment, leasing has grown so that now it is possible to lease an entire factory plus all the equipment in it. Lease agreements are offered by most commercial banks, financial institutions, insurance companies and equipment manufacturing companies through captive leasing subsidiaries and independent leasing companies. The lease arrangement can be either a direct lease, a leveraged lease or a sale and leaseback lease.

A direct lease involves two parties and occurs when the lessee leases equipment or other assets from the lessor, who already owns or acquires the asset. The lessor is a manufacturer or leasing company that is providing the asset and its financing to the lessee. This is the most common form of lease arrangement and is particularly widespread in Ireland for office equipment and car fleets.

A leveraged lease involves three parties and occurs when a lender provides funds to the lessor in order to purchase the assets that are leased to the lessee. The leverage refers to the financial leverage used by the lessor in structuring the lease, with the risk associated with default by the lessee partly borne by the third party lender. The lender may insist on a lien on the asset, an assignment of the lease or lease payments and/or a direct guarantee from the lessee or other third party as part of the agreement in providing the finance. Leveraged leases normally involve only very large assets due to the complexity and expense of structuring the lease arrangement.

A sale and leaseback lease involves two parties and occurs when the lessee sells land, buildings or equipment to a lessor who simultaneously enters into an agreement to lease the property back for a specified period under specific terms. If the property consists of machinery and equipment, this form of lease would be deemed medium-term financing. If land and buildings are involved — which is the most common situation — then the maturity of the lease would be long-term. This is discussed in more detail in Chapter 11.

Equipment leasing has grown rapidly in Ireland. From a total figure of less than £12 million in 1972 it was approximately £700 million in 1994.

Table 10.1 Irish Assets Financed by Leasing	
Year	Amounts (£m)
1988	346
1989	483
1990	540
1991	698
1992	660
1993	690
1994	670 (est.)
Source: Lease Europe Annual Reports.	

It is estimated that at its peak leasing financed 32 per cent of all equipment investment in Ireland.

The principal products financed by leasing in 1994 are shown in Figure 10.2 and the main users in Figure 10.3.

Lease agreements can take one of two forms, an operating lease or a finance lease. They typically differ in terms of the length of the leasing arrangement and whether the lease can be cancelled by the lessee.

Operating leases, also called service or maintenance leases, provide the lessee with use of the asset on a period-by-period basis and are usually characterised by the following features:
(a) The lease can be cancelled by the lessee prior to its expiration, with options to renew.
(b) The lessor provides service, maintenance and insurance.
(c) The sum of all the lease payments by the lessee does not necessarily fully provide for the recovery of the asset's cost. Subsequent leases or a sale of the assets are required to recover the investment.

194

As a rule, operating leases provide goods that are not peculiar to one kind of industry — that is, office equipment, computers, fleets of cars and trucks — and relate to goods that have a relatively short product life cycle — that is, less than five years.

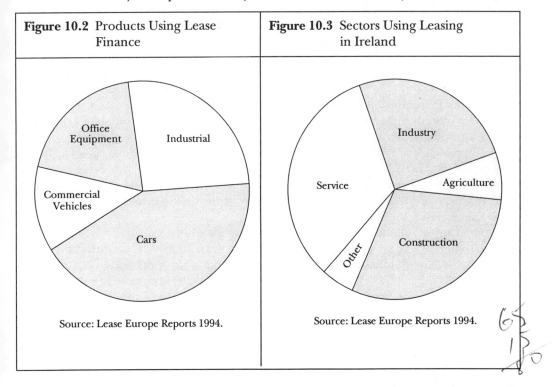

Figure 10.2 Products Using Lease Finance

Source: Lease Europe Reports 1994.

Figure 10.3 Sectors Using Leasing in Ireland

Source: Lease Europe Reports 1994.

Financial leases, also called capital leases, are a longer-term commitment and are usually characterised by the following features:
(a) The lease **cannot** be cancelled by the lessee prior to its expiry date.
(b) The lessor may or may not provide service, maintenance and insurance for the asset.
(c) The asset is fully amortised over the life of the asset.
   A finance lease is now required to be shown on the Balance Sheet as an asset at fair value and as a liability for future lease payments. The key distinction is 'cancellability'.
   Most commonly, financial leases are entered into by lessees as a means of acquiring the use of land, buildings and heavy manufacturing equipment, and apply to most sale and leaseback leases and leveraged leases.
   Under a leasing agreement, the 'lessee' obtains assets from the lessor, who maintains ownership of the assets. The lessee makes regular tax-deductible payments to the lessor for the use of the assets; these payments are a contractual liability and so failure to meet them could lead to bankruptcy.
   A typical lease agreement covers four topics:
(a) The life of the lease.
(b) The timing and amount of payments.
(c) Agreements on renewing the lease or on purchasing the asset at the end of the lease period.
(d) Arrangements concerning repairs, insurance and other expenses.

The cost of leasing depends on the asset being leased, the creditworthiness of the lessee, the period of the primary lease, interest rates and service charges. The cost is somewhat reduced by the tax-deductibility of leasing costs. However, these costs must be offset against the loss of depreciation allowances in computing taxable profits. Given the low level of manufacturing profits tax — 10 per cent versus the 40 per cent tax rate on services — it is easy to see why service industry is the main user.

A firm considering a leasing arrangement should shop around to find the best leasing terms. It should then compare the cost of the leasing agreements with the costs and benefits that would arise through purchasing the asset using alternative sources of finance. In attempting a 'lease or buy' analysis it is particularly important to examine the availability of cash discounts, government grants and the annual allowances granted by the tax authorities.

Leasing in Ireland used to differ from practice in the United States and United Kingdom due to the following:

(1) The availability of capital grants in Ireland, which were paid to the owner rather than to the user of the asset: hence the lessor and not the lessee gained an advantage. These have largely disappeared.

(2) Liberal annual allowances in Ireland. These too have gone.

(3) Tax relief on export profits, which meant that many Irish manufacturing firms had no tax liability. Purchasing an asset in those circumstances provided no tax shield. Leasing an asset allows the lessor to gain a tax advantage, thus enabling the lessor to provide finance to the lessee on terms cheaper than those of purchasing the asset. Note that export tax relief applied only to firms exporting manufactured products prior to January 1981 and ended on 5 April 1990.

(4) A 10 per cent tax rate on manufacturing company profits compared to 40 per cent on service company profits. As such, a manufacturing company obtains a low tax shield on depreciation plus interest payments should it buy the asset, while a service company leasing the equipment to a user has a 40 per cent tax shield on the depreciation and the interest.

The very rapid growth in leasing in Ireland in the 1970s and 1980s was due to artificial incentives created by the state. It was based on the ability of owners (lessors) to use the 100 per cent depreciation allowances and to take advantage of liberal capital grants. By the mid-1990s the free depreciation allowances were abolished while capital grants had declined to a nominal amount.

Because it is the use of assets and not their ownership which is essential for profitable operations, leasing facilities offer several advantages. The major advantage is that the firm does not have to tie up scarce resources to obtain the use of assets. This can be of vital importance to the smaller business in the conservation of working capital and gives rise to the possibility of up to 100 per cent financing with few or no restrictions. The benefits of flexibility and convenience allied to the ease in obtaining leases by firms with poor credit ratings is also worth considering. Furthermore, the owners of certain assets may refuse to sell them as they wish to reserve for their own benefit any capital gain that may be realised as the property appreciates. This may apply particularly to land with mineral or oil rights or to the use of patents. An additional advantage is that the most modern equipment can be obtained without the outlay of capital and should the asset become obsolete during the lease period the lessee has the option to trade in for the up-to-date model, though a fine is levied for changing the lease. The primary disadvantages of leasing are the cost and the loss of any appreciation in the asset's value.

The very swift growth of leasing in Ireland came to an end with the abolition of the tax advantage during the 1980s. Specialist leasing firms had entered the market. They had few overheads, access to capital and skills. Their mix of business ensured that little, if any, tax was payable; that is, they mixed assets on which capital depreciation was free — such as industrial machines — with cars. These firms were cheaper, quicker and more flexible than the more traditional industrial banks.

But the bubble burst in the early 1990s. Leasing firms found it difficult to obtain finance in the high interest, tight credit circumstances of the early 1990s. Economic recession caused a slowdown in expansion and an increase in bad debts. The elimination of free depreciation allowances and the reduction in capital grants further reduced the opportunities for leasing companies.

By 1994 there were seventeen members of the Irish Finance Houses Association, almost all associates of associated banks or European or American banks. Member firms of the IFHA control in excess of 90 per cent of all leasing.

A special case is the role played by leasing firms located in Shannon. There, a highly specialised large ticket leasing business has developed as a result of a very favourable tax regime and free depreciation. Firms such as Guinness Peat Aviation (GPA), Shannon Air Services and International Air Services (IAS) came to dominate the world aircraft leasing business while other specialised leasing firms evolved to service the printing industry and textile machinery trade. Here too recession took a toll, with the virtual collapse of GPA and a decline in most other leasing companies.

2. HIRE PURCHASE

Hire purchase in its widest meaning embraces two different systems for purchasing goods on an instalment basis; hire purchase agreements and credit sales agreements. The major difference between the two is the date of the transfer of ownership. Under hire purchase agreements ownership remains with the seller until the last payment. The agreement covers the rental of the goods with an option to purchase at a nominal price at the end of the hire purchase. Credit sales agreements transfer ownership immediately to the purchaser, who agrees to pay for the goods over a specified period.

The range of goods that can be obtained through hire purchase is extensive. Motor vehicles form the largest category but other categories of importance to businesses are industrial machinery, furniture and office equipment and contractor's plant.

Hire purchase agreements are between three parties: the purchaser, the seller and the financier, which is generally a company dealing exclusively with hire purchase transactions. Normally, the financier is skilled in credit evaluation. Frequently, as in the case of television sales, the retailer enters into hire purchase agreements with the purchaser. A block of such agreements is sold to a finance house, usually for 80 per cent of the face value. This process is known as 'block discounting'.

The objective in hire purchase, or 'equipment financing' as it is sometimes known, is to have the market value of the asset always above the sum owed to the financier. Hence only a percentage of the purchase price is advanced and the period of the agreement rarely goes over three years.

Hire purchase can be a very expensive form of finance. The rate of interest charged is calculated on the initial sum borrowed, not the amount outstanding at any one time. A simple method of calculating the true rate of interest being paid is as follows:

$$\frac{\text{Stated Interest Rate per Annum} \times 2 \times \text{Number of Instalments}}{\text{Number of Instalments} + 1}$$

It can be seen from this formula that the true rate of interest is approximately twice the stated rate. In 1995 the true rate was almost 20 per cent per annum.

The advantages claimed for hire purchase as a source of finance are that (a) it enables a firm to obtain the use of assets without large outlay, (b) all costs are tax-deductible and (c) annual depreciation allowances can be claimed on the full retail price of the goods.

Relative to other sources, hire purchase finance is expensive. Another disadvantage is that the total instalment due on hire purchase contracts will be detailed on the liability side of the Balance Sheet. If the amount is substantial, it will adversely affect the firm's efforts to raise further debt finance. Firms with no tax liability would be well advised to seek alternative sources of finance.

Despite the high cost of finance, in 1994 there was over £700 million extended under hire purchase and instalment credit agreements. Over 70 per cent of the total was advanced by industrial banks, 9 per cent by hire purchase companies and the balance by trading companies and state-sponsored bodies.

The principal users of hire purchase are private individuals and small firms which often find it the only source of finance available to them, though a surprising number of large companies hire car fleets and office equipment.

3. TERM LOANS

One consequence of rapid economic growth in Ireland has been an increase in demand for capital. The banking system, which for many years had exported capital, now found internal demand greater than supply. Much of the new demand was for investment in fixed assets. The traditional bank overdraft form of lending was not suited to this demand and so term loans were introduced. A term loan is usually for a fixed period of time with repayments of principal and interest on an agreed periodic basis. The average term loan is granted for periods between three and seven years.

Term loans are tailored to suit the requirements of the individual firm and consequently provisions are flexible: that is, there may be a remission of all repayments in the first year, large payments (balloon payments) may be permitted at the end of the term, and so on. It is also not uncommon for the lender to require the borrower to keep a percentage of its loan balance, say 10 per cent, on deposit as a compensating balance. This effectively increases the interest cost of the loan as not all of the face value of the loan is available to the borrower. Other features of the term loan facility could include the borrower negotiating a line of credit and then drawing down all or a portion of that amount as he sees fit. This is primarily short-term and is generally seen to be either seasonal or self-liquidating.

Alternatively, for the more medium-term, the borrower may enter into a revolving credit agreement whereby the lender offers credit up to a given amount during a specified period.

The rate charged will depend on the source of the finance, the term of the loan, the creditworthiness of the firm seeking the loan and current interest rates. In general it will be at least one half of one per cent above bank overdraft rate but may be much higher depending on the risk of the venture. As in the case of commercial bank loans, interest

charges are tax-deductible. In addition alternative methods may be used in calculating interest, such as:
— regular interest: percentage of principal charged periodically.
— discount interest: interest deducted at start of loan.
— instalment interest: computed on total principal for total life of loan with fixed monthly repayments of both principal and interest.
— variable interest: fluctuates in line with market conditions.
— fixed interest: remains at agreed fixed rate for specified period of loan.
    The term loan structure of interest rates in Ireland is shown in Table 10.4.

Table 10.4 Selected Lending Rates

	1984	1988	1992	1994	1995
Central Bank Short-Term Facility	14.00	9.50	(a)	6.25	6.75
Associated Banks Prime AAA	14.75	10.50	19.00	5.85	6.50
AA Overdraft	15.75	12.50	15.75	10.25	11.00
1–3 years	15.75	13.00	15.00	10.00	10.50
3–5 years	16.25	13.50	16.00	9.25	10.00
5–7 years	16.75	14.00	17.00	9.75	10.50
Over 7 years	17.25	15.00	18.50	11.00	10.50
A Overdrafts and Term Loans	17.25–19.25	14.5–16.00	18.25–19.75	11.00	11.50
House Purchase Loans	14.75	10.5	13.75–14.45	6.75–7.45	7.50
Building Societies' Mortgage Rates	11.75	10.25	13.75–14.45	6.85–7.45	7.50

(a) Short-term facility suspended at end 1992

Source: Central Bank Quarterly Reports.

Table 10.4 gives a flavour of the volatile nature of interest rates which face business people in Ireland. Over the decade 1985–95 the short-term interest rates for prime customers varied by 250 per cent. At an extreme, towards the end of 1992 the Central Bank was forced to suspend all dealings at the short-term rate which it would lend to banks. This was at a time of major currency instability. To protect the Punt by attracting in overseas capital, interest rates in Ireland rose to unprecedented levels, e.g. 200 per cent per annum for overnight money.

    The decline in rates over the period reflects falling inflation. Money which is loaned out at no risk is estimated to have a real cost of 3–5 per cent annually. To that figure must be added inflation and if appropriate a risk premium. The relatively high interest rates in the mid-1980s reflected the high levels of inflation at that time.

    The term loan agreement is a legal contract often stretching to many pages. Borrowers would be well advised to read carefully each line of the contract and to have lawyers explain any complex provision. The contract usually covers the following:
(a) The amount of the loan.
(b) The term of the loan.
(c) The purpose of the loan.

(d) Repayment dates.

(e) Interest rate and how it may vary.

(f) Commitment fees and drawdown fees.

(g) Annual management fees.

(h) Security provisions and protective covenants.

(i) Preferential share purchase schemes.

(j) Prepayment penalties and provisions.

(k) Life insurance on essential executives — so-called key man insurance.

(l) Any guarantees.

Many of the above provisions may bear hard on management, so it is wise to be fully aware of the implications of all the provisions of the contract.

The security provisions and protective covenants specified by the term agreement are determined by the borrower's credit standing and size. Term loans to small firms tend to be secured more than those to large firms, although there is an increasing tendency for all term loans to be secured. Security provisions can take the form of fixed and/or floating charges on assets of the business — thus restricting asset management, an assignment of receivables, inventories and/or payments under a specific contract, cash surrender value of a life insurance policy, or the pledge of marketable securities held by the borrower. The protective covenants could fall into any of the following categories: affirmative, negative, restrictive or default.

An affirmative covenant outlines actions the borrower agrees to take during the term of the loan, such as provide periodic accounts, maintain minimum amounts of working capital to protect liquidity, or comply with management structure guidelines acceptable to the lender.

A negative covenant outlines actions the borrower agrees not to take without the written approval of the lender. These could include pledging any of its assets to other lenders or selling its receivables, entering into any merger or consolidation agreements, and making or guaranteeing any loans to others.

A restrictive covenant restricts the scope of the borrower's action, typically by placing limitations on dividend payments, salaries and bonuses and any advances to management or employees. In addition restrictions could be placed on the borrower's total borrowings or its investment in new property, plant and equipment. In essence these provisions force the borrower to increase its equity base and thereby increase the security available to the lender.

A default provision outlines the likely consequences of failure by the borrower to honour any of the loan agreement conditions. All term loans have a number of default provisions that allow the lender to insist upon immediate repayment of the loan should the borrower fail to make payments when due or to observe any of the affirmative, negative or restrictive covenants specified in the loan agreement.

Share option schemes can prove expensive if the business does grow. Lenders argue that they are entitled to share in the success of a business if they provide 'finance for growth'. This point is debatable but usually the borrower is in a weak position since the funds are required. Commitment, legal and other fees are usually charged by term-lenders. Though small, these fees increase the effective interest rate. Joint and several guarantees are onerous since each individual bears full responsibility for all the debt. In the event of business failure the investor will probably be ruined. Possibly of greater concern is the fact that other lenders will be less willing to advance funds to individuals with outstanding guarantees.

Borrowers would do well to seek funds from their commercial bank prior to approaching other banks and thereby capitalise on their track record and proven banking relationship. Non-associated banks can be very flexible in their approach to lending while the commercial banks are more rigid. Increasing competition among banks makes it essential to shop around. One can often find a variation in interest rates of 1 or 2 per cent, which can make a significant difference in the rate of return on the equity investment.

It is important to negotiate a term loan. That does not mean asking for the money and signing the contract. Each provision in the contract should be negotiated. It is possible that certain provisions can be deleted or adapted. Particularly in growing companies, restrictions on capital expenditure may prove unwise.

Preparing a Term Loan Application

Practically every business will require medium-term finance at some time or other. Before seeking a term loan, management should prepare a detailed package for submission to the bank, including the following:

(a) The audited accounts for the company for recent years.
(b) An outline of the proposed project, including markets, capital cost and some operational details.
(c) A financial analysis, as outlined in previous chapters, which examines projected cash inflows and outflows and estimates the return on investment.
(d) A proposed repayment schedule.
(e) The nature of the security, if any, being offered as collateral for the loan.

While some of the above requirements seem onerous, it should be remembered that sensible management will already have prepared most of the data for its own purposes. Furthermore, submissions for capital grants or assistance from the government must be accompanied by detailed figures on any proposed project.

Term loans are especially useful to firms not wanting to raise permanent or long-term finance, and to those businesses expanding rapidly with a time lag between expenditure and the resultant cash inflows. Managements short of the cash necessary to make profitable investments or those with large semi-permanent bank overdrafts should examine the possibilities of putting their businesses on a stronger financial footing by raising a term loan. It is equally important for management to maintain a continuing relationship with the lender during the period of the loan. The lender has funds at risk in the business so it should be given up-to-date, candid information on its condition. Having accepted the terms of the loan contract, management must live up to the provisions and not attempt to circumvent them. The purpose of these provisions is to safeguard the interest and capital repayments of the term loan. It is important to remember that they are negotiable both before the term loan is accepted and during the life of the loan. The lender will be quite willing to reconsider the provisions if management can show that they are restricting the profitable expansion of the business.

CONCLUSION

Medium-term financing covers those financial instruments with lives of between one and seven years. Such instruments have developed swiftly in Ireland. This chapter has covered the three principal forms of intermediate-term financing — leasing, hire purchase and term loans. The explosive growth in leasing was explained. Hire purchase was shown to be a widely used but very expensive source. Term loans, which have become the staple source of business finance, are useful but expensive. In terms of risk, leasing and term loans have contractual obligations which if defaulted upon can lead to loss of the business. With hire purchase, default normally means the repossession of the asset. Term loan agreements have the most restrictive control effect, and unless negotiated carefully can dilute the control of the owners. This does not apply to leasing or to hire purchase.

FURTHER READING
Investor's Chronicle, Leasing Survey, 4 September 1993, pp. 65–71.
C. Drury, *Lease Financing* (Hull, MCB Press, 1989).

QUESTIONS
Question 10.1
Describe the major differences between an operating lease and a finance lease.

Question 10.2
What are the main points contained in a leasing agreement?

Question 10.3
What are the advantages and disadvantages of hire purchase?

Question 10.4
What types of firm would be particularly interested in a term loan? Why?

Question 10.5
Explain, with examples, the term 'off balance sheet' financing.

Question 10.6
What is the difference, if any, between hire purchase and credit sales agreements?

11

Long-Term External Loan Finance

Most businesses are going concerns. This means that they have no definable life. Some live for centuries. The Rathborne candle business in Dublin has lasted for over 500 years while the Smyth clothing company in Balbriggan was a relative youngster of around 250 years' experience when it closed in 1980. Few if any business people look centuries into the future but many do expect to be in business for decades. Certain investments, such as land, buildings and some plant, have very long lives. Less clear perhaps is the long-term element in working capital. Though all working capital should turn over rapidly, a part is a long-term or permanent investment.

Firms always need external funding to supplement funds generated internally. Success is often the problem. An increase in sales brings an obvious need for more raw material but brings also an increase in the amount of money owed to the business as accounts receivable. Greater turnover leads to requirements for new machines which may need new buildings. It is said that the major cause of business failure is overtrading, i.e. having too little capital to finance the level of business. A growing profitable business often generates a good cash flow but it rarely covers the need for finance. Firms may also need financing when economic activity begins to slow down — a sales decline causes a drop in internally generated funds, with levels of labour and investment in capital and inventory continuing as before until they can be adjusted downwards to reflect the slowdown in economic activity.

The fact that business is long-term with long-term financial needs means that much of the money invested in the business should also be long-term. The idea that business people would use a short-term bank overdraft to construct a factory which will take years to build and longer again to produce positive cash flows should surprise people but it has been done and is being done. Uses of finance should be matched to sources of finance. In this chapter the role of long-term debt finance is examined. This is money which is borrowed in one way or another for a long period. The strengths and weaknesses of this type of money are examined below. Long-term debt finance has very specific income, risk and control effects. From the point of view of an income effect, debt finance can be very beneficial to the owners if the use to which the money is put generates profits above the cost. The risk effect may be substantial. Interest and capital are fixed payments. Miss a payment and the business may be put into receivership. The control effect is beneficial. Owners get the use of Other People's Money (OPM) without having to give up voting or ownership rights.

From the borrower's perspective the major advantages of long-term finance could be summarised as follows:

— It can have a low after-tax cost due to the tax-deductibility of interest. This is not as significant in Ireland with 10 per cent corporate tax rates on manufacturing profits.
— It normally does not involve giving up voting or share control of the firm.
— It is not permanent and permits flexibility in its scheduling.
— It gives rise to the possibility of increasing earnings per share by achieving favourable financial leverage through the introduction of debt into the capital structure, i.e. investing the money to obtain a return greater than the cost.

There are disadvantages and they can be summarised as follows:

— The interest payments and repayment schedule create a fixed burden on the firm's financial resources which in certain cases can lead to default and ultimately bankruptcy.
— The lender may impose restrictions on the management's freedom to act as part of the loan agreement.
— The earnings per share may fall as a result of the debt introduction, due to the rate of interest on the debt exceeding the rate of return on the assets purchased with the debt finance.

The sources of finance examined in this chapter are:

    (1) Debentures.
    (2) Sale and Leaseback.
    (3) Section 84 Loans.
    (4) Project Financing.

The above sources are usually available only to substantial, profitable businesses. Most privately owned Irish-based companies would not be in a position to raise substantial long-term loans. Project financing is a very particular type of finance available only to large resource-based projects.

1. DEBENTURES

Debentures are promises to pay interest and principal.

Long-term debt is generally classified according to whether it is secured by specific assets. A **mortgage debenture** usually describes secured debt issues while issues not secured by specific assets are simply called debentures. The term bond or debenture is used to denote any type of long-term debt issue. The words are used interchangeably. Long-term debt comes in many varieties, shapes and sizes. It may be arranged privately or sold publicly. If sold publicly, bonds are graded for their creditworthiness, which will determine the level of interest cost.

All debt instruments possess five characteristics:

— Maturity: long-term debentures as a rule means ten to thirty years.
— Security: this refers to the recourse, if any, to the debt holder.
— Repayment provisions: these vary widely and depend on the borrower's history, cash flow, profitability, management and other factors.
— Interest (coupon) rate: frequently, the rate is fixed and set equal to market interest rates on bonds of comparable quality and maturity so as to ensure it sells at or near

par value. Floating rate bonds are common among private issues and in time of economic uncertainty.

— Denomination: normally in thousands of units of the relevant currency.

A bond is therefore a long-term loan with specific maturity, interest and repayment provisions and an average life of between ten and thirty years. The lenders of long-term funds are creditors of the borrowing company. Generally, the relationship between borrower and lender is covered by a legal contract known as an 'indenture'. This contract is similar to the term loan contract.

An indenture details the nature of the debt issue, specifies the manner in which the principal must be repaid and lists any restrictive covenants placed on the firm by the lender. The bond holder's interest in a public issue of long-term debt is represented by a trustee, usually a bank or trust company designated in the indenture to act on his behalf. The primary responsibilities of the trustee are to ensure:

— that all legal requirements are met before issuing the bond,
— that the terms of the indenture are carried out,
— that appropriate action is initiated on behalf of the bond holder if the firm defaults on any of its obligations or payments.

As long as the borrower operates within the confines of the indenture, the lenders have little or no control over the business. Should the terms of the contract be breached, the firm is 'in default' or in breach of loan covenants and the lenders may obtain a voice in management and may end up running the business or even closing the business. Apart from having fixed maturities and interest payments, bonds have preferential rights to repayment in the event of a corporate liquidation.

Bonds issued for the first time are called new issues whereas those that have been on the market for some time are called seasoned or outstanding issues. Bonds may be sold publicly through an underwriter, who is usually an investment banker, or through private placement directly with institutions.

The frequency with which firms raise long-term debt varies considerably. At one extreme large firms may raise millions of pounds every few years while small firms raise less than a million pounds during a lifetime. The array of debt instruments available outside of Ireland, and the possible complexities involved, has resulted in bond rating agencies offering independent assessment of the quality of the investment. The two major world rating agencies are Moody's Investors Service and Standard and Poor's Corporation. They provide an estimate of the bond's investment quality and its risk of default. This can range from those that fall within 'gilt edge' or 'investment grade' category to those with a high degree of speculation, so-called 'junk bonds'. Ratings are very important in determining a firm's ability to raise additional long-term finance and effectively determine the interest rate and size of the issue. Generally speaking, a low rating is translated into higher interest costs to cover the higher default risk and may preclude institutional investors from participating by law or by custom. This can seriously limit the number of potential purchasers of the bond and threaten the success of the issue at any rate of interest.

Debentures are not a significant source of capital for Irish business. Studies in the 1980s and early 1990s have demonstrated a serious lack of long-term debt finance. The pension funds and insurance companies which provide the bulk of long-term debt finance in Germany, the US and Japan have not been active in creating an Irish market. The small size of indigenous Irish business, with 97 per cent of all firms having fewer than 100 employees, is a major disincentive to investors who equate small size with higher risk.

Small companies and a small stock market mean that investors shy away from long-term loans because they are illiquid, i.e. they are difficult if not impossible to sell. High levels of inflation in Ireland have eroded the value of fixed coupon debentures and militated against new issues.

Finally, the low level of corporate taxation on manufacturing and, until the early 1990s, liberal depreciation allowances meant that bonds had few or no tax advantages.

Types of Debenture

(a) Unsecured Debentures. The lender of an unsecured debenture has no security apart from the profitability of the business. Such instruments are used when the business in question is either very strong or so weak as to have no security to offer. Generally, unsecured debentures are issued only by extremely strong firms. The holders of these bonds have a claim on assets prior to that of the owners but equal to that of the other unsecured creditors. The bond indenture frequently contains a 'negative pledge' clause, prohibiting the firm from pledging assets to other creditors without the permission of the bond holder. Examples of unsecured bonds are the 7 ¾ per cent Unsecured Loan Stock issued by Guinness and redeemable in 2001, the 8 per cent Debenture Stock issued by CRH and redeemable between 1986 and 1991, and the 11 per cent Unsecured Loan Stock issued by Seafield PLC, redeemable between 1976 and 1996. This latter issue is an interesting example of the dangers of being unsecured. When the debentures were issued Seafield was a strong company. By the mid-1980s successive annual losses had weakened it. The loan stock was selling in 1994 at £65 per £100 of stock, thus giving a running yield of over 16 per cent and a redemption yield of over 30 per cent.

(b) Mortgage Bonds. This is the most common method of long-term debt financing. The lender obtains a lien on specific assets, usually buildings and/or land. Often the lender takes a 'floating charge' over all present and future assets of the business. The details of the mortgage must be registered with the Registrar of Companies. Where more than one mortgage exists, debentures will be ranked by number. In the event of default the trustee may foreclose and sell the asset, the proceeds of which are used to compensate the mortgage bond holder. If the proceeds of sale prove insufficient, the mortgage bond holder has an equal claim with the rest of the creditors to the firm's other assets. The mortgage may be open-end or closed-end. Open-end permits a firm to issue additional bonds under the same lien whereas closed-end stipulates that additional bonds secured by the same property cannot be issued.

(c) Guaranteed Debentures. Some businesses in Ireland are able to raise long-term money because their debts are guaranteed, usually by their parent companies. The subsidiaries of large American-based multinationals find it easy to raise finance on foot of the guarantee of their parents. So too do state-sponsored companies, such as the Electricity Supply Board and Bord na Móna, which have state guarantees supporting them.

(d) Convertible Debentures. This method of raising long-term loans has grown in recent years. The lender is given the right to convert the debt into ordinary shares of the firm at specific prices on or before specified dates. In this way the lender is allowed to share in the fortunes of the firm. If the business is a publicly quoted company and share prices rise rapidly, the loan holder has the right to buy shares at fixed prices at agreed times. Over time the conversion price usually rises. If the business does not do well and/or share prices do not rise on the stock market, the lender can continue to hold his loan and receive interest payments plus eventual capital repayment. Debentures such as these are subordinate and not protected by a mortgage. The return required falls between that required by secure bond holders and ordinary stock holders. Convertibles are used by venture capital companies, particularly in 'second round' financings (see Chapter 12). The investor is not very sure about the future of the business which is getting the finance so he protects himself by having an income in the form of a coupon. By having conversion rights, the investor can participate in any capital gain which may arise if the business is successful. There are a few examples of convertible debentures on the Irish Stock Exchange. The Bank of Ireland has a 10 per cent Convertible Loan Stock, and CRH has a 5.75 per cent Convertible Bond.

(e) Debentures with a warrant. In order to raise debt finance and avoid paying too high a coupon rate, a firm may offer a mix of interest and capital gain potential. As well as an agreed coupon and repayment schedule, the investor is offered warrants. These warrants are also known as an 'equity sweetener'. They are of two types:

(i) convertible, where the warrant allows the debenture holders to convert into ordinary shares at agreed prices at agreed times

(ii) straight, where the holders have the right to subscribe for new ordinary shares at agreed prices at agreed times. In addition the investor gets his principal back at the appropriate redemption date.

If the firm expands to the stage that it can 'go public' then the loan holder may exercise his warrants, sell his shares and realise a profit. This sort of financing is used mainly for small to medium-sized private firms with good potential. Investment banks are the usual lenders of this type of debenture. They may insist on the appointment of a director to advise the firm and safeguard their interest. Investment banks like to see ahead to the 'take out' point when they will have the opportunity to realise their investment. They may be content to see the company grow in value and receive interest for a long period. The logic of a sweetener is that the debenture holder is putting funds into a risky venture. All he would normally receive is his interest, plus his original investment. The downside risk is the loss of all his investment. On the other hand, the holder of equity has the same downside risk but has far greater potential for profit. Should the venture succeed, the holders of shares will make handsome returns. The warrant allows the debenture holder to participate in profits.

(f) Subordinated Debentures. A subordinated debenture is an unsecured debt which is junior to all other debts: that is, other debt holders must be fully paid before the subordinated debenture holder receives anything. This type of debt will have a higher interest rate than more senior debt and will frequently have rights of conversion into ordinary shares. It is a very useful means of finance in that it does not restrict further issues of debt because it is subordinated. From the owner's point of view it is as good as debt because it will not affect control.

Subordinated debt is often called mezzanine finance because it ranks between equity and standard debt. Many United States companies establishing subsidiaries in Ireland use subordinated debt in their capital structure. If profits are generated in Ireland, instead of being repatriated to the United States, where they will be taxed, the subordinated debenture is repaid. Since this is a repayment of capital no tax is due. Hence the parent receives the full repatriation of cash.

(g) Junk Bonds. The phenomenon known as the **Junk Bond** or high yield security became a widely used source of finance in takeovers and 'leveraged buyouts' during the 1980s and 1990s. Firms with low credit ratings were willing to pay 3 to 5 per cent more than high grade corporate debt to compensate for the greater risk. Michael Milken of the investment banking firm Drexel Burnham Lambert helped create a market for these bonds that surpassed $200 billion in size and accounted for over 25 per cent of all corporate debt outstanding.

Milken noticed that the extra yield on low grade bonds more than covered the extra risk of default. His findings led to an increase in the demand for junk bonds among investors and in the supply of such bonds by corporations.

The real importance of junk bonds lay in their use to finance the merger/takeover boom of the late 1980s. Firms specially created to mount takeover bids could raise vast sums of money by paying higher interest rates. Over a period of eight years a large percentage of US business felt the impact of these bonds.

The industry virtually collapsed when many of the principals were charged and some — including Milken — jailed for securities offences. High interest rates and recession led to serious losses for many investors.

However, 1994 saw the rehabilitation of the sector. Once again junk bonds were issued to finance leveraged buyouts and other types of takeover. The junk bond phenomenon had little impact in Ireland.

(h) Perpetual Debentures. These are bonds issued without finite maturity dates. The bond issuer promises to pay interest indefinitely and there is no contractual obligation to repay the principal. This is a very rare animal. The only example in existence in Ireland was the 4 per cent Perpetual Debenture Stock of the Alliance and Dublin Consumers Gas Company. In 1866 when the stock was issued, individuals thought that the right to receive 4 per cent interest in perpetuity was a good investment. In 1985 the company went into liquidation. The debenture holders were repaid in full.

(i) Income Bonds. They are the weakest form of debt bond a firm can issue, in that they are unsecured debt requiring interest to be paid only if profits are sufficient. While interest payments may be passed, unpaid interest is generally allowed to accumulate for some period and must be paid before ordinary stock dividends. This cumulative interest feature provides the bond holder with some security. The advantage to the issuer is protection from default should earnings fall.

They are issued only in the case of reorganisations and firms emerging from receivership and bankruptcy. As one investment banker has put it, they have the 'smell of death' about them.

(j) Indexed Bonds. Inflation has already been mentioned as having a very damaging effect on debentures. Fixed income and fixed sum repayments are uneconomic in times of rapid inflation. When uncertainty regarding the purchasing power of money is great, investors are unwilling to acquire fixed income bonds unless an explicit purchasing power guarantee is included in the agreement. Numerous attempts have been made to develop a financial instrument which retains the security and fixed income of the debenture but which also provides some safeguard against inflation. The objective is to tie the interest and principal to some index of the general price level. Club Mediterranée, in the 1980s, launched a sixteen-year debenture with an 8.5 per cent coupon rate but with two additional bonuses: (a) an increased payout to debenture holders if occupancy of a new holiday resort rose above 60 per cent and (b) a bonus related to rises in the prices of vacations. The very low interest rate on the debentures and the fact that the issue was heavily oversubscribed suggests that the new financial instrument may finally bridge the gap between debt and equity. The first bonus, on occupancy, offers a participation in profits while the second bonus, on prices, makes an allowance for inflation. The benefit to the borrower is the low rate of interest and the fact that higher rates will not be paid until the venture in which the funds are being invested is successful.

It is thought that this type of finance will be attractive to any business which can identify the breakeven threshold and whose prices match or exceed inflation.

(k) Zero Coupon Bonds. These are also known as deep discount bonds or simply 'Zeros'. An example will best explain the type. An Irish manufacturer issues £1,000 of five-year deep discount bonds at a price of £621 per £1,000 worth. The bond pays no interest but at the end of five years pays £1,000 for every £621 invested. This is a rate of 10 per cent per annum compounded, i.e. $£1,000/(1.10)^5 = £621$.

There may be certain tax benefits for holders receiving capital rather than income. In addition interest rates are locked in for the duration of the bond. This form of debenture is rare.

Widespread innovation has characterised the long-term debt market in recent years with the stimuli for this arising from volatile interest rates, changes in both the taxation system and the regulatory environment, and extensive research on the operation of efficient capital markets. Ireland has seen little development in this area. There is no effective bond market.

Most bonds are registered by a registration agent for the issuing firm, usually a bank. This records ownership with respect to principal and interest. Bearer bonds where possession is the primary evidence of ownership are also issued, but to a much lesser extent than previously, due to risk of loss.

Characteristics of Debentures

The characteristics of debentures can be evaluated by means of their risk, income and control effects. The risk to the borrower of using bonds is the inability to meet annual fixed commitments. Every increase in borrowed funds increases this risk, the 'financial' risk. The income effect arises from the possibility of investing fixed interest funds to produce a return higher than the cost. Control considerations arise if interest or capital payments are missed.

Debt financing involves the firm in fixed annual commitments as to interest and perhaps capital repayments. This is the great advantage of this source and also the great disadvantage: each is related to the concept of leverage or gearing. If a firm raises a loan at, say, 9 per cent and invests this money to yield 15 per cent, the difference is an extra profit to the owners. However, if the firm is unable to get any return from the investment of borrowed money and cannot pay the 9 per cent annual interest, the debenture holders are entitled to foreclose on the firm. This may best be explained by a short example.

Two firms, A and B, have investments of £50,000 each but firm A financed £20,000 of this investment by means of a debenture with net interest payment of £1,200 per annum. Both firms earn £5,000 after taxes, which equals an earnings yield of 10 per cent for firm B: that is, £5,000 ÷ £50,000. However, after paying out interest of £1,200 the owners of firm A have £3,800 left, which represents a yield of 12.6 per cent on their investment of £30,000.

Table 11.1 Effect of Gearing

	Firm A		Firm B	
Year	1994	1995	1994	1995
After-Tax Earnings	£5,000	£1,000	£5,000	£1,000
Interest on £20,000 at a Rate of 6% After Tax	£1,200	£1,200	-	-
Net Profit on Owner's Investment	£3,800	(£200)	£5,000	£1,000
Owner's Investment	£30,000	£30,000	£50,000	£50,000
Earnings Yield	12.6%	- 0.65%	10.0%	2%

Now consider the effect of an 80 per cent drop in after-tax earnings — that is, earnings of each firm drop to £1,000. Firm B now yields 2 per cent on owner's investment. Firm A is unable to pay its interest. The debenture holders may have the option of foreclosing on firm A and selling off the assets to receive their £20,000. Because of the fixed charge commitment of long-term debt, the risk to the owners and creditors is automatically increased.

In most countries debentures are a cheap source of finance. This is because interest rates are tax-deductible. In Ireland the 10 per cent manufacturing profits tax rate means that for many the tax shield on interest rates is small. An estimate of the cost of a debenture is as follows:

$$\text{Net Cost} = \frac{\text{Annual Interest}}{\text{Net Proceeds of the Issue}} \times (1 - \text{tax rate})$$

For Irish manufacturing industry the tax rate is often zero but at most could be 10 per cent so that the net cost approximates to the gross cost. This compares to a net borrowing cost of half the gross cost in most countries and a cost of 60 per cent in service industry in Ireland i.e. a 10% loan costs 6% after tax.

Straight debenture issues are rare. Service industries such as banking and insurance use them but they are costly for many firms and unattractive to most investors. Inflation can make a nonsense of debentures. Anyone buying £100 of debentures knowing that they will be repaid £100 in twenty years' time would need a very high rate of interest to compensate for the time value of the money, the risk of not being repaid and the loss in real value caused by inflation.

Deciding on the amount of long-term debt to raise involves the balancing of the risk, income and control aspects of the firm. However, certain guidelines can be applied to the firm's operations to discover its debt capacity.

In evaluating a debenture, a lender will attempt to measure the potential ability of the borrower to meet his future obligations. This aspect has been mentioned in Chapter 3 and is noted further under the ratio heading of debt/equity, times interest earned and times burden covered.

(1) Debt/Equity Ratio. This is the ratio of the amount of long-term debt to the amount of permanent or ownership capital in the business. The lower the proportion of debt to equity, the less risky a firm appears. The rule of thumb applied to the average firm with average earnings is an optimum debt equity ratio of 25 to 35 per cent. A 1994 investigation of the proportion of debt to equity in Irish business revealed that long-term debt made up 21 per cent of the long-term capital structure. Larger businesses with more than 100 employees had an average of 37 per cent.

(2) Times Interest Earned. This measures the cushion of earnings available to a prospective lender. For example, for Ardmore Limited:

	1994 (Actual)	1995 (Forecast)
Earnings before interest and taxes	£251,000	£320,000
Interest payments (including overdraft interest)	£64,000	£52,000
Times interest earned	3.9	6.2

(3) Times Burden Covered. It is common for debentures to be repaid by annual instalments rather than in a lump payment at the end of the term. The total of interest and annual capital repayments is called the burden. A cover of two — that is, earnings twice the annual burden — is a rule of thumb which investors and bankers frequently use.

2. SALE AND LEASEBACK

Many businesses have substantial investments in property. Older firms often find themselves the owners of prime property. It is possible to sell property to financial institutions which are seeking outlets for their funds and thereby 'unlock' frozen equity in real estate assets. This gives the vendor cash but no premises. The buying institution usually wishes to rent or lease the property. Who better to lease it to than the original owner?

Leases are usually for a period of twenty-one years with renewal options. The leases normally carry a provision allowing revisions of rent every five or seven years. Insurance, maintenance and rates are generally paid by the lessee.

The cost of this source of finance depends not only on the annual lease payments, but on the frequency of rent reviews. Management should press for as few rent reviews as possible during the lease period. A further factor in estimating the cost of sale and leaseback is the fact that the firm loses the capital appreciation on property. In times of inflation and/or heavy demand the value of property can increase rapidly. It is equally true that in deflationary times property prices can decline. However, it may be valid to say that commercial firms are not property developers and therefore should not employ their resources in property. This is logical only if a firm can more profitably use resources released from property.

It is important that the premises be marketable. The lessee must also be a tenant of substance as the lessor does not want problems during the period of the lease. These two reasons have restricted sale and leaseback to prime properties in large towns and cities and restricted leases to well-known businesses. In isolated cases big foreign firms in Ireland have managed a sale and leaseback on their premises. These may involve parent company guarantees.

In recent years the technique has developed to the stage that it is now possible for a user to design a totally new building, have an insurance company finance its construction and then lease the premises. As a general rule, sale and leaseback is effected through insurance companies and institutional investors, such as pension funds, more often than commercial banks. A firm should answer carefully the following questions before it uses sale and leaseback:

(a) Does it need the funds that will be provided?

(b) Will the cost of leasing the building back exceed the return anticipated from the capital created through the sale and leaseback technique?

Sale and leaseback may be an especially costly source of finance. The companies which sold their premises in the early 1970s lost capital appreciation and so paid a high price for the funds. However, property prices fell through the years of the 1980s, so firms which sold in the late 1970s would have a very cheap source of finance. Selling a premises loses an asset widely acceptable as security.

3. SECTION 84 LOANS

[handwritten: NOT examined]

In the late 1970s astute tax accountants in Ireland developed a hybrid form of long-term loan which carried almost all of the protection of a loan but had the tax efficiency of equity. The trick lay in splitting the payment on the loan into two components — an interest payment and a tiny dividend. As such, since the total payment could vary with the profits of the company, the Revenue authorities regarded it as a distribution of income, and not an interest payment. This meant that the income to the bank was regarded as 'franked investment income' and so was not taxable in their hands.

The net effect was a lower rate of interest to the borrower and a tax-free revenue stream to the Irish lender — usually a bank. The critical requirement was a written statement that the payment on the loan was related to the profitability of the borrower.

In December 1991 the state restricted new lending under this technique to projects on a list agreed with the Industrial Development Authority, as it was estimated that the loss in tax revenue was £100 million a year. By the mid-1990s almost all domestic Section 84 loans were repaid.

4. PROJECT FINANCING

Two events coincided in recent years to make the financing of many projects

[handwritten: in general]

extraordinarily difficult. Technology in a lot of industries changed so that efficient production required massive capital-intensive projects. At the same time inflation caused capital costs to soar. The net result was that a number of big projects, particularly in natural resources, became almost impossible to finance. New instruments had to be and were developed. Now major capital projects are financed by means of a custom-tailored package, known as project finance. In Ireland project finance has been used on the £100 million Tara zinc/lead mine at Navan and the £100 million Marathon gas field off Kinsale. In the United Kingdom a special package of over £1,000 million was raised to finance British Petroleum's Ninian oil field in the North Sea. The Euro Disney project in France and the Channel Tunnel are further evidence of projects that required specialised financing.

Apart from the sheer size of once-off projects, additional problems arise with large capital-intensive projects:
(1) Often construction and development take years. During that period the parent company would have to fund interest and other carrying costs with no revenue arising from the project.
(2) Attempting to consolidate huge debt sums on a Balance Sheet would totally distort the apparent financial strength of the company. For example, up to the day the Ninian field came on stream, British Petroleum had little to show for its investment, but debts of £1,000 million. This has also been a problem for Euro Disney.
(3) Any one financial institution could hardly afford the risk attaching to such loans. Few banks would survive a £1,000 million write-off. Remember the Bank of Ireland Group with over £15,000 million of assets produced £350 million in profits in the year ended March 1995.

Although the term project financing has been used to describe many types and kinds of financing, both with and without recourse, the term has evolved in recent years to allow a more precise definition:

A financing of a particular economic unit in which a lender is satisfied to look initially to the cash flows and earnings of that economic unit as the source of funds from which a loan will be repaid and to the assets of the economic unit as collateral for the loan.

Industries engaged in the production, processing, transportation or use of raw materials and energy have been especially attracted to project financing techniques. Boards of directors are receptive to proceeding with projects which can be financed entirely or substantially on their own merits.

The objective in project financing is to arrange borrowing for a project which will benefit the sponsor and at the same time be completely non-recourse, i.e. not in any way affecting the sponsor's credit standing or Balance Sheet. Indeed, project financing is sometimes called off balance sheet financing. This can be accomplished by using the credit of a third party to support the transaction.

There is considerable room for discussion between lenders and borrowers as to what constitutes feasible project financing. Borrowers prefer their projects to be financed independently off balance sheet. Lenders, on the other hand, are not in the venture capital business. They are not equity risk takers. Lenders want to feel secure that they are going to be repaid by either the project, the sponsor or an interested third party.

Therefore, the key to successful project financing is structuring the financing of a project with as little recourse as possible to the sponsor while at the same time providing sufficient credit support through guarantees or undertakings of the sponsor or third party so lenders will be satisfied with the credit risk.

A proposal which qualifies for project financing will usually have all of the following characteristics:

(1) The project must be backed by strong supporters. This backing may be provided by the sponsor or by a third party. The backing may be limited to the critical construction and start-up period rather than extending for the life of the project. It may take the form of direct or indirect guarantees, take-or-pay contracts, or economic necessity. These types of support can often be structured so they do not have the same impact as debt on the sponsor's Balance Sheet. They may be off balance sheet for the sponsor if support is provided by a third party. In the case of Euro Disney the Disney company provides support. In the case of the Channel Tunnel the UK and French governments are the supporters.

(2) A credit risk is involved rather than an equity risk or a venture capital risk. This means that the lenders want the business risk reduced as much as possible. As noted previously, lenders are lenders. They are not in the business of taking equity risks even if compensated as equity risk takers. Long-term sales contracts reduce this risk.

(3) The financial viability of the project must be shown. Conservative projections of assured internally generated cash flows must be prepared and justified by appropriate independent feasibility and engineering studies. The cash flow projections must be sufficient to service any debt contemplated, provide for cash needs, pay operating expenses and still provide an adequate cushion for contingencies.

(4) Supply contracts for product and/or energy to the project must be assured at a cost consistent with the financial projections.

(5) A market for the product or service must be assured at a price consistent with the financial projections. If take-or-pay contracts are being relied upon, they must be tight.

(6) Transportation for product into the project and product produced by the project must be assured at a cost consistent with the financial projections.

(7) The expertise of the contractor who is to construct the project facility must be well established.

(8) The financial capability and the technical expertise must be available to cover cost overruns and complete the project so that it operates in accordance with cost and production specifications.

(9) The project is not a new technology. The reliability of the process and the equipment to be used must be well established. The technical reliability and commercial viability of the project must be clear. If a new technology is in question, more than a lending risk is involved.

(10) The principal or the beneficiary of the sponsorship must have available the expertise to operate such a facility. In other words the project cannot be a start-up situation dependent upon going to the outside to hire the expertise to operate the new facilities.

(11) In addition to operating expertise, management personnel must be available to manage the project. If the sponsor is already short on management personnel, the

project is suspect.

(12) The properties and facilities being financed must have value as collateral. A flooded Channel Tunnel is not very valuable nor is a mine without ore.

(13) The political environment for the location of the project and the type of project must be reasonably friendly and stable.

(14) The sponsor must make an equity contribution consistent with its capability, interest in the project and risk of the project. The greater the perceived business, political and legal risks, the greater the equity.

(15) An adequate insurance programme must be available during both construction and operations.

(16) Government approval must be obtained.

(17) An environmental impact study (EIS) must be prepared to counter any or all planning objections.

In structuring a specific package the following steps may be taken:

(1) The project is developed by a subsidiary company; thus the parent can in many cases simply consolidate the equity investment in the subsidiary and not take on board the debt.

(2) One bank agrees to become the 'lead bank'. The lead bank attempts to organise a consortium of banks willing to take part in financing the project. The consortium might be as large as 200. Depending on the industry, certain banks are likely to be interested: Texan banks in oil, New York banks in iron ore mining and Toronto banks in base metal mining. International banks such as the European Investment Bank and World Bank are now involved.

(3) The banks commission a feasibility study which examines the physical and commercial viability of the project.

(4) Assuming it to be viable, the consortium designs a set of loans with repayments based on the cash flow of the project. The repayment schedules are usually related to a percentage of revenue, say 20 per cent, or a percentage of net cash flow, say 80 per cent. The repayments will vary with the level of production and the price of the output. Due to high depreciation write-offs in the early years tax is seldom paid so cash flows tend to be large.

(5) Shareholders rarely receive any dividends until all of the debt is repaid. This is not as harsh as it first appears since shareholders generally put up only a small percentage of the capital cost. The debt package may run as high as 90 per cent of the total cost.

(6) The lending consortium appoints one or more experts to monitor the capital expenditure, the operation of the project and the loan repayments.

(7) A detailed contract, often running to numerous volumes, spells out the relationship between the consortium and the principal.

(8) The package of debt finance frequently involves subsidised loans for capital exports, loans from international organisations such as the World Bank or European Investment Bank.

(9) The cost of the funds provided by the banks themselves is usually based on London Interbank rates or on Eurodollar rates.

Despite the analyses not every project works. The best way to appreciate the concerns of lenders to a project is to review causes for project failures, which are as follows:

(1) Delays in completion with consequent delay in the contemplated revenue flow.
(2) Capital cost overrun.
(3) Technical failure.
(4) Financial failure of the contractor.
(5) Government interference.
(6) Uninsured casualty losses.
(7) Increased price or shortages of raw materials.
(8) Technical obsolescence of the plant.
(9) Loss of competitive position in the marketplace.
(10) Expropriation.
(11) Poor management.

In order for a project financing to be viable these risks must be properly addressed and avoided.

Ideally, the project is financed on a non-recourse basis to the principal. Few big companies are willing to take 'bet the company' gambles. In addition sponsors wish to avoid damage to Balance Sheet ratios, problems with restrictive covenants, etc. Where large projects are financed — remember some are not — there is usually some recourse to the principals. Frequently, this takes the form of the principal agreeing to put up in equity any cost overruns.

When large projects fail or look like failing, the sponsors come under strong pressure to invest again. The financial difficulties at Euro Disney in the 1990s are a good example. The sponsor, Disney, resisted pressure to take full control and financial responsibility for the debt. The recurring problems in the Channel Tunnel project are yet another example. There the unfortunate shareholders continued to put up new equity time and again as delays, cost overruns and bureaucratic interference eroded the commercial value of the project.

In Ireland in the mid-1990s two projects are likely to proceed using project finance — the Arcon lead zinc mine at Galmoy and the Ivernia lead zinc mine at Lisheen.

CONCLUSION

This chapter has broadened the sources of finance to include long-term external sources of borrowed funds. Over time, a wide variety of long-term debt instruments has evolved to meet the needs of investors who want security but who also want participation. Inflation, interest rate volatility, taxation policies and regulatory control have been the catalysts for widespread innovation in the type and variation of long-term debt instruments available. Ideally, the maturity of the debt should be aligned with the maturity of the assets being financed to comply with the maturing matching principle. The objective is to develop an agency relationship between lenders and borrowers so as to minimise the risk of default and possible financial distress.

FURTHER READING

J.C. Van Horne, *Financial Management & Policy*, 9th ed. (New Jersey, Prentice-Hall, 1992).

R.C. Moyer et al., *Contemporary Financial Management*, 5th ed. (New York, West Publishing, 1992).

J.W. Kensinger & J.D. Martin, 'Project Finance: Raising Money the Old-Fashioned Way', *Journal of Applied Corporate Finance*, 1, pp. 69–81 (Fall 1988).

QUESTIONS

Question 11.1

When would a sale and leaseback agreement arise?

Question 11.2

What are the advantages and disadvantages of long-term debt?

Question 11.3

What is subordinated debt also known as? How and why did it become popular?

Question 11.4

What is the most common form of debenture?

Question 11.5

In your opinion what type of business would be interested in Section 84 loans and why?

Question 11.6

How was project financing a response of the financial community to obsolete traditional methods of finance?

Ownership Sources of Finance

The sources of finance discussed to date have two things in common — they are all other people's money and they all have to be repaid. But business should not be financed solely by borrowed sources of finance. A business venture, no matter how good, has an element of risk. Lenders are paid for the use of their funds. They may receive a risk premium but it is usually only a token payment because debt finance is not risk finance. A business has an indeterminable life. It should outlive all of the debt sources of finance. This leads logically to the concept of owners' funds as a source of finance: that is, the risk capital which is invested by people. This capital is generally permanent. It bears the financial and business risks of the venture. In the event of a liquidation all other sources of finance are repaid before the owners receive anything. Offsetting the risk disadvantages of ownership funds are the income and control advantages. Debt capital has a fixed return. After interest is paid the remainder of the profit is available to the owners. In successful ventures the profits can be very substantial. Borrowed funds rarely give any control to the lenders. The equity investors own and run the business.

Table 12.1 Sources of Past Equity in Irish Companies %

		No. of Employees				
	Total %	3–9 %	10–19 %	20–50 %	51–99 %	100+ %
Private Sourcing	49	59	55	38	40	75
BES	27	19	25	32	40	25
Venture Capital	12	9	10	18	13	
Other	12	13	10	12	7	
	100	100	100	100	100	100
Companies Issuing Shares	129	32	40	34	15	8

Source: Department of Enterprise & Employment.

This chapter looks at ownership funds. The importance of equity can be gauged from a 1992 study of 400 Irish firms where 31 per cent had raised equity in the previous three years while 58 per cent felt that they would need new equity within the following three years. Four out of five respondents thought it difficult to raise equity. The ownership sources of finance discussed here are preference share capital, equity share capital and retained earnings. The role of venture capital and the Business Expansion Scheme in providing equity is examined. Principal sources of past equity funding in private Irish business is shown in Table 12.1.

1. PREFERENCE SHARE CAPITAL

Some investors are not willing to take the full risk which attaches to owners' funds. Instead, for a lower expected rate of return they seek a lower risk. Preference shares are designed to meet such needs. As the title suggests, preference shareholders have preference or priority over ordinary shareholders but are subordinate to debt holders and creditors with regard to the firm's dividends and assets. They occupy an intermediate position between long-term debt holders and ordinary shareholders or equity holders. Investors receive a dividend payment, usually fixed, instead of interest payments and in the event of liquidation or bankruptcy usually rank ahead of ordinary shareholders. The non-payment of dividends does not force the firm into bankruptcy as can failure to pay interest on long-term debt. Preference shares participate in risk and profits but not to the same extent as ordinary shares. They combine some of the characteristics of both debt and equity. Owners tend to regard preference shares as similar to debt while lenders regard such issues as equity or near equity.

From the ordinary shareholder's point of view, apart from the cost, there is little to choose between preference shares and long-term debt, particularly if the firm has a stable earnings record. An ordinary shareholder will not receive a dividend as long as either interest or preference dividend payments remain unpaid. An ordinary shareholder expecting to receive dividend payments will consider the preference share dividend as much of a fixed charge as interest payments on debt. Looked at in this light, preference shares are an expensive form of long-term debt. The expense arises from the fact that dividends on preference shares are a distribution of profit, not an expense, and as such they are not tax-deductible.

Control of a firm is rarely affected by issuing preference shares. Generally, the shares are non-voting except where the dividend has been passed. Control may also be affected to the extent that an arrears of preference dividends may restrict management's actions or involve some participation by the preference shareholder, such as a seat on the board of directors.

Types of Preference Share

Over time a number of variations on the basic form of preference share have evolved. The variations are designed to meet the varying needs of investors and take account of changing tax legislation.

(1) Straight Preference Shares. These shares have fixed dividend coupons. They are non-cumulative, which means that dividends not paid in one year are lost. Such issues are rare. The two main banking groups in Ireland have them. Essentially, these issues are long-term loans issued as preference shares to be tax-efficient to the holders.

(2) Cumulative Preference Shares. Practically all preference issues are cumulative. This means that dividends not paid accumulate. All arrears must be cleared prior to paying dividends to the ordinary shareholders. The cumulative provision is an important

protection for the preference shareholder and goes some way towards minimising the risk of no dividend in the case of a firm which doesn't practise a stable ordinary shareholders' dividend policy. There are many examples of cumulative preference share issues on the Irish Stock Exchange. Examples include Heiton's 4.5 per cent Cum. Pref. and CRH 7 per cent Cum. Pref.

(3) Redeemable Preference Shares. Preference shares are technically part of the firm's equity and as such are a permanent part of the shareholders' funds with no specific maturity date. However, many investors do not wish to make a perpetual investment at a fixed rate of return. To cater for such investors a finite life is given to certain preference shares – usually twenty years or longer. This is done to give the issuing firm some degree of flexibility in its financing plans and to allow it to take advantage of falling interest rates. This process of retiring stock is not attractive to investors and generally involves a once-off premium should the option be exercised. Some firms quoted on the Irish Stock Exchange have issued redeemable preference shares, i.e. the 7 per cent Red. Cum. Pref. issued by Unidare.

(4) Participating Preference Shares. Some investors want the security of an annual dividend but they also want the chance to participate in the profitability of the business. To cater for such needs, participating preference shares were developed. These shares are entitled to a fixed dividend coupon and to a further dividend which is related to the dividend paid on ordinary shares. This is not a widely used feature and is included only when the issuing firm needs to make the offer more attractive to an otherwise unwilling investor. An example is the Ryan Hotels PLC issue of 9 per cent non-cumulative participating shares. After a payment of 22 per cent on the 5 pence ordinary shares, the preference holders obtain a further 3.5 per cent.

(5) Convertible Preference Shares. In recent years a number of preference share issues have attracted subscribers by offering conversion rights into ordinary shares. This is now a growing feature of such issues as it makes them more desirable and may reduce the cost to the company. It allows the preference shareholder at his discretion to convert his shares into a predetermined number of ordinary shares. It is a 'sweetener' often used by small to medium-sized firms with low credit ratings and higher than average gearing to guarantee the success of the issue. It is also used by firms with high growth rates and little or no security available as collateral. Consequently, it tends to be subordinated and unsecured. It is in essence a form of delayed equity financing used by high risk companies to raise funds at a relatively favourable rate. The disadvantage is that it can limit the flexibility of the firm to raise additional finance and can result in a shift in the firm's capital structure should the convertible preference shareholders exercise their option. In the mid-1980s Heiton's issued a 6 per cent convertible preference issue. One of the most complicated issues is a Convertible Cumulative Redeemable Participating Preference share issued by Youghal Carpets. European Leisure has a 6 per cent Convertible Cumulative Preference share convertible up to 2005 on the basis of 1.16279 ordinary shares for £1 of preference shares.

(6) Export Preference Shares. The 1970s/1980s saw an increase in the number of preference shares issued in Ireland. These shares were generally redeemable preference shares with a life of less than ten years, though twenty-year redeemable preference shares were issued. The normal channel for these issues was an institution which purchased the entire issue. The cause of the resurgence in preference share issues was the tax relief granted on exports, not only for corporation tax but also for

income tax. A firm exporting a large part of its output paid a much reduced rate of tax. The dividends declared by this firm also qualified for tax relief. Consequently, export-oriented firms were able to issue preference shares at lower rates than long-term debentures. The net after-tax income to the holders of the shares was often larger than the net income resulting from a higher interest rate. The greater the proportion of exports in a firm's total output the greater the advantage of preference shares over long-term debt. The facility was discontinued in the late 1980s.

From the viewpoint of an Irish manufacturing company preference shares have attractions. Few manufacturing companies have a substantial tax bill, therefore the lack of tax-deductibility is not serious. Furthermore, preference share financing is flexible in that the dividend does not have to be paid and the average preference issue, being irredeemable, is in fact a permanent loan. Preference shares expand the equity base of the company and make it more attractive to lenders.

The principal reasons for the decline in preference shares are fear of inflation and lack of control. From an investor's viewpoint debt often has more attractions than preference shares.

2. EQUITY SHARE CAPITAL   *Not Examined*

Investors in ordinary shares are the real owners of a business. They invest in hope and expectation. They are the driving force behind the spirit of entrepreneurism that gave birth and continues to give birth to a nation's largest and most powerful firms. If hopes are realised then a stream of earnings and dividends will accrue to the owners. The amount of finance provided by the investor in ordinary shares serves as a 'cushion' for the creditors, which in turn increases the creditworthiness of the firm. If the venture is unsuccessful then the owners will in all probability lose their total investment.

The ordinary shareholder is the risk taker who controls the company. The objective of every business must be the maximisation of the long-term wealth of this shareholder. Such shares differ from all other sources of finance in that, depending on the success of the company, the value of ordinary shares can rise or fall spectacularly. In general, debentures and preference shares have a maximum redemption price. The price of these securities will hardly rise above their redemption prices no matter how well the business does but they can and do fall if the company is doing poorly.

Ordinary shares carry with them no right to repayment and no right to a dividend but they almost invariably possess the right of ownership and, in theory, control. The ordinary shareholders must have regular opportunities, usually annual, to elect a board of directors and to vote on issues such as whether a dividend is to be paid. In small firms the management, board of directors and shareholders are normally one and the same and ownership and control are not divorced. In medium to large firms the ordinary shareholders may have only a passive involvement, with their influence dependent upon their collective ability to reach a consensus on issues proposed by management or the board of directors, and their effect on the market value of their shares dependent upon their buying and/or selling them.

Once the directors are elected the shareholder has a right to expect them, as his agents, to administer the affairs of the firm in its best interest. In practice the shareholder's control is somewhat limited. Management recommends the composition of the board of directors and other important issues and, whether through shareholder inertia or apathy, generally succeeds in its proposals. Further, the directors may abdicate their responsibility and thereby ensure that the management controls the firm. This in turn sets up the potential for ongoing conflict by which a divergence of interests between the management and shareholders is allowed to exist. Passive ownership in this context can be detrimental to the ordinary shareholder's best interest.

The ordinary shareholders have the right to the income remaining after all commitments to other sources of finance have been met. The remaining income can all be paid out as a dividend of so much per share but more often the directors propose, and the shareholders usually accept, that a percentage of the income be retained in the business. The expectation is that retained income or 'retained earnings' will be used to generate even more profits for the ordinary shareholders.

The option to declare a dividend or not is a major advantage of ownership funds. When multiple investment opportunities exist, management can reduce or forego dividend payments. The type of investor who purchases ordinary shares is one prepared to take the risk of an uncertain income flow. In return he gets the opportunity of capital appreciation and/or higher income plus a voice in control.

In large, publicly quoted companies the risk and control aspects of investing in ordinary shares are more apparent than real. Companies such as Smurfit, Cement Roadstone and the banking groups have a near perfect record of paying dividends. The average shareholder with his few votes can attend the annual general meeting of these companies but he will wield no power. Nevertheless, the underlying theory of ultimate risk holds true. The riskiness of investing in equity shares can be seen by looking at the performance of equity shares on the Irish Stock Exchange. Cambridge — a darling of the Exchange in the late 1980s — failed in the 1990s. Shares in companies such as European Leisure, Yeoman Group and Xtravision collapsed by over 90 per cent in a few years. Even more spectacular was the performance of some exploration shares. Aminex, mentioned in Chapter 8, rose from 20 pence to £12.70 per share only to decline back to pennies after a restructuring where one new share was issued for every ten old shares. The price later rose again on new exploration hopes. Atlantic Resources rose tenfold but then declined by 99 per cent and was eventually merged into Arcon at pennies per share.

One of the most important financial judgments made by management is the decision to issue new equity shares. It is important for two reasons: the first is that new shares carry rights to vote and as such may affect the control of the firm; secondly, except in special circumstances ordinary shares are irredeemable and consequently participate in all future profits and dividends of the firm.

The admittance of new shareholders is likely to be considered in every business from the small one-man private firm to the big public company. In the small private firm the owner/manager may find that his talents are in one particular field — say, marketing. He may seek a partner experienced in production or financial matters who would invest in the business. If the firm grows, the partnership may discover that extra ownership finance is required. This can be raised by admitting more partners or by forming a limited company and admitting more shareholders. A further expansion of the business may be partially financed by retained earnings with additions of short-, medium- and long-term debt but ultimately the firm may require a stronger ownership interest. The owners of a profitable growing firm may wish to release some of the capital tied up in the business and may elect to sell shares to the public through the stock market. Finally, public companies often require extra ownership finance either to fund expansions or to secure and consolidate their existing position.

In general it can be stated that each ordinary share carries a vote and is entitled to a proportional share of earnings and dividends. Non-voting ordinary shares have been issued but they tend to be frowned upon as they place owners in the unenviable position of being forced to accept decisions affecting their interests without any say in the matter.

Deferred ordinary shares are another form of equity which have been issued in special circumstances. Shares such as these would not qualify for dividends except where abnormally large profits are made, and may not have voting rights until a specified date or until annual earnings have reached a certain figure. Deferred ordinary shares may arise on a reconstruction of a company where new equity capital is required and the original ordinary shareholders become 'deferred' in order to attract new shareholders. A number of examples of deferred shares exist on the Irish Stock Exchange, e.g. Kenmare Deferred 20 pence shares, Power Corporation Convertible Redeemable Deferred 10 pence shares. They are often valueless.

Risk Levels of Equity Capital *Not Examined*

It may surprise some to know that not all equity issues are of equal risk. Though all ordinary shares face the same financial risk insofar as they get repaid only after everyone else is paid, the level of business risk varies enormously. Investors seek the type of investment which best suits their own personal risk profile. The risk classes of equity capital can be categorised as (a) seed capital, (b) venture capital, (c) development capital and (d) ongoing equity capital.

Figure 12.2 outlines the stages of new project equity financing.

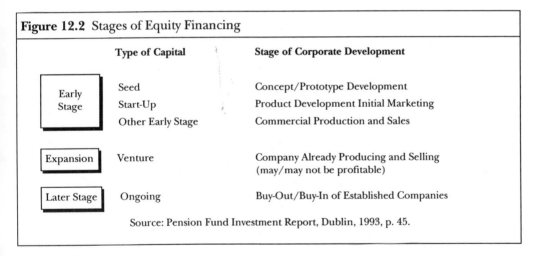

Figure 12.2 Stages of Equity Financing

	Type of Capital	Stage of Corporate Development
Early Stage	Seed	Concept/Prototype Development
	Start-Up	Product Development Initial Marketing
	Other Early Stage	Commercial Production and Sales
Expansion	Venture	Company Already Producing and Selling (may/may not be profitable)
Later Stage	Ongoing	Buy-Out/Buy-In of Established Companies

Source: Pension Fund Investment Report, Dublin, 1993, p. 45.

Seed Capital. Usually, this is the first source of capital raised and effectively the start-up equity capital. Very often this 'Seed Capital', as it is known, is the most difficult source to tap. The individual with the good idea frequently has no cash; he is often at an age where capital has not been accumulated; there is no history of success — that is, there is no so-called track record. In practically every new venture the first moneys spent come from the entrepreneur's savings, the sale of personal or business assets, an inheritance or friends'/relatives' funds. These funds are the capital at most risk. Many ventures never get off the ground. A business is in most danger during its first year of life, which is when any weaknesses emerge. Over 50 per cent of new firms which close do so in the first two years. The nature of seed capital is such that few organisations or individuals apart from friends or family of the entrepreneur are prepared to take the risk. Certain exceptions do exist. Brave souls called 'business angels' do invest in start-ups. They are generally wealthy individuals who have made money and are prepared for a high level of risk.

Seed capital is notoriously difficult to come by in Ireland. Apart from friends and relatives the only likely sources are well-off individuals. A few small organisations such as the Bolton Trust and Liffey Trust provide very limited funds.

Venture Capital. Venture Capital is generally thought to be equity capital, but it should be stressed that it can take the following forms: equity, debt and convertible debt. The term is also confusing in that there is no one precise definition for it. The key elements of a venture capital investment are:
— it is equity in orientation,
— it is long-term,
— it is aimed at companies with rapid growth potential,
— it offers higher expected returns to compensate for the higher risk,
— it is aimed at unquoted companies,
— it emphasises capital gain.

Table 12.3 Sectoral Distribution of Venture Capital Investment

Sector	% Funds Invested		
	USA %	Europe %	Ireland %
Software and Services	27.1	3.9	19.6
Medical/Healthcare	17.4	4.0	3.2
Telephone and Data Communications	14.4	3.9	1.3
Biotechnology	10.3	1.3	0.0
Consumer-Related	7.7	19.4	39.9
Other	23.1	67.5	36.0
Total	100	100	100

Source: Pension Fund Investment Report, Dublin, 1993

Venture capital is supplied usually by specialist firms which target certain companies, industries and in some cases locations. They could be subsidiaries of manufacturing or banking companies or firms set up to manage funds provided by pension contributions, individuals or companies. Though venture capital practice can be traced back to the 1950s, it was not until the 1980s that the market reached a stage of any significance and this period saw the foundation of most of today's firms in the area. Initially, venture capital firms had a preference for promising businesses in the high technology or speciality retailing area and for those located in high potential growth economies. There is now an increasing emphasis on non-technology service companies with innovative approaches to new or existing markets. They are also prepared to invest in ailing companies that they believe can be 'turned around' with the introduction of new management and a proper capital base. In addition to raising finance, venture capital firms can provide management and marketing know-how that many new companies lack, and ultimately allow the entrepreneur to unlock all or part of his equity by bringing the company to the market some years later. Recent trends have also shown venture capitalists to be particularly interested in companies that expand through mergers and acquisitions and leveraged buyouts.

Table 12.3 shows the sectoral distribution of venture capital investments. Table 12.4 gives an industry breakdown.

Table 12.4 Venture Capital Investments by Industry 1992

	Europe	Ireland
Communications	3.9	1.3
Computer-Related	3.9	19.6
Other Electronics-Related	2.9	4.3
Biotechnology	1.3	0
Medical/Health-Related	4.0	3.2
Energy	3.7	0
Consumer-Related	19.4	39.9
Industrial Products and Services	12.4	12.0
Chemicals and Materials	3.9	0
Industrial Automation	1.7	0
Transportation	3.0	4.0
Financial Services	5.6	0.5
Other Services	11.0	1.7
Other Manufacturing	13.8	3.1
Agriculture	1.2	0
Construction	4.1	10.4
Other	4.2	0
Total	100	100

Source: EVCA Reported in Pension Fund Investment Report, Dublin, 1993.

Once a project takes shape the level of risk often decreases. The individual who spends money to build a prototype has a tangible product instead of a vague idea. The project has more attraction if the market potential has been surveyed and likely customers identified. With a market survey, a product and even a limited history of production, investors will examine the potential. It is at this stage that the venture capitalist, if presented with a thorough business plan, a credible management team and the enthusiasm of the entrepreneur, is most likely to be interested. The carrying out of a 'due diligence' test and the intense negotiation of issues such as ownership, amount of finance required, management structure, control and the medium-term development of the firm should provide the basis of a formal contractual agreement in the interests of both parties.

Development Capital. Projects which get into production usually grow or fold. Growing projects require additional cash. The original investors find that their own resources and any profits emanating from the venture are insufficient to allow for rapid expansion. Development Capital is required. A venture capitalist, whether involved before or approached for the first time, may be interested in providing all or part of the necessary finance at this stage. It may simply be a question of luck and timing in matching up the surplus funds and ethos of the venture capitalist with the capital needs of the firm. Venture capitalists have shown an increasing tendency to spread their risk across a diversified portfolio of investments at various stages of their development and to respond to tax legislation initiatives. Development capital can also come in the form of a term loan.

Ongoing Equity Capital. The final type of equity arises from the needs of companies which find that their equity base is becoming too small in relation to the size of the business. Very often a new investment or a diversification opportunity requires some additional equity. Such finance can be called Ongoing Equity Capital. It is raised from existing shareholders by means of a rights issue, or from new investors by placing shares. Alternatively, expansion can be an acquisition paid for by an issue of new shares. This expands the equity base. Firms at this stage of financing are typically growing, have already a proven earnings capability and are confident of continued earnings growth.

VENTURE CAPITAL MARKET IN IRELAND

The United States is widely recognised as a world leader in the area of venture capital and has the most open environment for general investor participation in private enterprise. In the 1980s the United States venture capital business witnessed spectacular growth and success. The current funds pool in the mid-1990s amounts to approximately $30 billion with new investments of around $3 billion per year.

Pension funds contribute over 40 per cent of the venture funds. Two-thirds of the new investments go to companies over ten years old with less than 8 per cent invested in companies under five years old. The average return on investment has been 20 per cent annually.

The UK is the most developed venture capital market in Europe with over 100 venture capital companies supplying more than 40 per cent of all funds invested in Europe.

While risk equity was available in Ireland from private sources for many years, the development of the venture capital industry dates no further back than the mid-1970s. During the early years, the industry concentrated almost solely on investment in established companies but in recent years there is increasing evidence that the industry is investing more money in start-up situations.

Among the current batch of companies quoted on the Stock Exchange, many grew with the support of venture capital; examples include Barlo, the radiator manufacturer, Woodchester, the leasing company, Tullow, the exploration company, Dakota, the paper and packaging company, and even CRH, the building materials group.

Private companies which performed well with the support of venture capital include Cablelink, Poldys, the food manufacturer, Cahill May Roberts, the pharmaceutical company, Allegro, the food distributor, Imari, the freight shipping group, and Emmets, the cream liqueur company.

Venture capital tends to be a high risk, high return prospect and there have been many cases where venture capitalists backed companies which did not prove successful. For instance, Allied Combined Trust lost millions of pounds on its investments in Mahon and McPhilips, the engineering company, Galway Crystal and the Golden Grid lottery. Similarly, ICC lost out on investments in Memory Computer and Etos International Computers.

Despite this activity, the Irish venture capital market remains underdeveloped by international standards. In particular, pension funds have tended to give venture projects a wide berth. In 1992, for example, Irish pension funds did not supply any venture capital at all. Contrast this with the situation in the US, where 42 per cent of new venture capital finance came from private pension funds, and the UK, where 37 per cent came from such funds.

The Irish venture capital market shrank in the early 1990s as Allied Combined Trust (ACT) scaled down its activities, Development Capital Corporation (DCC) changed its strategy away from venture capital to become an industrial holding company, and the government closed down the National Development Corporation. At the same time UK investors, such as 3i, withdrew from the Irish market. After a review of the situation a number of new venture capital companies were formed in 1993 and 1994.

The new ACT fund was backed by — among others — AIB, which invested £15 million, Mercury Asset Management and Murray Johnstone, two leading UK venture capital funds, and a number of institutions and pension funds, including New Ireland Assurance, Norwich Union, Ulster Bank Investment Managers, AIB pension fund, RTE pension fund, Player and Wills pension fund and the Telecom Éireann pension fund.

ACT invests sums of between £300,000 and £5 million in medium-sized expanding companies which offer an exit opportunity within a ten-year time span. Two other firms, ICC and Delta Partners, have also begun to trade. Unlike ACT, ICC, with £120 million of a fund, expects the most likely exit mechanism to be a trade sale rather than a stock market flotation. Delta, which is backed by the Investment Bank of Ireland, has a fund of £20 million to invest and concentrates on technology ventures.

The main objective of the venture capital company is to have a minority shareholding in its investee companies. The venture capital investor will normally insist on a shareholder's agreement ensuring him certain minimum rights despite his minority status. The required rate of return will depend on the individual assessment of the risk attaching to each specific proposal. In Ireland an overall rate of 30 per cent per annum is, generally speaking, required.

The Irish Venture Capital Association (IVCA) was set up in January 1985, in order to provide a forum for, and a stimulus to, the venture capital industry in Ireland. According to the IVCA, the number of companies in which their members have equity shareholdings amounts to approximately 300. These companies have a combined turnover in excess of £500 million, export 30 per cent of their goods and provide employment for over 8,000 people. The funds pool is estimated to be in the order of £400 million, including the recent Enterprise Partnership Fund of £150 million set up by the government in association with the financial institutions.

Table 12.5 gives a list of equity providers in Ireland.

BUSINESS EXPANSION SCHEME (BES)

A major development in Irish corporate finance was the creation of tax incentives for equity investment, as part of the government's job creation strategy. This was achieved primarily through the Business Expansion Scheme (BES), set up in 1984, whereby an investor got a tax rebate at his marginal rate (1995 rate: up to 48 per cent) on the full value of his investment up to £25,000 in any one year. If more than £25,000 is invested or

Table 12.5 Directory of the Key Equity Companies in Ireland — Enterprise Development

Name	Total Funds Managed	Minimum Investment	Maximum Investment	Types of Funding	Stages of Investment	Share-holding Level
Allied Irish Banks — Allied Combined Trust	£65-£70m	£500,000	Open	Equity and quasi equity, MBO financing	Development	20%-40%
Allied Irish Banks — First Venture Fund	£4m	£50,000	£1m	Equity and quasi equity	Start-up	20%+
BCP Stockbrokers	£25m (BES Funds)	N/A	N/A	Equity only	Development	N/A
Business and Trading House Investment Company	£4-£5m (BES Funds)	£250,000	£500,000	Equity only	All except start-up	25%-51%
DCC Ltd	£130m	£500,000	£10m	Equity and MBO	Development	Large stake
Dublin Business Innovation Fund	£1m	£25,000	£75,000	Equity	Start-up	Open
Early Start Technology Fund — SFADCo	£200,000	£10,000	£50,000	Equity	No preference	Open
Woodchester Credit Lyonnais Bank Enterprise Fund	£10m	£25,000	£150,000	Loan finance	No preference	Open
Enterprise Equity (Ireland) Ltd — International Fund	£8.1m	£75,000	£750,000	Equity and quasi equity	No preference	N/A
Enterprise Trust Fund	£2m p.a.	£5,000	N/A	Equity	Development	25%-35%
Equitas Investment Ltd	£19m (BES Funds)	£150,000	£500,000	Equity	Start-up and restructuring	20%-30%
First Step	N/A	None	£10,000	Interest-free loan finance	Preferably established	N/A
Guinness Workers' Employment Fund	£30,000-£60,000 p.a.	£5,000	£15,000	Loan finance	Development	N/A
Hill Samuel Fagan Investment Management	£2m	£100,000	£250,000	Equity	Mature	N/A
ICC Bank BES Fund	£3m	£500,000	£500,000	Equity	Development and MBO	10%+
ICC Venture Capital	£3-£5m p.a.	£200,000	£1.5m	Equity and loan finance	Development	10%-50%
Riada BES Fund	£2m p.a.	£200,000	£500,000	Equity	Development	N/A
Smurfit Job Creation Enterprise Fund	£10m p.a.	£100,000	£500,000	Equity and loan finance	Preferably established	N/A

Source: Chapman, Flood and Partners, 1994.

insufficient income arises in the current year, the benefit may be carried forward.

The BES offers two types of investment vehicle, the managed fund and the individual project. The managed fund is where the investor's money is spread over a large number of projects, selected and administered by the fund manager. This should minimise the risk for the individual investor, who has no direct interest in any one project while at the same time gaining the tax advantage. The individual project is where the investor's money goes to one specific project and he has direct exposure to that specific sector. He also puts his faith in that particular management team.

Various changes have taken place since its inception, principally in regard to the life of the scheme, the restrictions on the amounts of money to be raised, the operational details and what constitutes an approved scheme. The chief operational details legislate that the investment must remain in place for a minimum of five years and that:
— an individual claiming relief must be resident in Ireland for the year in which relief is claimed,
— qualifying companies must be incorporated and solely resident in the state and
— must be an unquoted company for three years from the date of the shares issue or from the commencement of trading, if later.

Initially, only manufacturing firms were included. Subsequent relaxations allowed the scheme to apply to software companies and to tourist developments. This led to an upsurge in property-backed hotel development-type projects which subsequent tightening regulations have effectively ruled out. The criterion is now that the project should have a genuine tourism development focus and carry the approval of Bord Fáilte, rather than merely serve the local market. The Finance Act of 1993 extended the life of the scheme to April 1996 when it will cease. It also removed the lifetime cap of £75,000 per investor, thereby bringing back into consideration the large-scale investor, but maintained a cap of £1 million which can be invested in any one company.

Table 12.6 BES Funds Raised 1984–1993

	No. of Firms	Total Value £m
1984/85	6	0.9
1985/86	42	4.4
1986/87	91	6.9
1987/88	161	9.9
1988/89	188	25.5
1989/90	239	78.0
1990/91	237	61.3
1991/92	271	61.3
1992/93	169	21.7
Total No. of Firms	1,404	
Total Investment		£270 million
Estimated Cost to Exchequer		£140 million

Source: Revenue Commissioners Reported in Pension Fund Investment Report, Dublin, 1993, p. 41.

It is especially important that investors and companies wishing to take advantage of BES incentives use competent advisors at an early stage, as despite the attractive tax incentives and glossy brochure presentations this is not a risk-free investment.

Me elamo CIARAN.

After a very slow start, the BES scheme flowered. In the ten years 1984–93 the BES has raised over £270 million and provided capital to approximately 1,400 companies. It has led to the development of a significant service industry whereby specialist firms and professional advisors have been set up to seek and manage investments on behalf of clients. Previously established advisors have also expanded their practices to provide this service to existing and new clients.

In 1993 a total of one hundred and sixty-nine companies received BES funds, 83 per cent going to manufacturing industry. Of the companies raising funds, seventy-four raised less than £50,000 each, with a further seventy-one raising less than £400,000 (Table 12.7). Only twenty-four companies raised over £400,000, and between them these companies absorbed half the funds raised. Because of the £1 million ceiling on BES investment in a company, these figures understate the proportion of funding which would go to companies requiring over £400,000 in the absence of a constraint.

Table 12.7 Spread of BES Investment by Company Size 1993

Firm Size	% of Money	% of Firms	No. of firms
Small (below £50,000)	7	44	74
Medium (£50,000–£400,000)	43	42	71
Large (above £400,000)	50	14	24
	100	100	164

Source: Revenue Commissioners Reported in Pension Fund Investment Report, Dublin, 1993, p. 42.

The main impact of the BES scheme is twofold:
(1) An expansion in the range of seed capital and venture capital available.
(2) A reduction in the cost of equity capital to companies. The tax incentives mean that promoters can finance equity issues at a higher price, thus reducing both the cost of equity and the loss of control.

Following threatened redundancies in a number of multinational companies in the early 1990s, particularly Digital Equipment Corporation, a new tax incentive known as Seed Capital Relief was introduced. This encouraged high earners who were made redundant to invest their lump sum redundancy payment in their new business, subject to certain conditions. If they qualified for the relief, they could set off their investment against their taxable income over the previous five years. The conditions of the scheme were very strict and to date it has not been widely taken up.

3. RETAINED EARNINGS

Each year the directors of the firm make a dividend decision whereby they pay to the ordinary shareholders part, all or none of the profits earned during the year. Most firms do not pay out all their earnings all the time but prefer to keep some in the business either as reserves or for investment projects.

In deciding on the dividend, the board of directors is also deciding for the shareholders how much they should invest. The following explains the procedure. Tax complications are ignored.

Net earnings	£70,000	This belongs to the shareholders.
Dividends declared	£20,000	The shareholders receive this in cash.
Retained earnings	£50,000	The directors have decided to keep this amount of the shareholders' money in the business.

Had the £50,000 retained earnings been paid to the shareholders they would have been able to use the money as they wished. The directors, by keeping the money in the business, have decided that the shareholders will derive greater benefit by increasing their investment in the firm. By retaining earnings, the directors are providing funds for further investment. They should be quite certain that the return on the proposed investment will be higher than the return which the shareholders could achieve if they had received the funds.

Retained earnings provide industry with much of the funds needed for investment. Very often these funds are retained without considering the implications of the decision. In a private firm the directors are normally the owners and consequently there is no possibility of an incorrect decision being reached. In a public company the directors may represent only a part of the total ownership and so they must be very careful to make decisions in the best financial interests of the shareholders.

The advantages of retained earnings as a source of funds are that:

(a) There is no change in the control pattern of the firm.

(b) Retained earnings, being equity capital, reduce the financial risk of the firm: that is, lower the debt/equity ratio.

(c) The funds are readily available and do not involve expensive issuing costs.

(d) There are no fixed charges.

(e) There is no fixed maturity, as equity capital is a perpetuity.

(f) There is no increase in the number of shares, so even a small return on the investment of retained earnings will increase the earnings per share to all existing shareholders.

The disadvantages of retained earnings are that:

(a) Management may not be as careful with retained earnings as it would be with an alternative source of capital.

(b) Retained earnings may not be the most suitable source of capital: that is, a firm with no debt and stable earnings may be able to raise debt capital more efficiently than using retained earnings.

(c) The 'cost' of retained earnings may be high.

The last disadvantage is often difficult to explain to managements which look on retained earnings as a costless source of finance. They point out that retained earnings have no issuing costs, and that no new dividends arise. This serious error has led many a management into a serious trap. If retained earnings are viewed as a costless source of finance, management is tempted to reduce dividends. Paying out low dividends often causes share prices to remain low. High levels of retained earnings, if properly invested, increase assets per share. Over time, assets per share may greatly exceed the share price. This makes the company vulnerable to a takeover bid, which can result in management personnel losing their jobs.

Since retained earnings are equity, their cost is the same cost as that of raising new shares, with the exception of the issuing costs attaching to new shares.

DIVIDENDS VERSUS RETAINED EARNINGS

As stated already, the amount of earnings retained is a function of the dividend policy followed by a business. In practically every case the dividend is a cash payment to shareholders, a payment which reduces the value of the business. The power to declare a dividend rests with the board of directors of a company, and they are usually declared twice yearly. An interim dividend is declared when the half-yearly results are announced and a final with the annual results. The dividend decision is voted on at the annual general meeting. Dividends need not and cannot be declared unless profits have been made, or unless reserves of undistributed profits exist. It is illegal to declare a dividend out of subscribed capital.

In attempting to define a policy on dividends, the directors must remember that the objective of the business is the maximisation of the long-run wealth of the owner. In practice this means maximising the share price in the long term. The effect of dividends or the lack of dividends on the share price has been the subject of much theoretical debate. In the early 1960s Modigliani and Miller put forward a well-argued thesis that the value of a business was defined totally by its earning power. It therefore did not matter whether a firm paid dividends; in terms of net worth to shareholders, there could be no difference between paying dividends on the one hand and allowing retained earnings to reflect themselves in share price rises on the other. The model used assumed a world of perfect certainty and no taxes. Modigliani and Miller suggested further that investors would invest in firms with dividend policies which suited their own needs.

Other researchers take a very different view. In a world of uncertainty, dividends are relevant because investors are receiving cash now instead of an uncertain gain in the future. The evidence available tends to support the view that firms paying dividends are in general more highly valued than firms retaining all earnings.

Differing taxation policies also affect the issue. In Ireland capital gains tax at rates between 27 and 40 per cent is lower than the average income tax paid by investors on dividend income. This suggests that many investors would prefer lower rather than higher dividends. Offsetting this to some extent is the tax credit available on dividends paid out by many companies.

The factors that influence a dividend policy can be outlined as follows:

(1) The informational content of dividends. Paying regular cash dividends leads investors to expect that they will continue. Changing dividends either upward or downward provides information to the shareholders. The new information is likely to lead to a change in expectations. This in turn leads to a change in the share price.

(2) Industry 'norms'. Over time, the financial community comes to expect firms in certain industries to perform in certain ways. A maverick company may worry the financial community. This can lead to a flight of investors.

(3) Reinvestment opportunities. Firms may have or, equally importantly, be perceived to have certain investment opportunities. If opportunities are limited, as they might be in mature businesses such as brewing or tobacco, investors would expect profits to be paid out as dividends. Other companies, such as high technology communications or information processing firms, will have many potentially profitable investments. Investors might expect companies like this to retain some or all of their profits.

(4) Restrictive covenants in lending agreements might place a limit on dividends.

(5) The tax status of the shareholders may influence the proposed policy.

(6) Revenue regulations on the dividend policy in private firms will have an effect. The

Revenue Commissioners are keen to prevent owners of small private companies from retaining earnings which would be taxed as income if declared as dividends. In some circumstances they will impose a 20 per cent surcharge on the undistributed service and investment earnings of small private companies known as close companies.

(7) The availability of cash. Irrespective of all other considerations, a business may lack the ready cash with which to pay dividends. Lenders rarely like to see their funds being paid out as dividends.

In practice companies tend to follow a stable, conservative dividend policy. Investors are assumed to prefer a stable level of cash income to a fixed percentage of earnings, which would mean a drop in income in poor years. Studies of dividend policy in Ireland have shown that management changes the level of dividends only when it expects to be able to maintain the revised payout levels.

It is important to note the distorting effect of taxation on Irish dividend policies. Profits arising from export sales in companies exporting prior to 1981 were exempt from both corporation tax and income tax. This created a bias in favour of paying dividends rather than retaining earnings. Special rules which applied to manufacturing dividends reinforced this bias. However, 27 per cent capital gains tax on private Irish companies now creates a bias in favour of capital gain.

It is possible that Irish management has been too conservative in dividend policies. Increasing the level of dividends has repeatedly been shown to increase the value of the company though in fact the net worth is reduced by the payout. Higher dividends lead investors to expect higher income. Discounting a future stream of expected dividends leads to a higher price unless the discount factor is also increased. Evidence suggests that this does not occur.

Today the average Irish dividend-paying, publicly quoted firm is paying out 33 per cent of its profits as dividends.

METHODS OF RAISING NEW EQUITY CAPITAL

The major means of raising new equity funds are:

(1) Owners increasing their investment. This method is frequently used where the firm is very small and the owners have outside sources of funds. It involves no change in the control of the firm, if each owner can supply his share of the new investment.

(2) Introducing new partners or members. Small private firms starved for capital may accept funds from private individuals wishing to become involved in the business. In many cases the new members are willing to forego all control in return for the opportunity to invest. This method is occasionally adopted by a new investor providing a high interest term loan in return for the right to buy a certain percentage of the issued shares.

(3) Institutions providing term loans and accepting an equity interest. Small and medium-sized firms with good potential are often able to secure badly needed capital from financial institutions. These institutions provide a term loan and usually take a proportion of the total equity capital. The shares would be bought at par or at a valuation rather less than current value.

(4) Selling shares to suppliers or customers. If a firm is an important supplier to or purchaser from a company, the management of the company may consider it worth while to provide some equity capital for it.

(5) 'Going public'. A firm with a strong earnings record and good potential may benefit from 'going public' — for example, obtaining a Stock Exchange quotation and selling shares through the market. The mechanics of obtaining a quotation were dealt with in Chapter 8.

Basically, therefore, new equity capital can be raised through either a private placement or a public issue. Once a firm has become established and built a track record, it can remain private and still raise capital from institutional investors, usually with the help of an investment banking service. This is primarily the domain of small to medium-sized firms. A public issue, on the other hand, is much costlier, takes longer and is generally undertaken only by large firms. While there are a number of considerations — noted below — that influence the choice between private and public financing, size is one of the major factors.

Not Examined

CONSIDERATIONS IN RAISING NEW EQUITY

In reviewing new equity sources of capital, management should take into account — in addition to size — the control, risk and cost effects. These should be related to the capital structure required to provide the necessary base for the firm's future activities.

New equity is very much a long-term source of funds and it should be considered in conjunction with the long-term future of the business. Another important concern, especially in relation to public issues, is the time factor involved. Negotiating and issuing new capital may take many months and so management must anticipate the need and plan well in advance.

In summary the principal considerations are that:

(a) The issue of equity capital to outside interests can result in changes in control: that is, dilution of control. In addition management has less flexibility in running the business and, in the case of a public issue, faces significant disclosure requirements and regulatory control procedures.

(b) Equity issues generally tend to lower the financial risk of the firm and will thereby enable the firm to raise more debt.

(c) The cost of equity issues is difficult to define but it may be excessive. The cost is related to the fact that each new share qualifies for a proportion of all future earnings of the firm: that is, dilution of earnings may arise.

(d) Investors find the shares of publicly held companies more attractive because they are liquid and can usually be sold at any time in the marketplace. They automatically carry a market valuation, which can assist in raising other types of finance.

In contrast private placements can allow the firm to work more closely with specific investors whose expectations and strategy are closely matched. This should lead to a closer partnership between management and shareholder, which can be difficult to achieve in the case of a public issue.

CONCLUSION

This chapter has discussed ownership sources of finance. It was suggested that preference share financing, though related to equity financing, had many characteristics in common with debt financing. New equity finance is an area fraught with complexity. Equity reduces risk and relieves the burden on management but it is costly and may result in dilution or loss of management control. New equity enhances the future borrowing capacity of the firm, creditors preferring to lend to firms with a substantial equity base. Equity finance is needed at various stages of a company's life and is usually hardest to find when it is most needed — for instance, at start-up and in times of financial difficulties. The Business Expansion Scheme in Ireland greatly enhances the attraction of issuing new equity. Venture capital firms are expected to contribute to the pool of equity available in the late 1990s.

Retained earnings are a widely used and substantial source of finance. Though commonly held to be costless, they are in fact only slightly cheaper than issues of new equity. The amount of earnings retained is a function of dividend policy. In deciding on that policy, a firm must take into consideration a number of factors, such as legal constraints, investment opportunities, earnings stability, taxes, and the use of dividends as a way of sending signals to investors about current financial strength and future profit potential.

Decisions regarding ownership finance, especially new issues of ordinary shares, are taken only after serious soul-searching. Practically every other source has a finite life, so even if a mistake is made it will disappear some day. Not so with ordinary shares: they are a permanent feature of the company.

FURTHER READING

J.C. Van Horne, *Financial Management & Policy*, 9th ed. (New Jersey, Prentice-Hall, 1992).
R.C. Moyer et al., *Contemporary Financial Management*, 5th ed. (New York, West Publishing, 1992).
Pension Fund Investment Report, Dublin, 1993.
European Venture Capital Association Annual Reports.
Investor's Chronicle Supplement, *Private Equity*, 21 October 1994.

QUESTIONS

Question 12.1
What should be taken into consideration when defining a policy on dividends?

Question 12.2
What are the advantages and disadvantages of preference shares as compared to ordinary shares and long-term debt?

Question 12.3
Why was there seen to be a need for the Business Expansion Scheme?

Question 12.4
Why does a public quotation increase the risk of a firm being taken over? When a company goes public what additional pressures are created?

Question 12.5
In financing investment by retained earnings what are the costs and taxes incurred by shareholders?

Question 12.6
What are the main features and characteristics of ordinary shares?

13

State Aid in Financing Business

Ireland, as a small island located on the periphery of Europe, has a number of significant disadvantages for business. Location is an obvious problem, as is the small domestic market. As a province of a larger economic unit, Ireland, until 1922, developed few businesses apart from agriculture and service industries. Agriculture, based mainly on cattle, supplied raw materials for processing in the United Kingdom. Service industries, such as retailing, banking and insurance, reflected the structure existing throughout the UK and so were relatively advanced.

A priority of the first Irish government was to promote agricultural development on the premise that prosperity in farming would filter through to the rest of the economy. It was quickly realised that development required capital. Existing financial institutions were reluctant to lend to farmers. In 1923 the state established the Agricultural Credit Corporation to provide capital for agricultural development. The policy of developing agriculture did little for the economy as a whole.

In the early 1930s there was a change in policy. A new administration believed that the future prosperity of Ireland lay in industrial development. Manufacturing industry, it was held, offered the best solution to the twin problems of emigration and poverty. The thinking of the time was that imported goods could be made in Ireland. Tariffs and quotas were placed on a host of imported products. Investment capital was in short supply, so the state established the Industrial Credit Company (ICC). The ICC was to provide finance which would complement the various other sources of finance then available.

In the late 1940s a further policy change evolved. The strategy of economic development by means of import substitution was seen to have limitations. In a market as small as that in Ireland there were few products with a market demand sufficient to enable economic production. Small production runs produced high cost items, often of inferior quality. After the first rush of establishments during the 1930s, few other firms set up. There was insufficient demand to create any noticeable backward linkage. This meant that the demand for machines to make sweets, knit vests and roll cigarettes was not large enough to lead to the setting up of a machinery business, all of which in turn meant little or no demand for the output of a steel plant.

The new economic strategy which evolved during the 1950s was based on export markets. If Irish business were to grow it needed to export; the Irish Export Board, An

Bord Tráchtála, was established to promote exports. It was realised that Ireland lacked four ingredients essential to success: technology, access to markets, management and capital.

The easiest way to acquire all of the essentials was to attract overseas companies to establish manufacturing operations in Ireland. This strategy became known as development by means of export-oriented foreign direct investment.

In order to attract investors to a poorly located island with a limited infrastructure, a series of agencies and incentives was created, among them the Shannon Free Airport Development Company (SFADCo), the Industrial Development Authority and Údarás na Gaeltachta. Capital grants, tax incentives and liberal depreciation policies were introduced. During the 1960s and 1970s, economic development policy extended the range of assistance and incentives available. Agencies such as Bord Fáilte, Bord Iascaigh Mhara and AnCO (now FÁS), to name but three, grew rapidly and developed a range of subsidised financial instruments. After spectacular success in attracting hundreds of foreign companies in the 1960s and early 1970s, the momentum faltered.

In the late 1970s the policy changed again. The native Irish entrepreneur was recognised as a crucial part of the economic development process. Schemes and incentives were made available to promote Irish-owned businesses. Emphasis was placed on employment rather than capital.

By 1990 unemployment was at the highest level ever in the country. A number of studies into industrial development policy were carried out. Chief among these was the Culliton Report and the subsequent Moriarty Task Force Report. The government's response to these reports was the creation in 1993 of new state agency structures. Under this bill three new bodies were created — Forfás, Forbairt and the Industrial Development Agency (Ireland) — IDA. Forfás was to be in overall charge of industrial policy with Forbairt dealing with domestic industry and the IDA handling overseas companies.

In taking this step the government was accepting that the existing industry support agencies instead of helping were in fact inhibiting the most efficient and effective development of industry generally. It was agreeing with the conclusions of the Culliton Report that while the industrial development agencies were important in creating jobs, they could play only a limited role and could not be held solely responsible for the failure to meet the country's employment needs. The establishment of the new agency structures was but part of a range of government initiatives responding to the recommendations of the Moriarty Task Force, recommendations covering the areas of taxation, energy, ports, communication, transport, environment, commercial state enterprises, education and training, competition policy and the legislative process. In effect the Task Force report was setting out an agenda to deal with the requirements of employment and enterprise development in the country against the background of too much dependency on overseas investment and the opening up of the large European market through the internal market process. It was also trying to develop closer linkages between overseas and indigenous companies and between companies in different sectors. In essence Forfás was to be the link in the policy chain between the two operational agencies, Forbairt and the IDA, and the government department responsible, the Department of Enterprise and Employment.

There are a great many state agencies involved in Irish business. This chapter looks at the following:

(a) Forfás, Forbairt and the IDA
(b) Shannon Free Airport Development Company (SFADCo)
(c) Údarás na Gaeltachta
(d) ICC Bank
(e) FÁS
(f) An Bord Tráchtála/The Irish Trade Board
(g) The Agricultural Credit Corporation (ACC Bank)
(h) Bord Fáilte
(i) Bord Iascaigh Mhara (BIM)
(j) Custom House Docks Financial Services Development.

FORFÁS, FORBAIRT AND THE INDUSTRIAL DEVELOPMENT AGENCY (IRELAND) — IDA

The creation of these agencies in 1993 was a major change in the development and implementation of industrial policy in Ireland. Up to then the Industrial Development Authority, also denoted by the initials IDA, was the main job-creating agency. It was formed in 1949 and became a potent force during the 1960s, a time when over 80 per cent of all new private capital investment came from foreign companies. Employment in IDA-assisted firms rose during the 1980s, reaching almost 200,000 people by 1992 or approximately 20 per cent of all employment. While its incentives and services were adapted and updated over the years, the principal incentives were

— employment grants,
— non-repayable cash grants towards the cost of fixed assets,
— training grants,
— rent subsidies,
— provision of advance factories,
— leasing subsidies,
— loan guarantees,
— interest rate subsidies,
— feasibility study grant,
— product and process development grants.

The IDA ran a Small Business Division aimed at grant-aiding start-ups, primarily manufacturing and targeted to the poorer or designated areas in special need of assistance. Services included a comprehensive enterprise development programme, a graduate placement scheme, a national linkage programme aimed at building formal connections between Irish suppliers and larger, often multinational, purchasers, and support for the creation and development of co-operatives under its Industrial Co-Operative Incentive programme. Its incentives were available to service companies as well as manufacturing companies.

Throughout the 1970s and 1980s the IDA was one of the principal financial institutions in Ireland, and over thirty years it spent up to £3,000 million by way of grants and other incentives.

Notwithstanding the successes, the pace of job creation was unable to come close to meeting the requirements of the Irish economy, giving rise to the search for a solution through the Culliton and Moriarty reports. The new structure set up under the Industrial Development Bill 1993 saw the creation of three autonomous agencies, Forfás, Forbairt and the Industrial Development Agency (Ireland), each with a distinct mission and goal and its own board of directors. However, all three agencies will operate within a framework which facilitates co-operation and mutual support.

Forfás is responsible for overall policy co-ordination and administration. It works closely with various Departments of State to ensure that the company development role of Forbairt and the export development role of An Bord Tráchtála is maximised.

Forbairt and IDA now offer the following range of incentives.

Feasibility Study Grants of up to 50 per cent of the cost of eligible expenditure are available for companies investigating the feasibility of new products or markets.

Product Development Grants are provided towards the cost of developing new products and processes.

Capital Grants are provided towards the cost of fixed assets, including site development, buildings, new machinery and equipment. The IDA also provides Rent Subsidies towards the cost of leased premises.

Training Grants are provided towards the cost of implementing training programmes for workers in new greenfield industrial projects.

Development Grants of up to £30,000 per person, or 50 per cent of eligible costs, can be made available to companies which implement a sustained programme designed to build management capability.

Interest Subsidies and Loan Guarantees can be provided for Irish companies on loans raised for fixed asset investment.

Equity Participation may be taken in companies which the IDA assists, when this is desirable and possible. At the end of 1992 some 180 equity stakes were held. Generally, the stake was less than 10 per cent of issued equity.

Forbairt can provide an additional range of incentives for native firms. These include:

Employment Grants for additional jobs created.

Management Development Grants, in conjunction with FÁS. Up to 90 per cent of costs may be paid to help small companies develop their management skills and improve competence in business and strategic planning.

Product and Process Development Grants of up to 50 per cent for new product research.

The normal range of Forbairt grant incentives for new projects is supplemented under the Enterprise Development Programme as follows:

Forbairt guarantees loans towards the working capital requirements of the project as well as grants towards interest payments. These incentives normally apply only to the first stage (covering approximately three years) of a new enterprise.

To encourage companies to investigate and acquire new technology or products through licences, patents or know-how agreements, Forbairt can provide grants of up to 50 per cent of the direct costs of negotiating and acquiring the technology. Grants are subject to a maximum of £250,000 for any one project.

The Industrial Development Agency (Ireland) — IDA is responsible for attracting overseas industry to Ireland. Currently, three-quarters of Irish industrial exports come from foreign firms and those same firms employ half the total workforce in manufacturing. Ireland's success in the field of attracting mobile investment has been obscuring the relative failure of indigenous industry. The separation of responsibility for indigenous and overseas firms between the two agencies, Forbairt and the IDA, was done to ensure clarity and maximise the return to Ireland from the attraction of mobile international investment at the minimum cost to the taxpayer. The IDA must demonstrate the attractiveness of Ireland in terms of grant support package, quality of the labour force, clean environment and other infrastructural assets such as the telecommunications system.

In carrying out its primary responsibility, the promotion of industrial development in Ireland, the IDA offered a series of incentives and services under the following headings:

(a) New manufacturing and service industries or a major expansion of existing ones.
(b) Re-equipment of existing manufacturing industries.
(c) New or existing small industries, defined as manufacturing firms with up to fifty employees and fixed assets of £300,000.
(d) Enterprise development, which provides IDA guarantees for loans raised towards working capital needed for a project, grants towards the interest payable on loans raised to provide working capital, as well as normal financial assistance.

New Industries or Major Expansions. A wide range of financial incentives is available to overseas projects. The main elements of the incentives are:

(1) Every new job created will be eligible for a once-off grant of £5,000.
(2) Corporation Profits Tax for all manufacturing industry will be at 10 per cent from 1 January 1981 until 31 December 2000.
(3) A rate of 100 per cent initial capital allowances applies to qualifying service companies in the Custom House Docks area and the Shannon Customs Free area. Outside of those areas, writing down and wear and tear allowances of 15 per cent for plant and machinery, 4 per cent for industrial buildings and hotels and 10 per cent for farm buildings apply. The rate for plant and machinery was 100 per cent up to 1988 but has been reduced gradually to 15 per cent since then as part of an overall reform of the corporate tax system.
(4) Dividends paid to overseas shareholders, both corporate and individual, will be fully exempt from Irish income taxes and there will continue to be no withholding taxes.

Non-repayable cash grants towards the cost of fixed assets — defined as site, site development, buildings, new machinery and most equipment — are negotiable in certain circumstances in designated areas. The designated areas are Counties Donegal, Sligo, Leitrim, Roscommon, Longford, Cavan, Monaghan, Galway, Mayo, Clare, Kerry and parts of Counties Cork and Limerick.

Non-repayable cash grants are available towards approved capital costs of product and process development facilities, including R & D units in IDA research parks. The grants are negotiable up to a maximum of 40 per cent of eligible costs in designated areas and 25 per cent of eligible costs in non-designated areas.

Training grants of up to 100 per cent are available towards the costs of wages, travel and subsistence in Ireland or to parent companies abroad; salaries, travel and subsistence of training personnel; management training; and, where necessary, the cost of hiring training consultants.

Grants are made available towards factory rent in IDA industrial estates, IDA advance factories or commercially operated estates, as are loan guarantee and interest subsidies and IDA equity participation, where desired and possible.

IDA development services to new industrial projects comprise:

(a) Assistance with project development and financing, including expert advice on taxation and legal aspects.
(b) Provision of advance factories on IDA industrial estates and other locations.
(c) Advisory service on site selection, factory building cost control, and planning and pollution control requirements.
(d) Manpower information and advisory services.
(e) After-care services in initial production stages.

Re-Equipment/Modernisation of Existing Industries. Re-equipment grants may be available towards the cost of modernisation of plant and machinery in existing industries. The grants are payable up to a maximum of 35 per cent of eligible costs in designated areas and 25 per cent elsewhere. They are administered selectively on the basis of defined criteria for different sectors of industry. Forbairt provides development services to existing manufacturing firms as follows:

(1) It assists certain firms in commercial difficulties to organise appropriate packages of financial aid. In each case, assistance is given where there are prospects of commercial viability without continuing subsidy.
(2) Restructuring of sensitive sectors. Certain sectors of Irish industry have been experiencing serious trading difficulties following the introduction of free trade. The IDA encourages mergers or acquisitions within selected industries through the provision of grants towards the interest payable on a loan raised in connection with an acquisition or merger, and may also act as guarantor for the repayment of money borrowed for the same purpose.
(3) Promotion of joint ventures between Irish and overseas industrial companies.
(4) Promotion of product licensing and subcontracting opportunities for existing industrial companies.
(5) Assistance with identification of product development opportunities.
(6) Grants towards current costs of R & D projects negotiable up to a maximum of 50 per cent of such costs or £50,000 per project, whichever is less.
(7) The IDA assists in-house feasibility studies which assess the viability of new project possibilities, with up to 50 per cent of eligible costs grant-aided. Eligible expenditure includes executives' salaries, travel costs and expenses. The studies must involve the normal commercial and technical considerations, provided the work is related to products not already being manufactured by the company. It must also lead, if positive, to a new investment in fixed assets or an R & D project.

Small Industries. Under the Small Industries Programme of Forbairt, capital grants are available to new and existing small manufacturing firms up to a maximum of 60 per cent of fixed asset costs in designated areas and 45 per cent in non-designated areas. Training grants, product development grants, rent subsidies for up to five years, and a recent innovation, employment grants of £5,000 per job instead of capital grants, are also approved under the programme.

Enterprise Development Programme. Forbairt's normal range of grant incentives for new projects is supplemented under the Enterprise Development Programme by additional benefits including: a guarantee for loans raised towards the working capital needs for a project, grants towards the interest payable on loans raised to provide working capital, and equity participation if necessary.

The normal incentives cover capital grants on fixed assets, loan guarantees for fixed assets, rent reduction grants and training grants.

The capital incentives are available for service companies as well as manufacturing companies.

Since 1982 the IDA, now Forfás, has introduced new policies and programmes in keeping with the government White Paper on Industrial Policy. These new policies have culminated in a greater focus on the realism of market, profit and job projections; an assessment of the 'value-added' to the Irish economy as well as direct jobs created within the firm; the totality of the state's financing commitments compared with the promoting firms and the linking of payments closely to performance. The days of new capital equipment expenditure giving rise to 'automatic grants' are over.

The core change allied to the structural changes discussed earlier is that the state will seek to ensure that the arrangements it negotiates guarantee the state value for money from its investment. The main methods used are:

(1) Performance clauses.
(2) Explicit parent company guarantees of the subsidiary's liabilities.
(3) The introduction of an element of repayability into the financial package and the greater use of equity and preference shares.

For some years now the IDA has been using financial appraisal techniques to assess proposals submitted to it. These systems were of a standard sort and ensured that the proposal was coherently structured and did not lay the promoter open to a cash shortage over the period of the project or, indeed, an unwarranted cash surplus.

More recently, it has been using an economic appraisal system designed to calculate the anticipated return to the state on its investment. An assessment is made of the total cost to the state, expressed in terms of Net Present Value, of grants and tax foregone on any leasing. This is then compared to the benefits in terms of the NPV of the stream of value-added created during the life of the project, or over seven years if that is shorter. The three chief components of value-added are direct wages and salaries, Irish raw materials and Irish services. These elements are not necessarily taken at full value but may be downweighted because of 'leakage' — that is, one local raw material is not as local as another. In order to ensure a positive return to the state it is understood that Forfás requires a benefit:cost ratio of the order of 4:1 for a project to receive approval.

Obviously, this whole sophisticated appraisal process is so much wasted effort if the project does not proceed in the way outlined. Thus it is a natural development of the process that Forfás should seek to ensure that it gets what it has agreed to pay for, by an extension of the value-for-money principle. Specific assurances are sought from industrialists as to the accuracy of their proposals in the areas of job creation and/or other key aspects of their project on the basis of which grants are approved. As a corollary to this, specific provisions are being inserted in grant agreements whereby the company will be liable, on demand, to repay a proportionate part of capital grants where projects are not met within an agreed time scale — normally three to five years (the 'clawback approach'). A variation of this principle is to withhold payment of part of the grants pending achievement of the projections (the 'holdback approach'). The middle course, which is the course now most usually followed, is to review progress of the project at the end of each year and to withhold subsequent payments until prior projections have been met (the 'annual review approach').

THE SHANNON FREE AIRPORT DEVELOPMENT COMPANY (SFADCO/SHANNON DEVELOPMENT)

Shannon Development has responsibility for regional economic development in the Shannon region, which encompasses Counties Clare, north Tipperary, west and south-west Offaly and north Kerry. As part of that mandate, Shannon Development has particular responsibility for the development of industry in the Shannon Free Zone, including aviation-related projects in the greater Shannon Airport area, the development of indigenous industry, rural development and the development of the Eurotechnopole project at Plassey, Limerick. Shannon Development is also responsible for the development and growth of trade, passengers and services at Shannon Airport and for the development of tourism in the Shannon region.

In 1947 the Shannon Airport area was designated a 'free port', thus becoming the first such zone in the world. Companies were encouraged to establish there. They could import products without custom duties, tariffs or quotas as long as they were later exported. Shannon Free Zone is now home to 100 international manufacturing and service operations employing circa 5,500 people and utilising two million square feet of factory space. Its location on the threshold of the European Union makes it an ideal base for any international company seeking to serve this enormous and profitable market.

The incentives available for overseas industrial investment at Shannon are:

• Capital Grants:
These are cash payments based on a percentage of fixed investment. Eligible fixed assets include equipment, sites and buildings. The actual amount is a matter for negotiation in each case and depends on the overall attractiveness of the particular project to Shannon.

• Training Grants:
These are payable at up to 100 per cent of the training costs of agreed programmes. Costs covered include sending personnel abroad for training, salaries, travel and subsistence expenses of training personnel, management training expenses and the costs of hiring training consultants.

• Rent Reduction Grants:
Rent subsidies reducing gross rental by an agreed percentage over a period of time.

• Ready-to-Occupy Factories:
There is ready-to-occupy purpose-built distribution space or fully serviced sites to facilitate those wishing to construct their own factories.

In addition to the above incentives, Shannon Development can, in certain cases, guarantee loans, subsidise interest charges and take equity stakes in new ventures.

In recent years Shannon Development has undertaken a more expanded regional development role for the Shannon region, with particular responsibility for the integrated promotion of the region. In fulfilling this responsibility the promotion and development of the region's indigenous industry sector is one of its principal activities. It provides a range of incentive and support programmes to established firms and those starting up. They can be summarised as follows:

Incentive Programmes

• Feasibility Study Grant — to qualifying entrepreneurs who wish to investigate the commercial and technical viability of a proposed project, covering up to 50 per cent of the cost of wages, salaries, travel, subsistence, consultancy fees and the development of product prototypes.

• Employment Grant — to companies increasing their employment, with half paid on recruitment and the remainder after six months' employment.

• Capital Investment Grant — towards the cost of new machinery and equipment, site purchase and site development, construction and/or modification of industrial buildings and industrial rent reduction for up to five years.

• Management Development Grant/Mentor Grant — towards the cost of a firm strengthening its management capabilities and structures and obtaining the advice of an experienced business practitioner who acts as the firm's mentor.

• Research and Development Grant — up to 30 per cent of the cost of either researching and developing new products and/or manufacturing processes or of improving/modifying a firm's existing products and/or manufacturing process.

• Technology Acquisition/Joint Venture/Licensing Grant — up to 50 per cent of the cost of searching for, negotiating and acquiring/transferring a manufacturing or processing technology joint venture or manufacturing licence.

• Employee Training Grants — up to 100 per cent of the cost of an agreed training programme, available to qualifying new firms.

• An Enterprise Development Programme, aimed at experienced managers and/or professionals with potential, offers in addition to the above incentives loan interest subsidies, loan guarantees and equity participation by Shannon Development.

• The Early Start Technology Fund is a seed capital investment fund established by a core group of business organisations and companies within the Shannon region to assist the development of innovative, highly technological, protectable products or ideas.

In addition Shannon Development offers a range of support programmes including:
— a network of workspace centres providing start-up workspace
— enterprise centres
— a specialist food centre in Limerick providing start-up food processing ventures in a pure environment
— a special programme in natural resources covering start-ups in stone, minerals, aquaculture, floriculture and forestry
— an information centre
— an innovation centre in a joint venture with the University of Limerick
— an entrepreneurs' programme

Shannon Development has regional offices in Birr, Ennis, Limerick, Nenagh and Tralee which provide advice on a wide range of issues and are the first point of contact between entrepreneurs and the business community generally.

In promoting the development of the region's Tourism Sector, Shannon Development devised a range of quality tourist attractions such as mediaeval banquets at the restored and refurbished fifteenth-century Bunratty Castle; the Bunratty Folk Park — an open-air theme park featuring life-styles of the late nineteenth century; Craggaunowen Museum, which illustrates prehistoric Irish life-styles; the restored King John's Castle and its multimedia interpretative centre; and the Kilrush Creek marina. Its Rent an Irish Cottage project provides visitors with long- or short-term holiday accommodation in fully equipped, traditional, thatched cottages located in some of the region's most picturesque villages.

The early 1980s saw the establishment of a Technological Park at Plassey, Limerick which has at its core the University of Limerick. Located at the Park are Ireland's first Innovation Centre; the Microelectronics Applications Centre; a concentration of new indigenous, high technology companies; multinational corporations; research and development laboratories; international services businesses; and a variety of business and leisure services.

Shannon Development spent £48 million in 1992 and created approximately 1,700 first-time jobs.

ÚDARÁS NA GAELTACHTA

Údarás na Gaeltachta, the Gaeltacht Authority, is responsible for the economic, social and cultural development of the Gaeltacht (Irish-speaking) regions of Counties Donegal, Mayo, Galway, Meath, Kerry, Cork and Waterford. These scattered Gaeltacht areas have a total population of 83,268, with a labour force of over 28,500.

Údarás was established by the government in 1979, taking over the functions of its predecessor, Gaeltarra Éireann, which the government had established in 1956. It has a thirteen-member board, seven of whom are elected by the people of the Gaeltacht. The remaining six, including the chairperson, are appointed by the Minister. Údarás is the only state development agency in Ireland which has members of its board directly elected by popular vote.

The Údarás has fifteen wholly owned subsidiary companies trading in textiles, knitwear, food processing, plastics, information technology and hotels.

Údarás na Gaeltachta's incentive package offers a wide range of services to new and expanding enterprises, including financial, construction, legal, advisory and recruitment. An attractive package of grant aid is also available. This comprises employment grants, capital grants, interest subsidies, rent subsidies, feasibility study grants, research and development grants, training grants and technology acquisition grants. Employment grants vary from £3,000 to £9,000 per job and capital grants may be obtained for up to 50 per cent of the investment. Interest subsidies are available to small industry projects where the total grant aid is less than £100,000, and operates on a sliding scale of 100 per cent in year one, 75 per cent in year two, 50 per cent in year three and 25 per cent in year four. The rent subsidy is normally 40 per cent of the commercial rent and in exceptional cases can be paid for a period of up to ten years. Feasibility study and research and development grants of up to 50 per cent can be paid, with maximums of £5,000 and £100,000 respectively. Training grants of up to 100 per cent can be approved in conjunction with employment grants. A technology acquisition grant can be sought to cover part of the cost of a licence, technical consultants, salaries, research and development costs, etc. The technology must be capable of being produced in Ireland and must be innovative in relation to the company's existing level of technology.

To date the Údarás has developed an extensive range of indigenous industries while at the same time attracting new enterprises and skills into the Gaeltacht regions from other parts of Ireland and from the UK, Europe, Scandinavia and the USA. There are now almost 6,000 people employed in Údarás-supported industries in the Gaeltacht, such as textiles, engineering, electronics, aquaculture, other natural resources and communications.

An tÚdarás, in co-operation with University College Galway, has helped to pioneer the research and development of mariculture in the West of Ireland. As a result of this work there are now eight salmon farms and some seventy shellfish farms along the Gaeltacht coastline. Over 50 per cent of all salmon farmed in Ireland currently comes from Gaeltacht farms. Údarás's subsidiary company, Taighde Mara Teo., is very active in the area of shellfish research, and significant developments in this area include the establishment of a land-based turbot farm on Cape Clear Island (in partnership with University College Cork and Comharchumann Chléire) and a scallops enhancement programme in Beirtreach Buí Bay in Cill Chiaráin, Connemara.

Since 1979 Údarás na Gaeltachta has administered a Community Development Scheme, 'An Pobal Beo', which has encouraged many small Gaeltacht communities to take a more active part in shaping the future of their own area, with a strong emphasis on community education.

The Údarás has also played a pioneering role in the development of an audio-visual base in the Gaeltacht. A number of TV/video production courses have been organised in co-operation with RTE and there are now over a dozen small audio-visual production companies operating in the Gaeltacht.

In 1992 the Údarás spent about £15 million and created approximately 975 first-time jobs.

Údarás na Gaeltachta's headquarters are in Furbo, Galway and there are regional offices in Bunbeg, Co. Donegal, Belmullet, Co. Mayo and Dingle, Co. Kerry.

ICC BANK
The Industrial Credit Company was established in 1933 by the state to provide finance for the many new businesses being established behind the high tariff walls then being erected. Ireland at that time had underdeveloped financial institutions and so ICC had

to play multiple financial roles, such as issuing house, term lender and development bank. During the 1940s and 1950s it floated many new issues on the Irish Stock Exchange.

In the 1960s and 1970s ICC developed a full range of financial services, in response to a growing demand for short-term working capital finance, foreign currency export credit and commercial property financing. These developments reflected the bank's overall strategy of establishing a broader base in the financial services sector but remaining directed towards the business community and small to medium-sized enterprises in particular. Its loans, which can be fixed or variable, cover short-, medium- and long-term finance. Its long-term loans tend to be based on a longer repayment period than those of the commercial banks. In addition it provides venture capital to unquoted companies with potential.

In the early 1990s the ICC had discussions with the Department of Finance, its major shareholder, with a view to revising the legislative provisions under which the bank operated. This resulted in the passing of the ICC Bank Act 1992, which allowed the bank expand its range of services without any geographic restrictions, increase its borrowing powers, change its name to ICC Bank PLC and come under Central Bank supervision, in line with the majority of other financial institutions. This also reflected the changed situation in regard to its funding position. Up to the late 1960s the Department of Finance provided 100 per cent of the bank's funding requirements. This position then changed with the introduction of a deposit-taking service from bank and non-bank sources. Today deposits from companies, individuals and other financial institutions, both domestic and international, supply the bulk of its funding requirements. The Department of Finance still appoints the board of directors, which determines the overall policy of the bank, with day-to-day management delegated to a senior management team.

In line with normal banking practice ICC Bank PLC is now structured to provide a broad range of financial services to business. They can be summarised as follows:

- ICC Corporate Finance Limited is involved in fund-raising operations for companies, the provision of Stock Exchange, strategic and general corporate and financial advice.

- ICC BES provides individuals with an opportunity to invest in Irish businesses.

- ICC Investment Bank, a specialist savings and investments subsidiary, provides a quality and innovative service to its customers.

- ICC Finance Limited manages the group's leasing and hire purchase portfolio. New equipment and machinery finance is now being handled through ICC Bank's core lending facilities.

- Through International Development Ireland Ltd (IDI) ICC Bank provides international consultancy services.

In 1995 ICC was being suggested as a candidate for privatisation.

FÁS
In 1988 the state established FÁS to co-ordinate the activities of AnCO, the Youth

Employment Agency (YEA) and National Manpower Service. FÁS has a general responsibility for training and job placement.

FÁS runs six main programmes:

(a) Company-based training, where FÁS works on development programmes with company training personnel.
(b) Skills training, which consists chiefly of apprenticeship schemes.
(c) Individual training programmes in nine regional centres. Training courses are related to the skills required in the locality. Participants are paid training allowances and where necessary travelling and accommodation allowances.
(d) Management and supervisory training. In close consultation with the Irish Management Institute, FÁS offers grants of up to 50 per cent of the cost of attendance at courses for further training in supervisory and management skills.
(e) National Manpower Agency, which attempts to match employers and employees.
(f) A range of educational training and employment programmes for school leavers.

FÁS, which is funded by the EU, the state, a training levy on employers and a 1 per cent charge on incomes, is one of the largest employers in the state, with over 3,000 employees. Employers should note that 90 per cent of the levy is returnable if the company has an approved training programme.

AN BORD TRÁCHTÁLA/THE IRISH TRADE BOARD (ABT)

An Bord Tráchtála/The Irish Trade Board was established in 1991 to combine the activities of the Irish Goods Council and An Córas Tráchtála/The Irish Export Board. It is a state organisation with the chairperson and members of the board appointed by the Minister for Tourism and Trade. The chief executive is appointed by the board.

The functions of Bord Tráchtála are:

(1) to promote, assist and develop in any manner which the board considers necessary or desirable the marketing of Irish goods and such services as are specified by the Minister by order.
(2) to advise the Minister on matters affecting or connected with the marketing of Irish goods and services.

The successful development of Ireland's export trade was due in no small way to the range of services provided by Córas Tráchtála. These included market research, overseas office facilities, trade missions and retail promotions, introductions to overseas contacts and the resources of a large information centre. It resulted in a reduced dependency on the UK market and a rise in exports to other EU countries. This was achieved against the background of increased growth in manufactured goods despite reduced employee numbers in that sector.

A review of Ireland's exports in the 1980s led to the discovery that the growth was due almost entirely to a small number of foreign-owned firms in a small number of industries: computers, electronics, drugs and chemicals. Native Irish firms had, in general, not developed an export business. Various reviews of industrial policy and the support services resulted in two new schemes, the Marketing Activities Grant Scheme (MAG) and the Targeted Marketing Consultancy Scheme (TMC), focusing on native firms with export potential.

Under the MAG Scheme, the maximum annual non-repayable grant available for companies undertaking a broad variety of marketing activities (market research, market visits, sales personnel recruitment, trade fairs and exhibitions, advertising and promotion, tender costs, overseas customer visits, product design, sales literature and product testing) rose from £5,000 (based on company expenditure of £10,000) to £10,000 (based on company expenditure of £30,000).

Under the original TMC Scheme, companies were required to increase their marketing expenditure by a minimum of £150,000 over a two-year period to be eligible for assistance. Under the new Scheme, the minimum expenditure requirement was reduced to £60,000. As in the original Scheme, one-third of the implementation costs is eligible for a non-repayable grant and a further one-third is repayable in the form of royalties from sales. The maximum expenditure eligible for assistance is £750,000 over the two-year period with the maximum grant and the maximum repayable loan each being £250,000.

The European Scheme, under which Bord Tráchtála grant-aided for two years two-thirds of the cost of putting extra sales representatives on the ground in overseas markets, is part of the TMC Scheme. The reduction in the eligible expenditure requirements means that companies now seek support for a wider range of marketing activities.

In discharging its functions in 1993 the Board spent £34 million on market development and promotional programmes.

In addition to financial incentives, An Bord Tráchtála services include
— Identifying opportunities for indigenous industry
— Customised consulting to individual firms to turn opportunities into sales
— Organising promotions, trade fairs and the like.

The Board has six regional offices in Ireland: Dublin, Cork, Galway, Limerick, Sligo, Waterford, and has twenty-two offices world-wide, with access to trade consultants in countries in which it is not represented.

In 1995 export marketing assistance to the food and drink industries was moved from the Bord to the new Bord Bia.

THE AGRICULTURAL CREDIT CORPORATION BANK (ACC BANK)

The ACC Bank was established by the Irish government in 1927, under the title Agricultural Credit Corporation, with the specific aim of providing finance to the farming sector. It did this by making loans available for a wide variety of purposes, including:

(a) Purchase of livestock, feeding stuff, fertiliser, seeds.
(b) Purchase of machinery and equipment.
(c) Erection and repair of farmhouses and farm buildings.
(d) Installation of water supplies.
(e) Land drainage and reclamation.
(f) Fruit farming and horticulture.
(g) Working capital.
(h) Purchase of land and implementation of family settlements.

Loans were granted against the security of lands and could be up to two-thirds of the market value. It also offered in special cases loans at preferential rates of interest and special repayment arrangements to suit the borrower's individual circumstances. The bank endeavoured to operate within the framework of an overall farm development scheme designed to facilitate planned expansion and incorporating the wide range of grants and subsidies available to that sector from the Irish government and the European Community.

After spectacular growth in the 1960s and 1970s ACC suffered from the decline in agriculture. This resulted in many farmers not being able to repay loans having borrowed to buy land at inflated prices or make investments in non-productive assets. Significant bad debts all but wiped out the bank's capital base and meant that the Exchequer had to recapitalise its Balance Sheet. This situation forced it to rethink its overall strategy and in the late 1980s it got a mandate from its regulatory authority, the Department of Finance, to seek business outside of agriculture. It also adopted a new name, ACC Bank, to indicate more strongly that it is a bank and to help it project a stronger profile in the financial services industry as a broadly based commercial bank.

This new strategy saw it recovering the ground it had lost with a return to profit performance and a healthy Balance Sheet. It has done this by extending its business base, establishing new customer relations and providing a definitive range of products and services. Today the bank concentrates on four business sectors.

- Farming — it continues to offer a wide variety of products and services, tailor-made to the agricultural community's needs; from long-term lending and seasonal and environmental loans to attractive deposit facilities.

- Corporate Banking — it can provide a wide range of credit and leasing facilities, financial instruments, commercial mortgages and specifically structured deposit facilities to the corporate sector in a way that meets individual customer requirements.

- Small Businesses — it is developing a full range of banking services for small to medium-sized businesses, including attractive commercial mortgage facilities, leasing and working capital finance and investment facilities. Through its branch network, it can bring its banking services to many new customers.

- Personal Banking — it offers a variety of deposit and investment facilities, cheque book and cheque card accounts, Visa, foreign exchange facilities, personal loans, leasing and home mortgages — in effect a comprehensive range of personal banking services.

ACC Bank is now a fully fledged bank with the authority to lend to the total credit market. The future is unclear given the mention of a merger possibility with the ICC Bank. Such a merger would have wide-reaching implications for both management and staff and would involve addressing the question of the provision of adequate capital resources for its future development.

BORD FÁILTE

In 1994 the Irish tourist industry earned over £2 billion, of which 60 per cent came from out-of-state visitors and the balance from domestic tourism spending. Revenue from out-of-state tourism has increased by 77 per cent over the past five years, and dependent jobs by 25,000 to 90,000. Investment in infrastructure rose from an annual £50 million to £200 million in the same period.

Tourism was one of the first industries to be formally recognised by the state for the potential it possessed to bring benefits to less developed areas of the country. In the 1920s the Irish Tourist Association (ITA) and the Hotel Proprietors' Association were formed. The ITA opened the first tourist information offices at major centres and also produced guide booklets and maps.

In 1939 Bord Cuartaíochta na hÉireann, the first Irish Tourist Board, was set up and was given statutory powers for the registration of hotels. In 1952 An Bord Fáilte, which had responsibility for development work, and Fógra Fáilte, which was charged with the promotion of Ireland overseas, were established. They were amalgamated in 1955 into the new Bord Fáilte Éireann, literally the Welcome Board of Ireland.

Bord Fáilte's strategies and operations are framed within the national objective, set out by the government, of increasing tourism-supported jobs by 35,000 between 1995 and 2000 and foreign visitor revenue by £1 billion.

A six-year programme introduced in 1994 proposed an investment programme of £650 million, of which £370 million was expected to come from the EU, £80 million from the state and £200 million from private sources.

The aim of Bord Fáilte is to increase the level of economic activity in Ireland through stimulating demand within the tourism sector. Specifically, Bord Fáilte sets out to:

- Create additional employment.
- Attract foreign earnings and thereby contribute to the balance of payments.
- Increase the level of value-added and thus contribute to a higher level of gross domestic product.
- Generate increased Exchequer revenue through the expenditure of tourists.
- Contribute to an improved regional distribution of income.

The primary yardstick of performance is the foreign exchange revenue earned from tourism, since it is such 'export' earnings that bring the bulk of the economic benefits.

The strategic agenda for the 1990s and the immediate future is dominated by three key requirements.

The first is to increase the market for Irish tourism products, in particular the paid serviced accommodation sector, which has considerably expanded its capacity in recent years. The second is to grow off-season demand, especially in the major tourism centres. The third is to achieve growth in expenditure on a per capita basis by visitors.

These three priorities are fundamental to creating a sustainable and profitable tourism industry within Ireland.

In carrying out its function Bord Fáilte offers market development and capital investment grant aid. It does this under a number of funds and schemes, such as:

- The European Regional Development Fund, where grants range from 10 per cent to 50 per cent on projects such as sailing, equestrian, language learning, traditional craft facilities and leisure facilities generally. Assistance is also given to help promote tourism products in overseas markets.

• The Hotel and Guesthouse Improvement Scheme is designed to assist lower-grade hotels to improve the physical standard of their accommodation and facilities. The scheme is funded by the International Fund for Ireland, allows grants of up to 33 per cent of eligible expenditure and is confined to counties Leitrim, Louth, Cavan, Monaghan, Donegal and Sligo. Allied to this is the Tourist Amenity Scheme, whereby grants of up to 50 per cent may be given for developments such as angling, educational projects and interpretative centres. In addition community-based groups can get grant assistance of up to 75 per cent, with a maximum of £100,000. In all cases acquisition costs are excluded.

• The Business Expansion Scheme provides for the inclusion of certain tourism undertakings and Bord Fáilte is the agency responsible for certifying the bona fides of the undertaking from a tourism perspective. Initial abuses of these projects in high asset-backed, low risk schemes has resulted in a severe restriction in the qualifying activities under recent Finance Acts. The scheme finishes in April 1996.

Figure 13.1 Incentives Available to Tourism

In general the maximum aid rates for eligible public and private sector activity under the programme are 75 per cent and 50 per cent respectively. However, lower maximums will apply in the following cases:

Public Sector: % *of expansion*

Improved Caravan/Camping Parks
Disabled Access 50

Private Sector:

Equestrian Facilities
Sailing Facilities (excl. marinas/moorings)
New Lake and Sea Angling Boats 33
Bait/Drying Rooms etc.

Cycling Equipment
Golf Courses
Golf Clubhouses
Upgraded Sea Angling Boats
Additional Cruising Craft
Language Learning Facilities
Improved Hotel Conference Facilities 25
Accommodation-Related Leisure Facilities
Improved Caravan/Camping Parks
Horse-Drawn Caravans
Motor-Homes
Improved Accommodation at Equestrian Centres
Disabled Access/Hotel Conversion
Selective Accommodation Improvement Scheme

Upgraded Cruisers 20

Source: *Tourism 2000*, Dublin, 1994, p. 30.

BORD IASCAIGH MHARA (BIM)

BIM was established in 1952 to promote aquaculture. It concentrates on
— market development
— boat modernisation
— fish processing
— fish farming including shellfish and salmon.

In the thirteen-year period 1980–93 fish exports grew fourfold to £190 million while employment grew from 2,600 to 8,000.

A package of capital incentives is offered which consists usually of a capital grant ranging from 25 per cent to 50 per cent, subsidised term loans, and discretionary grants to assist exporters and processors with packaging and promotional material, participation in international food fairs and exhibitions, advertising and travel incentive schemes.

On the home market the objective is to increase the domestic market for fish and fish products, increase per capita consumption and effect import substitution. Discretionary grants are available on the same basis as that which applies in export development.

The BIM spent in excess of £5 million in 1994, with over 40 per cent of its grant-in-aid being capital development.

CUSTOM HOUSE DOCKS FINANCIAL SERVICES DEVELOPMENT

In 1987 the government introduced legislation offering significant tax incentives for financial service firms located in a particular area of Dublin Docks. A thirty-acre site downriver from the Custom House has been designated a financial services centre. The Dublin International Financial Services Centre is one of the foremost examples in the world of a new phenomenon — the 'onshore' financial services centre — where companies are clustering to transact cross-border business. By mid-1995 over 240 companies were in business and employment had grown to some 2,000, the vast majority being financial services professionals engaging in specialised international activities. A major step forward was the attraction of the Finex Exchange of the New York Cotton Exchange.

Since its inception the history of the centre has been one of constant evolution. Successive Finance Acts have developed and refined the fiscal environment and have responded to the ever-changing demands of a global industry. Parallel to this the Central Bank has developed its regulatory regime in a flexible and enlightened manner. As the centre has grown, four core activities have proven especially popular: asset financing, fund management, insurance and corporate treasury.

The attractions of the centre include:

(a) A special 10 per cent tax rate on profits. This special rate will be available to companies until the end of the year 2005. Broadly speaking, in order to qualify for this 10 per cent rate three criteria must be satisfied:
(1) the activities must be of a financial nature.
(2) the activities must be conducted with non-residents.
(3) transactions must not be denominated in Irish pounds.

(b) A range of other incentives, including zero Irish taxation on income and capital gains on certain funds, 100 per cent tax write-off on premises built, double allowances for tax in respect of rent, exemption from municipal rates for ten years and no capital and stamp duty on companies operating as collective investment undertakings.

(c) Double taxation agreements with more than twenty countries and others being negotiated. This allows the tax savings in Ireland to be maintained in the investors' home countries.

(d) EU membership.

(e) Well-educated English-speaking workforce with skills in banking, accounting and legal services.

(f) As a separate EMS currency centre Dublin has the financial institutions and skills essential to a national economy, such as a central bank, a Stock Exchange, a money market, a bond market, a finance ministry, a long-established banking system and a futures and options exchange.

(g) Attractive time zone between Tokyo and New York.

The rapid growth of the centre is also due to the revolution in international information and technology, which makes doing business in secondary and peripheral European centres as easy as in the major centres, i.e. London, Frankfurt and Paris, but much less expensive.

Many of the early projects in the centre were fundamentally tax-driven but through changes in Finance Acts and in other jurisdictions a shift in emphasis has taken place. It is evidenced by a rapid expansion in the funds management and global custody sector and the possible arrival of US mutual fund companies. This is in line with the original concept that the centre should be one of real substance and not just a tax haven in the classic sense.

RANGE OF BUSINESS INCENTIVES
State agencies provide a wide range of subsidies, which can be grouped as follows:

(1) Labour grants.
(2) Capital grants.
(3) Training grants.
(4) Low taxation levels.
(5) Liberal depreciation.
(6) Interest, rent and lease payment subsidies.

Labour Grants
Ireland has a large surplus of labour. In the late 1980s the IDA and other agencies recognised this fact and began offering labour incentives. Companies taking on employees may qualify for a once-off grant of £5,000 per employee, which can rise to £9,000 in designated areas.

Capital Grants

Many of the agencies examined above offer capital grants. The grants are normally permanent finance but in the event of liquidation part or all of the grant becomes repayable. Grants are usually given on new machinery or plant.

Capital grants are available on a wide range of fixed assets, including office equipment. Service industries which are not eligible for taxation incentives are eligible for grants.

Grants are paid after the installation and subsequent certification of the asset. It may be some months before the cash is received, so bridging finance is often necessary. Capital grants have declined in importance in the last few years. In certain cases they can be as high as 50 per cent but a figure of 25 per cent is more realistic. In 1994 the state gave more than £200 million in grants to industry.

Training Grants

Many modern projects require skilled staff. Training a workforce can involve huge inputs of both capital and time. In a business such as diamond cutting, glass blowing or software the biggest capital investment may be in the staff. Recognising the cost involved, the state established grants to enable manufacturers to train their workforce. Grants cover not only the direct wages cost but the costs of materials used and managerial costs associated with training. A training programme must be drawn up and approved in advance by the relevant authority and FÁS.

Low Taxation Levels

To maintain the attraction of Ireland as a base for manufacture, corporate tax on manufacturing profits was reduced to 10 per cent. This is one of the lowest levels of corporate tax in the world.

Liberal Depreciation

For many years the state provided liberal depreciation allowances. Free depreciation or the ability to write off assets against taxable profits was available to manufacturing industry for many years. This facility reduced the financial risk of new projects. Expanding businesses had continuous write-offs against profits and so paid little or no tax. In line with the bias towards labour grants there has been a reduction in liberal depreciation allowances over the years to current annual rates of 15 per cent for plant and machinery, 4 per cent for industrial buildings, 10 per cent for hotels and 10 per cent for farm buildings.

Interest, Rent and Lease Payment Subsidies

A high interest charge burdens a company with costly fixed expenses. This is particularly relevant to small businesses which often have a high proportion of borrowed funds in their capital structure. To reduce the cost, interest subsidies are available through the IDA, SFADCo, Údarás na Gaeltachta and, for fishery assets, BIM. These subsidies may be as high as two-fifths of the cost and may last for five years or the life of the loan, whichever is the shorter. Lease payments may be subsidised in the same way.

Grants towards rent payments are common. They can amount to a 50 per cent subsidy in the early years of a project.

Grants are undoubtedly a most attractive form of finance. Apart from being costless to the individual firm, they are non-repayable under normal circumstances, involve no risk to the business and do not affect control. Grants reduce the investor's risk as he can put up less capital. They reduce the lender's risk in that they rank behind all sources of borrowed funds and do not affect annual cash flows.

Apart from capital grants a bewildering collection of incentives exists: liberal depreciation allowances, subsidised loans, low taxes and a host of specialised grants for training and marketing.

The range of loans available complements that available from the private sector. Many of the state agencies are interested in development as much as profit and security so they may view a loan application differently to private financiers.

All business people should be aware of the range of incentives available to them.

FURTHER READING
Annual Report of each organisation examined.
B. O'Kane, *Starting a Business in Ireland* (Oak Tree Press, 1993).

QUESTIONS

Question 13.1
What are the main forms of financial assistance offered by the state?

Question 13.2
Between 1960 and 1988 80 per cent of new private capital investment was made by foreign investments. What were the causes of this?

Question 13.3
What new system has the IDA used to guarantee that the state gets value for money from any of the IDA-assisted foreign investments?

Question 13.4
What was the attraction of the Shannon Free Zone for development? Has the perceived success of Shannon led to other developments?

Question 13.5
Why was tourism targeted as having potential for development and what are its social and economic benefits?

Question 13.6
For what reasons were the ICC and the ACC set up? In your opinion would they have been perceived as a success?

The Cost of Capital and Capital Structure

hapter 6 examined in some detail methods of evaluating investment proposals. The output from each technique examined is a rate of return which measures the profit from the venture against the capital cost of undertaking the venture. This rate of return is meaningless unless it is compared with the cost of the funds used to make the investment. The cost of funds is known as the cost of capital, which has been defined as 'the rate of return a firm must earn on its investments for the market value of the firm to remain unchanged'. Accepting investments with a return below the cost of capital will reduce the value of the firm whereas accepting projects with a rate of return above the cost of capital adds to the value of the firm.

The cost of capital is normally an amalgam of several costs, because a project will seldom be financed from a single source. As a rule, capital projects have debt, equity and grant sources of finance.

The importance of the various types of finance in Ireland is shown in Table 14.1.

Table 14.1 Capital Structure of Irish Business

		No. of Employees				
	Total %	3–9 %	10–19 %	20–50 %	51–99 %	100+ %
Share Capital and Reserves	75	75	77	74	78	65
Borrowing Due After 1 Year	16	14	16	17	12	24
Grants	7	7	7	6	8	10
Other	2	4	–	3	2	1
	100	100	100	100	100	100
No. of Replies Analysed	276	74	83	85	22	12

Source: Deloitte & Touche: Report on Irish Business 1994.

Taken together, these sources are known as the capital structure of the firm. The effect of changes in the capital structure on the value of a business has been the subject of much learned debate. Some of the arguments put forward will be examined later but for the present it is sufficient to note that the capital structure of a firm determines the level of financial risk in the firm.

A business faces two classes of risk, business risk and financial risk. Business risk is the chance that the investments undertaken by the firm will prove unsatisfactory and refers to the variability or uncertainty of the firm's operating income. The factors that influence business risk include the variability of sales volume, prices and costs applicable to that firm, the degree of market power under its control, the extent of the product diversification practised, the growth history and prospects for that industry and the degree of operating leverage. The degree of operating leverage is defined as the percentage change in earnings resulting from a percentage change in sales or output. It is the multiplier effect resulting from the firm's use of fixed operating costs. Firms with wide fluctuations in sales can reduce their business risk by limiting the use of assets with fixed operating costs. Ultimately, the firm's business risk is a combination of all the issues noted above and is determined by the firm's accumulated investments over time. Typically, firms in consumer product industries, such as food processing, grocery retailing and public utilities, tend to have low levels of business risk whereas firms in durable product industries and airline services have higher levels of business risk.

Financial risk, on the other hand, measures the danger that the fixed charge sources of finance will force the business into insolvency and refers to the variability in earnings arising from the use of those fixed capital costs. The measure of the financial risk is the degree of financial leverage resulting from the financing decisions made. It is defined as the percentage change in earnings per share resulting from a given percentage change in earnings. The firm uses it to increase the returns available to the ordinary shareholders but at the expense of increased risk. The greater the percentage of fixed charge sources in a capital structure the higher the financial risk. Financial risk is, therefore, a function of the proportion of debt in the total financing of the firm. The word 'gearing' is applied to this proportion, though the American term 'leverage' is also used in practice. Chapter 3, under the heading Debt Ratios, covered gearing. Consider what happens as a consequence of a firm borrowing funds. Annual interest and capital repayments are fixed. These charges must be met irrespective of the profitability of the firm. Should there be a downturn in business, there may be insufficient cash to meet fixed charges and so the firm slips into liquidation. As the financial risk of a firm increases so too does the cost of capital. Lenders note the level of borrowings and so charge a higher rate of interest and/or exact more onerous repayment provisions. Ultimately, the objective of the firm is to find the right mix of capital so as to maximise the value of the shareholders' investment.

The cost of capital can be defined as follows:

$$k = f(r, b, f)$$

where

    k = cost of capital
    r = the pure rate of interest
    b = a business risk premium
    f = a financial risk premium.

A lender or consortium of lenders examining a request for capital must consider three elements in evaluating the price to charge. The first element is the pure time value of money or the riskless rate of interest. Secondly, lenders must evaluate the possibility that the business to which they are lending funds will collapse. The higher the probability the greater the premium. Finally, lenders look at the capital structure of the firm. The greater the proportion of fixed charge funds the greater the financial risk and so the higher the risk premium.

In practice this means that the cost of capital varies substantially across business. At one extreme, high-risk mineral exploration is such a risky business that no lender will provide funds; only risk-taking equity investors are prepared to balance the high level of business risk with the prospects of high returns. At the other extreme, investors in government bonds feel that there is virtually no business or financial risk and so they accept a rate close to the riskless rate of return.

Capital costs arise usually in relation to long-term sources of capital. Sections below examine the costs of the following sources of capital: mortgage/debenture bonds, grants, preference share capital and ordinary share capital.

THE COST OF MORTGAGE/DEBENTURE BONDS

The cost of long-term loans is the before-tax cost adjusted for the tax shield (subsidy) available to profitable firms, effectively the after-tax yield to maturity. It can be applied to the current debt structure, i.e. average cost, or to a new issue of debt, i.e. marginal cost. The latter case applies to a firm planning a new project or expansion, which requires financing and wants to know the minimum return necessary to meet the interest payments without any dilution in the ordinary shareholders' earnings.

The cost items are easily identified and are:

 ✳(1) Fixed interest payments.
 ✳ (2) Issuing costs such as legal fees, underwriting fees.
 ✳(3) Commitment fees.
 ✳(4) All premiums on repayment.
 ✳(5) Marginal tax rate.

Item 1 represents a periodic cost over the life of the loan. Items 2 and 3 represent a reduction in the actual amount received, while item 4 represents any excess to be paid on maturity. Item 5 notes the relevant tax rate.

An example would be a £500,000 sixteen-year term loan from the Industrial Credit Company. The borrower has to pay costs of £20,000 to obtain the funds; therefore the net proceeds are £480,000. The rate of interest payable semi-annually is 12 per cent. The lump sum of £500,000 is repayable in sixteen years and the marginal tax rate is 10 per cent.

The basic formula for calculating the cost of a debenture is

$$ki = \frac{I + \left(\dfrac{FV - N}{n}\right)}{\left(\dfrac{N + FV}{2}\right)} (1 - t).$$

where

ki = net after-tax cost of the loan	I = annual interest payment in £
FV = face value of the loan	N = net proceeds received by the firm
t = tax rate	n = period of the loan.

Assuming that the ICC loan above was negotiated in 1995 by a manufacturing firm, the cost is

$$ki = \cfrac{60{,}000 + \left(\cfrac{500{,}000 - 480{,}000}{16}\right)}{\left(\cfrac{480{,}000 + 500{,}000}{2}\right)} (1 - .10)$$

$$= \frac{60{,}000 + 1{,}250 \ (.9)}{490{,}000}$$

$$= 11.25\%$$

Note carefully that the borrower has only a 10 per cent tax shield. A service industry firm with a 40 per cent tax rate would have a net cost of 7.50 per cent.

In addition firms employ many different forms of debt and the formula noted above may need to be adjusted to reflect these differences. Also most firms see debt financing as a permanent part of their capital structure and in these circumstances the appropriate formula is simply

$$ki = \frac{I}{N} (1 - t)$$

This implies that the debt is irredeemable and issued in perpetuity. While individual debt instruments are retired over time new instruments are issued, thereby maintaining the same overall level of debt financing as part of the capital structure. The approach to be used is dependent on whether the firm is looking at its current cost of debt or planning a new issue as part of its capital structure.

As regards debt issues which are not marketable and with their value fixed by contract, the explicit cost is either the variable or fixed interest rate. Provided interest rates are constant over a period of time the interest cost adjusted for tax savings will reflect the cost of the debt. Should the interest rate be variable it may be preferable to take the current yield on a fixed interest security of the same maturity to calculate the cost and thereby reflect the market's best estimate of future interest rates. In addition it may make sense to include as part of long-term debt the permanent part, if any, of the firm's bank overdraft facility.

In theory a lender examines each loan application and applies business and financial risk premiums to the company. In practice lenders tend to divide businesses into two classes.

An A borrower i.e. small business and personal borrower might expect to pay up to 5 per cent of a risk premium compared to an AA borrower i.e. stable, well-financed business. Differences within categories tend to be nullified by the taking of collateral and the insistence on personal guarantees from the owners and/or directors.

THE COST OF GRANTS

Grants from organisations such as Forbairt, the IDA and SFADCo have been a significant source of long-term finance to modern business. Apart from being available, grants are virtually costless. Should the business cease within ten years of grants being paid, then a portion may be repayable. There is a sliding scale rate of repayment tied to the period which has elapsed since the grant was obtained.

In the purely theoretical sense grants do have costs:

(1) Since many grants are payable only on new assets the business might be forced to use new higher cost equipment instead of adequate second-hand and cheaper equipment. This has often been claimed in Ireland.

(2) The availability of labour grants may result in more labour-intensive activities and possibly higher costs of production.

(3) The state normally insists on a certain equity contribution by the promoters of the project. If this is higher than would be required were no grant obtained then it is possible that obtaining grants leads to higher costs on the remainder of the capital structure. Equally relevant is the likelihood that the presence of grants reduces not only the financial risk, in that no fixed charges apply, but the business risk, in that lenders know that the grantor has examined the proposed project and is satisfied with the viability. These effects could reduce the cost of debt capital.

In general it is safe to assume that capital grants have no cost to the individual company.

THE COST OF PREFERENCE SHARE CAPITAL

Preference share capital has some of the characteristics of debt, such as fixed annual charges, and some of the characteristics of ordinary share capital in regard to dividends. In addition preference dividends rank behind debentures in terms of obtaining annual fixed payments and will not cause bankruptcy. As such it can be viewed as a hybrid form of finance, positioned between that of debt finance and the ordinary shareholder in terms of risk and expecting a rate of return to reflect that risk profile.

It is theoretically incorrect to state that preference dividends are fixed. Firstly, directors must declare the payment of the dividends annually. Secondly, dividends can be declared only out of profits — either current profits or distributable earnings. From the viewpoint of the ordinary shareholder preferred payments are fixed in that no distribution can be made on the ordinary shares until the preferred shareholders are paid. Since dividends are a distribution of after-tax profits no tax shield arises.

The cost of preference share issues is as follows:

$$kp = \frac{dp}{Np}$$

where

kp = cost of preferred share capital
dp = annual dividend in £ per share
Np = net proceeds received from selling one share.

If the issue is publicly quoted one can calculate the yield currently received by the existing preference shareholders, i.e. the present average cost, or the yield required to attract new funds of this type, i.e. the marginal cost. It is the dividend divided by the current market price per share.

In addition, using the net proceeds or effectively the market issue price less any flotation costs reflects the current opportunity cost of the capital. This reflects current market conditions and will usually not be the same as the fixed dividend (coupon) rate when the shares were first issued. Where a firm has a corporation tax liability preference shares are often more expensive than debentures.

THE COST OF ORDINARY (EQUITY) SHARE CAPITAL

There are two types of equity: new funds raised by an issue of shares, and retained earnings representing owners' funds not paid out as dividends but reinvested in the business. Estimating the cost of equity capital is extremely difficult in practice because there is no stated interest or dividend rate. In theory the cost of equity can be defined as the minimum rate of return that a firm must earn on its ordinary shareholders' funds in order to maintain the market price of its shares. This means that the return can be volatile as the firm's performance fluctuates with the consequent risk reflected in the share price value. High risk firms tend to have a low share market price and therefore a higher cost of equity relative to that of a low risk firm. Most firms are private so there is no market price for their shares.

Every ordinary share has the right to a proportion of all future dividends declared by the board of directors of a company. Investors examining the company make up their own minds as to the likely pattern of future dividends. Depending on the level of expectations, investors will be either buyers or sellers. If the future flow of dividends were known with certainty, the cost of equity could be found by discovering the discount rate, which would equate the flow of future dividends to the current market price.

Several methods of estimating the cost of equity capital are in use. Three are examined here: historical rate of return, dividend price/growth model and the capital asset pricing model. No method is free of problems and in practice more than one is used by the financial manager.

Historical Rate of Return

This involves taking the historical performance of the firm in terms of dividends and any change in the value of the shares since they were issued. It is a simple estimate of the return on the investment. Depending on the time period chosen it can give widely different results and should be used with great caution. It is based on the assumptions that there were no significant changes in investors' expectations, interest rates or attitudes towards risk during that period. Consequently, it is rarely a fair reflection of market reality and should be employed only as an initial benchmark calculation.

Dividend Price/Growth Model

This model is often referred to in finance literature as the Gordon Model in recognition of the pioneering work of Myron J. Gordon. Gordon developed a dividend price model which was subsequently developed into a growth model to reflect dividend payment patterns.

The price model is shown below.

$$MP = \frac{D_1}{(1+k_e)^1} + \frac{D_2}{(1+k_e)^2} \cdots \frac{D_n}{(1+k_e)^n}$$

where

MP = current market price
D = dividend per share
k_e = the cost of equity.

For the sake of simplicity rather than theoretical accuracy many observers suggest that investors expect dividends to grow at a constant projected rate. Investment advisory services offer some help in this area by analysing possible market values arising from earnings forecasts. The historical earnings patterns and subsequent forecasts are seen as a strong indicator of dividend policy and help to provide direct measures of the expectations that determine market values. This is particularly true of mature firms that have reached a stable stage of development and are characterised by controlled growth and sound professional management. For high growth young firms or those subject to wide fluctuations in performance a realistic estimate of future growth is important. Analysis simply based on the past without extracting the once-off or non-recurring features will give rise to a gross overestimation of the true cost of equity. This could then lead to bad decision-making in the overall financing mix decision-making process.

Using this parameter the growth model can be rewritten as follows:

$$MP = \frac{Do(1+g)^1}{(1+k_e)^1} + \frac{Do(1+g)^2}{(1+k_e)^2} \quad \cdots \quad \frac{Do(1+g)^n}{(1+k_e)^n}$$

where

Do = the current dividend rate
g = the expected annual growth rate in dividends.

From this the cost of equity capital can be estimated as

$$k_e = \frac{D_1}{MP} + g$$

This means that the cost of equity is the expected dividend yield, using next year's dividend plus a growth factor. The above method of costing equity is most appropriate to retained earnings. Very often management assumes that retained earnings are costless. This is untrue. Retained earnings are, in fact, dividends foregone. Shareholders could have had the use of this money but instead the directors chose to retain it. In theory the cost of retained earnings must be calculated by assuming that the full sum was paid out to shareholders who then decided to reinvest the sum. This effectively involves estimating the opportunity cost of funds by using the firm's own resources. As was shown in Chapter 12 taxation policies in Ireland distort the value of dividends versus new equity investment. The differences between (a) retaining earnings and (b) issuing new shares to the same amount are issuing costs such as underwriting, advertising, printing and price discounts. New equity is usually issued at a discount against the existing market price. Therefore the cost of new equity is

$$k_{ne} = \frac{D_1}{NP} + g$$

where

K_{ne} = the cost of new equity capital

D_1 = expected dividends per share next year

NP = net proceeds per share

g = expected annual growth rate in dividends.

Note that the cost of new equity is almost always above the cost of retained earnings since the net proceeds per share will be below the market price of the share.

NOT DONE *

The Capital Asset Pricing Model

A more advanced method of identifying the cost of capital was developed in the 1970s — the capital asset pricing model.

A firm in deciding on its investment programme and financing mix sets out to maximise the value of its ordinary shares. In so doing, it is helpful to have an objective measure of risk. Risk measurement procedures are generally based on probability distributions and their characteristics in terms of the mean-variance rule. This is done through calculating the expected mean return of the investments, by getting the arithmetic average of the possible outcomes weighted by their probabilities. The variance measures the dispersion of the returns around the mean value.

When investments are combined in an efficient portfolio, part of each investment's total risk, its standard deviation, is reduced. This is achieved through the process of positive/negative correlation, i.e. diversification, whereby high return investments and low return investments form part of the total portfolio. The degree to which diversification stabilises the overall return on the portfolio depends on the strength of the relationships between the individual investments and the degree of uncorrelation with the overall market. This type of risk is called diversifiable or unsystematic.

The other element of risk, non-diversifiable or systematic, cannot be reduced by diversification. This stems from general market fluctuations, i.e. inflation, general economic conditions, government policy, etc. and is that part of the variability in returns which is correlated with the overall market.

The capital asset pricing model provides a single measure of an investment's risk, called beta. It also allows one to assess the significance and impact of both risk components, systematic and unsystematic, on investors' decisions. It can be defined as the required rate of return being equal to the risk-free rate of return plus a risk premium based on the expected return on the market portfolio and the investment's systematic risk as measured by beta. It is formally expressed as

$$R_s = R_i + (Rm - R_i)\beta$$

where

R_s = required rate of return

R_i = risk-free rate of return

R_m = expected return on the market portfolio

β = measurement of the systematic risk of the investment.

The risk-free rate of return is based on the current rate for government-secured bonds. The market risk premium, i.e. $R_m - R_i$, is calculated by taking the difference between the expected long-run average market return and the rate on government bonds. When interest rates are high the premium is usually low and vice versa. The beta for an investment can be obtained from published sources or estimated by the financial manager. It reflects the contribution of an investment to the overall risk of the market portfolio and is dependent on the degree of correlation between investment returns and portfolio returns. It reflects the expected volatility of the investment in relation to the market generally as shown by the stock market, which has a beta of 1.0. Investments with a beta of 1.0 are expected to move in line with the average risk. Risky investments whose returns tend to fluctuate up and down faster than the general market have a beta greater than 1.0.

Although beta can be estimated solely on the basis of subjective beliefs, it is common practice to use historical data to estimate future betas. Statistical methods are used to estimate the beta risk coefficient; these are seen as being outside the scope of this text.

The capital asset pricing model, like any abstract theory, has weaknesses. Notwithstanding its theoretical nature, assumptions and wide acceptance academically, there is concern that issues such as the firm's size, timing of investment and the lack of empirical evidence are important considerations. An alternative theory has been developed in this area, called the arbitrage pricing model. This considers multiple economic factors in determining the investment's rate of return and could be seen as complementary to the capital asset pricing model, given its concentration on systematic risk.

In general, new equity is thought to be the most costly source of finance. This may not be true in Ireland, where tax incentives on dividend payouts and tax-deductibility on approved equity investments (BES) increase the attractiveness of equity as an investment. As a result, the cost is lower.

THE OVERALL COST OF CAPITAL

Having identified the cost of each specific source of finance, it is now possible to develop a means for determining the overall cost of capital. This is the rate that must be earned to satisfy the firm's investors for a given level of risk. This figure can then be used as the cut-off or hurdle rate for investment evaluation. Two methods are presented below: the weighted average cost method and the marginal cost method.

The Weighted Average Cost of Capital (WACC)

Most investment projects use a mixture of grant, debt and equity capital. Consequently, if the project does not materially change the firm's overall risk profile, the appropriate cut-off or hurdle rate is the weighted average cost of capital (WACC). The WACC is defined as the rate that reflects the costs of individual sources of finance, weighted by their share in the firm's capital structure. The weights may be either the historical proportions in the capital structure of the firm or the actual proportions of each source used to finance a particular project. Traditionally, the historical weights are used.

In computing the WACC we are assuming that the firm's financial mix will not change, that it will continue to invest in projects of about the same risk as it has in the past and that it will not change the percentage of earnings paid out in dividends to its shareholders.

Market values should be used as a basis for WACC calculations, when available, in preference to book values.

Table 14.2 shows the weighted average cost of capital of financing the Ardmore Limited stainless steel tank project. To recapitulate, Ardmore Limited was considering an investment of £188,000 to establish a stainless steel tank engineering project. The capital was being subscribed by Forbairt, a bank and the owners.

Table 14.2 Weighted Average Cost of Capital for Ardmore				
Source	*Quantity* £	*Weight* %	*Cost*	*Weighted Cost*
Grant	40,000	21.0	0	0.00
Bank Loan	100,000	53.0	13.5	7.16
New Equity	48,000	26.0	56.0	14.56
	188,000	100		21.72

The following are the assumptions:
(1) The grant has no cost.
(2) The cost of the bank loan is $(15.0)(1-.1) = 13.5$ per cent. The loan has a seven-year term and a 15 per cent interest rate. There is a tax shield of 10 per cent.
(3) The owners intend to begin paying dividends at the end of the current year. The amount of dividends attributable to the £48,000 of equity will be £17,500 in year one. This is expected to grow at the rate of 20 per cent per annum. The cost of equity in this case where there are negligible issuing costs is

$$\frac{£17,500}{£48,000} + 20\% = 56\%$$

The weighted average cost of capital of 21.72 per cent is close to the rough estimate of 25 per cent used to evaluate the investment proposal in Chapter 6.

The Marginal Cost of Capital

This method takes into account the fact that raising additional funds may change the overall cost of funds to the firm. This can best be understood by considering a situation where a company borrows 100 per cent of the funds required to undertake a project. Existing lenders looking at the new fixed cost funds are concerned with the rising level of financial risk so they increase the financial risk premium on existing funds.

At the opposite extreme a company with a high level of equity may find it possible to fund a project with only grant and debt finance. Equity holders may view this decision as improving dividend prospects and so may pay a higher price for the share.

If the overall cost of capital rises as a result of introducing new finance to fund an investment programme, the marginal cost of capital should be used as a cut-off or hurdle rate. This is to allow the evaluation of the investment in line with the basic economic principle of marginal analysis, i.e. up to the point where marginal revenue (internal rate of return) equates to or is closest to marginal cost.

VALUATION AND CAPITAL STRUCTURE

For many years now a heated debate has raged among financial theorists. One group, the traditionalists, believes that there is an optimum capital structure. By this it means that one particular combination of all long-term sources of finance provides the least expensive cost of capital to the firm. On the other hand, a group of researchers supports the Modigliani-Miller approach, which states that changing the mix of capital sources does not affect the valuation of the business.

The Traditional Approach to Capital Structure

At the simplest level the traditional approach suggests that using cheap fixed interest debt will provide higher earnings for the ordinary shareholders. Investors seeing a higher rate of profitability will be prepared to pay more for the shares of the company and so the total value of the company will rise. Since the objective of the business is to maximise the long-run wealth of the shareholders, it is correct for management to manipulate the capital structure. The approach is presented graphically in Figure 14.3.

Figure 14.3 The Overall Cost of Capital

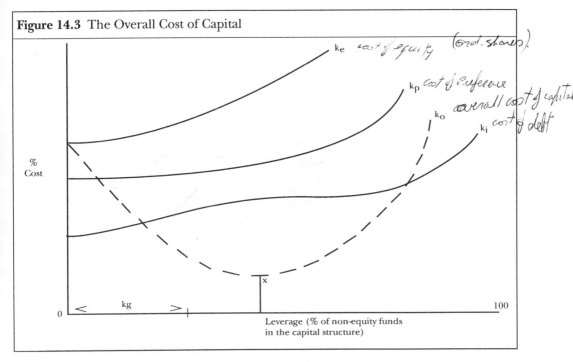

In this example a firm is considering financing a project with 100 per cent equity. As an alternative the managers may obtain a grant for part of the cost. The effect of the grant–equity mixture is to reduce the overall cost. As the ratio of no cost grant to high cost equity increases, the average cost decreases. Once all available grants are used, debentures are substituted. Since debentures are often cheaper than equity, the average cost continues to decrease. Sooner or later lenders become worried about fixed costs so they charge a risk premium which rises rapidly as the percentage of debt increases. Likewise preference share capital can be used to bring down the average cost. At point x in Figure 14.3 the company has an optimum capital structure.

The Modigliani-Miller Approach

The MM approach, as it is known, has two basic elements:

(a) That the market value of a firm and its cost of capital are totally independent of the capital structure of the firm.

(b) That as cheaper debt funds are used in a structure the cost of equity rises proportionally.

Figure 14.4 shows the MM approach using two sources of funds, debt and equity. The theory states that two firms alike in every respect except capital structure must have the same total value. If not, arbitrage will be possible, causing their values to come into line quickly. Arbitrage is the process of buying and selling in more than one market so as to make a riskless profit and quickly eliminate differentials across different markets.

If the market for capital were perfect, if there were no taxation anomalies, if all relevant information was free and available to all investors and if there were no transactions costs then the MM thesis would hold. In a perfect capital market investors can substitute personal leverage for corporate leverage. The net effect is that the capital structure could not affect the market value of the business.

Figure 14.4 Modigliani-Miller Approach to the Cost of Capital

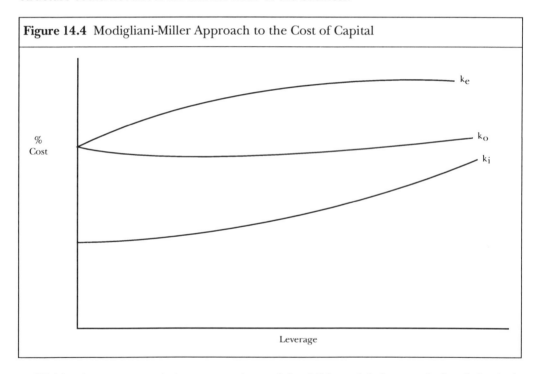

Within the many restrictive assumptions of the MM model the conclusion is logical. However, this argument cannot be supported in a practical world, for it is extremely doubtful that personal investors would substitute personal leverage for corporate leverage, since they do not have the same risk characteristics. In a world of uncertainty, imperfect capital markets, poor diffusion of information and a battery of tax incentives, the proposition does not stand up. Nevertheless, the propositions and their criticisms should be carefully studied since they will aid an understanding of capital structure theory.

CONCLUSION

This chapter has discussed two important topics, the cost of capital and capital structure. Calculating the cost of capital is essential if a firm is to have a realistic cost against which returns on investments can be compared. Methods of calculating the cost of debt, preference and ordinary share capital were presented. The importance and zero cost of grant capital was noted.

Capital structure and the changes in financial risk as leverage changes were examined. The weighted average cost of capital was calculated. Finally, we examined the thorny question of capital structure and the valuation of the firm. While the theoretical Modigliani-Miller model has its merits, a successful capital structure policy must be based on understanding and exploiting market imperfections. In brief, the financial manager in assessing the capital structure of the firm should look at the tax rate, the degree of dependence on tangible assets, the amount of business risk and the target capital structure. Given the traditional approach to capital structure and giving due weight to the reasons for using debt financing, the trade-off theory recognises that structure will vary from firm to firm. Firms with safe, tangible assets and high taxable earnings to shield should have a high debt ratio. Unprofitable firms with risky, intangible assets should rely primarily on equity financing. This should lead to rational financing decisions, moderate debt ratios and the existence of norms or patterns emerging by industry or clusters of industry.

However, there are some contradictions that cannot be explained by the trade-off theory. This is evidenced by the existence of highly profitable firms with little or no debt. The pecking order theory, which places internal equity at the top of the list, goes some way towards explaining this situation. This type of firm, with a restrained dividend policy, a preference for internal funds and an aversion to raising outside finance, is showing rational economic behaviour in building up financial slack so as to be well placed should any investment opportunities arise. In practice firms will tend to come to rely on the historically tested and conventional capital mix for that industry or sector.

On an international level firms have to take into account other factors, such as exchange rate risk, particular standards and financial incentives in host countries, the risk of expropriation and the degree to which the political and economic country is diversified.

As regards small firms their lack of equity sources leads to a greater reliance on debt, both long-, medium- and short-term. This magnifies the risk of insolvency and reduces the options available in determining the optimum capital structure. It could be helpful to use the indifference point technique, which indicates the level where the earnings per share are the same, regardless of alternative capital structures. At earnings levels above the indifference point, more financially levered capital structures will produce higher levels of earnings per share, and similarly for less financially levered capital structures with earnings below the indifference point. Allied to this the small firm may use the standard deviation technique to measure the risk associated with the firm's earnings and thereby be better able to calculate the amount of debt to be used. In the final analysis the critical question may not be the amount of debt but rather the type of debt. The ability of the firm's management to synchronise its cash flow as part of its cash insolvency analysis may be the dominant issue.

FURTHER READING

J.W. Petty et al., *Basic Financial Management*, 6th ed. (New Jersey, Prentice-Hall, 1993).

F.M. Wilkes and R.E. Brayshaw, *Company Finance and Its Management* (UK, Van Nostrand Reinhold, 1986).

QUESTIONS

Question 14.1

If a company is planning to issue a £50 par preference share capital that pays £6 dividends per year and the firm is expected to realise £48 per share, what is the cost of preference shares issued?

Question 14.2

What is the cost of a debenture with a £200,000 twelve-year term loan with costs of £22,000 and a rate of interest payable semi-annually of 14 per cent? The borrower pays corporation tax at 50 per cent.

Question 14.3

A company is expected to pay a dividend of £2 on common stock in the coming year. The stock is currently selling at £50 per share. Dividends are expected to increase at a rate of 12 per cent per year. What is the cost of equity?

Question 14.4

If the cost of equity for a stock were 14.8 per cent with a dividend of 9p per share and expected future dividends were to grow at 10 per cent per annum, what would be the current market price of the share?

Question 14.5

The Balance Sheet of a company is as follows:

Source of Finance	Current Market Value	Marginal Cost
Equity	£1,000,000	12%
Preference Shares	£500,000	16%
Long-Term Debt	£500,000	20%
Total	£2,000,000	

Calculate the weighted average cost of capital (WACC).

Question 14.6

The capital structure of a company shown in its Balance Sheet is as follows:

	£
200,000 £1 Ordinary Shares	200,000
Retained Profit	100,000
Shareholders' Funds	300,000
10% Debentures (repayable in ten years)	150,000
	£450,000

270

The current market value of an ordinary share is £2.50 and a dividend of 10p has just been paid with constant growth of 8 per cent over the next ten years. The debentures, with a nominal value of £100, are quoted on the market @ £90. Assuming that the capital structure will be maintained over the next ten years, calculate the company's weighted average cost of capital. Assume corporation tax is at 50 per cent.

15

Mergers
and Acquisitions

Mergers move in cycles. The first half of the 1990s was a low stage in the cycle whereas the decade of the 1980s saw an unprecedented growth in the number and size of corporate mergers and acquisitions. In the 1980s business dealers such as Michael Milken and Carl Icahn in the US, James Hanson and James Goldsmith in the UK and Dermot Desmond in Ireland caught the imagination of the public as they 'wheeled and dealed'. Terms such as 'Dawn Raider', 'White Knight', 'Leveraged Buyout' and 'Junk Bonds' were used by people far removed from the centre of financial takeovers. Ireland experienced considerable takeover activity. A number of top-quality Irish companies — CRH, Smurfit's, Kerry and Waterford — became significant multinational entities by means of international acquisitions.

This period of high merger activity has to be viewed against the cyclical nature of such activity over the previous century. During the twentieth century merger activity has been seen to be closely correlated with variations in macro-economic trends and stock market prices. While the earlier merger waves were greatly influenced by technological growth, the 1980s brought forth raiders armed with a large arsenal of 'junk bond' financing that was used to attack some of the world's biggest corporations. This changed the outlook of corporate management, which had not previously been exposed to such formidable outside threats, and was clearly seen as a hostile process.

But that phase also passed. World economic slowdown in the late 1980s and early 1990s, rising interest rates and changing social attitudes towards corporate acquisitions led to a virtual cessation of merger activity. Some of the major players went bankrupt while others went to jail. Much was written and more was said about the 'uniqueness' of the 1980s merger mania.

In the mid-1990s the cycle turned up again. Economic growth, low interest rates and cheap assets led to the beginning of another round of mergers. What was thought to be unique in the 1980s was merely another stage in the ongoing cycle.

A detailed examination of mergers and acquisitions is beyond the scope of this text. This chapter sets out some of the basic factors involved and attempts to give a flavour of a subject which generates massive business, political and social risk.

TYPES OF MERGER AND ACQUISITION
Why do mergers occur? Growth in income is a fundamental objective of all private

enterprise businesses. Such growth usually requires an increase in the activities of the firm. Very often increasing activity means expanding the product range of the company, expanding the market served by the business or diversifying into totally new businesses. Expansion can be internal or external. Mergers mean external growth: that is, growth by acquisition.

The amalgamation of one firm with another through a merger or acquisition is now an established and well-accepted part of commercial life. Legally, mergers may be distinguished from acquisitions but from a financial viewpoint there is rarely a significant difference. A merger or acquisition is defined here as an amalgamation of two or more firms into one organisation with common ownership and management. Reasons for amalgamation are many, but it is important to remember that there are at least two sides to a merger and the reasons for acquiring a firm may differ substantially from the reasons for disposing of a firm. There are a number of differing strategies involved in acquisitions. These can be seen in the following major categories of acquisition activity:

(1) Conglomerate Takeover.
(2) Diversification by Takeover.
(3) Horizontal Takeover.
(4) Vertical Takeover.
(5) Leveraged Buyout/Management Buyout.
(6) Shell Operations.

Conglomerate Takeover

Conglomerate takeover occurs when a firm acquires another firm in an unrelated industry. The word conglomerate fell out of favour in recent years. Such firms are now known as 'Industrial Holding' companies. The logic behind these ventures centres on a core of financial/management skills in the acquiring firm being used in the acquired firm. The golden era of conglomerates was the late 1960s/early 1970s. In Ireland conglomerates such as Fitzwilton, Brooks Watson, Moore Holdings, James Crean and Ferrier Pollock were formed. Note that only two survived into the 1990s, Fitzwilton and James Crean, and they too had problems.

Conglomerates are formed and grow through five stages of development:
(1) Creating a management group which will appeal to the investing public. This usually involves managers with proven track records. In Ireland Tony O'Reilly formed Fitzwilton, Ray McLoughlin formed James Crean, while in the late 1980s a well-respected venture capitalist, Tony Mullins, formed Barlo.
(2) Getting the backing of a financial group. The founding group puts up some of its own equity then raises debt.
(3) Obtaining a quotation by injecting large amounts of cash into a small moribund publicly quoted company called a 'shell'. By taking shares in return for the cash injection the promoting group gets control of the original company.
(4) Using the cash in the public company to take over high earning, privately held companies. This explains the tendency of early Irish conglomerates to purchase builders and distribution operations. Both of these industries were expanding rapidly in the 1970s. Neither was capital-intensive. Purchasing earnings with cash causes the earnings per share of the original company to rise. If investors value a company on the basis of earnings per share, then the share price will rise as earnings are purchased.

(5) Buying assets. Ideally, the group is by now composed of high income earners with little asset backing. By merging the high earnings/low asset company, with a low earnings/high asset company, a more stable operation is supposed to ensue. In addition making the group larger widens the number of shares issued and is supposed to diffuse ownership. This should allow the initial investors to sell off part of their shareholding if they desire.

Conglomerates fared badly in bear markets. Many were dismembered and some went bankrupt. In Ireland Ferrier Pollock, Moore Holdings and Braids closed, while Brooks Watson and Fitzwilton were reduced to shells. Ultimately, Brooks Watson was acquired. Unrelated activities based on high levels of borrowing did not survive economic recession. Internationally, conglomerates fared little better. In the US, UK and Australia they folded, burdened by high debt and low declining mature industries. Yet some survived. Hanson and BTR in the UK continue to grow into world-wide companies.

In the late 1980s the phenomenon appeared again. In the UK a series of companies was created to purchase cheap assets while in Ireland the Barlo group expanded rapidly from a basis of simple engineering into acquisitions in the UK and mainland Europe. It ran into difficulties in 1994.

Fitzwilton developed through a series of ventures into engineering in Ireland (Novum and Rennicks), car leasing in the UK (Keep Trust) and grocery wholesaling (Mark 6). These activities did not please the investing public so new directions were pursued — a share in Waterford/Wedgwood and the purchase of the Wellworth retail chain in the North of Ireland. Earlier acquisitions were disposed of generally at a loss.

Diversification by Takeover

Diversified companies operate in more than one country and/or business. A strategy of diversification is often followed when a firm has proprietary technology, specialised skills, efficient distribution networks, or strong brand names. A company may have a combination of strengths which leads it towards a diversification strategy.

Certain Irish companies have followed such a diversification strategy. Smurfit's has diversified internationally within the packaging industry. CRH has expanded abroad in related activities.

Smurfit, from a Dublin base, has expanded into the third largest paper and packaging company in the world, with significant production operations on most continents. Despite their size and success Smurfit has found that the cyclical nature of the packaging industry still has an impact on performance. In 1994 Smurfit profits were a fraction of what they were in 1989 though they rose again in 1995.

CRH expanded from Ireland into the UK, US and mainland Europe in the building products industry.

Independent Newspapers purchased papers in the UK, Australia, New Zealand and South Africa.

On the other hand, numerous Irish companies have found it difficult to expand abroad. The two major banking groups spent hundreds of millions on purchasing banks in the UK and US. For many years the investments failed to yield a return. Smaller financial groups such as Yeoman, Cambridge, Anglo and Reflex suffered heavy losses on overseas ventures.

The main Irish food companies all expanded internationally by acquisition in the 1980s and 1990s. They assumed that their domestic production skills and management expertise could be transferred to foreign environments.

Horizontal Takeover

Horizontal takeovers are undertaken to capture specific markets, to increase market share or to eliminate competitors. Capital-intensive industries with high breakeven points often find it cheaper to buy market share than to develop new sales. For many industries higher sales mean more economies of scale and lower production costs so the more you grow the lower your costs and the bigger the potential profit. In the 1970s/1980s major waves of horizontal takeover activity took place in the Irish printing and packaging industry and in the concrete trade. In the 1980s the co-op movement also consolidated. This will continue in the 1990s.

The retail grocery trade in Ireland provides a good example of horizontal takeover activity. Over a twenty-year period literally hundreds of acquisitions have led to the creation of two dominant forces in Irish grocery retailing — Dunnes Stores and Quinnsworth. Over the years these two firms have bought market share which enabled them to bulk purchase, thus giving lower costs. They also bought geographic advantage to consolidate their position. The battle, which began in Dublin, has spread throughout the country and has seen the demise of many hundreds of small retailers and a number of large chains such as Five Star and H. Williams.

Vertical Takeover

Vertical buyers are seeking acquisitions that will enable them to gain greater efficiencies through integration, either forward by buying distributors and/or outlets, or backward by acquiring supply and/or manufacturing capability. Agribusiness in Ireland has also seen a number of forward integration takeovers.

Internationally, resource producers have strong reasons to integrate forward to protect sales of their raw materials. The international oil producers acquired transport, refineries, petrol stations and chemical companies in their drive for survival and profit. A more detailed example is that of BHP, the biggest resource company in the world. After it became a coal producer almost by accident, it examined its strategies. It decided to provide energy to end users by systematically buying into coal, gas and oil producers. It also bought and built pipelines to transport its raw energy and acquired refineries, petrol stations and electricity power stations to process the raw materials to finished products.

Leveraged Buyout/Management Buyout

The most spectacular development in recent years in the takeover arena has been the growth in 'leveraged buyouts'. A leveraged buyout (LBO) is any acquisition of a company which leaves the acquired operating entity with a greater than traditional debt-to-equity ratio. The structure of the debt will always fall into one of the following quadrants:

	Type of debt financing	
	Secured	Unsecured
Asset acquisition		
Share acquisition		

Type of transaction

Secured financing occurs when the assets of the acquired operation are used to collateralise the debt. The difference between the secured debt and the purchase price is normally covered by a combination of equity contribution of the investing group and subordinated debt.

Unsecured financing normally involves some combination of venture capital, 'mezzanine debt' or subordinated debt (generally with an equity sweetener) and senior debt (generally owing to banks), aggregating to the total purchase price.

Asset acquisitions involve the formation of a new corporation (or utilisation of an existing corporation), which acquires the assets of the target company. If the acquired operation is a corporate division rather than a separate corporation, an asset acquisition is the only available type of transaction.

Share acquisitions take many forms: they can include stock redemptions, tender offers, pure stock acquisitions and reverse mergers. They generally involve the most complex structuring and the greatest number of legal issues. They are most commonly used if the target company is publicly held or if an asset acquisition will result in significant tax issues.

After the merger spree of the early 1970s new management believed in 'sticking to the knitting' so a range of businesses which no longer met the long-term strategic needs of diversified firms came onto the market. Investment bankers moved aggressively into the business of organising management buyouts, using the assets of the company being acquired as collateral for the deal.

An LBO involves borrowing from a financial source to acquire a target company. The proceeds are used to pay the seller. Internal cash flow and sales of assets are used to repay the lender.

Table 15.1 Industries Preferred for LBOs

	Ranking February '95
Industrial products	1
Engineering	2
Communications	3
Food & beverage	4
Healthcare	5
Electronics	6
Chemical	7
Computer services software	8
Energy	9
Publishing & education	10=
Leisure recreation	10=
Computer hardware equipment	12=
Other services	12=
Hi tech	14
Bio tech	15
Financial services	16
Advertising & marketing	17
Hotels & restaurants	18
Property & construction	19
Film industry	20

Source: *Investor's Chronicle*, 10 March 1995.

Over a time a series of rules of thumb have evolved to help identify companies suited to an LBO. Certain industries have the desired criteria. The characteristics of a classic

LBO and the industries preferred by investors are shown below.

(a) Saleable or non-industry specific assets.

(b) Stable cash flow.

(c) Good 'free' cash flow, i.e. after essential capital investment.

(d) Debt capacity.

(e) Modern plant and equipment.

(f) Modest future capital requirements.

(g) Reasonable market position in a mature industry.

(h) Low seasonality.

(i) Low risk of technological obsolescence.

(j) Few union problems.

It is not immediately obvious to most how an LBO works. Remember the objective is to use the underearned assets of the business being bought as the security for loans used to buy the shares of the business. The following is a simplistic model.

(1) New investors establish Newco for the specific purpose of taking over asset-rich Sleepyco. The initial investors, usually management, obtain a good percentage of the equity of Newco to 'incentivise' them.

(2) Newco obtains massive loan commitments from a 'junk bond' consortium. The loans to be used only to acquire Sleepyco and then to be repaid by selling assets or making them 'sweat'.

(3) Newco bids for and acquires Sleepyco.

(4) Now the loans are in Newco, the owner of Sleepyco which has the assets.

(5) Sleepyco in turn merges entirely with or takes over Newco. Now the Newco debt is on the Sleepyco balance sheet with the Sleepyco assets.

(6) Some of the assets of Sleepyco are sold to pay off the debt while the rest are sweated to produce a higher cash flow.

Table 15.2 shows the level of LBO deals in Europe in 1992 and 1993.

Most LBO deals are in the £20 million to £80 million band.

Table 15.2 Buyouts by Country — 1992–1993

	No. of deals		Est. total value mEcu		Est. ave. value mEcu	
	1993	1992	1993	1992	1993	1992
Austria	0	2	0	35	0	17.7
Belgium	2	1	26	10	12.8	9.7
Denmark	0	1	0	62	0	62.4
Finland	1	0	11	n/a	10.6	n/a
France	12	15	388	797	32.3	53.1
Germany	11	7	364	280	33.1	39.9
Ireland	3	0	90	n/a	30.1	n/a
Italy	6	5	266	296	44.4	59.2
Netherlands	5	1	181	43	36.2	43.2
Portugal	1	1	10	182	10.0	182.4
Spain	0	3	0	192	0	63.9
Sweden	8	5	723	178	90.4	35.5
Switzerland	1	0	18	n/a	17.5	n/a
Intn'l	4	4	551	351	137.8	87.8
UK	49	48	2,491	2,549	50.8	53.1
Total	103	93	5,119	4,975	50.4	53.5

Source: *Investor's Chronicle*, March 1994.

Shell Operations

In the mid-1980s a new takeover phenomenon appeared on the Irish scene. Control of a number of Irish publicly quoted companies was partially acquired by UK-based investors to be used as vehicles or shells for United Kingdom acquisitions.

The principal cause of this interest was that Irish companies were part of the London Stock Exchange. These new shell companies concentrated on purchasing UK property assets. In the booming property markets of 1987–8 fortunes were quickly made. When the property bubble burst in 1989 most of the shells were caught with high borrowings and totally illiquid property assets. The majority took massive losses and survived only by the grace of their bankers. Share price collapses of 95 per cent were common. By the mid-1990s only the rare exception has managed to recover. A new form of the shell activity appeared in 1993, when depressed exploration companies were acquired and directed into new areas. Again the cause was a public listing. Irish companies on the Exploration Market have their shares quoted each day in London and in the financial press. This was sufficient to use the shells as vehicles.

MERGERS/ACQUISITIONS MOTIVES AND CAUSES

There are many diverse motives, which can be generally classified into three groups. The first group consists of those motives that deal with 'synergy': that is, those which claim to create real net gains to the merged or acquired firm, causing the value of the two firms combined to be greater than the sum of the two parts. This can be subdivided into operating or financial synergy. Operating synergy refers to efficiency gains or operating economics. Financial synergy refers to the possibility that the cost of capital can be lowered by combining two or more companies. The second group of motives is 'based on the perceived *undervaluation*' of the target firm, which is then seen as offering a 'good buy' to the acquiring firm. Undervaluation may be identified through information, in-depth analysis or confidence that better management or marketing can improve the firm's performance. The third group of motives comprises a wide range of '*managerial motives*' based on the self-interest of corporate managers. These include power needs, growth, executive compensation and the pride of the managers in the acquiring firm. In these cases the economic gain to the acquiring firm is not the sole or even the primary motivation. An interesting hypothesis by Richard Roll posits that managers seek to acquire firms for their own personal motives, explaining why they might pay a premium for a firm that the market has already correctly valued. Roll's view is that pride allows management to believe that its valuation is superior to that of the market.

Specific causes of mergers as seen from the buyer's perspective include the following:

(1) The desire of a company to obtain a scarce technology controlled by another.
(2) The desire of a company to acquire the management or special skills of another.
(3) To safeguard a source of supply. Examples of this include the acquisition of small private oil companies with North Sea interests by large multinational oil firms.
(4) To reduce or eliminate competition. Alternatively, the acquisition may be simply to stop a competitor from increasing its strength. The attempt by Irish Distillers to acquire Cooley Distillery fits here.
(5) To obtain economies of scale. This can be by horizontal integration where one firm buys up competitors.
(6) To obtain growth by diversification due to maturity in the existing product range of

the company. The efforts of the tobacco industry to diversify are an example.

(7) To improve the spread of investment risk. It may be possible to purchase a contracyclical or contraseasonal business. An illustration would be a snow ski manufacturing company purchasing a tennis equipment manufacturer.

(8) A need for rapid expansion in capacity. Increasingly roundabout methods of production mean that adding new capacity can take years. It is often quicker to buy existing capacity.

(9) The discovery that it is cheaper to buy than to build. Share prices were low for many years, particularly in relation to net asset values.

(10) To obtain synergy. An example is adding a sportswear company to a sports equipment company.

On the seller's side there may be numerous reasons for merging, such as:

(1) Tax or estate planning.
(2) Lack of management succession.
(3) Lack of technical know-how.
(4) To avoid being acquired by unwelcome suitors.
(5) Lack of fit with current or future strategic direction.
(6) Need to be part of a larger entity to maintain a competitive edge.
(7) Availability of a 'good price'.

ANTI-TAKEOVER MEASURES

Takeovers can cause problems. Not all are welcome, and they frequently generate a great deal of controversy. Corporate takeovers reached new levels of hostility during the 1980s. There were many innovations in the art of hostile takeovers, bringing about the development of anti-takeover defence tactics. Within a short while investment banks had teams of defence specialists who could work with the management of the target firm to counter the aggressive tactics of the acquiring firm. It is useful to divide the array of anti-takeover tactics into two categories: preventative and active measures.

Preventative measures are designed to reduce the likelihood of a financially successful hostile takeover by attempting to reduce the value that the hostile bidder can find in the firm. The presence of value-enhancing characteristics in a company, such as high and steady cash flows, low debt levels and a low stock price relative to the firm's assets or to the market generally, may make it vulnerable to a takeover. The preventative measures designed to alter these characteristics include 'shark repellents', 'poison pills', 'golden parachutes' and 'the crown jewels lock-up'.

Shark repellents are designed to make the target firm so unpleasant that it is attack-proof. They could include supermajority provisions, i.e. 80 per cent approval required for a merger; staggered board elections; fair price provisions to determine the price of minority shareholders' stock; and dual capitalisation, whereby the equity is restructured into two classes with different voting rights. Other examples include provisions in a loan covenant that makes debt instantly repayable and the firm insolvent in the event of a takeover, and an onerous commercial agreement if the hostile firm requires a certain level of shareholding.

Poison pills are often securities issued by the target firm in the form of rights offerings.

These allow the holders to buy stock in the acquiring (hostile) firm at a low price. They would be distributed after a triggering event such as the acquisition of 20 per cent of the stock of the target firm by any individual partnership or corporation. This process curtailed the possibility of friendly mergers and led to variations in the process used to allow for less than 100 per cent control of the target firm. Recent US court cases have limited the effectiveness of this type of poison pill as an anti-takeover defence. Other types of poison pill are long-term contracts and/or provision for withdrawing from contracts if control shifts.

Golden parachutes are unacceptably high compensation packages that must be paid to managers if they are forced to leave the firm. Managers have five- or ten-year contracts with provisions for full payments up front if they are forced to leave.

The crown jewels lock-up is a contract to sell the firm's most valuable assets at below market price if the hostile bid succeeds.

As a rule, each of these tactics is designed to protect the interests of an entrenched management at the expense of the shareholders whose interests they are supposedly defending. Consequently, their legality is often successfully challenged. While most of the above tactics are US-based, certain of them exist in Ireland. The Bank of Ireland has restrictive rights against shareholdings greater than 15 per cent. In floating Greencore the state insisted that restrictive provisions be installed against takeovers. Golden parachutes are common in Ireland.

As well as the negative anti-takeover measures, managements frequently pursue an 'active' policy.

'**Active**' measures are employed after a hostile bid has been launched and include the introduction of a white knight or squire, greenmail, standstill agreements, capital structure changes, litigation and the infamous pac-man defence.

A '**white knight**' is a company that comes to the rescue of a firm targeted for a takeover. The white knight may make an offer to buy all or part of the target firm on more favourable terms than the original bidder and promise not to disassemble the firm or lay off the management or other employees. It may be difficult to find a bidder willing to agree to such restrictive terms and some compromise by the target firm may have to be entertained. Generally, the search for a 'white knight' begins immediately a bid is launched.

A **white squire defence** is similar to the white knight defence in that the two parties, target firm and white squire, seek to implement a strategy to preserve the target firm's independence. This is done by placing assets or shares in the hands of a friendly firm or investor who is not interested in acquiring control of the target firm and will not sell out to a hostile bidder. This is rarely a long-term solution as the squire often sells on the shares or becomes a 'grey knight', i.e. makes a hostile bid himself.

Greenmail refers to the payment of a substantial premium for a significant block of shares in return for an agreement not to initiate a bid for control of the firm.

A **standstill agreement** occurs when the target firm reaches a contractual agreement with the potential bidder that he will not increase his holding in the target firm for a particular period. The agreement can take many forms, including the right of first refusal to the target firm if the bidder sells his shares and a commitment by the bidder not to increase his holding beyond a certain percentage in return for a fee. Standstill agreements are frequently accompanied by greenmail and are a clear example of the management entrenchment hypothesis referred to earlier.

Capital structure changes can be adopted by the target firm when a hostile bid has been initiated and are an extension of the shark-repellent tactics discussed as part of the preventative measures. The firm may issue new stock and place it in the hands of a friendly shareholder (white squire). It may buy back shares so as to ensure that they are not purchased by the hostile bidder or assume more debt in the form of bonds or bank loans. In addition it could decide to recapitalise, whereby it substitutes most of its equity for debt while paying shareholders a large dividend. This is called a leveraged recapitalisation and it places the firm in a dramatically different financial condition. In effect it allows the firm to act as its own white knight by seeking out a friendly bidder or attempting a management leveraged buyout. These tactics are rarely used in the British Isles as they are against the listing agreement of companies on the Stock Exchange.

Litigation is one of the most common anti-takeover measures and is often used as a delaying tactic. The temporary halting of a takeover can give the target firm time to mount more effective defences or allow the bidding firm improve its offer. It may also allow other bidders to enter the process or a white knight to be courted. The basis for the litigation may be found in the complex web of EC competition law or securities legislation.

The **pac-man defence** is called after the video game in which characters try to eat each other before they are eaten themselves, i.e. the firm under attack from a hostile bidder turns the table by bidding for the aggressor.

Other less prevalent forms of defence tactics include pension parachutes, use of overfunded pension funds and the negotiation of golden handcuff conditions which place limits on what the bidding firm can do with the target firm if and when it gets control.

Finally, fighting a merger may lead to a corporate restructuring by way of a divestiture. The different types of divestiture may be summarised as follows:

— sell-off: the sale of a subsidiary, division or product line
— spin-off: the separation of a subsidiary from its parent with no change in the equity ownership. While the management gives up operating control of the subsidiary, the shareholders retain the same percentage ownership in both firms through issuing new shares representing ownership in the divested assets on a pro-rata basis.
— liquidation: this is not a decision to close down or abandon the assets; it involves a sale to another firm with the proceeds being distributed to the shareholders.
— going private: the ownership of the firm is transferred from a large diverse

group of outside shareholders to a small group of private investors, usually the firm's management. The stock is no longer bought and sold on a public exchange. Most LBOs follow this route.

Occasionally, anti-takeover provisions are valid. Companies with long research and development periods may need protection while the results become apparent in sales and profits. But in general, anti-takeover provisions are not in the best interests of shareholders. While exotic takeover defences have been installed and used in the US, there has been little use of such techniques in Ireland.

FINANCIAL EVALUATION: DETERMINING THE PURCHASE PRICE

Value is the process whereby the worth of the target company is established. Purchase price is not always equal to value.

The price which one company is prepared to pay for the shares of another is a matter of bargaining and negotiation; there is no perfect theoretical method of determining the value of a firm but there are certain guidelines which may be of assistance in the bargaining process.

Six methods are used to value the equity of a publicly quoted firm: (1) Market price, (2) Balance Sheet Value, (3) Fair Value, (4) Liquidation Value, (5) Present Value of Future Cash Flows, (6) Comparative Value.

Market Value. Theoretically, the price of a share represents the market's appraisal of the future earnings and dividends attributable to that share. Prices over a period should be averaged, as fluctuations in price may have taken place due to speculation or rumours of a possible takeover bid. The price on the Stock Exchange is based on a price/earnings (P/E) ratio. This is simply the relationship between the price of an individual share and the earnings of the company divided by the number of shares. A company which is in a growth industry and which is increasing profits each year might be on a price ratio of 20, while a firm in a declining industry with a poor profit record might be valued at five times earnings. This would mean that the price of the share of the company was twenty times the earnings attributable to one share. If the market price is used as a guide to valuation the total equity worth of the company would be valued at twenty times its current earnings. P/E ratios are regularly calculated and are available in newspapers for all public companies. The problem with using the P/E ratio as a basis for valuing a firm is that historical earnings may be a very imperfect indicator of future earnings. The bidders for a firm are likely to understate anticipated increases in earnings while the owners are likely to project a very rosy picture of future earnings. The Blue Book rules on takeovers have strict guidelines on how earnings forecasts can be made.

Balance Sheet Value. This method values the firm by taking the stated Balance Sheet value of current and fixed assets. A company acquiring another as a going concern is not interested in the asset value of the business but in its earning ability. This method therefore is of little use even if the Balance Sheet figures are realistic appraisals of worth. It can be used as a preliminary indicator by takeover specialists to find undervalued firms and to act as a floor for calculating multiples of book value appropriate for that industry.

Fair Value. Instead of accepting the Balance Sheet figures, a firm may examine each asset individually to get an idea of the realistic value of the assets. This method is of particular importance if the Balance Sheet has fully written-down property and land assets. In situations where property makes up a large percentage of a firm's assets it is not uncommon for the fair value to be far higher than the book value of the Balance Sheet.

Liquidation Value. This is another indication of the company's floor value and is a measure of the value that would be derived if the firm's assets were liquidated and all liabilities and preferred stock paid. While it may be a more realistic value than the Balance Sheet value it does not measure the earnings capability of the assets. The value of the assets may vary significantly depending on the type and efficiency of the user.

Present Value of Future Cash Flows. This method examines the future cash flows and the value of the company at the end of the projection period. There can be a certain lack of precision inherent in these calculations due to the problem of estimating the synergistic gains from the possible merger. From the bidding firm's standpoint, a merger is another capital budgeting problem with the objective of achieving a positive net present value. The choice of the required rate of return should incorporate the risk nature of the target firm's projected cash flow and assets. The difficulties in estimating future cash flows and discount rates have been dealt with in Chapter 6.

Comparative Value. This involves comparing the prices paid in current acquisitions for companies operating in the same or similar industries. The difficulties again are obvious — few comparable deals in Ireland; each deal is unique.

The valuation process is complex and requires a well-rounded knowledge of finance and other related fields. Deficiencies in this area could prove to be an expensive process and threaten the survival of the bidding firm in the long term. What may represent a good investment may not be a good merger.

Example: An Irish Acquisition in the US
A publicly quoted Irish company has decided to invest in the United States. After a prolonged search a potential acquisition has been identified. The mergers and acquisitions team has put together a study for the board of the Irish parent which includes:

   (a) A detailed description of the company's products and services.
   (b) Its organisational structure, with biographical information on senior management.
   (c) Financial results.
   (d) Sources of raw materials.
   (e) Distribution patterns.
   (f) Customers.
   (g) Marketing policies.
   (h) Patents.
   (i) Sales force.
   (j) List of physical locations.
   (k) List of equipment.
   (l) Employees.
   (m) Competitive position.

The section on financial results includes historical operating results and Balance Sheets for five years. Explanatory statements are attached to describe unusual features or events that have affected the financial statements, including salaries and bonuses that would not be continued under new ownership, assets that are understated, or excess assets that are not necessary to the conduct of the business.

Table 15.3 shows the Balance Sheet value of the proposed acquisition together with an estimated fair market value and liquidation valuation.

Table 15.3 Valuations of Yankee Corp. ($'000)

Assets	Balance Sheet 31 December 1994	Fair Market Value	Liquidation Value
Current Assets:			
Cash	2,000	2,000	2,000
Accounts Receivable	5,000	4,500	3,500
Inventories			
Finished Goods	2,250	1,500	1,000
Work in Progress	2,500	1,250	500
Raw Materials	3,000	2,250	2,000
	14,750	11,500	9,000
Other Current Assets	250	–	–
Total Current Assets	15,000	11,500	9,000
Property, Plant and Equipment:			
Land	2,500	6,000	6,000
Buildings	10,000	9,000	9,000
Equipment	14,000	10,000	7,500
	26,500	25,000	22,500
Less Accumulated Depreciation	(13,000)	–	–
	13,000	25,000	22,000
Other Assets	500	–	–
	$28,500	$36,500	$31,500
Liabilities and Stockholders' Equity			
Current Liabilities:			
Accounts Payable and Accrued			
Charges	5,650	5,650	5,650
Bank	1,350	1,350	1,350
Total Current Liabilities	7,000	7,000	7,000
Long-Term Debt	500	500	500
Shareholders' Equity	21,000	29,000	24,000
	$28,500	$36,500	$31,500

The quoted market price of the company on the stock exchange is $35,000,000: that is, $5.00 per share for each of the seven million outstanding shares. In this case the market price is misleading as there is a very thin market in the shares. Takeover interest has focused on the company in recent times causing the share price to double.

Comparative prices are available for a range of businesses in similar industries. A number of recent acquisitions have taken place at P/E ratios of between twelve and sixteen times after-tax earnings. Yankee Corp. had 1994 after-tax earnings of $2.2 million, thereby placing a comparative value of between $26.4 million and $35.2 million on the company.

Table 15.4 shows the data required for the Present Value of Future Cash Flows method. Discount factors of 12 per cent, 14 per cent and 16 per cent are used.

Table 15.4 Net Present Value of Yankee Corp. ($'000)

Years	Yankee Corp.'s Projected Cash Flows	Present Value at 12%	Present Value at 14%	Present Value at 16%
1995	$3.33	$2.97	$2.92	$2.87
1996	3.46	2.76	2.66	2.57
1997	3.60	2.56	2.43	2.30
1998	3.74	2.38	2.21	2.06
1999	3.89	2.21	2.02	1.85
2000	4.05	2.05	1.85	1.66
2001	4.21	1.90	1.68	1.40
2002	4.38	1.77	1.54	1.34
2003	4.55	1.64	1.40	1.20
2004	4.74	1.53	1.28	1.08
Present Value of Cash Flows		$21.77	$19.99	$18.33
Present Value of Terminal Value of $38.5m in 2004		12.40	10.40	8.74
Present Value of Yankee Corp.		$34.17	$30.39	$27.17

Table 15.5 shows a summary of valuations.

Table 15.5 Valuations of Yankee Corp.

Method	Value ($million)
Market Value	35
Balance Sheet Value	21
Fair Value	29
Liquidation Value	24
Present Value of Future Cash Flows	
at 12%	34.17
at 14%	30.39
at 16%	27.17
Comparative Value	26.4–35.2

After long negotiations a deal was agreed whereby the Irish company paid $32 million cash for the company.

VALUATION OF A PRIVATE COMPANY

The methods used to value a public company can also be used to value a private company but they must be adapted. The major differences lie in the use of net profits as a basis for valuation and the question of the availability and reliability of financial data. Public and private companies are subject to different requirements with regard to the disclosure of financial information and have different constraints applied to them. In the case of a private company the profitability could be closely linked to the owner-entrepreneur's personal compensation and not subject to the pressures of the publicly quoted stock market. The company is as a result freer to manipulate its income, notwithstanding attempts in recent years to regulate and police this area more strictly. The analyst must therefore attempt to reconstruct the 'true' profitability of the privately held firm by a series of addbacks, i.e. pension contributions, personal insurance and expenses, and take a close look at its accounting policies in regard to depreciation and inventory valuation in particular. As the private firm has no market price valuation, it is usual to use times earnings as a base.

Here the profit figure, usually an average over a period of years, is taken. The bidder will tend to use historical earnings while the seller will try to use projected earnings. Usually, the valuation is on a pre-tax basis. The next step is to decide on a multiple: that is, how many times earnings will be paid. One way of getting an approximation on this is to examine the multiple being paid on earnings of a public firm in the same industry; for example, a quoted textile firm is selling at P/E of ten, a private textile firm might be valued at seven.

Almost without exception multiples in private companies will be lower than those in public companies because (a) shares in a public company are more marketable and (b) the advantages of a public quotation, discussed in Chapter 8, make the public firm less risky than a private firm. In deciding on the multiple, the bidder is taking into account projected earnings without the merger, projected earnings after the merger, the quality of the earnings — that is, how risky they are, and an implicit measure of the opportunity cost of investing money in this particular venture rather than in another project.

As was the case with publicly quoted companies, several asset-oriented approaches can be applied. These include Balance Sheet value, fair value and liquidation value. Ultimately, it comes down to the judgment, intuition and motivation of both parties as to how close the merger price is to the basic financial and operating fundamentals.

A recent development in mergers has been that of 'due diligence'. Private firms negotiating takeovers are required to allow the purchaser to undertake a thorough examination of the books and business of the vendor. Swarms of accountants and lawyers examine the current and historical activities of the business with a fine-tooth comb. In theory the examination is to help decide a price and to discover any weaknesses. In reality it is an intimidatory mechanism for pressurising the vendors and driving down the price.

Publicly quoted companies are not required to undergo due diligence examinations because of their existing obligation to make information available to the public.

Methods of Payment

There are a number of well-tried ways of paying for mergers/acquisitions. They can be categorised as:

(a) A total cash acquisition.
(b) A cash purchase of a majority stake.
(c) An instalment cash purchase.

(d) Payment by shares.

(e) Payment by issuing new fixed charge securities or convertible loan notes.

(f) Part cash and part paper payment schemes.

Cash Acquisitions

The simplest method of acquisition is where one company acquires the total ordinary share capital of another with the total payment being made in cash: that is, Company X pays cash to the shareholders of Company Y to acquire the total ordinary share capital. From that moment it controls the appointment of the directors of Company Y and therefore controls policy and operations. If Company Y has other classes of voting share it may also be necessary to acquire them. If Company Y has preference shares which carry no voting rights, one can simply acquire the ordinary shares, leaving the preference shares in the hands of their existing owners.

Cash Purchase of a Majority Stake

In this instance 51 per cent of the shares of the company is acquired. This is sufficient to gain control. In a case where a majority of the shares is acquired and the payment is for cash, the minority shareholders in the company acquired have certain well-defined rights. These rights can be found set out in the relevant Companies Acts. If the company which is being partly acquired is a public company — that is, with shares quoted on a Stock Exchange — it is usually necessary to make an identical offer for the entire equity to all the holders in the acquired company. This is a requirement of the City Code on Takeovers and Mergers, which is operated by the Stock Exchange, and it effectively stops an acquiring company from gaining a majority percentage while not making a similar offer to all the shareholders. In certain instances a 'white wash' may be obtained where a bidder does not have to bid for all shares. This is rare.

Acquisition for Cash on an Instalment Basis

An acquisition of shares may be made for cash but the cash may be paid in instalments, with or without interest, over a period. Sometimes the level of the instalments is related to the profitability of the company being acquired during a particular period, say one or two years after the date of acquisition. This method of paying cash in instalments can be validly used where there is doubt about the reality of the profits shown as earned or where the profits earned are increasing so rapidly as to make the price, paid immediately in cash, seem unrelated to the value of the company. It is known as an 'earnout'.

This method of paying for acquisitions is often used by publicly quoted companies buying swiftly growing private firms.

Payment by an Issue of Shares

In the previous examples acquisition for cash was assumed, and it is obviously necessary for the acquiring company to have access to cash to meet the payment. Alternatively, the acquiring company may exchange some of its own shares for the shares in the company being acquired. This raises the problem of valuing the shares of both companies. Where the acquiring company is a public one a market price is available on the Stock Exchange. This is frequently used to exchange the shares between the acquired and acquiring firms. It is possible then for those shareholders who have received shares to sell them on the Stock Exchange but this has the potential disadvantage that if a great number of shares is placed on the market at any one time, the price of the shares may fall, due to the normal operation of supply and demand. It may therefore be more desirable for the shareholders who are gaining the public company shares either to hold these and sell them gradually over a period, or to place their block of shares with an institution, normally an insurance company or pension fund. If this placing is carried out, the price obtained is less than the quoted market price of the share as the institution will buy 'at a discount'.

If the acquiring company is a private company the value of the shares which it is proposing to offer for acquisition must be worked out in relation to the results of that company in the same way as the value of the shares in the company being acquired is calculated.

Tax considerations in Ireland favour payment in shares. If shares in one company are being sold for shares in another no capital gains tax liability occurs until the shares are ultimately disposed of for cash.

Purchasing by means of a share issue can be very expensive. As Chapter 14 pointed out, new equity carries rights to dividends. If new shares are issued it is virtually impossible to estimate the amount being paid for the acquisition since each share will participate in all future earnings of the company as a whole.

Payment by Means of Bonds, Debentures, Preference Shares or Convertible Loan Notes

The acquiring company may pay for an acquisition by issuing either preference shares or loan stock. The dividend rate or interest rate attaching to the new issues will be determined by existing market conditions. It will be priced to allow the sale of the preference shares or loan stock in the market at par. Alternatively, the shares or loan stock may be placed with an institution. In this way the shareholders in the company being acquired are in receipt of a cash equivalent. The calculation of price is carried out in the same way as in any ordinary cash deal. If the acquiring company is paying by means of its own ordinary shares then the new shareholders decide on the growth prospects of the acquiring company, particularly after the acquisition of their old company, and on this basis decide whether to dispose of or hold the new securities. Leveraged buyouts (LBOs) are the principal users of this form of payment.

This leveraging up process forces a firm to become even more conscious of its cash flow. It is a way of imposing market discipline and encourages greater efficiency and productivity. It also makes the firm a less tempting takeover target because it has no unused debt capacity to take advantage of. The disadvantage is that the process is sensitive to economic and political conditions and was partially responsible for the increased number of divestitures in the late 1980s and early 1990s. A variation of the LBO process is the management buyout (MBO). This occurs when a group of investors, including members of the management of the target company, buys the target firm. The new company goes private and is financed primarily by debt.

There are two general categories of debt used in leveraged buyouts: secured and unsecured. Secured debt, sometimes called asset-based lending or senior debt, is typically obtained from a group of banks in a syndicated loan with a maturity of less than seven years. The loan indenture details the company's assets as collateral and refers to covenants regarding financial ratios and other borrowing procedures/obligations. The interest rate is almost always variable and ranges between two and five points above the prime rate. Some of the desirable characteristics sought in borrowers of this type in addition to valuable collateral include stable and experienced management, room for significant cost reductions, projected stability of costs and a reasonable equity cushion.

Unsecured debt, also called mezzanine, subordinated or junior debt, typically has a longer maturity than senior debt and because it is riskier will cost more. Some transactions are straightforward and are priced at about five percentage points above the prime rate. Others are more complex and could cost up to twenty percentage points above prime rate. Special features include interest rates that vary with the market price of the bond and equity-linked issues. The fact that the loan is not secured does not mean that the lenders are not protected by the firm's assets. They are entitled to receive the proceeds of sale of the secured assets after full payment has been made to the secured lenders. The main advantage of unsecured financing is the profit potential that is provided by either a direct equity interest or loans convertible into equity, an added potential that offsets the lack of security. There are often several types of unsecured debt structured in layers, each subordinate to the other. This source of finance is usually issued in the form of junk bonds, was primarily a US phenomenon and declined dramatically with the collapse of that market in 1989 only to rise again in the mid-1990s. LBOs continued into the 1990s at a much slower pace and often without the aid of this type of financing. Some of the desirable characteristics sought in borrowers of this type are similar to those of secured LBO candidates. The lack of collateral increases the importance of other forms of lender protection, such as larger dependable cash flows.

Part Cash and Part Paper Payments

Very often the purchase of a business involves both a cash payment and the issue of new shares. This method is used by publicly quoted companies which are acquiring private firms. Sellers obtain cash plus an interest in the new business.

NEGOTIATING THE DEAL

'Every deal dies nine times.' This is the rule of thumb used by experienced negotiators in the takeover field. Successful negotiation requires two things: one, keeping in mind objectives to be achieved during the discussions, and two, being well prepared for negotiations.

Both sides should recognise that the closer the two parties come to an agreement, issues about which there are strong feelings will emerge — some very trivial — that could keep them apart. At this time no problem is too small to merit the full attention of the selling and the acquiring chief executives.

Negotiations include discussions not only on price but on terms and conditions, including representations and warranties, tax, accounting and legal considerations, series of payments, employment contracts, reporting functions and other post-merger integration problems.

Negotiation is a team effort and requires the involvement of many participants at different points in the process, such as:

    (a) Principal Shareholders.
    (b) Officers.
    (c) Directors.
    (d) Accountants.
    (e) Lawyers.

(f) Investment Bankers.

(g) Operating Management.

The negotiating process cannot be reduced to a precisely calculated formula. Still, there are a few guidelines, basically common sense, that can facilitate negotiations and increase the chances of getting what you want. Some of the most important are discussed below. Keep in mind that the person across the table is following some of these same guidelines. The points below assume the seller's side.

(1) Know what you want. Even before you begin negotiating, you should have a clear idea of what you want and of what is important to you. For example, what is the minimum price you will accept? Is the form of payment — cash, stock in the acquiring company, long-term debt, and so on — important? Do you want to retain some control in the new organisation? How much?

(2) Try to determine what the other side really wants. Is the buyer interested in the technology, patents, fixed assets, market outlets, customer base? Knowing what the other side wants will save time and effort in offering useless concessions.

(3) Consider the use of an experienced negotiator. Negotiating is an art. It is a delicate process, one that often benefits from the use of an experienced, tactful, disinterested third party. Your own intimate knowledge of your business, certainly an advantage in the course of negotiations, may be offset by an inability to deal unemotionally and dispassionately with some aspects of the give and take of negotiating. It is sometimes difficult for owners to remain objective during discussions that seem to undervalue their creations. An experienced negotiator, with no direct interest in the outcome, is open to all ideas and is willing to give them a fair hearing. Also the negotiator is often better able to develop ideas and float 'trial balloons' that may advance the negotiations.

(4) Focus on particular issues. Separate the issues and deal with them on an individual basis.

(5) Do not back the other side into a corner. You should always leave a face-saving way out.

(6) Get something for each compromise.

(7) Listen carefully to what people say during negotiations. Words are merely one indication of what they mean. Gestures, facial expressions, and voice inflections are other important signals of what is taking place. 'Yes, I want that,' for example, can mean a whole host of things, depending on the way it is said — including, 'I don't care about that one way or the other.'

Similarly, be aware of what you say and how you say it. Words can be taken out of context; they can be subtly redefined and come back to haunt you. Think before you speak, and monitor carefully the nuances of what you say.

(8) Think ahead; have a response prepared for what the other side might say. Try to anticipate what the prospective buyer will come up with — objections, counterproposals, and so on. The more you are able to do this, the less chance you have of being caught off guard and, by default, agreeing to an unfavourable proposition.

(9) Don't allow yourself to be rushed. You don't have to respond to everything the other side says. And when you do respond, take enough time so that your response is well thought out. However, it is important to be aware of time constraints that may have an

effect on the negotiations — the approaching end of a reporting year, for example. On the other hand, a false sense of urgency is a tactic that can lead to unwise short cuts and concessions. Keep in mind what is truly important, and make your responses count.

The overall goal should be to obtain the highest price for your business. The goal of the buyer is to pay the lowest price. The actual price will undoubtedly be neither — falling somewhere in between the extreme expectations of both sides. However, if you have done the groundwork with care — valued your business accurately, attracted the appropriate buyer, and negotiated the sale skilfully — the final price you obtain for your company will be a fair one. It will satisfy you and it will satisfy the purchaser.

MERGER ACTIVITY

Mergers and acquisitions come in waves. Usually, late in a cycle of prosperity merger activity increases. Very often a wave of mergers spreads across the developed world. Bursts of activity in the USA in the 1920s, 1940s, 1960s and 1980s were repeated after a short time lag in the United Kingdom and Ireland. Ireland experienced a significant increase in mergers between 1960 and 1973 when one hundred quoted securities were either taken over, merged or liquidated on the Irish Stock Exchange. In that time, fifty-three quoted companies had major ownership changes. This activity reached a peak in the first three years of the 1970s, due mainly to the growth of conglomerates. During this period certain industrial sectors were prone to takeovers and mergers. Shoes and leather, paper packaging and the builders' providers sectors were reduced to virtually one company each.

In the early 70s the Irish Stock Exchange experienced a wave of acquisitions which ultimately produced a number of industrial holding companies or conglomerates. This development had been preceded by similar occurrences in the United States and United Kingdom. The acquisition of Crowe Wilson, which is now part of the Fitzwilton Group, began the movement. This was followed in rapid succession by Braids, Brooks Watson Holdings, Barrow Milling, James Crean and Ferrier Pollock.

In the 1980s a new merger wave took place, based on the philosophy that it was cheaper to buy than to build. The bear markets of the late 1970s had reduced share prices while inflation had in many cases increased the net assets per share. Divestment of unwanted assets was a significant factor in the development of the merger wave of the 1980s — led by leveraged buyouts (LBOs).

LBOs began in the United States. During the heavy conglomerate era of the 1960s, a number of entrepreneurs formed mini-conglomerates through the use of leveraged buyouts. The lender was normally a commercial finance company; commercial banks were not yet in this business. As a rule, the acquired company was a smaller one — generally with less than £10 million of sales volume. The underlying collateral for the loan was the accounts receivable, inventories and fixed assets of the acquired company.

In many cases the investor had no equity risk; in some he was not even asked to guarantee the loan personally. For that reason this type of financing was often called 'bootstrap' financing — the entrepreneur could lift himself by his own bootstraps into a position of wealth and success. The lender normally insisted on adequate security, measured in terms of distressed liquidation values, and the thrust of the lender's analysis was directed towards good security rather than towards cash flow. Because each transaction was relatively small, the flow of deals went virtually unnoticed except by those who were actively engaged in the business.

In the 1970s a second type of leveraged buyout began to emerge. This type involved situations where a lender would take an option on equity and subordinate its debt, rather than taking collateral. This combination of equity and subordinated debt would entice another group of unsecured lenders to lay on a level of senior debt, since the target company's cash flow could obviously service such senior debt. The subordinated debt holders, initially limited to a small group of aggressive insurance companies, were willing to take a significant downside risk for an even more significant upside gain. Because no one was secured in the transaction, however, the analytical emphasis by all financing sources was on cash flow rather than on collateral.

Both secured and unsecured lenders had certain common criteria. Since in both cases an additional layer of debt was being imposed on the target company, with additional debt servicing requirements, a company that was incurring heavy losses would not usually be a target for a leveraged buyout unless the loss was clearly a short-term phenomenon that could be quickly reversed. Second, the lenders in both cases normally wanted to have continuity of management, and most leveraged buyouts involved the management group's continued involvement. To assure this, the management group would often be given some part of the equity. In many cases, in fact, the driver behind the leveraged buyout was the management group itself, although in a number of cases a third party entrepreneur would promote the acquisition.

In the early 1980s a small number of US investment houses organised large-scale LBOs. This led to one of the greatest takeover booms ever seen in the world.

Inflation, which increased the value of fixed assets, a booming stock market and, most importantly, a wave of development decisions led to a rapid rise in takeover activity. In the eight-year period 1982–90 much of corporate America was restructured. A breed of financier known as a 'corporate raider' was able to obtain vast financial backing by issuing debt — that is, junk bonds.

Leveraged buyouts grew in size up to the $23 billion acquisition of R.J. Reynolds/Nabisco by former management. Junk bonds were the main weapons in this takeover frenzy.

In the 1970s Michael Milken as a young student completed an examination of second line debentures. He discovered that the additional interest rule paid on these debentures more than covered any additional risk. This discovery led to the introduction of a range of second line debentures at above market rates of interest. In the ten-year period 1975–85 there were few defaults on these debentures. From becoming a curiosity in the late 1970s they became, by the mid-1980s, the principal form of takeover finance. In the process Milken became one of the world's richest men and the firm which employed him, Drexel Burnham Lambert, became a world-ranked investment house.

In 1989 the junk bond market crashed and the decade of the deal came to an abrupt end. The merger environment changed dramatically. The junk bond market was dependent to a remarkable extent on one individual, Michael Milken, and his indictment and subsequent jailing brought the 1980s merger wave to an end. The fall of the junk bond market slowed the pace of mergers and leveraged buyouts to a crawl and changed the process to one where more equity and less debt was used to finance transactions. It also meant a return to a more specialised and focused merger process conducted by well-financed bidders rather than junk bond raiders.

By 1995 all had changed once more. Studies in the 1990s showed again that investing in junk bonds brought returns greater than average. While there were numerous collapses most mergers financed by junk bonds survived and many flourished. Lower interest rates from 1993 onward, an availability of capital, hungry merchant bankers and ambitious entrepreneurs resulted in a re-emergence of the use of junk bonds as a means of financing takeovers.

A new merger wave began, led in part by the need for the huge US defence industry to adapt to the drop in demand caused by the collapse of communism, and by the need for the telecommunications industry to gear up to the challenges of the 'information superhighway'. The 1995 $20 billion bid proposed by one man, Kirk Kerkorian, for Chrysler demonstrated that 'junk bond' financing was alive and well. In the UK renewed merger activity was spearheaded by the communications industry and the move by building societies into mainstream financial services. The £10 billion bid by Glaxo for Wellcome was expected to trigger many other large takeover bids.

RECENT MERGER AND TAKEOVER ACTIVITY IN IRELAND

The depressed state of the Irish economy during the early 1980s placed a damper on takeover activity, but by 1985 there were signs of a pick-up. The major activity in this period was a flight abroad by substantial Irish firms. Most of the top ten publicly quoted Irish firms acquired one or more overseas companies. Some, like Smurfit's and CRH, became true multinationals.

The move to shed unwanted divisions led to the emergence of leveraged buyouts in Ireland. Most of the leverage had to be supplied by the seller in the form of debentures. A number of US firms divested themselves of Irish divisions.

In 1987 confidence in the economy returned, the Stock Exchange was rising and takeover activity resumed. The total amount involved was in excess of £550 million. By 1989 this figure had grown to approximately £1 billion and was dominated by three sectors: food, print and packaging, and property. The big spenders were Waterford Foods, Smurfit's, the Power Group, and to a lesser extent Fitzwilton, IWP and the financial sector.

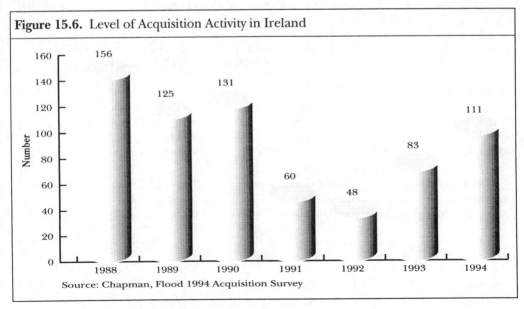

Figure 15.6. Level of Acquisition Activity in Ireland

Source: Chapman, Flood 1994 Acquisition Survey

As was the case internationally the world-wide recession and uncertainty in banking circles at the end of the 1980s put a halt to the growth in merger activity in Ireland. The total number of acquisitions reported in Ireland in 1992 was 48 as against levels of 156 in 1988. The effects of the currency crisis, the decreased activity in both the quoted and unquoted sector and the virtual absence of venture capital all contributed to this reduced level of activity. This culminated in acquisition activity being concentrated around a small number of companies. By 1993 activity had begun to pick up once more.

Table 15.6 shows the level of corporate acquisition activity in Ireland between 1988 and 1994

Table 15.7 Merger Activity in Ireland, 1994

Foreign Acquisitions by Irish Companies

Bidder	Target	Sector	Value IR£'000s
Jefferson Smurfit Group PLC	Cellulose du Pin (France)	Packaging	683,000
Kerry Group PLC	DCA Food Industries (USA)	Food Drink & AgriBusiness	250,000
Fitzwilton PLC	Wellworth (42.7% to 87%) (UK)	Retailing	42,900
Irish Life PLC	First Variable (USA)	Financial Services	34,770
Bank of Ireland PLC	Great Bay Bankshares Inc. (USA)	Financial Services	34,600
Anglo Irish Bank PLC	Canadian Imperial Bank of Commerce Mortgage Book (UK)	Financial Services	30,600
CRH PLC	The Marlux Group (Belgium)	Construction	25,000
Kerry Group PLC	Matteson Walls (UK)	Food Drink & AgriBusiness	25,000
CRH PLC	Balf Company (USA)	Construction	21,900
Dairygold Co-op	Horlicks Farms and Dairies (UK)	Food Drink & AgriBusiness	21,740
CRH PLC	A. Rotondo & Sons (USA)	Construction	14,600
CRH PLC	Templeglass Group (USA)	Construction	13,500
Clondalkin Group PLC	Nyffeler Corti AG (Switzerland)	Packaging	13,300
Clondalkin Group PLC	Vaassen Aluminium BV (Holland)	Packaging	13,300
IAWS Group PLC	United Fish Products Ltd (UK)	Food Drink & AgriBusiness	11,974
Kerry Group PLC	Productos Vegetales de Mexico (Mexico)	Food Drink & AgriBusiness	10,345
Musgrave Ltd	Dialsur 68% (Spain)	Retailing	9,000
Fyffes PLC	J.A. Kahl & Co. (70%) (Germany)	Food Drink & AgriBusiness	8,000
Bridgewater Food Holdings Ltd	Unipork Group (UK)	Food Drink & AgriBusiness	8,000
CRH PLC	Sullivan Lafarge (USA)	Construction	7,300
CRH PLC	Lebanon Rock (USA)	Construction	7,300
CRH PLC	P.J. Keating & Co. (USA)		7,300
Jurys Hotel Group PLC	Unicorn Hotel Bristol (UK)	Property	6,060
Silvermines	Molynx (UK)	Manufacturing	5,300
Independent Newspapers PLC	Capital Newspapers (66.6%) (UK)	Media	4,900
Aran Energy PLC	Louisiana Oil & Gas Field (USA)	Natural Resources	4,800
Adare Printing Company PLC	Great Northern Envelope Co. (UK)	Printing	4,235
Bula Resources	Aki-Otyr (51%) (Russia)	Natural Resources	4,000
CRH PLC	Bosse Concrete Products (USA)	Construction	3,850
CRH PLC	Schuster's Block Inc. (USA)	Construction	3,850

Kerry Group PLC	Dermet de Mexico Ingredients (Mexico)	Food Drink & AgriBusiness	3,449
Pharma Patch Ltd	Phametrix (Italy)	Health Care	3,400
Dealformatics Ltd	Desisco (UK)	Computers	3,289
Greencore PLC	Malting Business of HDM (Belgium)	Food Drink & AgriBusiness	2,600
Grafton Group PLC	Thrower Bros Group Holdings (UK)	Builders Merchants	2,550
Golden Vale PLC	Vejle Margarine Fabrik (Denmark)	Food Drink & AgriBusiness	2,550
Coyle Hamilton Ltd	Richardson Hosken Group Ltd (UK)	Financial Services	2,500
IAWS Group PLC	Nordos (UK)	Food	2,000
United Drug PLC	Robert Smith & Co. (Derry) Ltd (UK)	Health Care	1,790
Grafton Group PLC	Lumley & Hunt (UK)	Builders Merchants	1,630
AIB PLC	Deposits of Second National Federal Savings Association (USA)	Financial Services	1,300
Adare Printing Co. PLC	Label Convertors (UK)	Printing	1,220
Dana Exploration PLC	T.M. Oil Production (Russia)	Natural Resources	1,200
Fyffes PLC	Valley Gold (UK)	Food	1,000
Jones Group PLC	Hardy Craske (UK)	Distribution	920
Adare Printing Co. PLC	Alexander Pettigrew Ltd (UK)	Printing	860
IAWS Group PLC	Malton Fertilisers (UK)	Food	678
Musgrave Ltd	Cash Denia Sa (Spain)	Retailing	645
Minmet PLC	Sailsbury Garden Services (UK)	Natural Resources	211
Barlo Group PLC	Warmastyle Ltd (UK)	Engineering	N/D
Kenmare PLC	Slate Zinc Mine (Bolivia)	Natural Resources	N/D
Jefferson Smurfit Group PLC	Interlock Board Division (UK)	Printing	N/D
Inishtech PLC	Enwright (UK)	Packaging	N/D
Inishtech PLC	Wessex Interprint (UK)	Packaging	N/D
Inishtech PLC	Lochaber Base Co. (UK)	Packaging	N/D
AIB PLC	Bank of Ireland Deposit Book (USA)	Financial Services	N/D
Inishtech PLC	Print Permanising (UK)	Printing	N/D
Allen McGuire & Partners Ltd	Heller (France)	Toys	N/D
Allen McGuire & Partners Ltd	Humbrol (UK)	Toys	N/D
Monaghan Mushrooms Ltd	Middlebrook Mushrooms (UK)	Food	N/D
Glen Dimplex	Roberts Radio (UK)	Engineering	N/D
Australian Provincial Newspapers	Wesgo (Australia)	Media	N/D
Jefferson Smurfit Group PLC	Tower Park Leisure (UK)	Packaging	N/D
Woodchester Investments PLC	Slibal Portuguesa (80%) (Portugal)	Financial Services	N/D
Woodchester Investments PLC	Cl Finans Danmark (Denmark)	Financial Services	N/D
Aminex PLC	Off Shore Drilling Supplies (UK)	Natural Resources	N/D

N/D = Not Declared

Source: Chapman, Flood and Partners.

Domestic Acquisitions by Irish Companies

Bidder	Target	Sector	ValueIR£'000's
Anglo Irish Bank PLC	Irish Business Bank Loan Book	Financial Services	116,000
Green Property PLC	Na Mara Investments (Dublin City Properties)	Property	42,000
Irish Permanent PLC	Prudential Life of Ireland	Financial Services	30,500
Woodchester Investments PLC	Leasing Business of Highland Finance Ireland	Financial Services	25,000
Management Buyout	Comer International	Textiles	21,000
Green Property PLC	Companies owning Setanta Centre	Property	20,000
Management Buyout	Ballet International	Textiles	19,000
Heiton Holdings PLC	F&T Buckley Holdings	Builders Merchants	8,100
Irish Permanent PLC	Guinness Mahon	Financial Services	6,700
Management Buyout	Dakota Group	Print & Packaging	6,200
Management Buyout	Cara Computers	Computers	5,000
AIB Group PLC	Hill Samuel Fagan Investment Management	Financial Services	5,000
Dairygold Co-op	Tara Meats	Food Drink & AgriBusiness	5,000
United Pharmacists Co-op Society	Allied Pharmaceutical Distributors	Wholesale/Distribution	4,200
Barlo Group PLC	Business & Assets of Kingspan Veha	Electrical Engineering	4,000
Allegro Holdings Ltd	Fispak Holdings	Packaging	4,000
Brennan & Pettit family	Stillorgan Park Hotel	Property	3,600
Hibernian Foods Ltd	Beef Processing at Clones	Food Drink & AgriBusiness	3,000
Musgrave Ltd	Twomeys Stores (2 outlets)	Wholesale/Retail	2,500
IAWS PLC	Unifoods	Food Drink & AgriBusiness	2,100
ICC Bank PLC	Cambridge Venture Capital Fund (63%)	Financial Services	2,000
IAWS PLC	Malting Company of Ireland	Food Drink & AgriBusiness	1,500
Consortium	Drogheda Web Offset Printers	Printing	1,000
Magnum Ltd	Thorn Security Irish Operations	Security	1,000
DCC PLC	M. Casey (25% to 51%)	Health Care	825
Spectra Group Holdings Ltd	Photo King	Photo Processing	750
EBS Building Society	Midland & Western Building Society	Financial Services	337
Consortium of Cork businessmen	The Farm House Group	Food Drink & AgriBusiness	250
IFG PLC	Lawlink	Financial Services	200
Investor Unknown	Protea Pine	Wood Products	90
Lake Communications	Alpha Systems Network	Computers	N/D
Management Buyout	Business/Assets Avery Labels (Ireland)	Printing	N/D
Network SI Group	Act Computer Support	Computers	N/D
Management Buyout	Aer Turas	Services	N/D
Fexco	Diners Club International Irish Office	Financial Services	N/D
DCC PLC	Brodericks Holdings (41.2% to 54.9%)	Equipment	N/D

MacDonagh & Boland Ltd	Hugh McMahon & Co.	Financial Services	N/D
Hibernia Foods Ltd	Tallaght Deboning Plant	Food Drink & AgriBusiness	N/D
Messrs O'Ceide & Kelly	Aer Arann	Airline Company	N/D
The Marlborough Group Ltd	Professional Placement Group	Services	N/D
Callery Ltd	Biological Laboratories	Pharmaceutical	N/D
Management Buyout	Reflex Non-Software Assets	Computers	N/D
Management Buyout	Allegro Ltd	Wholesale/Distribution	N/D
Management Buyout	Draper Erin Ltd	Textiles	N/D
Management Buyout	Boss Trucks (Irl) Ltd	Importers/Agents	N/D

N/D = Not Declared

Source: Chapman, Flood and Partners.

Table 15.7 examines the acquisitions made by Irish companies in 1994. Over £1.3 billion was spent on foreign acquisitions and over £340 million on domestic acquisitions.

The growth in takeovers in 1994 was led by Smurfit's £630 million-plus European acquisition and a large £200 million US acquisition by the Kerry Group. The main reasons were the dramatic reduction in interest rates following the devaluation of the Irish pound against other European currencies and the economic recovery internationally. The willingness of financial institutions to arrange fixed rate borrowings, the continuation of a process of fiscal consolidation by the government and the substantial rises in share prices on the Irish Stock Exchange all added to the recovery.

The historical trend of most target firms being located in Ireland or the UK continued, with some exceptions such as CRH's acquisition of Braks BV (Holland), Avonmore's acquisition of Harzland Fleisch (Germany) and Spectra's acquisition of Hotel Fort Lauderdale (US). Aside from its geographic location and historical/economic linkages with Ireland, the popularity of the UK as a target country for acquisitions is due to its economic restructuring in the 1980s and an ongoing flexible legal code that lends itself to takeovers. Issues such as language, culture and economic differences have had a dampening effect on acquisition activity in Europe though this is changing. The average size of Irish acquisitions has been quite small at £20 million or less and funded conservatively. Both the absolute and relative amount of gearing has been low by international standards and such loans typically involve very high asset backing. The use of more sophisticated financing techniques such as earnouts and convertible loan notes is essential to attaining corporate growth through the acquisition process.

CONCLUSION

While there are undoubtedly good acquisitions and bad acquisitions it is hard to agree on whether acquisitions are beneficial on balance. Perhaps the best way to summarise the situation is to group all participants into two general classes: 'winners' and 'losers'. On the winners' side are clearly the shareholders of acquired firms. Managers of acquiring firms are also probably beneficiaries in that they use acquisitions for private ends, such as prestige, power, diversification of human capital, etc. Society at large is a beneficiary to the extent that mergers can be an efficient mechanism for replacing less efficient by more efficient managers, given the assumption that the market for executive labour and corporate control are functioning well. Other big winners include investment bankers, lawyers and accountants.

The losers are undoubtedly the managers of the acquired firms and perhaps to a lesser extent the shareholders of the acquiring firms. While the empirical evidence suggests that they do not lose much in market value, they lose indirectly in the time and attention spent by senior executives in waging futile takeover battles.

As a rule of thumb it is believed that one in three mergers works well, one in three fails while the outcome for the remaining third is uncertain. These figures are frequently cited as evidence against mergers but this ignores the fact that probably no more than one in three of all investment decisions works well. Business is uncertain, the future cannot be predicted so even the best mergers can and do go wrong.

This chapter has given an introduction to what is an area of growing importance. The free market in Europe will offer more opportunities to Irish companies to grow by acquisition. Equally, free movement of capital poses a threat to the continued independence of many Irish companies.

FURTHER READING

W. Davis, *Merger Mania* (London, The Anchor Press, 1975).

Issuing House Association, *The City Code on Takeovers and Mergers* (London 1994).

M.A. Weinberg, *Takeovers and Amalgamations*, 5th ed. (London, Sweet and Maxwell, 1986).

Investor's Chronicle Supplement, *Management Buy Outs*, 10 March 1995, London.

P. Gaughan, *Mergers & Acquisitions* (Harper Collins, 1991).

I. Walker, *Buying a Company in Trouble* (Gomer, 1992).

Chapman Flood, 1994 Acquisition Survey, Dublin 1995.

QUESTIONS

Question 15.1

Why would one company seek to take over another?

Question 15.2

What methods are used in establishing the purchase price paid on a takeover?

Question 15.3

What do you understand by the term 'leveraged buyout' (LBO)?

Question 15.4

Why would a company pay for a takeover by issuing shares rather than using cash? Is this a cheaper method?

Question 15.5

What factors are different when valuing private rather than public companies?

Question 15.6

To what can the development of conglomerates on the Irish Stock Exchange be attributed?

International Finance

Ireland has one of the most open economies in the world. This means that international trade plays a stronger role in the Irish economy than it does in most other economies. Total imports and exports in 1994 were in excess of £43,000 million as against gross national product for the year of almost £31,000 million. Belgium, Holland and Denmark rank alongside Ireland as open economies. Nations such as Japan, the United Kingdom, Italy, France, Germany, Canada and the United States derive a much lower proportion of their economic income from foreign trade.

As a small island economy Ireland had little option but to become involved in overseas business. Many of the conveniences of modern life are not produced in Ireland; they must be imported. New industries establishing throughout the country require plant and machinery which can only be found abroad. Irish agriculture and manufacturing industries need overseas markets to enable efficient levels of production.

The rapid development of the Irish economy since the 1960s was based on a policy which depended on export markets. The success of the country in attracting export-oriented projects to Ireland resulted in a twenty-five fold growth in manufactured exports in the period 1962–93. Accession to the European Community in 1973 led to a swift growth in agricultural exports.

In the early 1980s Ireland imported as much as was exported. By 1995 the picture had changed totally. A very strong export performance led to substantial surpluses on the balance of trade (exports minus imports). This was largely offset by profits, interest and royalties flowing out to foreign owners. Receipts from the EU amounting to almost £2 billion each year contributed to a high level of external reserves.

External reserves fund the trade of a country. Irish external reserves rose sharply in the 1980s from £975 million in January 1980 to peak at £3,800 million in mid-1992. The turbulence in the foreign exchange markets in the second half of 1992 contributed substantially to a reduction but a strong economy in 1993 and 1994 led to substantial inflows. In February 1995 the official external reserves stood at £4,210 million.

International business adds complexity and uncertainty to the job of management. Modern business is difficult enough without adding problems of language, culture and currency to the task. As long as the bulk of overseas business was with the United Kingdom then Irish business people muddled through. The United Kingdom had a similar language, culture and economic life. At least as important was the fact that parity existed between the British and Irish currencies. This meant that the same financial institutions operated in each country.

During the 1970s and 1980s overseas trade expanded into new markets. Many business people found themselves, for the first time, dealing with unknown institutions and handling little-understood currencies. The problems were magnified in the spring of 1979, when parity between sterling and the punt was broken. During the 1980s and 1990s further difficulties arose as currencies experienced major swings in value.

An understanding of the rudiments of international finance is an essential feature of every business person's training. This chapter sets out to provide an introduction to international business by examining the following areas: (a) the world monetary scene, (b) managing foreign exchange risk, (c) foreign currency borrowing, (d) international financial institutions.

THE WORLD MONETARY SCENE

In November 1979 an Irish exporter receiving dollars for a sale could have exchanged them for Irish pounds at the following rate: IR£1 = $2.04. Five years later the rate was IR£1 = $1.26. A year later the rate was IR£1 = $1.06. By 1992 the rate had returned to IR£1 = $1.70. In mid-1995 the rate was IR£1 = $1.65.

On 29 January 1993 the rate between the punt and sterling was IR£1 = 1.09stg. Seven days later the rate was IR£1 = 1.02stg. So what, you might say, a 7 per cent difference in a week! Consider the effect on a textile exporter operating on a gross profit margin of maybe 5 per cent. The currency swing if favourable would more than double his profits. If negative it could wipe out his margin and business. That in a week. What of the US businessman who invested in Ireland in 1980. He had a rollercoaster currency ride during the 1980s and 1990s.

Background to the Current System

The story of the modern system of international finance goes back to the latter days of the Second World War. A group of eminent economists met at Bretton Woods in the United States to decide on an international currency system for the post-war era. If every nation had fixed its currency against one medium of value, such as gold, there would have been no need for this meeting. On a gold standard, countries running a balance of payments deficit would cover the deficit by gold payments. Over time countries running deficits would adopt economic policies to stop the outflow. Such a simple system was not acceptable to the economists at Bretton Woods because many countries had no gold, others required time to rebuild and adapt their economies, and, most importantly, the discipline of a gold standard was too harsh.

Instead, the economists developed a system of fixed exchange rates, in reality not too unlike the gold standard system. The United States dollar had a price fixed in gold: $35 = 1 oz. gold. Every other country established a relationship with the dollar; for example, the United Kingdom initially established a rate of $4.00:£1. To allow flexibility, currencies could vary by 1 per cent on either side of the agreed parity; the 1944 dollar/pound rate, for instance, could vary between $3.96:£1 and $4.04:£1. Central banks were obliged to maintain the value of their currency within the agreed limits. Organisations were set up to assist the process of currency value maintenance. The International Monetary Fund was established to assist countries to weather short-term international difficulties. Structural or secular problems were to be handled by the

International Bank for Reconstruction and Development (World Bank). These institutions are examined in later sections.

The system of fixed exchange rates appeared to work well in the 1950s and 1960s. Trade expanded rapidly. Cracks did appear but they were papered over. The United Kingdom consistently ran balance of payments deficits. Major political importance was attached to the defence of sterling with the result that the country lived with a consistently overvalued exchange rate. This gave rise to expensive exports, cheap imports, balance of trade deficits, overseas borrowings and periodic devaluations. The Germans and Japanese reconstructed their economies with modern advanced technology. In the fifty years between 1945 and 1995 the deutschmark and the yen were undervalued, resulting in immense trade surpluses in each country.

As long as the dollar remained strong the system held. The Asian wars caused the United States to run balance of payments deficits. At first this was acceptable as there was a scarcity of dollars in the world. Indeed the Irish Export Board was established in the 1950s specifically to develop exports to dollar areas, as Ireland had little or no dollar reserves.

During the early 1960s a glut of dollars appeared. In theory central banks could submit their dollar holdings to the United States Treasury and obtain gold at the rate of $35:1oz. In practice most countries did not wish to offend the mighty United States, so they held their dollar assets in the form of United States Treasury bills. One group of institutions decided to loan dollars among themselves. This led to the development of the Eurodollar market.

The fixed rate currency exchange system developed major stress. In 1968 a two-tier gold pricing system was developed. This system allowed for a private market in gold where the price could find an equilibrium level and a central bank market where the price was maintained at $35 per oz.

By the early 1970s the system was in shreds. In August 1971 the United States decided that it would no longer convert dollars into gold. In effect this smashed the whole basis for the existing system. In December 1971 the Smithsonian agreement produced a revaluation of currencies against the dollar, a 10 per cent devaluation of the dollar against gold, and a widening of the bands around parities from 1 to 2.4 per cent.

By the end of 1973 the Smithsonian agreement had itself collapsed. The principal world currencies were allowed to float against each other. The theory behind a floating system is simple. The value of a currency against any other currency is decided by the laws of supply and demand. In reality no country allows a 'clean float'. Central banks intervene in exchange rates to ensure an orderly market and also to moderate the effect of exchange rate changes on domestic policies. A system of managed floating rates is known as a 'dirty float'.

The last half of the 1970s was a period of unprecedented uncertainty in foreign exchange markets. The United States ran a series of horrendous balance of payments deficits — mainly due to oil imports. The United Kingdom, for long the weakest member of the reserve currency club, found new oil-based economic strength. Sterling, which had declined from $4.00:£1 in 1944 to $1.58:£1 in 1975, rose to over $2.30:£1 by 1980, only to fall back to $1.00:£1 by 1985 rising to $1.60:£1 by mid-1995. The deutschmark and yen rose against most currencies. Oil producers built up large surpluses. Throughout the decade the role of the International Monetary Fund grew but it was not capable of solving singlehandedly the financial problems facing the world currency system.

During the late 1980s there was continuous upheaval in world currency markets. A dramatic reduction in oil prices led to the elimination of the huge surpluses built up by the main oil producing countries.

Third world countries found themselves totally unable to repay international loans. Brazil, Nigeria, Mexico, Argentina and Peru were among countries which had to restructure their obligations to international banks. There was a real possibility of massive defaults which would destroy the capital base of most large international banks and lead to the collapse of the existing world monetary system. A third factor affecting the world monetary system was a sustained economic boom in the United States. This had two effects:

(a) The US became an attractive market for investors, who bought billions of dollars worth of US assets, thus driving up the value of the dollar.
(b) The economic boom fuelled imports, which led to US balance of trade deficits of over $100 billion annually.

The pressure on the system grew until the convulsion on world Stock Exchanges in October 1987. The dollar collapsed against the yen and the deutschmark. The US authorities unsuccessfully moved to rectify major budget deficits as a world economic recession loomed.

As the 1980s drew to a close there was growing unease with the world monetary system of floating exchange rates. The expectation that floating rates would lead to automatic and easy adjustments of economic policies was not fulfilled.

In practice the system of floating rates hardly existed. A significant number of economies tied their rates to the dollar. The European Monetary System kept some limited form of control over European rates and rates between the two super-economies, the US and EU. All through the 1980s and early 1990s the Japanese continued to build huge currency surpluses. Taiwan, Hong Kong and Singapore all grew rapidly exporting to the US, which continued to run massive balance of payments deficits.

African and South American countries followed a policy of frequent devaluations against the major currencies.

The early 1990s saw the effective collapse of the European Monetary System into total chaos. The fundamental nature of the political and economic change which took place and is continuing to take place in Eastern and Central Europe, allied to the US government's strategy of reviving its economy through interest rate cuts alone, could be identified as the central issues that triggered the collapse. As the US Federal Reserve Board eased interest rates down, in Europe Germany was adopting a diametrically opposite monetary position to deal with the financial strains of reunification arising out of the removal of the Berlin Wall. The attempt by EU countries to respond to this situation by raising their interest rates was to lead to reduced economic growth and increased unemployment problems. The rejection of the Maastricht Treaty in June 1992 by the Danish people finally precipitated the collapse of the European Monetary System in all but name. This was evidenced by the ejection of sterling and the lira from the system and an overall realignment in January 1993.

The Irish situation was further complicated by the ending of exchange controls on 31 December 1992. This meant that the Irish pound now existed without a protective shield and could truly be regarded as an international currency.

EUROPEAN MONETARY SYSTEM (EMS)

In 1972 a group of European countries came together and produced an agreement to keep their currencies floating within a band of 2.25 per cent around a central parity. This system, known as 'the snake', was an important step along the road to European Monetary Union, the idea being to create within Europe a zone of monetary stability. This system floundered in 1976. In 1978 a new attempt was made to bring together, in some co-operative format, the nine currencies of European Community (EC) members. In March 1979 the European Monetary System (EMS) was established. All EC members with the exception of the United Kingdom were involved.

The ultimate objective of the EC is political union. An essential part of a political union is a common currency. No one could possibly envisage the United States of America with fifty differing currencies. As a first step on the road towards monetary union the European Commission proposed a system whereby a European Currency Unit (ECU) would be established. This ECU represents a weighted average of the economic strength of EC members. The initial weights and currency units as of March 1979 together with the revised position as of June 1989 are shown in Table 16.1.

Table 16.1 Composition of the ECU

		March 1979		June 1989	
		Weights	Currency Units	Weights	Currency Units
West Germany	DM	27.3	0.828	30.1	.6242
France	FF	19.5	1.15	19.0	1.332
United Kingdom	£stg	17.5	0.0885	13.0	.08784
Italy	Lira	14.0	109.00	10.15	151.8
Netherlands	DG	9.0	0.286	9.4	.2198
Belgium/Luxemburg	BF/LF	8.2	3.66/0.14	7.6	3.431
Denmark	DKr	3.0	0.217	2.45	.1976
Ireland	IR£	1.5	0.00759	1.1	.008552
Greece	Dra	–	–	0.8	1.440
Spain	Pta	–	–	5.6	6.885
Portugal	Esc.	–	–	0.8	1.393
		100%		100%	

Note that the Irish currency has a weight of only 1.1 per cent as of June 1989. Given that the values of the currencies change over time, so too do their weights. Further, a realignment of currency units was to take place every few years, to take account of the movements in inter-community trade during that period. It is clear from the above table that the only movements likely to affect the overall value of the ECU are in the currencies of West Germany, France and the United Kingdom.

Members of the EMS, except Italy and later the United Kingdom, agreed to keep their currencies within a band of 2.25 per cent on either side of the central parity. Italy and the UK agreed a band of 6 per cent. In practice if a currency crosses a divergent threshold, which is at 75 per cent of the maximum allowed spread, there is a presumption that the authorities concerned will correct this situation by adequate measures. When a currency reaches its maximum divergence — that is, it is at its limits with another currency — there is an automatic obligation on the two countries concerned to act. At the margins any or all of the following policies come into play:

(a) Intervention by a number of central banks.

(b) Monetary measures such as adjusting interest rates to relieve pressure on the exchange rate.

(c) Drawing on central credit facilities.

(d) Other external and domestic policy measures.

These four policies are the essence of the EMS and the process is known as the Exchange Rate Mechanism (ERM). The purpose is to buffer member economies from currency fluctuations. It was hoped that over time the 2.25 per cent bands could be reduced and finally eliminated.

In the early years of the ERM there were numerous realignments as countries sought to come to terms with the new system and because of divergent economic policies. From 1986 to 1992 the ERM achieved notable exchange rate stability between its member states. The number of realignments was reduced to negligible proportions.

However, in 1992 the effects of German reunification on the German economy and inappropriate policy mixes in Italy and the UK led to strains. Political problems contributed to the economic strains.

In the autumn of 1992 speculative pressures mounted and led to the devaluation of the UK pound sterling, the lira and the Spanish peseta. The UK left the ERM and Italy suspended its membership. This caused further uncertainty and the speculation spread to other currencies in the system. The Portuguese escudo and the Spanish peseta were both devalued in the autumn and winter of 1992.

The Irish pound was subject to speculation given the dramatic decline in sterling and the perceived interaction between the Irish and UK pounds. The Irish authorities preserved the ERM bilateral exchange rates in the period up to the end of January 1993 but only by using interest rate increases and intervention in the markets. In late January 1993, when the UK authorities unexpectedly cut interest rates again, the cost of defending the Irish pound in terms of a further increase in interest rates was considered too high and it was decided to realign the Irish pound by 10 per cent against its central rates in the ERM. This equated to about a 7 per cent change in the market rate for the Irish pound. Subsequently, the pound sterling continued to weaken but the Irish pound did not come under speculative attack — indeed substantial inflows accrued and domestic interest rates were reduced. The realignment of 10 per cent was more than the market had anticipated and was sufficient to calm the market.

In the summer of 1993 speculative pressures built on a number of currencies in the ERM. France and Denmark were the particular focus of attention although the Irish pound traded strongly against the deutschmark and inflows continued to be strong. Intervention and interest rate rises failed to calm this speculation and the ERM rules were changed in August 1993, to widen to 15 per cent the 2.25 and 6 per cent bands.

In the mid-1990s the goal of a single EU currency by the year 2000 looks unattainable. Notwithstanding this the move towards greater economic convergence and the internal market process was formalised by the coming into force on 1 November 1993 of the Maastricht Treaty. Governments of the European Union remain committed in varying degrees to the ultimate objective of monetary and political union. While the road to full integration and harmonisation will be bumpy the advent of a single economy with over 300 million consumers, a single currency and a simplified business environment offers enormous potential for increased growth and prosperity.

Supporters of the ERM claim that it is only by establishing a single currency that the full benefits of the European single market can be realised. They see the need for currency conversion as yet another barrier to trade which must be swept away if the single market is to function efficiently. The benefits can therefore be summarised under three main headings: the removal of exchange rate risk, a reduction in transaction costs (calculated at approximately one-half of 1 per cent of Gross Domestic Product for the Community as a whole) and greater price stability. Some proponents of monetary union go further, and contend that the 'natural' rate of unemployment (defined as the unemployment rate towards which the economy tends in the long run) will be reduced as well. This is based on the argument that high inflation rates and unstable exchange rates reduce the efficiency of the price mechanism and so lead to a misallocation of resources which makes the 'natural' rate of unemployment higher than it would otherwise be.

Probably the main drawback of a currency union is that each member state loses the use of exchange rate and monetary policies as a means of achieving domestic policy objectives. Consequently, some degree of sovereignty over economic policy should be retained by national government in the shape of fiscal policy. The possibility of running a budget deficit/surplus, the application of tax incentives, choice over type and rates of taxes levied and the nature of government expenditure would give governments some (demand-side and supply-side) influence over their domestic unemployment rates. This issue of sovereignty and wider political agendas both nationally and internationally have been major factors in fuelling the turmoil that has been associated with the concept in recent years.

Ireland Within the European Monetary System

The main effect of the EMS on Irish business life was that parity with sterling could no longer be maintained. Apart from introducing a variable exchange rate with Ireland's chief trading partner it also produced exchange controls between the two countries. This caused the loss of access to the London money market as a source of finance for Irish business, thus leading to higher domestic interest rates. This process was reversed with the ending of exchange controls on 31 December 1992 within the overall context of European Monetary Union. The break in the link with sterling also resulted in the introduction of a wide range of techniques by the Central Bank for the purposes of intervening in or influencing the financial markets and managing the liquidity of the banking system.

A second effect of the EMS was the discipline imposed on the Irish economy. Ireland is now a member of an economic grouping which has experienced much lower inflation than that usually obtaining in Ireland. If Ireland is to maintain membership of the EMS, cost increases cannot get out of line. Stated simply, if one country has a rate of inflation 10 per cent higher than another, then, assuming no productivity changes, the currency of the rapidly inflating country should devalue by 10 per cent. Because Ireland has accepted the discipline of a narrow band, domestic policies had to be adopted to bring inflation in line with that in other EMS member states. There is clear evidence of this happening in the 1980s and 1990s.

Membership of the EMS and the break with sterling led to the full integration in the 1980s of what had been happening gradually since the 1960s — namely, the domestic orientation of the management of bank liquidity, the development of local financial markets and the underpinning of ceilings on bank credit with penalties derived by reference to movements in the local interest rates. These developments paved the way for the establishment of the Irish Futures and Options Exchange (IFOX) in May 1989, closer supervision of the Stock Exchange in Ireland and the setting up of the International Financial Services Centre. It also led to the strengthening of supervision of all credit institutions, securities and investment activities.

MANAGING FOREIGN EXCHANGE RISK

From a business viewpoint the main effect of variable exchange rates is the problem of determining the local value of funds received from overseas sales. When a businessman sells abroad he expects a certain price in punts. In international trade the price set by the businessman might not equate with the funds actually received. Basically, a business trading abroad faces three types of foreign exchange risk:

(1) Transaction Exposure.
This type of exposure occurs whenever a company imports or exports goods or services with another country and is invoicing them in the other country's currency. The company then has an exposure to that country's currency from the time it knows how much currency is being charged, and not when the goods are delivered or warehoused. It is the most prevalent type of exposure in any company as it can be created by the day-to-day running of the company.

(2) Balance Sheet Exposure (Translation).
This type of exposure is of particular relevance in the case of multinational companies operating foreign subsidiaries. The problem is that the foreign company's investment is in the currency of the host country. When a foreign company sets up a plant in Ireland, it converts its own currency into Irish punts. From that moment it has an exposure in Irish punts. Notwithstanding its trading performance, the overall value of this investment in dollars swings with the changes in the dollar:punt exchange rate.

(3) Operational Risk.
This measures the impact of exchange fluctuations on all operational cash flows regardless of whether they require exchange transactions. It is conceptually a sound way of capturing the effects of exchange rate changes on the value of a firm. However, it is extremely difficult to measure and the various approaches used are outside the scope of this text.

Foreign exchange risk management seeks to reduce the exposure arising from international trade and activities. It should comprise both strategic and operational elements and should function within a precisely defined framework of decision making.

Strategic risk management is an integral part of the business planning process and is driven by the business and competitive environment in which a company operates, i.e. where raw materials are purchased, sales made or new plants established.

Foreign exchange policy should have clear objectives. Goals should be set down, as should the way in which they can be implemented. Policy options range from full hedging (cover everything) to the management of speculation through an aggressive risk management approach.

A recent survey of treasury management in Ireland showed that 78 per cent of firms have selective exchange cover, 15 per cent cover all and 7 per cent cover nothing. Foreign firms are more likely than Irish firms to leave exposures unhedged, as are small firms, out of either ignorance or lack of expertise.

The range of financial instruments available today allows a wide choice in covering exchange risk. In deciding which instrument to use, it is essential to have an understanding of the nature of the risk being managed and of the objective. This will influence the firm's choice in respect of cost, flexibility, security and maturity.

A businessman selling abroad has a number of specific options available:

(a) He can sell in punts, thus leaving the currency problem to the buyer. He can use a foreign exchange adjustment clause in the contract to cover currency changes. This is an unsatisfactory method of overseas marketing as the buyer is likely to have many potential sources of supply and may not accept these conditions. An Irish supplier pricing in punts is at an immediate marketing disadvantage.

(b) He can price in the overseas currency, immediately borrow the sum of foreign currency and convert it into punts, and repay the foreign currency loan when the overseas buyer pays. In this way the exporter protects the value of his sale. The cost of doing this is the cost of borrowing the funds less the interest profits earned in using the borrowed funds. The principal difficulties attaching to this method are that banks may be unwilling to advance funds and the term of the loan is subject to the time of payment by the buyer.

(c) He can insure against currency changes by 'selling forward', i.e. he can 'hedge' the risk of change. Some currencies have two exchange rates, the 'spot' rate, which is the current rate of exchange, and the forward rate, which is a rate of exchange projected 90, 180 or 360 days into the future. If a businessman expects to receive a sterling payment in ninety days' time he can insure against any changes by selling sterling for punts with a delivery date ninety days hence. This system of insurance is known as 'hedging' and is the most widely used by firms in Ireland. Variations of this hedging process include the use of options, swaps and futures contracts.

Options

The purchase of a currency option gives the buyer the right, but not the obligation, to exchange an agreed amount of one currency for another, for a specified period of time. The buyer/holder has, therefore, managed to lock into a predetermined exchange rate while still being allowed to make profits arising from a subsequent favourable spot rate movement. The exchange rate at which the currency amounts can be exchanged is called the strike price and the buyer pays the seller a premium for the flexibility associated with the contract. Options are basically a way of hedging contingent exposure and are a useful tool involving human judgment in regard to the strike price and premium to be paid.

Options can be European style, i.e. capable of being exercised only on a specific future date, or American style, i.e. capable of being exercised at any time up to and including a specific future date and traded on exchanges such as LIFFE in London, PHLX in Philadelphia and IFOX in Dublin.

Swaps

A swap is an exchange of streams of payments between two parties, either directly or through an intermediary. Swaps can be used to solve the problem of foreign exchange risk when financing cannot be obtained in the currency where the cash flows are generated and in particular when the period of exposure is upwards of a year in duration. They effectively match the needs of one party with the opposite needs of the other party. They are not limited to future exchanges of currency as they are also used as an interest rate hedging instrument. Firms can swap fixed interest loans for floating rate loans or convert floating rate loans that are tied to different base rates. In addition it is possible to swap commodities, i.e. whereby an oil company fixes its selling price to an index of oil prices while the other party pays the oil company a fixed stream of payments.

A swap is in effect a long-term agreement (two to twenty years plus) to exchange two currency amounts and to re-exchange them at a future date. Thus the rate is fixed for both currency exchanges. The relevant currency interest amounts are also exchanged for the period of the swap.

Futures

This is a contract to buy a commodity or security on a future date at a price that is fixed today. Unlike option contracts, future contracts are standardised and traded on organised exchanges and therefore can be of a smaller size. They are capable of being liquidated quickly and cheaply. In 1972 the Chicago Mercantile Exchange opened a market for futures contracts on a range of currencies and is joined today by a number of other exchanges world-wide. IFOX is the relevant exchange for the Irish market and today offers a market in the Irish £/$ exchange rate and government gilts among others.

In a perfect certain world there would be no difference between options and futures. The forward rate for a currency would represent the interest rate differentials between one currency and another. Interest rate differentials signify the difference in interest rates between similar financial instruments in different countries. If the annual interest rate on an Irish Exchequer bill were 15 per cent against a 10 per cent rate on United Kingdom Treasury bills, then, other things being equal, the punt should be at a 5 per cent premium against sterling in the twelve-month forward market. Alas, other things are rarely equal, with the result that forward rates often deviate from the interest rate differential rate.

Using futures as a hedge is possible only in widely traded currencies. Luckily, the vast bulk of Irish exports are to countries which have forward currency markets.

An Irish importer who has to pay for goods at some future date is in a similar position to the exporter. He faces the uncertainty of not knowing how many punts will be required to pay the overseas supplier. The three methods outlined above apply, but in reverse, to this situation.

Other techniques worthy of note available to the importer include leading and lagging, netting, the use of transfer pricing strategies and insurance.

Leading means accelerating payments, **lagging** means delaying payments. These methods were used before the development of financial products as a way of speculating on currency movements. Payments were accelerated on debts in currencies that were expected to appreciate and delayed on debts in currencies that were expected to depreciate. Today they are effectively obsolete due to the wide range of products that can do the job more efficiently, except in special cases as a means of shifting liquidity between subsidiaries and in order to take advantage of interest rate differentials.

Netting is another way of rationalising foreign currency management by reducing the transfer of funds between subsidiaries to a net amount. It involves setting up a control point in a carefully chosen location to handle all the financial transactions and thereby capitalise on the operational economies and market advantages of that location. It requires a solid administrative organisation, good bankers and advantageous banking terms allied to favourable exchange and tax laws. An extension of this process could be the setting up of a reinvoicing centre which has responsibility for all foreign exchange transactions and not just intergroup currency flows. The role of the reinvoicing centre is strictly financial and involves responsibility for financing current operations and managing the collection of accounts receivable. In effect the reinvoicing centre manages the exchange risk, is likely to be located in a low tax country and is evaluated as an autonomous profit centre.

Insurance is now available as an option to protect against foreign exchange risk. Most industrialised countries have organisations offering this type of cover. It is closely linked to the government and forms part of the export incentive programme. The decision to insure or not is dependent upon the firm's attitude to risk and the degree of certainty or uncertainty associated with the transaction. Good management practice suggests that a low risk strategy should be adopted, particularly for firms that cannot afford to be wrong or that lack the expertise to monitor the situation closely enough.

Managing foreign exchange requires not only a detailed knowledge of the exposure of the company over time on a currency-by-currency basis but an understanding of the spot and forward exchange markets and of the firm's investment and financing policies, and a view on the political risks inherent in multinational activity. It is more than a simple accounting exercise and if not managed correctly could seriously threaten the liquidity of the firm. As Irish business grows and expands abroad, this area has assumed a significance in the profitability of the firm. Extreme care must be taken in this area. Massive losses from currency speculation in multinationals, e.g. Allied Domecq and Metallgesellschaft plus the collapse of Barings Bank with $1 billion in currency losses, point to the dangers.

FOREIGN CURRENCY BORROWING

It is a measure of the growing sophistication of Irish business that the 1980s and 1990s saw the evolution of overseas borrowings by companies other than state-sponsored enterprises. The resort to overseas sources was due in part to serious credit restrictions in the domestic economy and to a realisation by some companies that they could finance overseas interest and capital repayments out of their export revenue. Foreign borrowing is of four types:

(a) Eurocurrency loans.
(b) Borrowing foreign currencies from Irish institutions.
(c) Borrowing foreign currencies from overseas institutions.
(d) Swap loans.

Eurocurrency Loans

Many years ago the Eurocurrency market was called a 'transatlantic telephonic money market'. Over time the market developed to encompass long-term debt and equity instruments.

The Eurocurrency market evolved from the dollar glut. Some dollar holders, for various reasons, did not wish to invest their funds in the United States. They lodged them in European-based banks which agreed to open dollar denominated accounts. Interest in dollars was paid on their accounts and the deposits were repayable in dollars. There were many borrowers only too eager to borrow dollars who were willing and able to repay loans in dollars. In the 1990s the Eurocurrency market attracted other currencies such as the yen, the deutschmark, the Swiss franc and sterling. An Asia currency market centred on Hong Kong also developed. Although the term 'Euro' stems from the origins of these markets in Europe, the market is not restricted to Europe but encompasses transactions in several non-European locations including the Caribbean, the Middle East and the Far East. The Eurocurrency markets have become the biggest international financial markets in the world, with London the major single centre of operations.

The Eurocurrency market is free of practically all regulation so that the rates of interest charged reflect supply and demand. This freedom from regulation has resulted in great flexibility. The sums traded are large, transaction costs are low and, because there are many lenders, loans of almost any maturity can be arranged. International banking markets helped recycle the so-called 'petrodollars' but this has resulted in serious problems. Some countries borrowed large amounts to finance industrial development, Mexico, Brazil and Argentina being the three biggest borrowers. These and other countries have experienced debt repayment and service problems, which has led to the need to reschedule debt repayments. Further problems in this area could create real difficulties for the banking community.

The most significant development in Eurocurrency markets in recent years has been the growing dominance of Japanese investors and bankers. In an attempt to offset its trade surpluses Japan has invested large sums overseas, often through the Eurocurrency markets. Japanese security houses and banks have bought into banks, stockbrokers and financial institutions in London and New York.

Few Irish companies are of such a size that they can borrow in the Eurocurrency markets. Sums of $10 million and upwards are typical. Businesses borrowing dollars usually do so from this source. The key interest rate in the market is the London interbank offer rate (LIBOR), the rate at which key banks in the London market will loan money to other banks. The interest rate is initially fixed at the present LIBOR rate plus a spread. The spread varies from loan to loan depending on the borrower's credit status and the availability of funds in the marketplace.

Due to increased international trade and competitive pricing, the Eurocurrency market has expanded rapidly and assisted in the greater degree of financial integration between different economies. It has operated against a background of the minimum amount of regulation due to the obvious difficulties of achieving multilateral co-operation in these matters. In practice undue domestic regulation has resulted in business being diverted to the Eurocurrency market, which is free of constraints. This has often acted as a stimulus for the relaxation of domestic regulations and made for a more competitive banking environment.

A second and more traditional market, the Eurobond market, provides a very flexible method for multinational corporations to raise long-term capital at short notice. Eurobonds are bearer securities and are primarily sold outside the capital market of the country in whose currency they are denominated. They generally have a maturity of no more than fifteen years and were originally issued at fixed rates. Floating rate bonds including index and option-like features are now becoming common.

Foreign Currency Borrowing from Irish Institutions

The availability and cheapness of foreign currency loans makes them very attractive to borrowers. However, the danger of a devaluation of the punt against the borrowed currency creates a risk of capital loss. Consider the following example.

Suppose an Irish clothing manufacturer borrowed 464,000 deutschmarks at a 10 per cent interest rate with a five-year term. Interest was to be payable annually and the capital sum was repayable in full at the end of year five. Assume an annual devaluation of the Irish punt against the deutschmark of approximately 5 per cent. Table 16.2 shows the effect of changes in currency rates on the borrower's punt repayments.

Table 16.2 The Effect of Exchange Rate Changes

		Deutschmarks		Irish Punts	
	Spot Rate	*Inflow*	*Outflow*	*Inflow*	*Outflow*
Year 0	2.32 DM:£1 IR	464,000		£200,000	
Year 1	2.20 DM:£1 IR		46,400[1]		21,090
Year 2	2.10 DM:£1 IR		46,400[1]		22,095
Year 3	2.00 DM:£1 IR		46,400[1]		23,200
Year 4	1.90 DM:£1 IR		46,400[1]		24,420
Year 5	1.82 DM:£1 IR		510,400[2]		280,440
					(254,945 + 25,495)

1. Interest at 10 per cent
2. Interest plus capital repayment

Note the outcome carefully. The Irish businessman borrows £200,000 in deutschmarks. He must pay his annual interest in deutschmarks but to do so each year he must set aside an ever-increasing number of punts. The real crunch comes when the capital must be repaid. To repay 464,000 deutschmarks in year five costs £254,945, not £200,000. The apparently cheap loan has increased to an annual rate of 15 per cent. Imagine the effect if the rate of devaluation were 10 per cent per annum.

Borrowing a non-EMS currency is even riskier. Certain Irish businesses have taken severe capital losses because of Swiss franc and yen loans.

Short-term borrowing is less risky, as short-term economic predictions can be made with some degree of assurance. Companies with revenues in overseas currencies can minimise the risk of exchange rate losses by borrowing only in those currencies in which they have revenues.

Because of the exchange rate risk, banks make foreign currency loans only to financially strong businesses.

Foreign Currency Borrowing from Overseas Institutions

An innovation in Irish lending has been the willingness of some European-based banks to provide foreign currency loans to Irish-based businesses. Ideally, the foreign lenders receive a loan guarantee from an Irish institution but in certain cases where the Irish borrower is well known to the European lender such guarantees are not required. This process has been assisted by the removal of all exchange controls on 31 December 1992. All restrictions or limits in respect of foreign currency borrowing by residents from authorised dealers or non-residents were removed. Compliance is now confined to informing the Central Bank of the transaction.

Swap Loans

An Irish business may wish to borrow punts but due to a credit squeeze or lack of collateral be unable to do so. However, the Irish business has connections abroad such as a sister or parent company which has liquid funds. The overseas company agrees to deposit funds in an overseas bank. The Irish branch, or associate, of the overseas bank now makes a loan to the Irish borrower. The bank has a lien on the funds deposited abroad. It usually pays interest on the deposit and charges interest on the loan. The 'spread' between the two rates depends on numerous factors but can be as low as 1 per cent. Such loans are also known as back-to-back loans.

INTERNATIONAL FINANCIAL INSTITUTIONS

A growing number of international or supranational organisations affect the operations of modern business. A small proportion of such organisations are financially oriented and it is these which are examined in this chapter: that is, the European Regional Development Fund, the European Investment Bank, the International Monetary Fund and the World Bank.

The European Regional Development Fund

The European Regional Development Fund (ERDF) was established in 1975 by the Council of Ministers of the European Communities. It is one of the funds which comprise the Structural Funds, the others being the European Social Fund (ESF) and the European Agricultural Guidance and Guarantee Fund (EAGGF). The purpose of the ERDF is to contribute to the correction of the principal regional imbalances within the Community, by participating in the development and structural adjustment of regions whose development is lagging behind and in the conversion of declining industrial regions. For ERDF purposes, Ireland is regarded as one region.

ERDF resources were allocated to member states on the basis of a range of upper and lower limits. Ireland's quota of the Fund ranged between a lower limit of 3.82 per cent and an upper limit of 4.61 per cent.

Reform of the Structural Funds

A fundamental reform of the Structural Funds took place in 1988. The major principles adopted were: concentration of resources, partnership, programming and additionality. The reform involved a switch from a project-based to a programme-based approach. The reformed regulations governing the activities of the Funds set five objectives for action:
1. Promoting the development and structural adjustment of the regions whose development is lagging behind.

2. Converting the regions, frontier regions or parts of regions (including employment areas and urban communities) seriously affected by industrial decline.
3. Combating long-term unemployment.
4. Facilitating the occupational integration of young people.
5. (a) With a view to reform of the Common Agricultural Policy, adjusting the production, processing and marketing structures in agriculture and forestry, and
   (b) promoting the development of rural areas.

The activities of the Structural Funds under the objectives are defined on a 'partnership' basis — in other words, close consultation between the Commission, the member state concerned and the competent authorities at national, regional, local or other level. Partnership covers all the operational phases of the activities: preparation, financing, monitoring and assessment.

In addition the activities of the Structural Funds have to be co-ordinated and consistent with the other Community policies.

The different implementation phases of Community action are as follows:
(i) The member state presents to the Commission a development plan for the regions and areas eligible under Objectives 1, 2 and 5b.
(ii) The Commission along with the member state draws up and adopts a Community Support Framework (CSF) for each objective and/or region which defines the priorities for joint action, an outline of the forms of assistance to be used and an indicative financing plan. The frameworks may cover a period of five years in the case of Objectives 1 and 5b and three years in the case of Objective 2.
(iii) The Commission adopts the forms of assistance provided for in the CSFs and for which the member state has requested funding.
(iv) The Community measures are monitored by means of monitoring committees and permanent dialogue with the competent authorities so that they can be adjusted where this is deemed necessary.

ERDF Activities
The ERDF's assistance in the Objectives 1, 2 and 5b areas takes the following forms:
(i) part-financing of operational programmes consisting of a coherent package of multiannual measures;
(ii) part-financing of infrastructure or productive investment projects;
(iii) global grants to be administered by an intermediary appointed by the member state with the approval of the Commission, which allocates the assistance in the form of individual grants to the final beneficiaries;
(iv) part-financing of a national aid scheme;
(v) support for preparation, monitoring and assessment measures needed to implement the regional action;
(vi) measures carried out within the framework of community initiatives, which cover schemes of especial interest to the Community not provided for in the initial plans.

The reform of the Structural Funds gave the Commission powers to act directly in the field of regional policy by means of measures not covered by the CSFs or in addition to them, in particular in fields which it considers essential for regional development and economic and social cohesion.

Community initiatives therefore constitute guidelines for the member states to submit applications for assistance on the basis of the objectives selected and according to the needs of the regions.

In Objective 1 regions — which includes Ireland — the Community contribution as a general rule is not more than 75 per cent of the total eligible investment cost and the contribution to investment in firms may not exceed 50 per cent of the total investment.

Table 16.3 Community Support Framework 1989–1993

Grants Received by Ireland	
Specific Priority	ERDF m. ECUs
Priority 1: Agriculture, Fisheries, Tourism and Rural Development	
— Rural Development	20
— Tourism	52
— Sanitary Services	114
— Other	11 297
Priority 2: Industry, Services and Supporting Infrastructure	
— Industry	534
— Other	13 547
Priority 3: Measures to Offset the Effects of Peripherality	
— Roads, Rail, Access Transport	645
— Other	74 719
Priority 4: Human Resources	
— Training	70 70
Individual Projects and Technical Assistance	13
Total	1,646

In the period 1989–93 Ireland received grants of 1,646m ECUs. Table 16.3 gives a breakdown by sector and priority.

Commitments are made on the basis of the Commission decisions approving the operations concerned:

(i) in one sum in the case of operations to be carried out over a period of one year;

(ii) in annual instalments in the case of operations to be carried out over a period of two or more years, with the commitments for instalments other than the first instalment being based on the financing plan for the operation and on the progress made in implementing it.

Payments are made in accordance with the corresponding commitments.

Provision also exists for the payment of advances equivalent to:

(i) 50 per cent of the amount committed;

(ii) 80 per cent of the amount committed in the case of a second advance being made and after it has been certified that at least half of the first advance has been used up and that the operation is progressing in accordance with the objectives laid down.

Payment of the balance is conditional on:

(i) a request being submitted to the Commission within six months of the end of the year concerned or of completion in practice of the operation;

(ii) the reports on progress in implementing the operation being transmitted to the Commission;

(iii) a certificate confirming the two preceding requirements being sent by the member state to the Commission.

Commission decisions, commitments and payments are denominated and carried out in ECUs.

In July 1993 regulations governing the Community's Structural Funds for the period 1994–9 were adopted by the Council. With a budget of 141 billion ECUs for this six-year period — in other words a third of the total Community budget — the Structural Funds are the favoured instrument of the policy of economic and social cohesion. Compared with the fundamental reform of the Structural Funds in 1988, the changes made were less far-reaching. The major principles adopted in 1988 are maintained or strengthened. However, new regions are involved, the programming arrangements have been amended and new types of measure may be part-financed by the Community.

The financial plan for the period 1994–9 is shown in Table 16.4 under the key development sectors and totals 2,562m ECUs (£2,000 m. plus).

Table 16.4 Community Support Framework 1994–1999

	Financial Plan for Ireland	
Specific Priority		ERDF m. ECUs
Priority 1:		
Productive Sector		
— Industry	720	
— Fisheries	25	
— Tourism	354	1,099
Priority 2:		
Economic Infrastructure		
— Transport	888	
— Energy and Communications	108	
— Environmental Services	78	
— Hospital Infrastructure	39	1,113
Priority 3:		
Human Resources		160
Priority 4:		
Local Urban and Rural Development		180
Technical Assistance		10
Total		2,562

The European Investment Bank

The European Investment Bank (EIB) was set up under the Treaty of Rome to contribute to the balanced and steady development of the Common Market in the interest of the Community. In accordance with Article 130 of its Statute, the Bank makes or guarantees loans for investment projects, principally in industry, energy and infrastructure, which further:

(a) The economic development of the Community's less developed regions;

(b) Modernisation or conversion of undertakings, development or introduction of advanced technology to improve the competitiveness of Community industry, fostering of co-operation between undertakings in different member countries;

(c) The improvement of communications between member states and other Community objectives such as energy policy and the protection of the environment.

The EIB finances capital investment which contributes directly or indirectly to an increase in economic productivity in general and which is economically and technically viable. Capital is subscribed by member states; however, the bulk of resources comes from borrowings on capital markets inside and outside the Community. The European Investment Bank also plays an important role in deploying development finance in the Mediterranean region and under the Four Lomé Conventions to African, Caribbean and Pacific countries.

In 1992 the Bank provided financing (including loans from the New Community Instrument for borrowing and lending) inside the European Community of over 16,963 million ECUs (£13 billion). Of this, approximately £230 million was provided to Ireland.

Loans are given for four different categories of project.

(1) Infrastructure projects financed by the Exchequer under the Public Capital Programme and for which the Exchequer borrows directly from the EIB.
(2) Projects undertaken by state-sponsored bodies for which they borrow on their own behalf from the EIB without any exchange risk cover from the Exchequer.
(3) Global loans from the EIB to the Irish banks for on-leading, for fixed asset investment to small and medium-sized manufacturing and agri-business firms as well as for tourism projects.
(4) Direct loans for private sector industrial projects.

Historically over half (62.4 per cent) of EIB loans to Ireland went directly to the Exchequer to finance investment in infrastructure. The sectoral breakdown of these loans from 1973 to 1993 is shown in Table 16.5. Telecommunications and energy are the most prominent sectors. Roads and sanitary services have also benefited substantially from EU loan finance while forestry has attracted substantial loans for a programme of its size. The education/training sector is also noteworthy. The EIB is strictly confined to assisting infrastructure of a clearly economic (rather than social) nature. In recent years Ireland has secured loans for FÁS and Teagasc training centres, for Regional Technical Colleges and for other institutions in the higher education sector such as University of Limerick, Dublin City University, the Dublin Institute of Technology at Bolton Street and Kevin Street, as well as for the National Microelectronics Research Centre in Cork. More recently, loans were granted in respect of the Regional Technical College at Tallaght, St Patrick's College Maynooth, UCC, UCG, and the College of Catering Dublin.

EIB lending to state-sponsored bodies has been concentrated on the ESB energy programme, mainly for the construction of the Moneypoint plant and for the development of a transmission network. It has also assisted Bord Gais in the modernisation of its gas distribution networks and the construction of the link between the Irish network and the UK supply system. The telecommunications programme has also benefited through loans to Irish Telecommunications Investments Limited. Industry and agriculture have been funded largely through the global loans to the Industrial Credit Corporation and the Agricultural Credit Company. Other loans have been to CIE, principally for the DART project, and to Irish Continental Lines for the purchase of car ferries.

Table 16.5 Sectoral Breakdown of Loans from EIB 1973–1993

	%
Energy	20.4
Telecommunications	18.2
Sanitary Services	14.3
Factories	3.7
Roads	12.9
Education/Training	3.5
Forestry	6.9
Arterial Drainage	0.6
Railways	2.0
Shipping	0.6
Harbours	0.8
Air Transport	6.5
Urban Renewal	0.4
Global Loans	8.8
Tourism	0.4
	100.0

The securing of EU grants and loans requires a co-operative effort between the Department of Finance, the sponsoring government departments/agencies and other bodies such as local authorities. The role of those bodies in charge of the actual implementation of the project is of particular importance. In most cases EIB financing is made available only on foot of an in-depth project appraisal, including an on-the-spot investigation carried out by a Bank team. This is standard procedure for all EIB financing.

Project implementation is closely monitored by the EU institutions and, in the course of construction and/or on completion, checks may be carried out by a number of such institutions, notably the Commission, the EIB and the European Court of Auditors. In addition the government is required to provide the European institutions with annual progress reports.

The International Monetary Fund

The IMF was first mooted in 1944 and commenced financial operations in 1947. The Fund was set up with a reserve of currencies supplied by members. Its objectives are:

(a) To assist in the development of international prosperity by helping members with balance of payments deficits.

(b) To implement guidelines for international monetary stability.

(c) To promote co-operation on international monetary matters.

The IMF acts internationally in a manner similar to that of a local commercial bank. The Fund provides temporary or emergency currency reserves to countries in balance of payments difficulties just as a bank provides overdraft facilities to a company. A member's maximum access to the Fund's reserves is determined by its quota, which is, effectively, its subscription to the Fund and which is subject to revision every five years or so.

A country running deficits can borrow from the IMF. As the level of borrowings increases so too do the restrictions imposed on the borrower. The objective is for the borrower to implement economic policies which will redress the adverse balance.

In the late 1960s the Fund membership agreed to the creation of Special Drawing Rights (SDRs). This was a major step towards the creation of a supranational central bank. SDRs are a form of international credit instrument. Countries can use them to cover deficits and/or they can be kept as reserves.

In the early 1990s the Fund played a pivotal role in the massive undertaking of supporting the transformation of the former centrally planned economies into market-based systems. A first credit tranche arrangement was approved for the Russian Federation, as well as upper credit tranche arrangements for each of the Baltic States and for many of the members in Central and Eastern Europe whose economies are in transition. In recognition of the unique challenges facing these economies, the Fund established in April 1993 a temporary Systemic Transformation Facility (STF). This facility was designed to provide financing to members facing balance of payments difficulties arising from severe disruptions in their trade and payments arrangements owing to a shift from major reliance on trading at non-market prices to multilateral market-based trade. Such members include those at the early stages of transition that have been unable, as yet, to formulate programmes which the Fund could support under its existing lending facilities. Members using the facility will undertake to move rapidly towards policies that could subsequently be supported under stand-by Extended Fund Facility or Enhanced Structural Adjustment Facility (ESAF) arrangements. In May 1993, in conjunction with a stand-by arrangement with the Fund, Kyrgyzstan made the first purchase for SDR 16 million under this facility. Russia made a purchase for SDR 1,078 million in early July 1993. The ESAF has proved to be effective in helping the low income countries to implement comprehensive macro-economic and structural policy programmes in order to strengthen their balance of payments positions, foster growth and attract external financing.

The Fund membership and financial resources continue to grow to serve the needs of an expanding world economy. By year-end 1994 its membership had reached 185 with a number of applications pending. Its SDR quotas were of the order of 145 billion at that point. The scope of the Fund's technical assistance and training activities has also grown in line with its membership and financial resources, as has the need for procedures to deal with members who failed to meet their obligations.

Ireland is an active member of the IMF. While we used the borrowing facility in the early years of our membership, we have not had recourse to it since 1970.

The World Bank

The World Bank was created at Bretton Woods as a new type of international investment institution to make or to guarantee loans for reconstruction and development projects. It was conceived originally to assist in the reconstruction of post-war Europe but soon evolved into an organisation to assist in developing third world countries, by fostering economic development through financial, technical and advisory aid.

Its fundamental objective is one of sustainable poverty reduction. Poverty reduction is the benchmark against which the Bank's performance is judged.

Underpinning this objective is a two-part strategy. The first element is to promote broadly based economic growth that makes efficient use of the poor's most abundant asset, labour. The second element involves ensuring widespread access to basic social services to improve the well-being of the poor and to enable them to participate fully in the growth of the economy. The strategy also emphasises the need to provide safety nets to protect the most vulnerable groups.

A crucial element of the Bank's poverty reduction efforts is the formulation of country-specific 'poverty assessments'. A poverty assessment provides the basis for a collaborative approach to poverty reduction by country officials and the Bank. The scope of the poverty assessment necessarily varies from country to country, depending on the country situation, the government's commitment to poverty reduction and the nature of the available data. The analysis can involve a review of sectoral reports that cover human resource development and food security and to a lesser extent population, environment and women-in-development issues.

The World Bank comprises a group of three affiliated institutions: the International Bank for Reconstruction and Development (also known as the World Bank), the International Development Association (IDA) and the International Finance Corporation (IFC).

The World Bank (IBRD) and IDA make loans for high priority projects and programmes in member countries to further their development plans. These loans are made to sovereign governments or to entities enjoying the full faith and credit of sovereign governments. In the case of the Bank these loans are made on commercial terms. The lending terms of the IDA, on the other hand, are very generous or 'soft' as IDA was established to assist the poorest countries, which could not afford to borrow money from the Bank on its normal terms. The purpose of the IFC is to assist developing countries in promoting private enterprise. The Corporation's investments take the form of both loan and equity financing of private sector projects in developing countries.

In the earlier years of its operations, the Bank concentrated its lending on capital infrastructure projects — primarily transportation, electric power, telecommunications, and irrigation and flood control. In the 1970s the development of such sectors as agriculture, education and industry was recognised by the Bank and IDA to be crucial to social and economic progress and lending was extended to those sectors. In recent years the Bank has increased the amount of loan finance which is not tied to specific projects but is conditional on national policies being adjusted to cope with balance of payments difficulties and to promote growth. This lending is known as structural adjustment lending. It is employed widely in Africa and South America.

The Bank's finances are based on increases in capital subscriptions made from time to time by its members. At the end of 1994 over 180 billion dollars had been subscribed but of this only about 6.36 per cent is paid in. The Bank's lending programme is financed in part through the paid-in capital, but mainly through commercial borrowing on the international capital markets.

The IDA's resources come predominantly from grant contributions, known as replenishments, from the richer countries among its membership. From its establishment to end 1994 IDA had issued over 62 billion dollars in credits to member countries.

As in the case of the World Bank, member countries subscribe for capital in the IFC. Paid-in capital amounted to over 2 billion dollars at the end of 1994. These subscriptions, in conjunction with borrowings, are used to fund the Corporation's investments.

Ireland is a member of all three World Bank affiliates. In early 1995 the total loan amounts outstanding to Ireland were less than 140 million dollars. Ireland no longer qualifies for World Bank loans because of the developed status of its economy.

CONCLUSION

The environment facing Irish business is increasingly international. No longer can a local firm rely on local markets, suppliers or financiers. As communications improve and as Ireland integrates further into the European Union, the opportunities and the threats posed by international business will grow.

From a financial management viewpoint there are two significant factors attaching to international business: the problem of exchange rate fluctuations and the possibility of raising finance from overseas sources. The foreign exchange market is complex and dangerous but needs to be understood by business people. All over the world, particularly in America, financial houses have come up with and continue to devise new financial techniques and instruments. Ireland through the International Financial Services Centre in Dublin is now in the mainstream of business in this area and an active participant in this dynamic and international marketplace.

This chapter provides only a limited introduction to international finance. Irish business people must become familiar with the global economy facing them in the twenty-first century.

FURTHER READING

International Bank for Reconstruction and Development Annual Reports, Washington.
International Monetary Fund Annual Report, Washington.
J. Kelly, 'The Development of Money and Foreign Exchange Markets in Ireland', Central Bank Annual Report 1992, Dublin, pp. 119–31.
D. K. Das, *International Finance* (London, Routledge, 1993).
A. C. Shapiro, *Foundations of Multinational Financial Management*, 2nd ed. (Allyn & Bacon, 1994).
R. Henderson, *European Finance* (McGraw-Hill, 1993).
J. Beecham, *The Monetary & Financial System*, 3rd ed. (Pitman Publishing, 1994).

QUESTIONS

Question 16.1
Briefly describe each of the three types of foreign exchange risk faced by a business trading abroad.

Question 16.2
What can a business do to reduce foreign exchange risk?

Question 16.3
In the context of international currency rates, what is the difference between a 'clean float' and a 'dirty float'?

Question 16.4
Why were the European Regional Development Fund and the European Investment

Bank set up? How has Ireland benefited from these institutions?

Question 16.5
How does the function of the IMF differ from that of the World Bank?

Question 16.6
How did the Eurodollar market develop?

Solutions

Chapter 1

Question 1.1

(a) A business owned by an individual. The individual is entitled to the profits from the business but must absorb any losses. Typically, no legal requirement must be met in starting the business, particularly if the proprietor is conducting the business in his own name.

(b) A business organisation in which two or more co-owners form a business, normally with the intention of making a profit. The relationship between the co-owners is dictated entirely by the partnership agreement, which may be an oral commitment or a formal document. Partnerships may be either general or limited.

(c) A corporation or joint stock company is a 'legal person' composed of one or more actual individuals or legal entities. It is considered to be separate and distinct from those individuals or entities. Ownership is reflected by ordinary share certificates designating the number of shares owned by its holder. The owner's liability is confined to the amount of the investment in the company, thereby preventing creditors from confiscating the shareholders' personal assets. Other characteristics include permanency and flexibility in making changes in ownership.

(d) A co-operative is a form of business enterprise operated by and for the benefit of all those involved. This includes workers as well as management. It can be formed by any group of seven or more people who are over the age of eighteen, and must be registered with the Registrar of Friendly Societies.

(e) Autonomous public bodies, other than universities; they are neither temporary in character nor purely advisory in function. Some are statutory corporations, some are established as public or private companies pursuant to an Act of the Oireachtas and others have been established or taken over by the state without any specific authority from an Act of the Oireachtas.

Question 1.2

In general partnerships all partners have unlimited liability. The relationship between partners is dictated by the partnership agreement. This should include the amount of capital invested by each partner and how profits and losses should be shared. General

322

partners may participate in the management of the firm.

A limited partnership permits one or more partner to have limited liability. This is restricted to the amount of capital invested in the partnership. At least one general partner has to remain with unlimited liability. The name of the limited partners may not appear in the name of the firm. The limited partner may not participate in the management of the firm. If any of these restrictions are violated a partner forfeits his right to limited liability.

Question 1.3

Advantages:
  (a) Maintains title to the assets.
  (b) Entitled to all profits from the business.
  (c) No legal requirements must be met in starting the operation.
  (d) The sole trader has no time limit on its existence.
  (e) The sole trader is independent and makes all the important decisions.
  (f) Simpler tax regulations.

Disadvantages:
  (a) The owner has unlimited liability.
  (b) One person can have difficulty in managing all the business.
  (c) In cases of absence or illness of the proprietor, mismanagement occurs often.
  (d) Death dissolves the organisation's legal form therefore causing succession problems.
  (e) Sole traders can have difficulty in raising the finances outside of their own funds.

Question 1.4

The Sole Trader:
• Absolute management freedom and minimum formal requirements.

Partnerships
• General Partnership:
Majority vote of partners needed for control and minimum formal requirements.
• Limited Partnership:
  General partners have the same guidelines as a general partnership.
  Limited partners are not permitted any involvement in management.

Corporations
• Shareholders have final control but usually the board of directors controls company policies.

Question 1.5

There are four types of joint stock company:

1. Private Limited Companies
• Between two and fifty shareholders.
• Right of share transfer restricted.
• Business can commence immediately on incorporation.
• Must file their financial statements with the Registrar of Companies.
• The public can subscribe for shares or debentures.

2. Public Limited Companies
• Must have a minimum of seven shareholders.
• Shares are freely transferable.
• Need a Trading Certificate to commence business.
• Accounts must be audited and filed with the Registrar of Companies.
• Can be quoted on the Stock Exchange.

3. Companies Limited by Guarantee
• This method is used by non-profit-making organisations.
• Members subscribe an agreed sum towards the company's assets in case of liquidation.

4. Unlimited Companies
• Formed by companies who do not mind losing the advantage of limited liability in return for avoiding having to file audited accounts with the Registrar of Companies.

Question 1.6
• Membership is voluntary and anyone can join.
• Purchased shares are not transferable.
• Co-operatives have a voting system of one person one vote.
• There is co-operation among co-operatives at all levels, i.e. local, international.
• The community is educated in the role of the co-operatives.
• At the end of the year any surplus is distributed among members depending on the proportion of business with the co-op.

Chapter 2

Question 2.1
(a) A Balance Sheet is a list of the assets and liabilities of a business grouped into relevant categories. The Balance Sheet equation is as follows: total assets = total liabilities + owners' equity.
(b) A Profit and Loss Account, also called an Income Statement, measures the result of operations during the period. It is calculated as net sales less the sum of cost of goods sold and operating expenses.
(c) The Cash Flow Statement combines information from the Income Statement and the Balance Sheet in order to show the volume of cash moving into and out of the business.
(d) Assets are economic resources owned by an individual or a company to which a money value can be attached and which are expected to provide a future benefit.
(e) Liabilities are legal financial obligations that must be paid by the firm in the short or long term in return for some current or ongoing benefit.

Question 2.2
Notes to a firm's financial statements are an integral part of these statements because they disclose the significant accounting policies used to prepare the financial statements and provide additional detail concerning several of the items in the statements.

They can include reference to:
• extraordinary items
• breakdown of stocks, investments, property and other assets
• contingent liabilities
• schedule of capital stock issued.
 They provide a wealth of information that is useful in financial analysis.

Question 2.3

(a) Current assets are more liquid as they are usually cash convertible within the operating cycle of the firm (normally a period of one year or less). Fixed assets, on the other hand, are usually held for a relatively long period, hence the term fixed, and are not for resale in the normal course of business.

(b) Current liabilities are due for payment within twelve months whereas other liabilities, such as long-term loans, debentures and leases, are repayable after more than one or several years.

Question 2.4

Although it furnishes useful information it does have its shortcomings.
• The information is based on a specific date and consequently may not be representative of the underlying performance of the organisation.
• The information identifies only symptoms not causes. It is summarised historical information and may not be the most appropriate for making a decision.
• Though many accounting methods are standard, some degree of variation is permitted, which could greatly change the amounts reported in certain accounts.
• The person preparing the Balance Sheet may make improper assumptions, mistakenly or otherwise.
• Assumptions as to when obligations have been incurred or revenues accrued can have marked effects on the Balance Sheet's final figures.

Question 2.5

(a) Since the house is not a business asset it should not be included. It is owned in a private capacity.

(b) Vehicles which are used by the management/employees of the business in carrying out their responsibilities would be classified as fixed assets whereas any vehicles on sale to the public would be trading stock and therefore classified as current assets.

Question 2.6

(a) Dr Rent, Cr Cash
(b) Dr Purchases, Cr Cash
(c) Dr Bank, Cr Rates
(d) Dr General Expenses, Cr Bank
(e) Dr Cash, Cr Commissions Received
(f) Dr T. Jones, Cr Returns Out
(g) Dr Cash, Cr Sales
(h) Dr Office Fixtures, Cr Bank
(i) Dr Wages, Cr Cash
(j) Dr Drawings, Cr Cash

Chapter 3

Question 3.1

Because a norm of twice current assets to once current liabilities has been accepted over the years as a starting-point for evaluating the ability of the firm to meet its short-term cash obligations. The 2:1 rule of thumb is an arbitrary standard and is subject to numerous exceptions and qualifications.

Question 3.2

     (a) Current Ratio = 3:1
     (b) Acid Test Ratio = 2.5:1

Given the above ratios the firm appears to be very liquid. In fact it would probably be open to the criticism that it is too liquid and not using its resources effectively.

Question 3.3

The five principal categories are:

(a) LIQUIDITY RATIOS

Indicate the ability of the firm to meet short-term obligations as they come due.

(b) ACTIVITY OR UTILISATION RATIOS

Indicate the efficiency or productivity with which assets are managed.

(c) FINANCIAL OR LEVERAGE RATIOS

Indicate the extent to which borrowed or debt funds are used to finance assets.

(d) PROFITABILITY RATIOS

Show the firm's effectiveness in terms of profit margins and rates of return on investment.

(e) MARKET VALUE RATIOS

Reflect the value which investors place on the company.

Question 3.4

     (a) Two times
     (b) 10%
     (c) 5%
     (d) 20%

Question 3.5

(a) DIFFERENT ACCOUNTING DATA

Since ratios are dependent on accounting information they are only as reliable as the data. In addition firms follow different accounting practices, thus making analysis more difficult as data has to be adjusted.

(b) WHAT IS A GOOD OR BAD RATIO?

It can be difficult to determine how good or bad a ratio is. An example would be the Quick Ratio. If it were high this would seem to show a high liquidity position but because the cash would be non-productive it would contribute very little to profits.

(c) Ratios are applied to past events and therefore may not always represent or indicate the present or future patterns. The analysis merely presents a starting-point and indicates areas that need to be investigated further. A series of statements forming the basis of some trend analysis and good comparative data can help to overcome some of the limitations in this area.

(d) Ratios based on financial statements are only as good as the quality of information presented. They are based on a snapshot of the organisation on a specific date and may or may not be a fair reflection of the underlying or ongoing activity of the organisation.

Question 3.6
Income Statement for Year Ended 31 December 1994:

	£
Sales	600,000
Less: Cost of Sales	420,000
Gross Profit	180,000
Less: Fixed Costs	150,000
Net Operating Income	30,000
Interest	(10,000)
Taxes	(20,000)
Net Income	£Nil

Balance Sheet of Gekko Oil Co. as of 31 December 1994

Fixed Assets			
Net Plant and Equipment			300,000
Current Assets			
Stock	25,000		
Cash	50,000		
Securities	25,000		
Accounts Receivable	100,000	200,000	
Less: Current Liabilities			
Accounts Payable	75,000		
Notes Payable	25,000	100,000	100,000
Total Assets Less Total Liabilities			£400,000
Financed by:			
Common Stock	150,000		
Debt	150,000		
Retained Earnings	100,000		400,000
			£400,000

Question 3.7

Income Statement of Modern Developments Limited for Year Ended 31 March 1995

	£
Sales	350,000
Less:	
Cost of Manufacturing	170,000
Gross Profit	180,000
Less:	
Administration Costs	90,000
Profit Before Interest	90,000
Interest	25,000
Net Profit	£65,000

Balance Sheet as at 31 March 1995

Fixed Assets

Land		105,000	
Buildings		110,000	
Plant and Machinery		185,000	400,000

Current Assets

Stock	40,000		
Debtors	90,000		
Cash	45,000	175,000	

Current Liabilities

Creditors		60,000	115,000
Total Assets Less Current Liabilities			£515,000

Financed by:

Creditors			200,000
CAPITAL AND RESERVES			
Share Capital	250,000		
Profit and Loss a/c	65,000		315,000
			£515,000

Appropriate Accounting Ratios:

Current Ratio	2.9 times
Acid Test Ratio	2.25 times
Long-Term Debt to Capital Employed	38.8%
Gross Profit Margin	51.4%
Net Profit Margin	18.6%

Chapter 4

Question 4.1
A cash flow forecast computes the future net cash position of the enterprise. It will help to explain how the cash and cash equivalents held by the enterprise have changed between one balance sheet and the next.

It is a critical integrating financial statement showing the effects of a firm's projected operating, investing and financing activities on its cash balance. The principal purpose of the statement is to provide relevant information about a firm's cash receipts and cash payments during a particular accounting period in order to be better able to determine its financing needs.

Question 4.2
The basic steps involved in financial forecasting are:
1. Project the firm's sales revenues and expenses over the planning period.
2. Estimate the level of investment in current and fixed assets that is necessary to support the projected sales.
3. Determine the firm's financing needs throughout the planning period.

Question 4.3
A pro forma statement is a carefully formulated expression of predicted results, including a schedule of the amounts and timing of cash repayments. It is sometimes called a budget.

Such statements have many uses in business.
• They compel management to plan ahead.
• They provide realistic goals.
• They assist in harmonisation of goals between various parts of the business.

Pro forma financial statements are the results of some assumed rather than actual events. They are a useful tool for analysing the effects of the firm's forecasts and planned activities. They can provide a benchmark or standard against which to compare actual operating results, and are therefore an instrument for controlling or monitoring the firm's progress throughout the planning period.

Question 4.4
Pro Forma Income Statement Leahy Motors Limited (£) 1995

	July £	August £	September £	Quarter £
Sales	400,000	500,000	450,000	1,350,000
Less:				
Cost of Goods Sold	280,000	350,000	315,000	945,000
Gross Profit	120,000	150,000	135,000	405,000
Less:				
Expenses	40,000	50,000	45,000	135,000
Depreciation	10,000	10,000	10,000	30,000
Net Profit Before Tax	70,000	90,000	80,000	240,000
Taxation	(14,000)	(18,000)	(16,000)	(48,000)
Net Income	£56,000	£72,000	£64,000	£192,000

Pro Forma Balance Sheet Leahy Motors Limited 1995

	July (£)	August (£)	September (£)
Net Fixed Assets	140,000	130,000	120,000
Current Assets:			
Accounts Receivable	400,000	500,000	450,000
Inventory	500,000	500,000	500,000
	900,000	1,000,000	950,000
Less:			
Current Liabilities:			
Accounts Payable	250,000	316,000	290,000
Taxation	14,000	32,000	0
	264,000	348,000	290,000
Assets–Liabilities	£776,000	£782,000	£780,000
Financed by:			
Net Income	56,000	62,000	60,000
Equity	440,000	440,000	440,000
Long-Term Debt	280,000	280,000	280,000
	£776,000	£782,000	£780,000

Question 4.5

This is the process whereby financial objectives and the means for their attainment are set by the company. Long-run financial plans produce forecasted statements for five- or ten-year periods. They are co-ordinated with capital budgets, which detail planned expenditure for facilities, equipment, new products and other long-range investments.

Short-run plans cover periods of up to five years and are essential for measuring the company's day-to-day performance.

Financial modelling is a technique, usually involving computer spreadsheets, whereby the behaviour of a business under different prospective sets of circumstances can be predicted. It can be a useful tool to management in forecasting the financial implications of its decisions.

Question 4.6

Month (£)	1	2	3	4	5	6	Total
Receipts (£)	–	–	10,000	10,000	10,000	15,000	45,000
Payments (£)							
Stock (£)(Permanent)			10,000				10,000
Stock (Replenishment)			8,000	8,000	8,000	12,000	36,000
Equipment	25,000						25,000
Machinery	10,000						10,000
Operating Expenses	4,000	4,000	4,000	4,000	4,000	4,000	24,000
Rent	300	300	300	300	300	300	1,800
Total Payment (£)	39,300	4,300	22,300	12,300	12,300	16,300	106,800
Cash Movement (£)	(39,300)	(4,300)	(12,300)	(2,300)	(2,300)	(1,300)	
Closing Bal. (£)	(39,300)	(43,600)	(55,900)	(58,200)	(60,500)	(61,800)	

Chapter 5

Question 5.1
Working capital refers to the difference in the firm's current assets and its current liabilities. It is the net current assets which circulate as an essential part of the profit earning process, and involves making simultaneous and interrelated decisions regarding investment in current assets and the use of current liabilities. The main objective is to minimise the time between inputting materials into operating processes and the eventual payment by customers for goods supplied. This is known as the cash operating cycle.

Question 5.2
In order to cater for any fluctuations in sales, production or purchasing, a portion of inventory is maintained as a safety stock or buffer. Determining the optimal safety stock involves balancing the expected costs of a stockout against the cost of carrying the additional inventory. It is a basic trade-off between possible customer dissatisfaction and lost sales due to a stockout, and the increased cost of carrying extra inventory.

In addition a company will keep some stock so that if a delivery is damaged or not up to specification, it can maintain an even flow of production. Finally, incremental stock may be held as a partial hedge against unfavourable movements in the market price.

Question 5.3

(a) EOQ $= \sqrt{\dfrac{2 \times 100,000 \times 30}{1.5}}$

$= 2,000$

(b) Reorder level $= \dfrac{100,000 \times 5}{50}$

$= 10,000$

The department store should therefore reorder 2,000 bottles of perfume whenever its stock falls to 10,000 bottles.

Question 5.4

(a) EOQ $= \sqrt{\dfrac{2 \times 300,000 \times 250}{.4}}$

$= 19,365 \text{ units (approx.)}$

(b) Reorder level $= \dfrac{300,000 \times 8}{48}$

$= 50,000 \text{ units}$

The department store should therefore reorder 19,365 units whenever its stock falls to 50,000 units.

Question 5.5

(a) EOQ $= \sqrt{\dfrac{2 \times 240{,}000 \times .02}{2}}$

$\qquad = 69$ units (approx.)

(b) EOQ $= \sqrt{\dfrac{2 \times 240{,}000 \times .02}{1}}$

$\qquad = 98$ units (approx.)

(c) EOQ $= \sqrt{\dfrac{2 \times 240{,}000 \times .01}{2}}$

$\qquad = 49$ units (approx.)

Question 5.6

In order to conduct a credit analysis, information is required on the creditworthiness and paying potential of a customer. The various sources include:

(a) FINANCIAL STATEMENTS

Based on a company's financial statement, an assessment of its stability and cash situation can allow one to make a judgment as to whether credit should be granted and how much.

(b) CREDIT RATING AND REPORTS

The best-known source is Dun & Bradstreet, which provides credit rating on over 30,000 Irish businesses.

A typical credit report includes:

(i) Summary of recent financial statements.
(ii) Key ratios and trends.
(iii) Information from firms' suppliers on their payment pattern.
(iv) Credit rating to indicate the agent's assessment of creditworthiness of a potential customer.

(c) BANKS AND FINANCIAL INSTITUTIONS

(d) TRADE ASSOCIATIONS

(e) COMPANY'S OWN EXPERIENCE

Credit analysis is a key part in the process of formulating and updating credit control policy and procedures. Creditworthiness is rarely assessable in terms of absolutes and will come down to a question of judgment of the risk in each case and a categorisation of the customer accordingly.

Chapter 6

Question 6.1
They are long-term projects undertaken by firms with a view to achieving profit maximisation. They usually involve an initial cash outlay leading to a flow of future cash benefits over a number of years. They can be grouped into projects generated by growth opportunities, projects generated by cost reduction opportunities, and projects generated to meet legal requirements and health and safety standards.

The basic principle in the process is that all projects should be accepted which promise a rate of return in excess of the cost of capital. This is signified by the emergence of a positive net present value calculation. One can also use a more sophisticated approach called the capital asset pricing model, which includes an analysis of risk. The four key steps in the process are:
(a) Generating investment project proposals.
(b) Estimating cash flows.
(c) Evaluating alternatives and selecting projects to be implemented.
(d) Reviewing a project after it has been implemented and post-auditing its performance.

Question 6.2
The accounting rate of return methods use accounting profits as a measurement tool whereas both the payback period method and the discounted cash flow methods use cash flows as a basis. In addition the discounted cash flow methods incorporate the concept of the time value of money whereas the others do not.

Question 6.3
To find the internal rate of return we must find the discount rate which gives a net present value of 0. This is done by trial and error.
Firstly, calculate the average rate of return.

$$£$$

Total returns	20,000
Less: Initial Investment	15,000
	5,000

$$= 1,000 \text{ per annum}$$

Therefore

$$\text{Return on average investment} = \frac{1,000}{7,500}$$

$$= 13.3\%$$

Since this does not take into account the time value of money the IRR is overstated. Therefore try 12%:

Year	Return £	Discount Factor (12%)	Present Value £
1	3,000	.893	2,679
2	2,000	.797	1,594
3	5,000	.712	3,560
4	6,000	.636	3,816
5	4,000	.567	2,268
	20,000		13,917
		Initial Investment	15,000
		Net Present Value	(1,083)

This leads to a negative Present Value, therefore try a lower rate.
Try 10%:

Year	Return £	Discount Factor (10%)	Present Value £
1	3,000	.909	2,727
2	2,000	.826	1,652
3	5,000	.751	3,755
4	6,000	.683	4,098
5	4,000	.621	2,484
	20,000		14,716
		Initial Investment	15,000
		Net Present Value	(284)

This again leads to a negative Present Value, try a lower rate.
Try 9%:

Year	Return £	Discount Factor (9%)	Present Value £
1	3,000	.917	2,751
2	2,000	.842	1,684
3	5,000	.772	3,860
4	6,000	.708	4,248
5	4,000	.650	2,600
	20,000		15,143
		Initial Investment	15,000
		Net Present Value	143

The actual rate would be about 9.4% and could be calculated by using the process of interpolation.

Question 6.4

Year	D.F.(11%)	Project X Actual Cash Flows	P.V.	Project Y Actual Cash Flows	P.V.
0	1.000	(120,000)	(120,000)	(120,000)	(120,000)
1	.9009	70,000	63,063	10,000	9009
2	.8116	40,000	32,465	20,000	16,232
3	.7312	30,000	21,936	30,000	21,936
4	.6587	10,000	6,587	50,000	32,937
5	.5935	10,000	5,935	90,000	53,411
		Net Present Value	9,986		13,524
		Internal Rate of Return	15.78%		14.19%

Net Present Value calculation says you should pick Project Y, while the Internal Rate of Return calculation says you should pick Project X.

Question 6.5

Cash Inflow (£)	Probability	Certainty Equivalent
30,000	.10	3,000
20,000	.20	4,000
15,000	.21	3,150
16,000	.06	960
8,000	.08	640
12,000	.15	1,800
14,000	.05	700
20,000	.15	3,000
	Expected Value =	£17,250

Question 6.6

(a) £200 × .7938 = £158.76

(b) £100 × .8573 + £200 × .7938 = £244.49

(c) £150 × 3.9927 = £598.905

Chapter 7

Question 7.1

Since banks primarily receive short-term funds from their depositors they tend to keep their lending short, which would be in the form of bank overdraft and bank loans. For those depositors who wish to withdraw at short notice some of their money is kept liquid.

Even though insurance companies receive contributions and premiums constantly, most of the obligations are long-term. Current maturing insurance policies and insurance claims can be met out of current receipts with a balance invested in long-term assets like property.

Question 7.2

When a company wishes to issue new securities, the investment bank will provide advice, market the securities and underwrite the amount an issue will raise. They also have a responsibility in setting a price.

Increased international investment in Ireland led to the entry of non-Irish banks operating here, which produced a dramatic increase in the number of banks providing investment-type services.

Question 7.3

A bank overdraft is a short-term source of finance that is repayable on demand. This makes it unsuitable for the financing of long-term investment projects, which can only be successful if their financing is secure for the life of the project. If a long-term project were financed by an overdraft it would carry a very high financing risk.

A bank overdraft would therefore be more suitable for short-term investment projects, such as stock or debtors. An overdraft facility is quicker and simpler to raise as it involves little or no cost to arrange. Long-term debt may not be suitable for short-term investment projects if it results in unwanted and surplus funds at times during a project.

An overdraft involves the payment of interest at a rate that varies whereas long-term loans usually carry a fixed rate of interest. Whether this would be an advantage depends on what happens to interest rates over the life of the loan. If interest rates are high but expected to fall, it may well make sense to use overdraft finance currently until interest rates fall and then take out some longer-term, fixed rate finance.

Question 7.4

A money market basically deals in short-term funds.

The Dublin money market is made up of the market for Exchequer Bills and Central Bank deposits. Other forms of international money market instrument are commercial paper, short-term loan notes and repurchase agreements (REPOs).

The Central Bank imposes credit restrictions by putting liquidity requirements on licensed banks and controlling the issue of Exchequer Bills. To be a money market security a financial asset must have little or no risk of loss to the purchaser.

Question 7.5

— Increased international trade
— Deregulation in the US and within the EU.
— Globalisation of financial markets.

Question 7.6

In Ireland at the end of 1986 legislation was passed in relation to building societies which permitted unsecured lending for specific purposes. This increased the power of the government to control activities of the societies.

Then in 1987 regulations were introduced for certain society activities which outlawed charging tiered mortgage rates and redemption fees. This obliged societies to pay their own legal fees. There was resistance to these changes which led to the Minister establishing a Working Party to review difficulties resulting from the legislation.

Changes in the UK have had an effect on societies in Ireland. With the passing of the Building Societies Act 1989, building societies now have the freedom to compete fully in the financial services market and are under the regulatory control of the Central Bank.

Pressure will also be put on Irish building societies by the introduction of barrier-free trade for credit institutions.

Chapter 8

Question 8.1
(a) To provide a market for shares; shareholders find it easier to sell shares in a wider market.
(b) To provide access to wider sources of finance; purchase of other companies is made easier by being able to offer shares instead of cash.
(c) To channel savings into investment.
(d) To reflect the business confidence in the country and how the economy is going.
(e) To provide a safeguard for investors.

Question 8.2
If a speculator believes that share prices will rise substantially during an account, he may buy far more shares at the beginning of the account than he can afford to pay for. Provided he sells before the end of the account he will not have to find any money but will receive a cheque representing his profit or loss on Settlement Day. This type of speculator is known as a bull.

A speculator expecting a fall in share prices may sell at the beginning of the account shares which he does not own. He then buys them at the end of the account and makes a profit on Settlement Day. This type of speculator is known as a bear.

Question 8.3
Advantages
(a) The lack of restriction on transfers of shares means that they are more marketable.
(b) Wider ownership of the shares results in no one shareholder being able to wield excessive influence on the company.
(c) The company should be able to raise capital for expansion more easily since it can offer issues of equity and debt to the general public.
(d) The shares are more attractive to investors since if they wish to sell they can do so through a broker without having to find a specific purchaser themselves.
(e) The quotation gives greater publicity to the company name.
(f) Expansion through takeover is also facilitated by the issue of shares to use as payment.

Disadvantages
(a) The company's results are public and therefore easily observed.
(b) The company has to comply with numerous statutory and Stock Exchange disclosure requirements.
(c) The chance of a takeover bid is increased.
(d) Costs of obtaining the quotation may be high.

Question 8.4

From 1982 it was known as the 'Great Bull Market' due to the large share price increase between 1982 and 1986.

After 'Meltdown Monday' the bull market crashed to be replaced by a bear market where weak share price rallies were snuffed out by precipitous falls. This bear market ceased when forced selling came to an end due to prices being too low.

These swings in the Stock Exchange can also be categorised by good times, where hopes are high and there exists a 'Bull Market', and bad times, with low expectations, when there exists a 'Bear Market'.

Question 8.5

The Unlisted Securities Market was introduced for companies not ready to comply with the stringent rules of a full listing. This market is being replaced in 1995 by the Alternative Investment Market (AIM). Junior markets for exploration stocks and small companies exist in Dublin. They are expected to merge into an AIM equivalent market in 1996.

Question 8.6

In general an investor will seek the advice of a broker in selecting a portfolio balancing secure low risk long-term holdings with more volatile short-term investments. The broker must establish what his requirements are as regards risk, expected income and expected capital gain.

Chapter 9

Question 9.1

The amount of trade credit available to a firm depends on:
(a) the proportion of raw materials in the product
(b) the terms of credit offered by a supplier
(c) the payment policies of the purchaser
(d) the volume of the purchases.

Question 9.2

It affects the business in three different ways:
(a) Risk
There is a risk that the business would not be capable of meeting financial commitments

relating to the source. The total risk of the mix of the capital sources is known as the financial risk of the business. This risk arises from the mismatch between the source of the funds and the uses to which such funds are put.

(b) Income

The income effect of financial sources relates to the cost of funds. Reducing the cost of funds should increase the owners' income. An example of this would be accounts payable.

(c) Control

This refers to the possibility of new sources of finance affecting management or ownership control. An example would be bank overdrafts, which usually have collateral that restricts the freedom of management to sell the assets. Also some forms of long-term debt, i.e. convertible bonds, can be converted into new ordinary shares of the borrowing firm, thereby diluting shareholder control.

Question 9.3

The three main types of tax which affect a business are VAT, income tax and corporation tax.

1. Value Added Tax (VAT)

VAT is a very important cash item as it can amount to 21 per cent on an invoice and is returned every two months to the state. Problems with lax credit policies of businesses can cause havoc with VAT.

2. Income Tax

Income tax and Pay Related Social Insurance are major business cost items. The Pay As You Earn system of income tax requires a business to deduct these taxes from salaries and wages, which is then remitted to the Revenue Commissioners on a monthly basis.

3. Corporation Tax

Business profits are liable for tax six months from the end of the accounting period, this is called corporation tax.

Question 9.4

Yes. There is a ready market in accounts receivable through debt factoring agencies. It should therefore be easier to realise cash from this source than from stock.

Question 9.5

Advantages

(a) Interest cost below overdraft rate.

(b) Simple and cheap negotiating procedure.

(c) Status and prestige connected with the ability to borrow by this method.

Disadvantages

(a) The paper market is very impersonal.

(b) It is very hard to get extensions from investors who hold the firm's paper when it encounters financial difficulties.

Question 9.6

A bank loan is for a fixed amount for a fixed period at a fixed rate of interest whereas a bank overdraft, although having an upper limit, may vary in amount from day to day as required by the borrower and be subject to a variable rate of interest.

Question 9.7

Instead of pledging its receivables, an alternative procedure employed by a firm is to sell (or factor) them. Through factoring, the firm sells its accounts receivable to a bank or other firm engaged in factoring. The receivables are sold outright so the factor assumes the total credit risk and incurs any losses from non-payment by the firm's customers.

Factoring operates in two different ways. With maturity factoring the factor purchases all receivables and once a month pays the seller for the receivables. With advance factoring the factor provides a loan against the receivables.

Question 9.8

Advantages

(a) It provides a source of cash when no other may be available.

(b) It saves administration costs in debt collection.

(c) It reduces uncertainty as to the value of the debts.

(d) It facilitates cash flow forecasting.

Disadvantages

(a) It is an expensive source of finance.

(b) It may reduce customer goodwill.

(c) Ultimately, it may lead to irrecoverable sales, as the creditworthiness of the customer is not seen as important. This in turn will lead to a lower price for the debtors sold to the factoring firm.

Chapter 10

Question 10.1

A Finance Lease:

(a) this is a non-cancellable contract providing for the payment of specific rentals over a primary period.

(b) the lessee is responsible for maintenance and insurance of the equipment.

(c) this arrangement is a way of financing use of an asset over its useful life.

An Operating Lease:

(a) this can be cancelled by the lessee prior to its expiration, with options to renew.

(b) the lessor is responsible for maintenance and insurance.

(c) the total rentals payable for the period do not fully repay the capital outlay for the lessor.

Under SSAP 21 a finance lease must be shown on the Balance Sheet as an asset of fair value and as a liability for future lease payments.

Question 10.2

The main points contained are:

    1. The period of the hire.

2. The timing and the amounts of the payments.

3. Agreements on renewing the lease or on purchasing the asset at the end of the lease period.

4. Arrangements concerning repairs, insurance and maintenance, and other expenses.

Question 10.3

Advantages of Hire Purchase:

(a) capital is released for alternative investments

(b) it is a readily available, easily negotiated finance when other credit is restricted.

(c) the most up-to-date equipment can be utilised to increase profits, out of which instalments can be paid.

(d) VAT is fully recoverable against outputs at the time of payment of the initial deposit.

(e) real cost of instalments will be reduced in times of high inflation.

(f) after sales service is often more forthcoming when instalments are still outstanding than if an asset is owned and fully paid for.

Disadvantages of Hire Purchase:

(a) it commits the hirer to a contractual payment that he may find difficult to meet.

(b) it can be an expensive form of finance.

(c) payments appear as a liability on the Balance Sheet.

Question 10.4

They are particularly useful to firms not wanting to raise permanent or long-term finance; also for businesses which are expanding and where there is a time lag between expenditure and the resultant cash inflow.

Question 10.5

The term 'off balance sheet' financing refers to sources of finance which do not show up as liabilities on the Balance Sheet. In a sense it is a misnomer because it refers to methods of avoiding the necessity to provide finance. Examples are leasing, debt factoring and project financing:

1. Leasing

This can apply to any fixed assets such as plant and machinery or motor vehicles. Instead of acquiring the assets, the company enters into an agreement with a leasing firm where it purchases the asset in question and then leases it on a long-term basis to the company. This would be shown in the Profit and Loss Account as a regular charge since no initial payment was made.

2. Debt Factoring

This applies to an important current asset, the debtor.

3. Project Finance

This applies to non-recourse project loans used to finance large-scale capital projects undertaken by the firm, e.g. development of offshore oil and gas fields. The lending institution issues the loan on a non-recourse credit basis. This means that it has no recourse to the assets of the firm other than the underlying assets in the specific project itself.

Question 10.6

Under a credit sales agreement, title to the goods passes at the start of the contract whereas under hire purchase it passes at the end.

Chapter 11

Question 11.1

A sale and leaseback agreement arises when a firm sells land or buildings or equipment that it already owns to a lessor and simultaneously enters into an agreement to lease the property back for a specified period under specific terms.

The lessor involved in the sale and leaseback varies with the nature of the property involved and the lease period. Where land is involved and the corresponding lease is long-term, the lessor is generally a life insurance company. If the property consists of machinery and equipment, then the maturity of the lease will probably be intermediate-term and the lessor could be an insurance company, a commercial bank or a leasing company.

Question 11.2

Advantages of Long-Term Debt
1. It is generally less expensive than other forms of financing because:
    (a) investors view debt as a relatively safe investment alternative and therefore usually demand a lower rate of return.
    (b) interest expenses are tax-deductible.
2. Debenture holders do not participate in extraordinary profits, as payments are usually limited to interest.
3. Debenture holders do not have voting rights although they can indirectly influence the running of the firm.

Disadvantages of Long-Term Debt
1. Debenture holders can restrict the discretionary powers of management by writing restrictive 'covenants' into the loan agreement. These are designed to minimise the risk of default on the part of the lender.
2. Debt results in interest payments which if not met can force a firm into bankruptcy.
3. Debt produces fixed charges thereby increasing the firm's leverage.
4. Debt must be repaid on maturity and involves substantial cash outflow at that stage.

Question 11.3

Subordinated debt is known as mezzanine finance, because its priority lies between secured debt and equity. It became popular in the US as a source of finance for takeovers.

Question 11.4

The most common form of debenture is a mortgage debenture which is secured by a lien on a property. Usually, the value of the real property being secured is greater than that of the mortgage debenture. It therefore provides a margin of safety in the event that the market value of the secured property declines. The details of the mortgage must be registered with the Registrar of Companies.

Question 11.5
Section 84 loans were attractive to profit-making companies which operated in a low tax regime, e.g. Shannon and ESR companies. Because of the significant loss of revenue, the Government effectively terminated their use in 1991 and today most of the loans raised in this way are repaid.

Question 11.6
Changing technology requires heavy capital investment for most companies and this is made more expensive by inflation. As a result many large potentially profitable projects become almost impossible to finance by conventional methods.

Chapter 12

Question 12.1
The following should be taken into consideration:
1. Legal restrictions which limit the dividends a firm can pay. This could be a statutory restriction, or it would legally not be able to pay the dividend if:
    (a) liabilities exceeded the firm's assets
    (b) the relationship between the proposed dividend amount and the accumulated profits.
    (c) the dividends were paid from capital invested in the firm.
2. Liquidity position. The firm must have cash available to pay dividends since liquid assets are basically independent of the retained earnings account.
3. An absence or a lack of other sources of financing.
4. Shareholders' requirements.

Question 12.2
Advantages of Preference Shares
1. They do not have any default risk to the business.
2. The dividend payments are generally limited to a stated amount, therefore preference shares do not participate in excess earnings as does stock.
3. Preference shareholders do not have voting rights except in extreme cases. Therefore the issue of preference shares does not create a challenge to the firm's owners.
4. In case of the firm going bankrupt the preference shareholders will be paid in advance of ordinary shareholders.

Disadvantages of Preference Shares
1. Because preference shares are riskier than bonds and because dividends are not tax-deductible their cost is higher than that of bonds.

2. Although preference shares dividends can be omitted, their cumulative nature makes payment almost mandatory.

Question 12.3

The BES was introduced to facilitate small Irish enterprises in raising cheap medium-term finance. If conditions are satisfied the investor obtains a full tax deduction for the investment made. Among the many conditions applying are the following:
1. The investment must be maintained for at least five years.
2. The company must be engaged in one of a list of activities including manufacturing, data processing, ship repair or some tourism trades.
3. The shares issued must be new ordinary shares.
4. The investor must not control the company.

Question 12.4

There is no restriction on the sale of shares. It may be relatively easy to acquire a large block of shares in a public company. Control may not rest in the hands of, for example, a single family.

A quoted company will be under pressure to perform at a level compatible with similar quoted companies. Failure to do so can affect the share price and result in the company being vulnerable to a takeover strategy.

Question 12.5

The shareholders incur the following:
— Depressed share price.
— Vulnerability to takeover as assets exceed share valuation.
— Capital gains tax on disposal of shares rather than income tax on dividends.

Question 12.6

Characteristics of Ordinary Shares
1. Claim on income
They have the right to residual income after debenture holders and preference shareholders have been paid, although clearly the firm's dividend policy will determine the extent of any payout.
2. Claim on assets
They also have a residual claim on assets in the case of liquidation but generally when a firm does go bankrupt the common shareholders' claims go unsatisfied.
3. Voting rights
They have the right to elect a board of directors and approve changes to the corporate charter.
4. Limited liability
Although the shareholders are the owners of the company, their liability is limited to their investment amount.
5. Pre-emptive rights
This entitles a common shareholder to maintain a proportionate share of firm ownership. When new shares are issued, common shareholders have the right of first refusal.
6. Risk
The ordinary shareholder is the risk taker in the company.

Chapter 13

Question 13.1
The main forms are:
- — Training grants
- — Capital grants
- — Low rent factories
- — Low tax regime
- — Access to cheap finance through BES, etc.
- — Loan guarantees

Question 13.2
A combination of grant aid; low taxation; free depreciation of assets for tax purposes; and schemes to simplify the operation of VAT and customs duties on goods. These, together with Ireland's low cost, English-speaking, highly educated workforce and location on the periphery of Europe, attracted many multinationals.

Question 13.3
The company's progress is reviewed annually and grants are withheld unless targets are met.

Question 13.4
Shannon has all the benefits normally associated with a manufacturing operation, i.e. low taxation, grants, etc. but without the requirements to manufacture. This means that service companies operating in the Shannon Free Zone around the airport obtain considerable grant aid, can rent low cost premises and are liable to tax at just 10 per cent. They could also avail of Section 84 lending, albeit on a somewhat restricted basis, and benefit from the significant infrastructural developments in the region.

The success of Shannon led to the creation of a similar 'zone' in Dublin for financial service companies called the Irish Financial Services Centre (IFSC).

Question 13.5
Tourism has a high potential for job creation, particularly in rural and isolated areas where other employment opportunities are not available. This helps to preserve community life in such areas and reduce the population drift to cities. Where a region derives much of its income from tourism, the native physical and cultural resources are its greatest asset and so are preserved.

Question 13.6
The ACC was originally formed in 1923 to assist farmers in improving their farms by investing in modern equipment. The ICC was formed in the 1930s to provide a similar service to new Irish industry. Both have effectively outgrown their original objectives and their future will depend on their ability to compete with other commercial banking enterprises.

Chapter 14

Question 14.1

The cost of preference shares is

$$kp = \frac{dp}{Np}$$

$$= \frac{£6}{£48}$$

$$= 0.125$$

$$= 12.5\%$$

Question 14.2

The cost of the debenture is

$$k = \frac{I + \left(\dfrac{FV - N}{n}\right)}{\left(\dfrac{N + FV}{2}\right)} (1 - t)$$

k = net after-tax cost of the loan
I = annual interest payment
FV = face value of the loan
N = net proceeds of the loan
t = tax rate
n = period of the loan

$$= \frac{28,000 + \left(\dfrac{200,000 - 178,000}{12}\right)}{\left(\dfrac{178,000 - 200,000}{2}\right)} (1 - 0.5)$$

$$= 7.89\%$$

Question 14.3

The cost of equity is

$$k_c = \frac{D1}{MP} + g$$

k_c Cost of equity
$D1$ Next year's dividend
MP Current market price
g Expected annual growth rate of dividends

$$k_c = \frac{2}{50} + 12\%$$

$$= 4\% + 12\% = 16\%$$

Question 14.4

The current market price of the share would be

$$k_c = \frac{D1}{MP} + g$$

$$.148 = \frac{.009}{MP(£)} + 10\%$$

$$MP(£) = \frac{.009}{.048}$$

$$MP = 1.875$$

Question 14.5

Source of Finance	Current Market Value	Weight	Marginal Cost	
Equity	1,000,000	.50	12%	6%
Preference	500,000	.25	16%	4%
Long-term debt	500,000	.25	20%	5%
Total	£2,000,000		WACC	15% p.a.

Question 14.6

Cost of ordinary shares:

$$\frac{.10\,(1.08)}{2.50} + .08$$

$$= .123 \text{ or } 12.3\%$$

Cost of debentures:

$$\frac{10\,(1-0.5)}{90}$$

$$= 5.5\%$$

Weighted Average Cost:

	Weight	Cost	WACC %
Shareholders' Funds	.667	12.3%	8.2
Debentures	.333	5.5%	1.8
		WACC	10%

Chapter 15

Question 15.1

The acquiring company may want to obtain the new technology, markets, suppliers, capacity or management skills of the target company. It may wish to diversify, or to eliminate competition or a 'middle man' in its core or associated operations. It may want to use the target company as a vehicle for transactions which are not possible or feasible in the existing company. It may also wish to balance risk by practising some degree of diversification.

Question 15.2
The methods used are:
- Market value using P/E ratio.
- Book value (Balance Sheet value).
- Fair value.
- Discounted PV of future cash flows.
- Comparative value if feasible.

Question 15.3
A leveraged buyout (LBO) is any acquisition which leaves the acquired company with an unusually high debt/equity ratio. It involves borrowing from a financial institution to buy the company, with the loan being repaid from the sale of assets and internal cash flow of the acquired company.

Question 15.4
The acquiring company may not have cash. It may wish to retain the sellers as shareholders in order to avail of their experience or to discourage them from competing. There are also tax advantages in many circumstances. This method seems cheaper, as no cash is used: however, it is usually more expensive as the new shareholders share profits and dividends indefinitely.

Question 15.5
A P/E ratio cannot be used, so a multiple of the company's earnings is used instead. This is generally lower than the P/E ratio of an equivalent PLC as private shares are less marketable.

Question 15.6
- The small size of the Dublin Stock Exchange.
- Buoyancy and a bull market.
- US and UK precedents.
- Improving opportunities in Ireland.
- Availability of 'shell' companies.

Chapter 16

Question 16.1
1. Transaction exposure refers to the risk of invoicing customers in a different currency to that in which your costs are paid.

2. Balance Sheet exposure is the risk relating to the difference between the local currency and the parent company's currency in an investment.
3. Operational risk measures the impact of all exchange movements on cash flows.

Question 16.2
(a) Sell or buy foreign currency forward to meet supply and demand.
(b) Invoice in currency of cost.
(c) Enter a hedge agreement.
(d) Enter a swap agreement.

Question 16.3
When central banks do not intervene in the free floating of currency rates this is known as a 'clean float'. In practice they always seek to manage the exchange rates, resulting in a 'dirty float'.

Question 16.4
The European Regional Development Fund (ERDF) is intended to compensate for regional imbalances within the EU by assisting in development of industry and infrastructure in peripheral areas. Ireland has received a great deal of money from the ERDF, mainly for infrastructure development such as roads.

The European Investment Bank (EIB) invests in projects which aim to develop the poorer EU economies, strengthen EU industry and foster co-operation within the EU. Most EIB loans to Ireland were spent on infrastructural development with some assistance to forestry and education.

Question 16.5
The IMF responds to temporary or emergency difficulties with balance of payments deficits by providing short-term limited currency reserves. The World Bank lends on a more long-term basis for reconstruction and development projects.

Question 16.6
During the years immediately following the Second World War and the ensuing 'cold war', many East European countries under the influence of the former Soviet Union held substantial reserves denominated in US dollars. For political reasons and the perceived risk that dollar denominated assets could be frozen by US banks in response to US government pressure, these funds were not invested in the US but rather in European institutions. The European institutions in turn lent the funds on to European borrowers. Hence, the Eurodollar market was born. This market later attracted other currencies.

Appendices

PRESENT VALUE TABLES (To be used in conjunction with Chapter 6)

APPENDIX A — Present Value of £1 Tables — Percentage

Year	5	6	7	8	9	10	11	12	13
1	.952	.943	.935	.926	.917	.909	.901	.893	.885
2	.907	.890	.873	.857	.842	.826	.812	.797	.783
3	.864	.840	.816	.794	.772	.751	.731	.712	.693
4	.823	.792	.763	.735	.708	.683	.659	.636	.613
5	.784	.747	.713	.681	.650	.621	.593	.567	.543
6	.746	.705	.666	.630	.596	.564	.535	.507	.480
7	.711	.665	.623	.583	.547	.513	.482	.452	.425
8	.677	.627	.582	.540	.502	.467	.434	.404	.376
9	.645	.592	.544	.500	.460	.424	.391	.361	.333
10	.614	.558	.508	.463	.422	.386	.352	.322	.295
11	.585	.527	.475	.429	.388	.350	.317	.287	.261
12	.557	.497	.444	.397	.356	.319	.286	.257	.231
13	.530	.469	.415	.368	.326	.290	.258	.229	.204
14	.505	.442	.388	.340	.299	.263	.232	.205	.181
15	.481	.417	.362	.315	.275	.239	.209	.183	.160

Year	14	15	16	17	18	19	20	21	22
1	.877	.870	.862	.855	.847	.840	.833	.826	.820
2	.769	.756	.743	.731	.718	.706	.694	.683	.672
3	.675	.658	.641	.624	.609	.593	.579	.564	.551
4	.592	.572	.552	.534	.516	.499	.482	.467	.451
5	.519	.497	.476	.456	.437	.419	.402	.386	.370
6	.456	.432	.410	.390	.370	.352	.335	.319	.303
7	.400	.376	.354	.333	.314	.296	.279	.263	.249
8	.351	.327	.305	.285	.266	.249	.233	.218	.204
9	.308	.284	.263	.243	.225	.209	.194	.180	.167
10	.270	.247	.227	.208	.191	.176	.162	.149	.137
11	.237	.215	.195	.178	.162	.148	.135	.123	.112
12	.208	.187	.168	.152	.137	.124	.112	.102	.092
13	.182	.163	.145	.130	.116	.104	.093	.084	.075
14	.160	.141	.125	.111	.099	.088	.078	.069	.062
15	.140	.123	.108	.095	.084	.074	.065	.057	.051

Year	23	24	25	26	27	28	29	30
1	.813	.806	.800	.794	.787	.781	.775	.769
2	.661	.650	.640	.630	.620	.610	.601	.592
3	.537	.524	.512	.500	.488	.477	.466	.455
4	.437	.423	.410	.397	.384	.373	.361	.350
5	.355	.341	.328	.315	.303	.291	.280	.269
6	.289	.275	.262	.250	.238	.227	.217	.207
7	.235	.222	.210	.198	.188	.178	.168	.159
8	.191	.179	.168	.157	.148	.139	.130	.123
9	.155	.144	.134	.125	.116	.108	.101	.094
10	.126	.116	.107	.099	.092	.085	.078	.073
11	.103	.094	.086	.079	.072	.066	.061	.056
12	.083	.076	.069	.062	.057	.052	.047	.043
13	.068	.061	.055	.050	.045	.040	.037	.033
14	.055	.049	.044	.039	.035	.032	.028	.025
15	.045	.040	.035	.031	.028	.025	.022	.020

APPENDIX B Present Value of £1 Receivable Annually
at the End of the Each Year

Year	1	2	3	4	5	6	7	8	9	10
				Percentage						
1	0.990	0.980	0.971	0.962	0.952	0.943	0.935	0.926	0.917	0.909
2	1.970	1.942	1.913	1.886	1.859	1.833	1.808	1.783	1.759	1.736
3	2.941	2.884	2.829	2.775	2.723	2.673	2.624	2.577	2.531	2.487
4	3.902	3.808	3.717	3.630	3.546	3.465	3.387	3.312	3.240	3.170
5	4.853	4.713	4.580	4.452	4.329	4.212	4.100	2.993	3.890	3.791
6	5.795	5.601	5.417	5.242	5.076	4.917	4.767	4.623	4.486	4.355
7	6.728	6.472	6.230	6.002	5.786	5.582	5.389	5.206	5.033	4.868
8	7.652	7.325	7.020	6.733	6.463	6.210	5.971	5.747	5.535	5.335
9	8.566	8.162	7.786	7.435	7.108	6.802	6.515	6.247	5.995	5.759
10	9.471	8.983	8.530	8.111	7.722	7.360	7.024	6.710	6.418	6.145
11	10.368	9.787	9.253	8.760	8.306	7.887	7.499	7.139	6.805	6.495
12	11.255	10.575	9.954	9.385	8.863	8.384	7.943	7.536	7.161	6.814
13	12.134	11.348	10.635	9.986	9.394	8.853	8.358	7.904	7.487	7.103
14	13.004	12.106	11.296	10.563	9.899	9.295	8.745	8.244	7.786	7.367
15	13.865	12.849	11.938	11.118	10.380	9.712	9.108	8.559	8.061	7.606

Year	11	12	13	14	15	16	17	18	19	20
1	0.901	0.893	0.885	0.877	0.870	0.862	0.855	0.847	0.840	0.833
2	1.713	1.690	1.668	1.647	1.626	1.605	1.585	1.566	1.546	1.528
3	2.444	2.402	2.361	2.322	2.283	2.246	2.210	2.174	2.140	2.106
4	3.102	3.037	2.974	2.914	2.855	2.798	2.743	2.690	2.639	2.589
5	3.696	3.605	3.517	3.433	3.352	3.274	3.199	3.127	3.058	2.991
6	4.231	4.111	3.998	3.889	3.784	3.685	3.589	3.498	4.410	3.326
7	4.712	4.564	4.423	4.288	4.160	4.039	3.922	3.812	3.706	3.605
8	5.146	4.968	4.799	4.639	4.487	4.344	4.207	4.078	3.954	3.837
9	5.537	5.328	5.132	4.946	4.772	4.607	4.451	4.303	4.163	4.031
10	5.889	5.650	5.426	5.216	5.019	4.833	4.659	4.494	4.339	4.192
11	6.207	5.938	5.687	5.453	5.234	5.029	4.836	4.656	4.486	4.327
12	6.492	6.194	5.918	5.660	5.421	5.197	4.988	4.793	4.610	4.439
13	6.650	6.424	6.122	5.842	5.583	5.342	5.118	4.910	4.715	4.533
14	6.982	6.628	6.302	6.002	5.724	5.468	5.229	5.008	4.802	4.611
15	7.191	6.811	6.462	6.142	5.847	5.575	5.324	5.092	4.876	4.675

Year	21	22	23	24	25	26	27	28	29	30
1	0.826	0.820	0.813	0.806	0.800	0.794	0.787	0.781	0.775	0.769
2	1.509	1.492	1.474	1.457	1.440	1.424	1.407	1.392	1.376	1.361
3	2.074	2.042	2.011	1.981	1.952	1.923	1.896	1.868	1.842	1.816
4	2.540	2.494	2.448	2.404	2.362	2.320	2.280	2.241	2.203	2.166
5	2.926	2.864	2.803	2.745	2.689	2.635	2.583	2.532	2.483	2.436
6	3.245	3.167	3.092	3.020	2.951	2.885	2.821	2.759	2.700	2.643
7	3.508	3.416	3.327	3.242	3.161	3.083	3.009	2.937	2.868	2.802
8	3.726	3.619	3.518	3.421	3.329	3.241	3.156	3.076	2.999	2.925
9	3.905	3.786	3.673	3.566	3.463	3.366	3.273	3.184	3.100	3.019
10	4.054	3.923	3.799	3.682	3.571	3.465	3.364	3.269	3.178	3.092
11	4.177	4.035	3.902	3.776	3.656	3.544	3.437	3.335	3.239	3.147
12	4.278	4.127	3.985	3.851	3.725	3.606	3.493	3.387	3.286	3.190
13	4.362	4.203	4.053	3.912	3.780	3.656	3.538	3.427	3.322	3.223
14	4.432	4.265	4.108	3.962	3.824	3.695	3.573	3.459	3.351	3.249
15	4.489	4.315	4.315	4.001	3.859	3.726	3.601	3.483	3.373	3.268

Index